Identity in American Revolution

Mark E. Bailey

Abstract

The American Revolution brought about a profound crisis of identification as the new nation struggled to distinguish its citizens and define its identity amidst political divisions that lacked outward distinctions. This crisis extended to insdividuals seeking citizenship and those caught in the conflict's periphery. Consequently, marginalized groups seized this opportunity to claim control over their own identities, while those asserting authority faced challenges in maintaining control during times of civil war and revolution.

To address this crisis, American and British authorities, along with various factions of "Americans," relied on paper instruments of identification, such as passes, passports, commissions, loyalty certificates, and letters of introduction. Though these instruments had a hierarchical and coercive origin, they were now adapted to meet the new challenges of the Revolutionary era. Demand for identification subjected Revolutionary Americans to levels of scrutiny and constraint previously reserved for the unfree, while subordinated groups experienced intensified regimes of control.

This book examines the history of identification and identification papers in early America during the Revolutionary period from 1774 to 1783. By analyzing how these instruments of identification were used to identify "Americans" both domestically and abroad, it sheds light on how the new United States were constituted through the process of individual identification. Uncovering the tensions between the ostensibly voluntarist, republican ideals of consent and equality and the exclusivity and coercion inherent in identification regimes, this study offers valuable insights into the complexities of forging a national identity during a time of upheaval.

Identity in American Revolution

Mark E. Bailey

Table of Contents

AAO	*American Archives: Documents of the American Revolution, 1774-1776*, Digitization Projects, Northern Illinois University Libraries
AAS	American Antiquarian Society, Worcester, MA
AHN	*America's Historical Newspapers*, Readex, NewsBank
AM	American Memory, Digital Collections, Library of Congress
AMDMR	*Archives of Maryland: Muster Rolls and Other Records of Service of Maryland Troops in the American Revolution, 1775-1783*, (Baltimore, MD: Maryland Historical Society, 1900)
ANB	*American National Biography Online*
APS	American Philosophical Society, Philadelphia, PA
APSED	American Papers of the Second Earl of Dartmouth in the Stafforshire Record Office, 1765-1782
CMHS	*Collections of the Massachusetts Historical Society*
CNYHS	*Collections of the New York Historical Society*
DLAR	David Library of the American Revolution, Washington Crossing, PA
EAI	*Early American Imprints, Series I*, Readex, NewsBank
ECCO	*Eighteenth Century Collections Online*, Gale
HL	Huntington Library, San Marino, CA
HNOC	Historic New Orleans Collection, New Orleans, LA
JCC	*Journals of the Continental Congress*, American Memory, Digital Collections, Library of Congress
LCP	Library Company of Philadelphia, Philadelphia, PA

<table>
<tr><td>LDC</td><td>Letters of Delegates to Congress, American Memory, Digital Collections, Library of Congress</td></tr>
<tr><td>MHS</td><td>Massachusetts Historical Society, Boston, MA</td></tr>
<tr><td>MPCC</td><td>Miscellaneous Papers of the Continental Congress, NARA, M332</td></tr>
<tr><td>NARA</td><td>National Archives and Records Administration, College Park, MD</td></tr>
<tr><td>PAA</td><td>Pennsylvania Archives</td></tr>
<tr><td>PBF</td><td>The Papers of Benjamin Franklin, Leonard W. Labaree et al eds., (New Haven, CT: Yale UP, 1959-2011)</td></tr>
<tr><td>PBFDE</td><td>The Papers of Benjamin Franklin, Digital Edition</td></tr>
<tr><td>PCC</td><td>The Papers of the Continental Congress, 1774-1789, NARA, M247</td></tr>
<tr><td>PGWDE</td><td>The Papers of George Washington, Digital Edition, Rotunda</td></tr>
<tr><td>PJADE</td><td>The Papers of John Adams, Digital Edition, Rotunda</td></tr>
<tr><td>PJMDE</td><td>The Papers of James Madison, Digital Edition, Rotunda</td></tr>
<tr><td>PTJDE</td><td>The Papers of Thomas Jefferson, Digital Edition, Rotunda</td></tr>
<tr><td>PWL</td><td>Carl E. Prince ed., The Papers of William Livingston, (Trenton, NJ: New Jersey Historical Commission, 1979-)</td></tr>
<tr><td>Wharton</td><td>Francis Wharton ed., The Revolutionary Diplomatic Correspondence of the United States, 6 vols., (Washington, DC: GPO, 1889)</td></tr>
<tr><td>WLCL</td><td>William L. Clements Library, University of Michigan, Ann Arbor, MI</td></tr>
</table>

Introduction

The crisis of political identity that gripped North America and fractured the British Atlantic world with the coming of the American Revolution was also and no less a crisis of personal identification. No divisions of language, accent, manners, dress, religion, culture, or race could be used to make clear distinctions among the shifting fragments of what had too recently been one "people." The Revolution divided but did not distinguish adherents of the two sides from each other: political differences were themselves invisible and intangible and could be manipulated as circumstances required and conscience would allow. Nor were these categories of identity stable. They continually evolved in the course of the conflict, no one quite knowing what forms they would ultimately take. The same crisis brought new challenges and opportunities to marginalized and subordinated groups who were notionally excluded from but deeply affected by the Revolutionary contest, as they struggled to navigate the crisis and, often, seize new control over their own identities. In all its facets, the crisis reflected a tension between the republican principles of the Revolution and the exclusive, coercive means of identification used to effect it. This study of the Revolutionary crisis of identification, from 1774 to 1783, examines the ways that "Americans" of many sorts employed paper and parchment instruments of identification to meet that crisis, both within the emerging states and abroad in Europe, and establishes that the new United States were constituted through the identification of individual "Americans." It is a study not of the formation of subjective identities but of practical identity, understood through the lived experience and practices of identification.

Discussion of identity is now common in early American studies, and multiple analytical frameworks have by now been developed to explain the formation of "American" identities. These include, most notably, an Atlantic-imperial analysis of creole identity formation, a closely related postcolonial analysis, and an analysis of the liminal character of America and the identities constructed there.[1] These approaches to American identity formation overlap, in turn, with the older, ongoing historiography of United States national identity, or nationalism.[2] However diverse their interpretive frameworks, these approaches share a common set of preoccupying questions: How did "Americans" come to see themselves as distinct from the rest of the world, and from European imperial peoples in particular? How did "Americans" come to see themselves as members of unified nations or states, sharing common sets of symbols, experiences, and aspirations? How did early "Americans" understand their relationship to the lands and peoples they had colonized? How did Native Americans and the Africans brought to the Americas as slaves (or the African Americans descended from them) see themselves in relation to America and to those European descendants who would appropriate the name "American"? What did it mean to be an "American," and who was considered or could consider themselves to be "Americans"?

The histories that have answered these questions are histories of categories and how they developed, were thought of, and were adopted or imposed. Older studies of this sort were predominantly pre-histories of nations-to-be, perhaps especially in the case of British North America and the United States. More recent scholarship has emphasized the contingency, ambiguities, and individual variations of the "American" identities under formation in this period,

---

[1] For the Atlantic-Imperial analysis, see Nicholas Canny and Anthony Pagden eds, *Colonial Identity in the Atlantic World, 1500-1800*, (Princeton, NJ: Princeton UP, 1987); Joyce E. Chaplin, "Creoles in British America: From Denial to

[2] Out of a very large historiography, see David Waldstreicher, *In the Midst of Perpetual Fetes: The Making of American Nationalism, 1776-1820*, (Chapel Hill, NC: University of North Carolina Press, 1997); Richard L. Merritt, *Symbols of American Community, 1735-1775*, (New Haven, CT: Yale UP, 1966); Elise Marienstras, *Les mythes fondateurs de la nation américaine : essai sur le discours idéologique aux États-Unis à l'époque de l'indépendance, 1763-1800*, (Paris: F. Maspero, 1976); Elise Marienstras, *Nous, le peuple: les origines du nationalisme américain*, (Paris: Gallimard, 1988); John M. Murrin, "A Roof without Walls: The Dilemma of American National Identity," *Beyond Confederation: Origins of the Constitution and American National Identity*, Richard Beeman et al eds., (Chapel Hill, NC: University of North Carolina Press, 1987); Carroll Smith-Rosenberg, *This Violent Empire: The Birth of an American National Identity*, (Chapel Hill, NC: University of North Carolina Press, 2010).

while still looking ahead to how later, familiar identity categories—now understood as multi-faceted and complex constructions—came to be. This study overlaps and builds on such analyses of the contingent formation and practice of identities in British North America and the early United States. At the same time it constructs a new way of understanding these histories by focusing on questions of practical identity and identification.

The Imperial Crisis and the Revolution, unsurprisingly, loom large in nearly all histories of North or British American identity, in many and various ways. This is the period, we are told, when inhabitants of the thirteen colonies who had long been loathe to acknowledge themselves as "creoles" or colonials—as anything other than full-fledged British subjects—came to redefine and embrace an identity as "Americans."[3] Through defending their objections to British policy from the Stamp Act through the Coercive Acts, and formulating their arguments against Parliamentary pretensions to legislate for the colonies, statesmen, pamphleteers, and protesters crafted an understanding of themselves and their place in the empire that gave greater emphasis to their self-creation, autonomy, and equality.[4] British violence and the apparent inhumanity manifest in the "Boston Massacre," the Boston Port Act, Lexington and Concord, and the burning of Falmouth, among others incidents, helped to alienate Americans from their "home" government, their "mother" country, and their "father" the King, who now seemed to have become "unnatural" and abusive parents.[5] By coming together to support—with donations, supplies, moral support, and

---

[3] See Chaplin, "Creoles in British America"; Murrin, "Roof without Walls"; Waldstreicher, *In the Midst of Perpetual Fetes;* Jack P. Greene, *Imperatives, Behaviors, and Identities: Essays in Early American Cultural History,* (Charlottesville, VA: University Press of Virginia, 1992); Brendan McConville, *The King's Three Faces: The Rise & Fall of Royal America, 1688-1776,* (Chapel Hill, NC: University of North Carolina Press, 2006).

[4] See Gordon S. Wood, *The Creation of the American Republic, 1776-1787,* (Chapel Hill, NC: University of North Carolina Press, 1969); Bernard Bailyn, *The Ideological Origins of the American Revolution,* Enl. ed., (Cambridge, MA: Harvard UP, 1992); Jack P. Greene, *Peripheries and Center: Constitutional Development in the Extended Polities of the British Empire and the United States, 1607-1788,* (Athens, GA: University of Georgia Press, 1986); James H. Kettner, *The Development of American Citizenship, 1608-1870,* (Chapel Hill, NC: University of North Carolina Press, 1978).

[5] Jay Fliegelman, *Prodigals and Pilgrims: The American Revolution against Patriarchal Authority, 1750-1800,* (New York: Cambridge UP, 1982); Peter Shaw, *American Patriots and the Rituals of Revolution,* (Cambridge, MA: Harvard UP, 1981);

arms—the Bostonians and New Englanders suffering and oppressed under the "Coercive" or "Intolerable" acts, inhabitants of all of the soon-to-be-rebellious colonies came to a clearer understanding that New England's cause was the cause of all Americans.[6] As they gathered in the Continental Congress, delegates from the several colonies who were inclined by long histories of comparative isolation from one another (not to mention inter-colonial conflicts over borders and wars with Native Americans) to distrust one another and think of their colony as their "country," came to think of themselves and their colonies as parts of a continental community and ultimately a confederation.[7]

On the local and personal level, committees of correspondence built both affective and organizational ties within and across colonies; committees of observation and safety and local vigilantes and militia defined and enforced conformity with an "American" or "Patriot" cause; and the experience of serving in committees, protests, and volunteer military companies gave rise to a greater and more continental or "American" political consciousness and sense of empowerment among "the people."[8] Newspaper coverage of resistance and rebellion throughout the colonies helped cement ideas of an American community and cause.[9] The pressure of political crisis, of committees and neighbors, and demands to subscribe boycotts, associations, and oaths of allegiance,

---

Gordon S. Wood, *The Radicalism of the American Revolution*, (New York: Vintage, 1993); T.H. Breen, *American Insurgents, American Patriots: The Revolution of the People*, (New York: Hill & Wang, 2010); Pauline Maier, *From Resistance to Revolution: Colonial Radicals and the Development of American Opposition to Britain, 1765-1776*, (New York: Vintage, 1974).

[6] Breen, *American Insurgents*; T.H. Breen, *The Marketplace of Revolution: How Consumer Politics Shaped American Independence*, (New York: Oxford UP, 2004); David Ammerman, *In the Common Cause: American Response to the Coercive Acts of 1774*, (Charlottesville, VA: University Press of Virginia, 1974).

[7] Maier, *Resistance to Revolution*; Wood, *Creation of the American Republic*; Murrin, "Roof without Walls; Jack N. Rakove, *The Beginnings of National Politics: An Interpretive History of the Continental Congress*, (Baltimore, MD: Johns Hopkins University Press, 1982); Bernard Bailyn, *The Origins of American Politics*, (New York: Vintage, 1970); Merrill Jensen, *The Founding of a Nation: A History of the American Revolution, 1763-1776*, (New York: Oxford UP, 1968).

[8] Breen, *American Insurgents*; Ammerman, *Common Cause*; Maier, *Resistance to Revolution*. See also Edmund S. Morgan, *Inventing the People: The Rise of Popular Sovereignty in England and America*, (New York: Norton, 1988).

[9] Waldstreicher, *In the Midst of Perpetual Fetes*; Merritt, *Symbols of American Community*; Benedict Anderson, *Imagined Communities: Reflections on the Origin and Spread of Nationalism*, (New York: Verso, 1983).

to resign royal commissions, or to take up arms against the Royal Army forced many to declare and live out more clearly than ever before a defined allegiance, while crystallizing new and more stark distinctions between Patriots and Tories, Americans and British, Loyalists and Rebels.[10] As political divisions hardened and new polities were created, individuals faced what was for many a novel opportunity—or a new and frightening ultimatum—to choose and declare their political identity and membership as "American" citizens or British subjects. This was a choice not only between sides but also between different conceptions of political membership—natural subjecthood or volitional citizenship.[11] The States and the Confederation as collective polities struggled at the same time to assert and defend their claims and self-definition as legitimate, autonomous sovereigns vis-à-vis both their own peoples and the established "powers of the earth" in the international realm.[12]

Service and suffering (on either side) added weight to individuals' commitment to their cause. The shared sacrifices and emblematic victories would become the first foundations of an American national mythology and of the "mystic chords of memory" that would give American national identity the affective power lacking in the civic, as opposed to ethnic, nationalism often considered distinctively central to the American Revolution and the formation of the Early

---

[10] See Breen, *American Insurgents*; Harold Melvin Hyman, *To Try Men's Souls: Loyalty Tests in American History*, (Berkley, CA: University of California Press, 1959); Maya Jasanoff, *Liberty's Exiles: American Loyalists in the Revolutionary World*, (New York: Alfred A. Knopf, 2011).

[11] Kettner, *American Citizenship*; Breen, *American Insurgents*; Douglas Bradburn, *The Citizenship Revolution: Politics and the Creation of the American Union, 1774-1804*, (Charlottesville, University of Virginia Press, 2009).

[12] David Armitage, *The Declaration of Independence: A Global History*, (Cambridge, MA: Harvard UP, 2007); Jerrilyn Greene Marston, *King and Congress: The Transfer of Political Legitimacy, 1774-1776*, (Princeton, NJ: Princeton UP, 1987); David C. Hendrickson, *Peace Pact: The Lost World of the American Founding*, (Lawrence, KS: University Press of Kansas, 2003); Patrick Griffin, *American Leviathan: Empire, Nation, and Revolutionary Frontier*, (New York: Hill & Wang, 2007); Samuel Flagg Bemis, *The Diplomacy of the American Revolution*, (New York: D. Appleton-Century, 1935); Jonathan Dull, *A Diplomatic History of the American Revolution*, (New Haven, CT: Yale UP, 1985); Warner Van Alstyne, *Empire and Independence: The International History of the American Revolution*, (New York: Wiley, 1965); Ronald Hoffman and Peter J. Albert eds., *Diplomacy and Revolution: The Franco-American Alliance of 1778*, (Charlottesville, VA: University Press of Virginia, 1981).

Republic.[13] Those serving in the Continental Army in particular—and especially, perhaps, the officers—frequently became more continental and less provincial in their perspective, developed a firm conviction of the need for unity and a central government to enforce it. These individuals came to form a large proportion of the committed nationalists and Federalists of the Confederation and Early Republican periods. Rank-and-file soldiers from throughout the colonies, brought together in the army, were exposed more than ever before to the denizens of the other colonies and gained a new sense of themselves as a continental people.[14]

Beginning in the first half of the eighteenth century, among small groups like the members of the Tammany societies, but gaining in intensity and scope during the Imperial Crisis and the Revolution, Euro-Americans began to lay claim to a distinctive status as "native Americans." They staked this claim by appropriating the symbols, costume, and history of Native Americans in protest, ceremony, and celebration; by formulating an archaeology and a natural history that would serve as the equivalent of Europe's ancient ruins and vindicate America and Americans against theories of degeneration and natural American inferiority; and by formulating defenses of the legitimacy of Euro-American displacement of Native Americans and of their now ostensibly superior claim to be the proper inhabitants and "natives" of North America.[15] With the coming of the Revolution,

---

[13] Sarah J. Purcell, *Sealed with Blood: War, Sacrifice, and Memory in Revolutionary America*, (Philadelphia: University of Pennsylvania Press, 2002); Marienstras, *Les mythes fondateurs*; Michael G. Kammen, *A Season of Youth: The American Revolution and the Historical Imagination*, (New York: Knopf, 1978); Caroline Cox, *A Proper Sense of Honor: Service and Sacrifice in George Washington's Army*, (Chapel Hill, NC: University of North Carolina Press, 2004); Rosenberg, *Violent Empire*.

[14] Cox, *Proper Sense of Honor*; Charles Royster, *A Revolutionary People at War: The Continental Army and American Character, 1775-1783*, (Chapel Hill, NC: University of North Carolina Press, 1979); John W. Shy, *A People Numerous and Armed: Reflections on the Military Struggle for American Independence*, Rev. ed., (Ann Arbor, MI: University of Michigan Press, 1990); Don Higginbotham, *War and Society in Revolutionary America: The Wider Dimensions of Conflict*, (Columbia, SC: University of South Carolina Press, 1988).

[15] See Philip Joseph Deloria, *Playing Indian*, (New Haven, CT: Yale UP, 1998); Peter S. Onuf, *Jefferson's Empire: The Language of American Nationhood*, (Charlottesville, VA: University Press of Virginia, 2000); Paul Semonin, *American Monster: How the Nation's First Prehistoric Creature Became a Symbol of National Identity*, (New York: New York UP, 2000); Antonello Gerbi, *The Dispute of the New World: The History of a Polemic, 1750-1900*, Rev. and enl. ed., (Pittsburgh, PA: University of Pittsburgh Press, 1973); David Kazanjian, *The Colonizing Trick: National Culture and Imperial Citizenship in Early America*, (Minneapolis: University of Minnesota Press, 2003); Anthony F.C. Wallace, *Jefferson and the Indians: The Tragic Fate of the First Americans*, (Cambridge, MA: Harvard UP, 1999).

Native American groups themselves made the choice to side with either the British or the rebellious colonists, thereby defining themselves in relation to the aspirant United States and within the newly restructured imperial space, while forming new coalitions and opening new enmities among themselves. Some Indian groups had begun their fight long before the Revolution and would, in their turn, continue it after the Anglo-American peace, refusing to allow their history and destiny be defined by others' decisions and timelines. Their struggle to maintain or reformulate their identities on their own terms would continue into the wars and pan-Indian movements of the late eighteenth century, through the era of "Indian Removal" and well beyond.[16]

African Americans, both free and enslaved, likewise found their own already ambiguous and oppressive circumstances and identities—as Africans, as Americans, and as persons or as property— cast into yet greater uncertainty, while at the same time they faced new opportunities to define, seize, and reshape or create identities. Did they identify more with the community where they were born or lived, or with their "race" or the African diaspora? Would they serve and defend their "masters" and the white American polities and governments under which they lived, or would they flee to the banner of the British? Would they take up arms and join the rebel forces—by choice or by coercion—either from political conviction or in hopes of gaining their freedom by reward? Would they remain where they were, as slaves or freemen, or would they take advantage of the confusion to flee their present circumstances and try to start anew in any number of possible far off places? Would they imagine their own struggle for freedom or equality as part of or in conflict with that of

---

[16] See James Hart Merrell, *The Indians' New World: Catawbas and their Neighbors from European Contact through the Era of Removal*, (Chapel Hill, NC: University of North Carolina Press, 1989); Colin G. Calloway, *The American Revolution in Indian Country: Crisis and Diversity in Native American Communities*, (New York: Cambridge UP, 1995); Alan Taylor, *The Divided Ground: Indians, Settlers, and the Northern Borderland of the American Revolution*, (New York: Alfred A. Knopf, 2006); Richard White, *The Middle Ground: Indians, Empires, and Republics in the Great Lakes Region, 1650-1815*, (New York: Cambridge UP, 1991); Gregory Evans Dowd, *A Spirited Resistance: The North American Indian Struggle for Unity, 1745-1815*, (Baltimore, MD: Johns Hopkins UP, 1992); Joel W. Martin, *Sacred Revolt: The Muskogees' Struggle for a New World*, (Boston: Beacon Press, 1991); Daniel K. Richter, *Facing East from Indian Country: A Native History of Early America*, (Cambridge, MA: Harvard UP, 2001).

the white rebels? Would they see themselves as citizens of the emerging polities, or would they see

oppression merely taking new form?[17]

Women among the Euro-American population faced similar and some additional dilemmas,

as the Revolutionary moment redefined their identities. Some had to choose on their own which

side they would support. Others were forced to decide whether they would abide by the decisions

and remain by the sides of husbands or families with whose political convictions they disagreed.

Many developed a new or more powerful political consciousness and American identity, very much

like their male contemporaries. Whatever their political convictions, free women commonly had to

negotiate treacherous social, political, and legal grounds on which they might or might not be held

accountable for their own, their father's, or their husband's political convictions or actions; where

they might or might not be able to maintain any claims to or practical control of property; and

where they sometimes, but not always, had greater freedom of movement and action precisely

because they were not considered political beings or likely threats. At the same time they were

driven to consider their identification, or lack thereof, with the communities and governments under

which they lived, during a period when numerous women were left to fend for themselves and their

families in dangerous and straightened circumstances. In the meantime they watched and

sometimes did what they could to influence the transformation of their role, practical and symbolic,

in political society and American culture, as they were simultaneously recast as republican mothers,

---

[17] See Sylvia R. Frey, *Water from the Rock: Black Resistance in a Revolutionary Age*, (Princeton, NJ: Princeton UP, 1991);
Douglas R. Egerton, *Death or Liberty: African Americans and Revolutionary America*, (New York: Oxford UP, 2009);
Cassandra Pybus, *Epic Journeys of Freedom: Runaway Slaves of the American Revolution and their Global Quest for Liberty*, (Boston:
Beacon Press, 2006); Jasanoff, *Liberty's Exiles*; Ira Berlin, "The Revolution in Black Life," *The American Revolution:
Explorations in the History of American Radicalism*, Alfred F. Young ed., (Dekalb, IL: Northern Illinois University Press,
1976), 349-382; Benjamin Quarles, *The Negro in the American Revolution*, (Chapel Hill, NC: University of North Carolina
Press, 1961); William J. Harris, *The Hanging of Thomas Jeremiah: A Free Black Man's Encounter with Liberty*, (New Haven, CT:
Yale UP, 2009); John Wood Sweet, *Bodies Politic: Negotiating Race in the American North, 1730-1830*, (Baltimore, MD: Johns
Hopkins UP, 2003); James Sidbury, *Ploughshares into Swords: Race, Rebellion, and Identity in Gabriel's Virginia, 1730-1810*,
(New York: Cambridge UP, 1997); Jane Landers, *Atlantic Creoles in the Age of Revolutions*, (Cambridge, MA: Harvard UP,
2010).

emblems of virtue, irrational and apolitical persons, adjuncts to their husbands, and weak or corruptible beings through which vices might enter the body politic and the national culture.[18]

Within these stories run stories still subtler. Over the last decade, innovative scholarship in the history of early America, the Revolution, and the Early Republic has added greater depth and sophistication to our understanding of the inner experience and self-fashioning underlying these more easily discernible, more aggregate, or coarser crises in subjective identity among all these groups, though especially among Euro-Americans, as well as to our understanding of the ways Americans of this period thought about inner identity, the self, psychology, self-fashioning, personality, the passions, and the soul.[19] Early American identities can now be understood, to a greater degree than ever before, in their innermost workings.

But identity has hitherto been approached almost exclusively as a subjective phenomenon—a matter of self-perception, affective group affiliation, or broad ascription of collective labels and status. What remains unclear—what has received less focused or substantive attention—is how these identities were made real and practical. How were they governed and practiced? What concrete forms did they take in everyday lives? What did it mean, in practical terms, to bear a particular identity for the individuals who lived through and participated in the histories of the Revolution? "Americans on Paper" provides a new and necessary perspective by examining what

---

[18] See Linda K. Kerber, *Women of the Republic: Intellect and Ideology in Revolutionary America*, (Chapel Hill, NC: University of North Carolina Press, 1980); Mary Beth Norton, *Liberty's Daughters: The Revolutionary Experience of American Women, 1750-1800*, (Boston: Little, Brown, & Co., 1980); Ronal Hoffman and Peter J. Albert eds., *Women in the Age of the American Revolution*, (Charlottesville, VA: University Press of Virginia, 1989); Joan R. Gundersen, *To Be Useful to the World: Women in Revolutionary America, 1740-1790*, Rev. ed., (Chapel Hill, NC: University of North Carolina Press, 2006).

[19] See Hoffman et al eds., *Through a Glass Darkly*; Mechal Sobel, *Teach Me Dreams: Transforming the Self in the Revolutionary Era*, (Princeton, NJ: Princeton UP, 2000); Nicole Eustace, *Passion is the Gale: Emotion, Power, and the Coming of the American Revolution*, (Chapel Hill, NC: University of North Carolina Press, 2008); Sarah Knott, *Sensibility and the American Revolution*, (Chapel Hill, NC: University of North Carolina Press, 2009); Daniel Walker Howe, *Making the American Self: Jonathan Edwards to Abraham Lincoln*, (New York: Oxford UP, 2009); Smith-Rosenberg, *Violent Empire*; Eric Slauter, "Being Alone in the Age of the Social Contract," *William and Mary Quarterly*, Series 3, Vol. 62, No. 1 (Jan., 2005), 31-66. See also Charles Taylor, *Sources of the Self: The Making of the Modern Identity*, (Cambridge, MA: Harvard UP, 1989); Dror Wahrman, *The Making of the Modern Self: Identity and Culture in Eighteenth-Century England*, (New Haven, CT: Yale UP, 2004); Roy Porter, *Flesh in the Age of Reason*, (New York: Norton, 2004).

might be termed practical identity, the bundle of categories and markers attached to an individual

that determined her or his social and governmental access, eligibility, privilege, status, and

possibilities. By focusing on instruments of identification themselves—including passports,

commissions, slave passes, loyalty oath certificates, and letters of introduction—"Americans on

Paper" illuminates the important but little-examined history of identification papers, while bringing a

new analytical lens to the history of the Revolution. While historians of this period have employed

instruments of identification as sources, they have rarely considered them as subjects of analysis in

themselves. In contrast, "Americans on Paper" uses these instruments to reconstruct how

"American" identities were negotiated by "Americans" of many descriptions.

The history of identification in Europe has been the subject of a growing historiography for

the last decade and more. This began roughly with the 2001 collection *Documenting Individual Identity:

The Development of State Practices in the Modern World*, edited by Jane Caplan and John Torpey, preceded

shortly by Torpey's own influential *Invention of the Passport* (2000).[20] Caplan and Torpey recognized

that though much attention had been devoted to the present-day dilemmas of identification

technologies, including practices and technologies of identification that were widely recognized as

essential to the modern state and "modern forms of public life," the historical background of these

practices and technologies had been "virtually ignored."[21] *Documenting Individual Identity* limns this

background, starting with a brief treatment of the "art" of identification in the Renaissance and

ending with discussions of the recent developments in biometric identification and its attendant

ethical dilemmas. Other historians have subsequently carried the project outlined in this collection

---

[20] Jane Caplan and John Torpey eds., *Documenting Individual Identity: The Development of State Practices in the Modern World*, (Princeton, NJ: Princeton UP, 2001); John Torpey, *The Invention of the Passport: Surveillance, Citizenship, and the State*, (Cambridge, UK: Cambridge UP, 2000). See Caplan and Torpey's bibliography for notable earlier works in the history of identification.
[21] Caplan and Torpey, *Documenting Individual Identity*, 3

forward in major book-length studies of identification in Europe from the late medieval period to

the twentieth century.[22]

But there has, to date, been very little study of the history of identification in America or the

United States, especially for periods before the Civil War. This is especially true of the history of

identification papers. Early American identification papers have been discussed almost exclusively

as incidental elements of other historiographies and rarely in detail: slave passes have been dealt with

in passing in histories of slavery, seamen's protections in histories of impressment, and so on.

National passports have received the most attention as a topic in themselves. This historiography,

however, has until lately been dominated by several successive internal histories and studies issued

by the United States Passport Office, the State Department, and Congress, capped by the last of

these in 1976.[23] Craig Robertson's recent history of the U.S. passport goes much further and is

much more sophisticated, but it begins only with the middle of the nineteenth century and still

focuses almost exclusively on the passport issued by the State Department.[24] (Torpey's study of the

passport considers the U.S. passport beginning only with the twentieth century.) Studies of the

history of surveillance in the United States, which necessarily intersect with the historiography of

identification, take a somewhat less narrow approach but have, similarly, emphasized the post-Civil

---

[22] See Valentin Groebner, *Who Are You?: Identification, Deception, and Surveillance in Early Modern Europe,* (New York: Zone Books, 2007); Vincent Denis, *Une Histoire de l'identité: France, 1715-1815,* (Paris: Champ Vallon, 2008); Edward Higgs, *Identifying the English: A History of Personal Identification, 1500 to the Present,* (New York: Continuum, 2011).

[23] U.S. Department of State (Gaillard Hunt), *The American passport; its history and a digest of laws, rulings and regulations governing its issuance by the Department of state,* (Washington, DC: Government Printing Office, 1898); Association of the Bar of the City of New York, *Freedom to Travel: Report of the Special Committee to Study Passport Procedures,* (New York: Dodd, Mead & Co., 1958); Library of Congress, Legislative Reference Service, *Passports and the right to travel: a study of administrative control of the citizen,* (Washington, DC: Government Printing Office, 1966); Leonard S. Goodman, "Passports in Perspective," Texas Law Review 45 (Dec. 1966): 221-279; U.S. Department of State, Passport Office, *The United States Passport: Past, Present, Future,* (Washington, DC: Government Printing Office, 1976).

[24] Craig Robertson, *The Passport in America: The History of a Document,* (New York: Oxford UP, 2010). Rebecca J. Scott and Jean M. Hébrard, *Freedom Papers: An Atlantic Odyssey in the Age of Emancipation,* (Cambridge, MA: Harvard UP, 2012) has recently offered an innovative study of identity and freedom in the history of a single family in late eighteenth and early nineteenth-century French Atlantic and Louisiana that will provide an illuminating comparative perspective and a useful starting point for further studies of identification and identification papers in the Americas and the United States.

War period and have privileged a very few topics, especially state recordkeeping and criminal identification, which is a focus in itself for other studies.[25] Christian Parenti's 2003 survey of surveillance in American history gives substantial primary attention to the documentation of identity in early America and the Early Republic, but does so only briefly and synthetically, while restricting its discussion for these periods almost exclusively to slave passes and criminal records.[26]

Little consideration has been given to identification as an overarching topic in the history of early America and the early United States—as a history embracing multiple regimes, genres, modes, and heuristics of identification and attending to the connections among them. At the same time, in the historiography to date, the colonial period, Revolution, and first several decades of the Early Republic appear only as a pre-history of the "modern" or "true" identification made possible by developments in bureaucracy, infrastructure, technology, or culture. Perhaps because identification in these earlier periods could not match present-day standards of reliability, the historiography has developed as though either identification was not a concern in these earlier periods or any pretensions to identification were implausible, at best highly imperfect versions of the techniques and instruments to be developed later. Yet work in other historiographies belies these presumptions.

Despite the relative lack of attention to documents of identification in early America and the early United States, several important historiographies have made clear that Americans in this period were preoccupied with problems of anonymity and identification and with how a rising use of print and various paper instruments might contribute to or mitigate these problems. Studies of confidence men and the fear thereof in early America and the Early Republic have demonstrated

---

[25] See Pamela Sankar, "State Power and Record-Keeping: The History of Individualized Surveillance in the United States, 1790-1935," PhD Diss., Communications, University of Pennsylvania, 1992; Simon A. Cole, *Suspect Identities: A History of Fingerprinting and Criminal Identification*, (Cambridge, MA: Harvard UP, 2001).

[26] Christian Parenti, *The Soft Cage: Surveillance in America, from Slavery to the War on Terror*, (New York: Basic Books, 2003)..

that Americans of the period were fascinated by the threat of fraud by impostors.[27] Other work has

revealed a pervasive and closely allied fear of duplicity during this same period, from concerns about

dissimulation of identity and character in a market economy to the fears of seduction channeled by

the sentimental novels popular at the time.[28] At the same time, an on-going historiography,

beginning roughly with Karen Halttunen's seminal 1982 study *Confidence Men and Painted Women*, has

argued that by the 1830s at the latest, increasing geographic mobility and urbanization had created a

"world of strangers" in mass urban societies. In this world, the systems of local community

knowledge and hierarchical social and family structures that had made it possible to easily identify

individuals were no longer operable. In response the urban middle classes struggled to develop new

modes of identifying and classifying strangers and of constructing their own public identities, in part

through adopting codes of social ethics meant to promote sincerity (the alignment of inward and

outward self) in social behavior and thus preserve "confidence" in society. For practical purposes

they turned to devices such as etiquette books and urban guidebooks, designed to help individuals

decipher, navigate, and protect themselves in these dangerous, anonymous worlds.[29]

---

[27] See Karen Halttunen, *Confidence Men and Painted Women: A Study of Middle-Class Culture in America, 1830-1870*, (New Haven, CT: Yale UP, 1982); Steven C. Bullock, "A Mumper among the Gentle: Tom Bell, Colonial Confidence Man," *William and Mary Quarterly*, Series 3, Vol. 55, No. 2 (Apr., 1998), 231-258; Thomas Kidd, "Passing as a Pastor: Clerical Imposture in the Colonial Atlantic World," *Religion and American Culture*, Vol. 14, No. 2 (Summer, 2004), 149-174; Robert A. Gross, "The Confidence Man and the Preacher: The Cultural Politics of Shays's Rebellion," *In Debt to Shays: The Bicentennial of an Agrarian Rebellion*, (Charlottesville, VA: University Press of Virginia, 1993); Stephen Mihm, *A Nation of Counterfeiters: Capitalists, Con Men, and the Making of the United States,* (Cambridge, MA: Harvard UP, 2007).

[28] See Jean-Christophe Agnew, *Worlds Apart: The Market and the Theater in Anglo-American Thought, 1550-1750*, (New York: Cambridge UP, 1986); Toby Ditz, "Secret Selves, Credible Personas: The Problematics of Trust and Public Display in the Writing of Eighteenth-Century Philadelphia Merchants," *Possible Pasts: Becoming Colonial in Early America*, Robert Blair St. George ed., (Ithaca, NY: Cornel UP, 2000), 219-242; Toby Ditz, "Shipwrecked; or, Masculinity Imperiled: Mercantile Representations of Failure and the Gendered Self in Eighteenth-Century Philadelphia," *Journal of American History*, Vol. 81, No. 1 (Jun., 1994), 51-80; Cathy N. Davidson, *Revolution and the Word: The Rise of the Novel in America*, Exp. ed., (New York: Oxford UP, 2004); Christopher J. Lukasik, *Discerning Characters: The Culture of Appearance in Early America*, (Philadelphia: University of Pennsylvania Press, 2011).

[29] Halttunen, *Confidence Men and Painted Women.*

These books were parts of what historians have identified as a great proliferation of print in the Early Republic.[30] Since the publication of Benedict Anderson's *Imagined Communities* (1983) and Michael Warner's *Letters of the Republic* (1990), print has been understood as a principal medium through which Americans imaginatively constructed the United States as a nation, beginning in the pre-Revolutionary period, through the construction of themselves as a unified reading public of mutual strangers.[31] As David Henkin describes in his study of antebellum New York City "urban texts," *City Reading* (1998), American cities were, as part of the proliferation of print and construction of anonymous mass public life, papered with signs, posters, handbills, banners, newspapers, and currency. These all served, Henkin argues, to allow strangers to navigate the city and communicate without the need for personal acquaintance, local knowledge, or social networks—these urban texts facilitated, even encouraged (selective) anonymity while at the same time allowing new modes of imaginative self-presentation.[32] Stephen Mihm likewise argues in *A Nation of Counterfeiters* (2007) that the paper money that inundated the Early Republic in bewildering varieties issued by numerous banks was based on and served to facilitate the impersonal economic exchange that seemed inevitable in the increasingly mobile and populous nation.[33] Other works have suggested that a substantially integrated system of public print—combining, for instance, newspapers and wanted posters—was used in some cases to regulate mobility and police social

---

[30] See, for instance, David D. Hall, "The Uses of Literacy in New England, 1600-1850," *Cultures of Print: Essays in the History of the Book,* (Amherts, MA: University of Massachusetts Press, 1996).

[31] Anderson, *Imagined Communities,* esp. ch.4; Michael Warner, *The Letters of the Republic: Publication and the Public Sphere in Eighteenth-Century America,* (Cambridge, MA: Harvard UP, 1990). David Waldstreicher, François Furstenberg, and Trish Loughran have all qualified and developed these understandings, encouraging us above all to understand the institution and physical limits of print markets and print mediums and to understand the constitution of national discourses through print as a technology of governance. See Waldstreicher, *In the Midst of Perpetual Fetes*; Furstenberg, *In the Name of the Father: Washington's Legacy, Slavery, and the Making of a Nation,* (New York: Penguin, 2006); and Loughran, *The Republic of Print: Print Culture in the Age of U.S. Nation Building, 1770-1870,* (New York: Columbia UP, 2007).

[32] David Henkin, *City Reading: Written Words and Public Spaces in Antebellum New York,* (Columbia UP, 1998).

[33] Mihm, *Nation of Counterfeiters,* 11.

order. Thus, as David Waldstreicher and John Wood Sweet, among others, have argued, ostensible

masters of alleged fugitive slaves often depended on the cooperation of the public, who, having read

a descriptive runaway slave advertisement, might capture the fugitive or give information as to his or

her whereabouts.[34]

Even as print might have been used to coercively fix social identity, it also offered at least

some individuals, other historians have argued, the opportunity to claim new, even multiple,

identities. Warner, along with Larzer Ziff and others, has argued that, beginning in the early

eighteenth century, print and the public sphere it constituted gave Americans new opportunities to

construct public personae distinct from their everyday selves, giving new scope for self-fashioning.[35]

At the same time the work of Mechal Sobel suggests that, rather than merely a matter of

manipulating outward appearances, the practice of writing new selves, and particularly exhibiting

them in public, may have been a way by which individual Americans reshaped their self-conceptions.

Sobel has argued that in British North America in the eighteenth century increasing numbers of

individuals began to conceive their selves as discrete, unique, and moldable. As a consequence, they

increasingly sought to take control of their inner lives and to fashion themselves—through

introspection, the interpretation of dreams, self-discipline through documentation of their thoughts

and lives, and the writing and, ultimately, publishing of life narratives.[36]

Though printed texts may have been used to police social order or by individuals to reshape

themselves, historians have also argued that anxiety over print's potential anonymity contributed to

---

[34] David Waldstreicher, "Reading the Runaways: Self-Fashioning, Print Culture, and Confidence in Slavery in the Eighteenth-Century Mid-Atlantic," *The William and Mary Quarterly*, Third Series, 56:2, (Apr., 1999), 243-272; Sweet, *Bodies Politic*, ch.2.

[35] Warner, *Letters of the Republic*, ch.3; Larzer Ziff, *Writing in the New Nation: Prose, Print, and Politics in the Early United States*, (New Haven, CT: Yale UP, 1991).

[36] Sobel, *Teach Me Dreams*. For similar studies of eighteenth-century American fashioning of the self—in this case seen as in a constant state of "liminality"—see Hoffman et al eds., *Through a Glass Darkly*. It is now a well-established point that we cannot take for granted that present-day conceptions of selfhood and identity were shared by inhabitants of earlier historical periods. See on this point Taylor, *Sources of the Self*; Wahrman, *The Making of the Modern Self*.

the more general crises of confidence. Even as the fashioning of personae through print described by Warner and Ziff could empower the individual, it could, at the same time, undermine public confidence in published material.[37] Henkin points to how, in the Early Republic, the proliferation of print, and in particular the growing prevalence of newspapers and their increasing dominance as a primary source of information, inevitably raised questions about the reliability of printed material, often precisely because it was anonymous and separated from the author's accountability. This produced ambivalence over the growing authority, yet distrust of print, as newspapers and other urban texts created a seemingly official discourse of impersonal authority while at the same time serving as the medium for notorious hoaxes, slander, and heated disputes (as in the case of runaway advertisements).[38] Mihm likewise describes how the Early Republic's paper money supply was riddled, and known to be riddled, with counterfeit and worthless bills, prompting elaborate efforts to distinguish good bills from bad by means of counterfeit detector books and other tools.[39]

In parallel with these historiographies of print in the Early Republic, a growing body of work examines the ways in which appearances were "read" and a variety of heuristics—such as physiognomy—deployed to interpret them. Most recently, Christopher J. Lukasik has presented an intriguing study of "the culture of appearance in early America"—focused on the reading of faces— and the ways it shifted from an emphasis on performance and malleable appearances to an emphasis on fixed, involuntary appearances, including racial categories. But Lukasik emphasizes literary analysis and the cultural and intellectual history of this aspect of identification rather than quotidian practicalities.[40] Other studies, embracing the colonial and Revolutionary eras as well as the Early

---

[37] Ziff, *Writing in the New Nation.*

[38] Henkin, *City Reading*, esp. ch.5.

[39] Mihm, *Nation of Counterfeiters.*

[40] Lukasik, *Discerning Characters.*

Republic, have shown how manners, clothing, and other dimensions of personal appearance and

presentation were freighted with and read for political, class, and gendered identities, among other

significations.[41] Still other work has explored how race and class were read off and onto the body in

early America.[42] These and other histories dealing with appearance, presentation, performance, and

material culture, if extended to comprehend early America and brought together, might serve to

construct a history of the bodily and other non-textual dimensions of identity and identification.

Even so, that synthesis would be unable to convey the past experience of practical identities, which

this study of the history of paper instruments of identification will provide.

What is needed to complement both the historiography of identity in early America and the

multiple historiographies of print, public life, and appearance is an understanding of the means by

which the imperatives of identification were met on a practical, day-to-day level, by means of

instruments of identification. A historiography of identification is lacking for early America in

general. But the American Revolution, the focus of this study, may be a particularly good starting

point. Civil war, revolution, and the shift in categories of political membership from subject to

citizen brought questions of identity out into the open and gave instruments of identification a

particularly salient public role. As such, understanding how identification functioned during the

---

[41] See Richard L. Bushman, *The Refinement of America: Persons, Houses, Cities*, (New York: Vintage, 1993); Simon P.
Newman, *Parades and the Politics of the Street: Festive Culture in the Early American Republic*, (Philadelphia: University of
Pennsylvania Press, 1997); Simon P. Newman, *Embodied History: The Lives of the Poor in Early Philadelphia*, (Philadelphia:
University of Pennsylvania Press, 2003); Michael Zakim, *Ready-Made Democracy: A History of Men's Dress in the American
Republic, 1760-1860*, (Chicago: University of Chicago Press, 2003); Kathleen M. Brown, *Foul Bodies: Cleanliness in Early
America*, (New Haven, CT: Yale UP, 2009); Jay Fliegelman, *Declaring Independence: Jefferson, Natural Language & the Culture of
Performance*, (Stanford, CA: Stanford UP, 1993).

[42] See Nancy Shoemaker, *A Strange Likeness: Becoming Red and White in Eighteenth-Century North America*, (New York:
Oxford UP, 2004); Alden T. Vaughan, *Roots of American Racism: Essays on the Colonial Experience*, (New York: Oxford UP,
1995); Winthrop D. Jordan, *White over Black: American Attitudes toward the Negro, 1550-1812*, 2nd ed., (Chapel Hill, NC:
University of North Carolina Press, 2012); Matthew Frye Jacobson, *Whiteness of a Different Color: European Immigrants and
the Alchemy of Race*, (Cambridge, MA: Harvard UP, 1998); Brown, *Foul Bodies*; Newman, *Embodied History*; Lukasik,
Discerning Characters.

Revolution will help us to better understand identification in early America and the Atlantic era of revolutions more generally. This study documents at length the pervasive concern with identification during the Revolution, and explains the ways in which instruments of identification were deployed accordingly. At the same time, even as a study of identification during the Revolution can help advance the larger historiography of identification, it can help us reach important new understandings of the Revolution itself. If we are to understand how the Revolution took place and was practiced in concrete terms, if we are to understand how individuals experienced and lived the Revolutions, we need to understand the changing structures, methods, practices, and instruments of identification that were vital to the day-to-day practice of revolution.

When the North American colonies broke from Britain they created new citizens. The new American governments had to find ways to identify these new entities—those they claimed to govern, from whom they demanded loyalty and service, and who might in turn demand their protection or claim rights against them. Indeed, to be states as such they had to identify citizens they could claim to represent, serve, protect, and govern.[43] The new polity and nation could be constituted and identified as such only through the identification of the individuals that composed them. For states that were committed to volitional citizenship but were embroiled in civil war as they fought for independence, it could not be assumed that those who had been subjects under the

---

[43] On the preoccupation of the erstwhile colonies with establishing themselves as states, a recognized but newly proliferating form of polity, within an international system of states, and for some attention to the relation between the newly defined political populations and statehood, see Armitage, *The Declaration of Independence*, 16-19, 30, 34, 64-65. On the period understanding of the American states as fully sovereign states within the confederation, see Hendrickson, *Peace Pact*. On the nature of political legitimacy during the Revolution and the importance of practical governance to achieving it (in the case of the Congress), see Marston, *King and Congress*. And on the developing ideas of the relationship between "the people" and the state leading up to and during the Revolution, see Morgan, *Inventing the People*.

colonial regime would choose to be citizens of the new states.[44] To prosecute their wars, the

Continental Congress and the individual state governments needed also more generally to

distinguish Patriots from Loyalists.[45] They had to assemble bodies of soldiers—at first largely

volunteers but increasingly conscripts—who were to be governed by coercive regimes of

surveillance and identification. And they had to police the boundaries of citizenship (including

military service) defined by gender, race, age, and autonomy. Potential citizens themselves had to

consider not only where their loyalties lay—they might wrestle with their consciences and inner

selves—but they had also to determine how they would secure and prove the identities they chose

(even if only for the moment) and discern the "true" identities of those who surrounded them.[46]

Indeed, as Americans of all stripes and in all places struggled to decide who they would be, many of

them forced the same decision upon their neighbors.

---

[44] On "volitional citizenship," see Kettner, *American Citizenship*, ch. 7. On the distinctions between subjecthood and citizenship and the greater exclusivity of the latter, see (besides Kettner) Bradburn, *Citizenship Revolution*), ch. 1; and Rogers M. Smith, *Civic Ideals: Conflicting Visions of Citizenship in U.S. History*, (New Haven, CT: Yale UP, 1997), chs. 3-4.

[45] In addition to the common and common sense assumptions that spies, opportunists, profiteers and the like were to be guarded against, and the suspicion and caution fostered by the highly fraught contests and conflicts between revolutionaries and Loyalists, the Congress and the states had their suspicions heightened by their own engagements in espionage; the shock of Benedict Arnold's betrayal; the arrivals of strangers from abroad offering their services to the Revolution, seeking supply contracts, or claiming diplomatic standing; and the warnings of their agents abroad. In response to early warnings from Silas Deane, stationed in France, the Committee of Secret Correspondence would write to the commissioners in France of their conviction of "the necessity of invincible reserve with persons coming to France as Americans and friends to America about whom the most irrefragable proofs have not removed all doubt," Committee of Secret Correspondence to Franklin, Deane, and Lee, 21 December 1776, Wharton, II: 230. Franklin, several years later, would nevertheless feel the need to send warnings again that "that we have in America too readily, in various instances, given faith to the pretensions of strangers from Europe, and who offer their services as persons who have powerful friends and great interest in their own country, and by that means obtain contracts, orders, or commissions to procure what we want, and who, when they come here, are totally unknown, and have no other credit but what such commissions give them; or, if known, the commissions do not add so much to their credit as they diminish that of their employers," Franklin to Committee of Foreign Affairs, 26 May 1779, Wharton, III: 192. He would in turn be cautioned that "there may be Arnolds at Paris," Franklin (acknowledging the warning) to Searle, 30 November 1780, Wharton, IV: 168-169. On espionage during the war see, e.g., John A. Nagy, *Invisible Ink: Spycraft of the American Revolution*, (Yardley, PA: Westholme, 2010). For examples of the anxieties raised by particular strangers from abroad, see (re. Holker) Committee of Foreign Affairs to the Commissioners at Paris, 21 June 1778, Wharton, II: 627; (re. Berkenhout) the correspondence quoted in Wharton, I: 655-657n.

[46] Kettner, *American Citizenship*, ch. 7; Hyman, *To Try Men's Souls*, chs. 3-4. See also Nellie Protsman Waldenmaier ed., *Some of the Earliest Oaths of Allegiance to the United States of America*, (Lancaster, PA: Lancaster Press, 1944).

At one level, addressing these challenges meant determining in fact what qualified an individual to be considered a citizen. The new governments, setting out to prosecute their revolution and secure their independence, did not create citizenries that were neatly contained in their home territories, whose locations and identities were readily and clearly known. In part this was because the basic qualifications for citizenship, as well as the meaning of that status, were and would remain substantially unsettled through and beyond the Revolutionary War. Nor was it clear who among those eligible would ultimately choose to give their allegiance to the new governments. It was clear from the dissension within the states and the actions of Loyalists that mere residence, or even nativity, was insufficient to determine who was or was not a citizen of the new governments that founded their legitimacy upon the right of the people to choose their government and governors. Indeed, it was largely unsettled how individuals were to prove (or officials to judge) that they met the qualifications for citizenship—whatever they were—or that they had previously been granted or had established their citizenship.

The story of how colonial Britons became Americans, of how a periphery of the British Empire became the United States—first plural, then singular—emerges familiarly from this crisis and has been retold many times in a quest to discern the essence and origins of the American identity. Much less familiar are the means by which these evolutions of identity were made real and put to work in the practice of everyday life. The conjoined political and military conflicts were contests not only to define identities but also to embed them in institutional, administrative, and material forms by which they could be monitored and enforced. As individual Americans were compelled in some manner to commit themselves to one side or the other, these commitments needed to be made durably legible, portable, independently verifiable, and thus enforceable. At the same time, on all sides, those who claimed mastership over their fellow Americans—and the right to determine their dependents' identities, or deny them any independent identity at all—struggled to preserve established regimes of social and documentary control and to prevent the upheavals from diminishing their authority over their servants, slaves, children, and wives. Many of these same "dependents" indeed saw in these disruptions opportunities for liberation, self-determination, and reinvention. As they strove to claim new, independent identities, these—often scattered and isolated—social, familial, and racial rebels had to find ways to manipulate the practices and documentary regimes of identification, old and new. The struggles to define, enforce, and contest Revolutionary identities reveal the ways the notionally voluntarist, republican Revolution was effected through regimes of identification both exclusive and coercive.

For individual Americans of all ranks and walks of life, the Revolution brought a destabilization of their identities—intense and radical suspicion and scrutiny on all sides, and proliferating demands that they prove who they were, in all senses. Any given day might bring demands to declare or prove—once and for all, or yet again—whether they were friends or foes, Patriots or Loyalists. On either side, those counted among friends lived through continual suspicion that they were not who or where they were supposed to be. Were they soldiers or civilians? If civilians, were they supposed to be, or should they be made soldiers? Were they adults or minors, and what did that mean? Free or unfree? Men or women? Whether soldiers or civilians, were they where they were supposed to be, attending to their duty, acting in accord with their professed allegiances and sympathies? Were they honest and trustworthy, or were they smugglers, profiteers, unreliable opportunists? Mobility, travel beyond the bounds of communities and places of residence, would only increase suspicion concerning identities, both among those left behind and those met abroad. But even persons who remained at home or resettled after being displaced were liable to be scrutinized repeatedly, by fellow residents, or by representatives of civil and military authorities. The Revolution brought to the general populace, accustomed to comparatively little scrutiny and relative freedom of movement, modes of identification—like pass regimes—and a level of surveillance traditionally reserved for bound labor, criminals, and soldiers. Meanwhile, marginalized and subordinated persons, such as enslaved African Americans, faced an intensification of surveillance, largely through the same patrols, pass requirements, and other measures by which they had been governed before the Revolution.

Apart from the activities of vigilantes and partisans, the suspicions sparked by the Revolution were channeled through institutions of governance at multiple levels, from local committees and militia patrols to the sentry lines, guards, port officials, patrols, boats, and ships of the provincial, state, imperial, or Continental armed forces, and the committees of provincial, state, and Continental governments. Civilians and soldiers were subjected to partially distinct but entangled regimes of identification. In part because an individual's identity as a civilian or soldier could never be taken for granted—perhaps he was a deserter or spy—and in part because civil and military interests, always overlapping, might both be threatened by either, civilians and military personnel were subject to regulation from representatives of both civil and military authorities. Both civil and military authorities, likewise, sometimes in cooperation and sometimes in conflict, regulated the identities and mobility of persons both civil and military.

Governance of identity and mobility on all fronts was effected predominantly through paper and parchment instruments of identification—passes and passports, loyalty oath certificates, and many others. The well-known instruments of state creation, sovereignty, and nationhood—the Declaration of Independence most prominent among them—were therefore parts of a larger complex of documents by and through which the Revolution was enacted and contested and new peoples and polities were defined and governed: national and individual identification were inextricably bound up one with the other. Individuals of all descriptions were forced to navigate a fractured landscape of identity by means of such instruments. These instruments, issued by civilian governments, military commanders, and prominent private individuals, proliferated in both number and genre with the advent of the Revolution, and assumed an importance in the identification of individuals not accorded to analogous peacetime documents.

Identity and identification (and the documents that embodied or enacted both) rested at bottom on the knowledge of individuals accrued and maintained by local communities and societies of which they were or had been members; by networks of their social connections and correspondents; and by networks of merchants, lawyers, and others with whom an individual might have been associated or in contact for commercial or other reasons, at various times. In practice this meant that those possessed of greater social resources, of more connections, with greater standing, credibility, influence, or power, and who were more readily able to draw on these connections when demanded, across distance and time, could exercise greater power over their own identification and identity in practice vis-à-vis the other parties to their identification. At the same time, access to instruments of identification was unequally distributed. "Gentlemen" had almost exclusive access to commissions, paroles, and letters of introduction. Dependents and socially marginalized people—including women, servants, children, and African Americans, enslaved and free—were generally not eligible for loyalty certificates or passes in their own right. Even among those eligible for a particular genre of instrument, the ease with which they could be acquired and the forms they would take varied with the social resources of the applicant. Instruments of identification were, as such, instruments of privilege and exclusion, the embodiments of individuals' unequal power over their own identities.

The Revolution grew out of and was fought across a varied array of social geographies, from frontier hamlets and villages, to the clusters and networks of New England towns, to the burgeoning urban centers of Boston, Philadelphia, and New York. The different characteristics of these geographies constituted the disparate social and material conditions of the identities of those who inhabited or traversed them. Greater or lesser isolation, extents, population, and population densities—among other factors—determined the degree to which either anonymity or identity was possible or, from another perspective, inescapable. The same factors made strangers more or less noticeable in particular locales. The Revolution brought with it a proliferation of such strangers, as it spurred or forced numerous people to become much more mobile, travelling greater distances from home, more frequently, often through communities that had never seen so many strangers. Men deployed in state militia units travelled far afield within their own states and, sometimes, across state lines. Others joined the Continental Army and travelled great distances from home and throughout the states for long periods. Provincial congresses and the Continenal Congress gathered together delegates, often unacquainted with and disinclined to trust one another, from across states and eastern North America, and then subsequently dispatched agents, military commanders, and messengers to all points of the colonies or states, North America, and the Atlantic world. British soldiers and seamen, accompanied by Hessian mercenaries, arrived from abroad to quell the rebellion and occupy the colonies. Provisioners, wagoners, and other contractors and civilian auxiliaries preceded and followed the armies, or scoured the countryside around them. Native American war parties, as allies of either side or on their own account, visited, travelled through, and raided Euro-American communities far afield, along the full sweep of the "backcountry." Refugees displaced by political persecution and war flooded communities throughout the colonies. Prisoners of war and parolees most often made their temporary homes among strangers.

The British Empire and the Atlantic World into which the American Revolution erupted were made of paper and ink. Their denizens constructed extended selves, stretching across oceans, out of layers and chains of documents. Over the course of the eighteenth century, the families, commercial networks, a republic of letters, and imperial bureaucracies that were spread around the Atlantic and the world maintained relationships and coordinated their multitudinous activities through increasingly voluminous correspondence.[47] Newspapers created communities of knowledge.[48] Bills of credit, bills of lading, and numerous other commercial instruments kept goods and money flowing through the extended channels of trade.[49] Powers of attorney and letters of introduction identified lawful agents and worthy associates among the numerous strangers travelling the globe. Commissions identified legitimate officials.[50] Volumes and sheaves of written records maintained the knowledge and continuity of empires and firms.[51] Passports authorized travel through restricted realms. Even those who were illiterate or lacked access to the tools and materials of literacy had their paper persons. They were often documented and bound by written regimes not of their own making, as were the slaves subordinated by passes, bills of sale, cargo manifests, and fugitive advertisements.[52] Neither the importance of paper to defining persons nor the genres of instruments of identification thus employed were innovations of the Revolution. The story of identification in the American Revolution is a story of the creative adaptation of familiar media and instruments to novel crises and new imperatives of identification. Often it is a story of instruments embodying a hierarchical social order used to create a new republican polity and society still significantly defined by privilege, exclusion, and coercion.

---

[47] See Emma Rothschild, *The Inner Life of Empires: An Eighteenth-Century History*, (Princeton, NJ: Princeton UP, 2011); Konstantin Dierks, *In My Power: Letter Writing and Communications in Early America*, (Philadelphia: University of Pennsylvania Press, 2009); Sarah M.S. Pearsall, *Atlantic Families: Lives and Letters in the Later Eighteenth Century*, (New York: Oxford UP, 2008).

[48] See Ian Kenneth Steele, *The English Atlantic, 1675-1740: An Exploration of Communication and Community*, (New York: Oxford UP, 1986); Anderson, *Imagined Communities*; Waldstreicher, *In the Midst of Perpetual Fetes*.

[49] See Mary Poovey, *Genres of the Credit Economy: Mediating Value in Eighteenth- and Nineteenth-Century Britain*, (Chicago: University of Chicago Press, 2008).

[50] See Chapter 3.

[51] See Miles Ogborn, *Indian Ink: Script and Print in the Making of the English East India Company*, (Chicago: University of Chicago Press, 2007); Raman Bhavani, *Document Raj: Writing and Scribes in Early Colonial South India*, (Chicago: University of Chicago Press, 2012); Daniel R. Headrick, *When Information Came of Age: Technologies of Knowledge in the Age of Reason and Revolution, 1700-1850*, (New York: Oxford UP, 2000); Ben Kafka, *The Demon of Writing: Powers and Failures of Paperwork*, (New York: Zone Books, 2012).

[52] See Chapters 6 and 7. See also Walter Johnson, "White Lies: Human Property and Domestic Slavery aboard the Slave Ship *Creole*," *Atlantic Studies*, Vol. 5, No. 2 (Aug., 2008), 237-263; Scott and Hébrard, *Freedom Papers*.

"Americans on Paper" analyzes the instruments of identification that Americans employed in the era of the Revolution, as part of the recreation of American polity and society. At the same time, it explores how the practice of identification connected the daily and material life of individuals with the construction of governance and civil society. "Americans on Paper" explores this history of identity and identification in practice through a cluster of questions: How did one go about being a person and what did it mean in practical terms to be a person, of any number of different varieties and many-faceted identities, in the midst of civil war? How did one prove who one was, create a new identity, or prove one was not who another said one was? How did these same persons—as part of governments, militaries, or society—identify or govern the identities of others? What degree of power did disparate "Americans" of this period possess in practice over their own and one another's identities? How were the political and social transformations of the period experienced and enacted by individual "Americans" through everyday practices of identification?

"American on Paper" is divided into eight chapters, which take a variety of approaches to explore how Americans of all stripes experienced and navigated the Revolutionary crisis of identification through the use of instruments of identification. Chapter 1 explores the early stages of the crisis by following the story of Major Robert Rogers, as he attempted to reconstruct his identity and navigate the fractured landscape of Revolutionary America. This chapter provides an integrated picture of one experience of the crisis of identification, and the concomitant role of instruments of identification, as a complement to later chapters, which follow particular threads of these histories across a variety of individual stories.

The next four chapters each take up one major genre of the many Revolutionary instruments of identification and explore it in depth, while at the same time suggesting how these different genres functioned in relation to one another. Chapter 2 explores how the American revolutionaries constructed networks of trust and collaboration to prosecute their revolution, and how individual mobility and access were enabled in ways that blurred the official and the unofficial, by means of letters of introduction and recommendation. Chapter 3 traces how the Revolution was marked by and enacted through the revolution of commissions that took place from the autumn of 1774 through the first two years or so of the Revolutionary war, as the colonial resistance and, later, separatist movement worked to displace British authority and its emblems and instruments by deploying new instruments of their own. Chapter 4 shows how individual political loyalties, by their nature invisible and changeable, were parsed, made legible, and mobilized through loyalty oath certificates and allied instruments. Chapter 5 examines the intersection of mobility and identification in the Revolution by mapping pass regimes and analyzing the passes issued by both civil and military authorities to control the flows of persons, goods, and information in the midst of a civil war.

The final three chapters each examine a particular context or realm of identification. In these chapters "Americans on Paper" returns to more integrated histories of Revolutionary identification, comprising multiple genres of instruments. At the same time, these chapters explore dimensions and interstices of the Revolutionary crisis and history of identification that are obscured by a focus solely on the principal instruments of identification. As such, they provide alternative ways of framing or tying together the preceding chapters. Chapter 6 explores how the boundaries between military and civilian identities were regulated and how military identities were constructed and enforced. Chapter 7 considers how marginalized persons—particularly women and African Americans—experienced and turned to their own purposes the regimes of identification from which they were excluded or which were designed to subordinate them. And Chapter 8 looks at how Americans were identified abroad during the Revolution, when what it meant to be an "American" was still very uncertain. The conclusion considers how elements of the Revolutionary crisis of identification extended beyond the Revolution itself to shape the challenges of identification faced by Americans of the Early Republic, even as new histories of identity and identification began.

The result is a story of how "American" identities were fractured and cast into crisis; of how "Americans" of all sorts worked out new identities in paper and ink; and of how new states were constituted through the identification of individual "Americans." It is at the same time a story of how instruments and regimes of identification embodying privilege, exclusion, and coercion were used to effect a Revolution in the name of consent and equality. The story begins at the intersection of two travails of identification—one of an entire nation in the making, and the other of a single enigmatic man.

Chapter 1

An American on Paper

In Philadelphia, the summer morning of Monday, July 1st, 1776, opened with a flurry of

paper and ink. "This Morning is assigned for the greatest Debate of all," wrote John Adams: "A

Declaration that these Colonies are free and independent States, has been reported by a Committee

appointed Some Weeks ago for that Purpose, and this day or Tomorrow is to determine its Fate."[1]

Meanwhile, Major Robert Rogers had equal, though very different cause to meet the morning with

anxiety, for his own fate would come before the Congress that same day. The preceding Saturday—

the day after the proposed Declaration was reported by the drafting committee—Rogers had arrived

in Philadelphia under guard, confided by General George Washington to the custody and judgment

of Congress. Received by the President of the Continental Congress, John Hancock, he had been

confined to the city barracks, where he had remained for the last two days.[2] What would become of

him depended on what was made of the passel of letters and documents found on his person. As

the entangling of these two stories—revolution and Major Rogers—will make clear, the history of

the American Revolution must be told and understood not only through the familiar great pieces of

parchment, but likewise through the small, sometimes grubby, quotidian scraps, sheets, and sheaves

that constituted individual identities and the animate body politic through ink, paper, and wax.

---

[1] John Adams to Archibald Bullock, 1 July 1776, *PJADE*, IV: 201. William Whipple, delegate from New Hampshire, expressed similar anticipation and trepidation in his morning letter to the governor of his home colony: "This day comes on the grand Question," he explained, "the Declaration is prepared, & in my opinion a very good one but I am fearful it will not be mended in Grinding over, You know good things have often been injur'd in a certain house, by endeavoring to suit perticular Humours," William Whipple to John Langdon, 1 July 1776, *LDC*, XXV: 580.

[2] John Hancock to George Washington, 1 July 1776, *PGWDE*, Revolutionary, V: 167. For the reporting of the Declaration of Independence, see *JCC*, 28 June 1776, V: 491.

Rogers' recent arrival and imprisonment had drawn considerable attention and excited speculation, even at this moment of greater crisis in the affairs of the United Colonies. Rogers was a celebrity of sorts—a homegrown, American hero from Britain's last great imperial war, when he had made his name as the famously artful leader of "Rogers' Rangers" in partisan warfare against the French and the Indians. Having suddenly returned to America a little less than two years earlier, after a long absence in England, Rogers had provoked both fascination and intense suspicion wherever he travelled. Though he insisted he was retired and had no plans to take part in the emerging civil war in America, he was widely suspected of being a covert agent of imperial tyranny. Now rumors and speculation about the reason for his arrest were running high. Even as Rogers himself had approached Philadelphia, reports had left the city in the letters of Congressmen that "the famous Major Rogers" had been seized as a party to the "damnable Plott" recently discovered in New York to assassinate General Washington.[3] On the very day the question of independence was taken up in Congress, Thomas Jefferson—architect of the Declaration—remarked in his only letter of that day that "The famous Major Rogers" was "in custody on violent suspicion of being concerned in the conspiracy" against the life of Washington.[4]

The proceedings of the Congress had no sooner opened that morning in the State House (present-day Independence Hall), than the great question of the day was delayed by "Sundry letters"—about twenty in number—that "were laid before Congress and read." Among these was the letter from General Washington—written on the 27th of June to President Hancock and conveyed "by an Officer who attended to guard Major Rogers to Philadelphia"—that would

---

[3] Joseph Hewes to James Iredell, 28 June 1776, *LDC*, IV: 332 ("damnable plot"; "the famous Major Rogers"); John Penn to Samuel Johnston, 28 June 1776, *LDC*, IV: 333: Penn here referred to Rogers as "The famous Rogers that was so active last war," and as "The famous Rogers that was so much talked of last war" in another letter of the same substance and date to an unknown recipient (IV: 333-334).

[4] Thomas Jefferson to William Fleming, 1 July 1776, *PTJDE*, I: 412.

illuminate why he had ordered Rogers to be arrested and sent to Congress to decide his fate.[5]

Washington explained that, "Upon information that Major Rogers was travelling thro' the Country under suspicious circumstances I thought it necessary to have him secured." Rogers had claimed he was on his way from New Hampshire, "the Country of his usual Abode," to Philadelphia, where he intended to make to Congress "a secret Offer of his Services" in the war with Britain. Rogers had explained that he had felt the need to conceal the object of his journey so that if his offer were rejected, "he might have his Way left open to an employment in the East Indies to which he is assigned, and in that Case he flatters himself he will obtain Leave of Congress"—presumably in the form of a passport—"to go to Great Britain." Yet his course of travel, as he himself had described it, was "so far out of his proper and direct Rout to philadelphia" that, combined with "the Length of Time he had taken to perform his Journey, his being found in so suspicious a place as Amboy, his unnecessary Stay there, on pretence of getting some baggage from New York, and an expectation of receiving Money from a person here of bad Character, and in no Circumstances to furnish him out of his own Stock, the Major's reputations, and his being an half pay Officer has encreased my Jealousies about him."[6]

The case, however, had been complicated by the sheaf of papers in Rogers' possession— passes, paroles, permits, and letters. Because Rogers, on his return to America, "had been put upon his parole by Congress," Washington explained, "I thought it would be improper to stay his progress to Philadelphia, should he be in fact destined thither." There had, moreover, been found upon Rogers "Letters...which from their Tenor seem calculated to recommend him to Congress."

---

[5] *JCC*, 1 July 1776, V: 503. Adams had received already one letter from Samuel Chase of Maryland "by the Post this Morning," and would receive another, enclosing the Maryland Convention's unanimous vote in favor of independence, "brought into Congress this Morning, just as We were entering on the great Debate," Adams to Chase, 1 July 1776, *PJADE*, IV: 202. For the arrival and reading of the Maryland resolution shortly after the opening parcel of letters had been read, see *JCC*, 1 July 1776, V: 504.

[6] Washington to Hancock, 27 June 1776, *PGWDE*, Revolutionary, V: 122-123.

Though such letters of recommendation would, under normal circumstances, serve to support the character of the bearer, Washington seemed to consider that those found upon Rogers simply substantiated an intention to deceive. "To prevent imposition" and ensure that Rogers kept to his professed course, Washington sent him onward to Congress, "but...under the Care of an Officer." Clearly wishing to defer to his civilian superiors, as was his wont, Washington nevertheless did not veil very thickly his opinion as to the proper response to Rogers' projected offers, concluding simply that he would "submit it to [Congress's] Consideration, whether it would not be dangerous to accept of the Offer of his Services."[7] The Congress, however, was not prepared to take up the question of Rogers' fate just yet. Writing that same day to inform Washington that Rogers was now imprisoned, President Hancock explained that the prisoner would remain where he was and his fate undecided for the time being, "the Congress having by a particular Appointmt had under Consideration a momentous matter this day, which prevented their Attention to Major Rogers."[8]

Rogers would not sit idly by, however. Nor could the questions and anxieties he raised be put wholly aside or out of mind as the delegates turned to consider their "momentous matter." Even as he prepared for debate on "the grand Question," Congressman William Whipple of New Hampshire had received a note from Rogers explaining that he had a letter for Whipple from John Langdon, governor of his home colony—likely one of the same letters "found upon him" that Washington had deemed so suspect—and "desiring me to call there [at the barracks] for it, as it is open." This news was highly unsettling to Whipple. Sending a servant to retrieve the letter, he immediately wrote home to Langdon in terms of deep concern. Though Whipple had not yet

---

[7] Washington to Hancock, 27 June 1776, *PGWDE*, Revolutionary, V: 122-123. When originally arrested, Rogers had been brought before a Council of General Officers at New York, headed by Washington himself, which had given as their unanimous opinion "that he should proceed to Philad. under an Escort & that at the same Time a Letter be wrote to Congress informing them that under all Circumstances he is not to be sufficiently relied on," Council of General Officers, 27 June 1776, *PGWDE*, Revolutionary, V: 114.

[8] Hancock to Washington, 1 July 1776, *PGWDE*, Revolutionary, V: 167.

received the letter, and "therefore dont know the contents," he supposed "it to be somthing in the Recommendatory way." It would "give me great pain," he explained to Langdon, "if it proves to be a recommendation for undoubtedly Rogers has shewn it, & you may rely on it that General Washington has not apprehended him without sufficient Grounds." Since his arrest and his arrival in Philadelphia, indeed, Rogers had "made no application to Congress," as he had claimed he meant to. "[And] if he shod," Whipple concluded, I think him a man of too infamous a Carrecter to be imploy'd in the Cause of Vertue."[9] The enigmatic, even sinister Major, languishing in the barracks while Congress debated other matters, might have been a spy, an assassin, a devious opportunist, or a treacherous double agent. The connections and identities he had built among his countrymen, embodied in the worrisome papers he bore—or that it was imagined he might secretly bear—meant that Rogers might both threaten the fragile, fledgling "American" cause and implicate any number of unsuspecting and well-meaning Patriots in his infamy.

At the same time, these papers made clear that it was far from easy to discern the true characters and inner commitments of fellow "Americans" caught up in the current crisis but not clearly committed to any of the several sides on offer. The opportunities for ambiguity and dissimulation were too great. But as Rogers himself had discovered, there were very real constraints on the possibilities for self-(re)fashioning—many parties had a stake in his identification, and the paper instruments of identification through which he might claim or reshape the identity he chose had to be negotiated with these many parties. These same instruments, indeed, might ultimately trap him, entangling him in identities not of his choosing and demonstrating the limits of personal control over identity.

---

[9] Whipple to Langdon, 1 July 1776, *LDC*, XXV: 580. Josiah Bartlett later reported to Langdon that "Major Rogers was taken up by order of General Washington and having your letters of recommendation to us, the General ordered him to Congress to be examined," 15 July 1776, *LDC*, IV: 460.

Over the next four days, Rogers' fate remained in suspense and his true character an enigma, even as the Congress debated the identity of the people and polities they represented: Would they be the United Colonies or the United States? Would they continue as a periphery of the British Empire or stake a claim to independence on their own stretch of the Atlantic rim? Would their constituents and they themselves be (British) subjects or ("American") citizens? On what grounds might an independent identity be founded, and what form should the declaration of this identity take? By the 2nd of the month, the question of independence had been resolved, and on the 4th, after two days of revisions, the Declaration of Independence was adopted. In this instrument, the Continental Congress purported to document an established and certain identity—"That these United Colonies are, and of right ought to be, FREE AND INDEPENDENT STATES"—while by the same instrument claiming and enacting a "separate and equal station" among "the powers of the earth." The Declaration of Independence was one of a cluster of state papers—including the Articles of Confederation and the Model Treaty, drafted concurrently with the Declaration—by which the representatives of the newly United States sought to resolve the identities of their polities, severally and collectively, and to constitute them as de facto and bona fide sovereigns. By means of these instruments they could be recognized and form relationships in the international community of sovereign states and could claim legitimate authority to govern their peoples.[10]

At the same time these documents of state creation, and, perhaps, especially the Declaration itself, as an act and a document, carried much more personal implications. Creating, contesting, or transforming the identities of states meant contesting or transforming the identities of those who constituted, acted for, and lived under those states. Revolution, war, independence, and governance

---

[10] "Each of these documents," as David Armitage argues, were "designed to be an expression of state sovereignty under the contemporary law of nations," Armitage, *The Declaration of Independence: A Global History*, (Cambridge, MA: Harvard UP, 2007), 35. For the concurrent drafting of the Articles of Confederation even as the Declaration was coming up for debate, see Josiah Bartlett to Nathaniel Folsom, 1 July 1776, *Papers of Josiah Bartlett*, Frank C. Mevers ed., (Hanover, NH: University Press of New England, 1979), 82.

were fundamentally personal, enacted by real persons from day to day, with stakes defined in the lives and fortunes of individuals. The Declaration itself began with a declaration of equal natural rights for "all men," and concluded with the considerably less abstract declaration by the signers that "for the support of this declaration, with a firm reliance on the protection of Divine Providence, we mutually pledge to each other our lives, our fortunes, and our sacred honor." The personal risk and the contentious questions of political identity implicated in the Declaration on a grand scale, were simultaneously playing out in the fragmentation and reconstitution of communities throughout the colonies.

Considered in light of this ongoing process, the Declaration and allied documents took on a much more concrete and immediately instrumental character. When John Dickinson prepared answers to the arguments in favor of the Declaration, he identified the fourth such argument as that it would "hasten the suppression of Toryism—ascertaining Offenders, trying them; prevent publication of Tory [declarations?]"[11]—casting the Declaration as an addition or adjunct to the battery of loyalty tests by which the enemies of the country might be ferreted out. For Jefferson himself, the Declaration itself took on the role of a personal instrument of identification. Noting with concern his poor showing in the recent election in Virginia and expressing some anxiety that in his absence his character had become the subject of "secret assassination without a possibility of self-defence," Jefferson reflected that "If any doubt has arisen as to me, my country will have my political creed in the form of a 'Declaration &c.' which I was lately directed to draw. This will give decisive proof that my own sentiment concurred with the vote they instructed us to give."[12]

---

[11] John Dickinson, Notes on Arguments Concerning Independence, [1? July 1776], *LDC*, IV: 357. Dickinson did not deny that the Declaration would serve this purpose, but rather that "That purpose will be effectually answered by establishing governments," without the same degree of risk.

[12] Jefferson to William Fleming, 1 July 1776, *PTJDE*, I: 412-413.

The "great and important question of Independance" was, indeed, not so far removed from

the pending question of the identity and fate of "the famous Major Rogers."[13] In the midst of a

crisis of identities, the elusive Major Robert Rogers was a particularly troubling reminder to

"Americans" of the challenging imperatives of identification. Two days after adopting the revised

Declaration of Independence, the Continental Congress resolved to send Rogers "to New-

Hampshire, to be disposed of as the Government of that State shall judge best."[14] That same day,

President Hancock appended a postscript to the copy of the circular announcing the Declaration of

Independence that he directed to the Provincial Congress of New Hampshire, in which he noted

that "Major Rogers, of your Colony, is now here" and that he had been sent to them to be disposed

of as they saw fit.[15] Congress had discovered, member Josiah Bartlett noted, "no absolute proof...of

his ill designs," yet "his conduct appeared so very suspicious" that they had felt justified in

continuing his arrest and consigning him to the discretionary power of his home state's

government.[16]

Rogers was never conveyed to the north. On the 9th of July 1776 he escaped. The

Pennsylvania Committee of Safety offered a £50 reward for his capture and return.[17] But the

---

[13] John Penn to Unknown, 1 July 1776, *LDC*, IV: 334 ("the great and important question of Independance").

[14] *JCC*, 6 July 1776, V: 523.

[15] John Hancock, Letter from the President of Congress to the States of New-York, Massachusetts, Connecticut, Rhode-Island, and New-Hampshire, *AAO*, Series 5, I: 33.

[16] Bartlett to John Langdon, 15 July 1776, *LDC*, IV: 460. It is not clear precisely why the task of disposing of Rogers was delegated to his home state rather than taken on by Congress. It may have been meant to avoid any resentment that might arise in New Hampshire were Congress to punish one of their citizens on its own authority. It may have been that Congress supposed that Rogers, by his (suspected) infamy had most offended the state from which he hailed and those inhabitants of New Hampshire who had been unwittingly implicated in his deceit and dishonor as among his social connections and patrons—those who helped to create and certify the character and identity that he had, it was supposed, abused so cynically. It may have been that precisely these social connections and the local knowledge concerning Rogers that had necessarily accumulated in New Hampshire made the inhabitants of his home state most qualified to judge of his true character and reshape his public identity as appropriate.

[17] Pennsylvania Committee of Safety, 10 July 1776, *AAO*, Series 5, I: 1291. William Ellery, member of Congress, reported in a letter to his brother on the 10Th that "Major Rogers who was under Guard here made his Escape last Evening. He may do Mischief, if he should not be taken," *LDC*, IV: 430.

cunning Major Rogers proved elusive. Where had he gone? Who was he to begin with? And who

had he become? To make sense of Rogers and his encounter with the Revolution we must begin by

tracing his earlier efforts to remake his identity and navigate the increasingly troubled American

landscape.

By the end of the French and Indian War (the Seven Years War), Robert Rogers had become

a hero, especially to his fellow Americans who were resentful of British denigration and dismissal of

"provincial" soldiers and officers. Benjamin Franklin, who would long remember being lectured by

General Edward Braddock in 1755 upon the superiority of the King's regulars, pointed in 1759 to

Rogers as a key example in refutation of such prejudice, noting "That one ranging Captain of a few

Provincials, Rogers, has harrassed the enemy more on the frontiers of Canada, and destroyed more

of their men, than the whole army of Regulars."[18] But in the years of peace that followed the war,

Rogers' fortunes had declined and his trials had mounted. Floundering for lack of direction, faced

by mounting debts and low prospects, Rogers had ventured to England in 1765 seeking either a new

position in the imperial military or support for his proposed venture to discover the Northwest

Passage. By the time he set out for England, Franklin had already offered him a recommendation.

To Franklin, Rogers was an emblematically American provincial and a useful polemical touchstone

for his work to support American equality within the empire. Once in England Rogers had turned

to Franklin and others for their influence in support of his petitions and proposals to the

government and the lords of the empire. Months of lobbying had brought him an appointment as

commander of the fort at Michilimackinac, and he had returned to America in early 1766 bearing

---

[18] Franklin, "To the Printer of the London Chronicle," 9 May 1759, printed in *The London Chronicle: or, Universal Evening Post*, May 10-12, 1759, *PBFDE*. Franklin recalled in his autobiography how, upon pointing out to General Braddock the vulnerabilities of his army, to attack by the Native Americans, Braddock had "smil'd at my Ignorance, and reply'd, 'These Savages may indeed be a formidable Enemy to your *raw* American Militia; but upon the King's regular and disciplin'd Troops, Sir, it is impossible they should make any Impression'," *Autobiography of Benjamin Franklin*, 2nd ed., Leonard W. Labaree et al eds., (New Haven, CT: Yale UP, 2003), 224.

letters of recommendation and orders in his favor from both Secretary of State Conway and the

Secretary of War, on the strength of which he was grudgingly given his promised appointment on

the northwest frontier by General Thomas Gage, who distrusted and despised Rogers as an

uneducated, unprincipled, and cunning parvenu.[19]

Questionable dealings in his new station and the continuing animosity and suspicion of Gage

led to his court martial for treason and a brief imprisonment, though he was ultimately acquitted.

After his release, Rogers made a second venture to England in the hopes of renovating his

professional, social, and financial prospects.[20] Caught up in his own troubles even as the crisis

between the British Empire and his native America deepened, Rogers once more turned to Franklin

for a portion of the influence and patronage that might allow him to restore his reputation, badly

damaged by years of financial difficulties and professional scandal. In 1770 he offered Franklin his

"Estimate and account of the Peltry and Firr Trade in the District of Michilimakinac made from

many Years carefull Observation whilst I commanded in that Country," possibly in hopes Franklin

would support his efforts to have Michilimackinac made a separate province.[21] Two years later

Rogers sought "the Doct[or's] Interest" in support of his "Petition for a Tour thro' the North

American Continent"—yet another proposal to undertake the discovery of a Northwest Passage.[22]

Franklin had certainly not forgotten Rogers, and though he could offer him little assistance in his

---

[19] John R. Cuneo, *Robert Rogers of the Rangers*, (New York: Oxford UP, 1959) 179-180, 183-187, passim; Peter Marshall, "Colonial Protest and Imperial Retrenchment: Indian Policy, 1764-1768," *Journal of American Studies*, V: 1 (Apr. 1971), 15.

[20] Cuneo, *Robert Rogers of the Rangers*, 179-180, 183-187, passim.

[21] Rogers to Franklin, 4 May 1770, *PBFDE*. For Roger's plan for Michilimackinac and the possible role of this letter to Franklin, see Cuneo, *Robert Rogers of the Rangers*, 249.

[22] Rogers to Franklin, 20 February 1772, *PBFDE*.

present difficulties, their connection would reemerge, if on very different terms, on Rogers' return to America three years later.[23]

Rogers' second journey to England, in search of back-pay and a new position, won him little more than three successive stints in debtor's prison, before obtaining his release under new bankruptcy laws and securing a retirement as a Major on half-pay.[24] As a bankrupt, formerly charged with treason, and now on half-pay, Rogers had sunk low in credit, character, and station—despite a nominal promotion—and was once again without a well-defined identity in either Britain or America. What patronage and influence he had been able to secure from the ministry and from Franklin, among others, had been deployed with little lasting effect in the face of misfortune, the countervailing efforts of Gage and other enemies, and his own missteps and mismanagement.

Rogers' post-war career had been defined by his attempts to navigate the streams of influence flowing through the British Atlantic world, largely in the form of letters of introduction and recommendation, and to secure the patronage that would allow him to claim a new position or launch a new career. When Rogers returned to America, however—sailing from England in early June 1775 and making landfall on Virginia's eastern shore in early September—he returned with no letters of recommendation (as far as is known) and no new patronage or influence clothing his person. It had been more than a decade since his exploits had won him renown in war against the French and Indians, and nearly seven years since he had last left America. New issues and new heroes had since risen to prominence. But Rogers' fame endured in some measure. Even as he was

---

[23] Indeed, since Rogers' return to England, Franklin had purchased a published edition of his journals from the French and Indian War: Inventory of Franklin's library, 1790, *PBFDE*. The inventory indicates that Franklin purchased the *Journals* in London in 1759. Because the first edition of Roger's *Journals* did not appear until 1765, it is likely that the 1759 date should instead be 1769 (when Franklin could have purchased the first edition, or a second edition that appeared that same year).

[24] For Rogers' life, service during the French and Indian War, and interwar career, see John F. Ross, *War on the Run: The Epic Story of Robert Rogers and the Conquest of America's First Frontier*, (New York: Bantam, 2009); Robert J. Rogers, *Rising Above Circumstances: The Rogers Family in Colonial America*, (Bedford, Quebec: Sheltus & Picard, 1998), 114-187; and, esp., Cuneo, *Robert Rogers of the Rangers*.

crossing the Atlantic from England, American newspapers were printing and reprinting reports that both recalled his bravery and prowess from the past war and linked him to the rising emblem of American patriotic, military leadership. "The late Duke of Newcastle," it was reported, "scrupled not to acknowledge Colonel Washington and Major Rogers 'two of the bravest and most experienced Officers in the King's service.'" Now, the papers pointed out, "The Colonel is...in his own service; and if he could fight so courageously for his King, there is no doubt of his displaying a redoubled valour for himself."[25] Clearly Washington was the new focus of attention, but Rogers was placed on an equal footing. The implicit question may now have been whether Major Rogers, should he return, would follow the Virginia Colonel's example and turn his bravery and experience to the service of the American cause.

After an absence of nearly seven years, Rogers found his native land roiling with conflict and suspicion. He would soon find, indeed, that as an officer in the British army, suddenly returned during this moment of crisis after years of absence in England, his own identity had been destabilized and his character and loyalties rendered suspect by the shifts of the political landscape. Nonetheless, he was, in a certain sense, emblematic and, in an extreme form, illustrative of the predicament of "Americans" and America in general. Having been born and spent most of his life in North America, he had dedicated his professional life to the service of the British Empire, as an officer first in the provincial forces and later in the Royal Army. Though his relationship with his military superiors and with the ministry in Britain had been far from smooth, it was nonetheless to these same figures and to the imperial metropolis that he had been repeatedly forced to resort for possible aid or relief in his distress. He now returned to his homeland, where his wife and family lived and where he owned land, still in the pay of and closely identified with the forces now cast in

---

[25] *Pennsylvania Journal,* 5 July 1775, 2; *Pennsylvania Mercury,* 7 July 1775, 1; *Virginia Gazette,* 21 July 1775, supplement, 1; *Norwich Packet,* 24 July 1775, 3. *AHN.*

the role of tyrants by so many of his compatriots. Rogers faced a challenge, to choose and to secure

an identity in the midst of a crisis both personal and imperial in scope. In both his navigation of the

interstices of the early Revolution and his efforts to secure an acceptable and practicable identity,

Rogers would wrestle with the limits imposed and the opportunities offered by the instruments of

identification—actual and imagined—by which he would find himself defined and through which he

would craft and practice several possible, compound identities in paper and wax.

Though Rogers had fought in the past war as a provincial officer, he had since held royal

commission as governor and now held a commission in the Royal Army as a Major on half-pay.

Since the Stamp Act crisis, commissions to particular offices under the crown—stamp agent,

customs officer, and others—had marked out individuals for abuse, ostracism, and vilification as

agents of corruption and tyranny and enemies of the liberties of America.[26] Since the imposition of

the Coercive Acts the year preceding Rogers' return, acceptance or use of a Royal commission under

or in service of the new policies had become a damning crime against the "American cause," first in

New England and then throughout colonies, as sympathy and mutual support were consolidated.

Since Lexington and Concord and Bunker Hill, a commission in the Royal Army had become a sure

mark of an enemy. (The Revolutionary contest for and transition of authority, both civil and

military, would be enacted through campaigns to force the resignation of Royal commissions, and

issue new commissions, first in the King's name, then on the authority of the local polities

themselves: See Chapter 3.)

---

[26] T.H. Breen, *American Insurgents, American Patriots: The Revolution of the People*, (New York: Hill & Wang, 2010), 83, 89, 130, 135; Pauline Maier, *From Resistance to Revolution: Colonial Radicals and the Development of American Opposition to Britain, 1765-1776*, (New York: Norton, 1991), 14, 16, 85, 97, 98, 129, 279. In December of 1773, the destruction of property in the Boston "Tea Party" was preceded, a week before, by efforts to persuade those to which the tea had been consigned to "resign their Commission," a step refused by the Boston consignees but which the Boston opposition was informed had been acceded to by the consignees of New York and Philadelphia, who had "declar'd without Reserve they would not have the lest Share in executing a Commission so disagreable to their Fellow Citizens." Samuel Cooper to Benjamin Franklin, 17 December 1773, *PBFDE*.

Rogers' renown as a brave and cunning military leader endured. But now—through the one instrument of identification he bore on his return, his commission—his fame identified him as a potential, and perhaps actual, instrument and agent of ministerial tyranny. In this context, his commission as an officer on half-pay made him a particularly ambiguous figure. The system of half-pay commissions had been established to cope with the population of demobilized officers produced by the reduction in size of the armed forces during intervals of peace. The officers put on half-pay became a sort of reserve force, liable to be recalled to active service (and full pay) when the needs of their country demanded it. Yet it functioned for the many officers who were never recalled as a kind of retirement pension.[27] When Rogers later explained himself to Washington by letter during his travels through Massachusetts, he would affirm that, "I have leave to retire on my Half-pay, & never expect to be call'd into the service again."[28]

Despite his commission, then, Rogers could be seen as only nominally an officer of the Royal Army. Another American half-pay officer—Lieutenant Colonel Charles Lee—had in fact already become a leading figure in the new American military establishment. As early as October of 1774, the British ministry had been informed that Lee "has lately appeared at Boston," where "he associates only with the enemies of government" and "encourages the discontents of the people by harangues and publications, and even advises to arms."[29] Less than a year later, he was commissioned one of the first Major Generals of the new Continental Army.[30] Rogers could well prove a similar resource to the American cause. But he had as yet given no such overt signs by his

---

[27] Richard Holmes, "Half-Pay," *Oxford Companion to Military History*, Richard Holmes ed., (New York: Oxford UP, 2001).

[28] Rogers to Washington, 14 December 1775, *PGWDE*, Revolutionary, II: 549-551.

[29] Lord Dartmouth to General Thomas Gage, 17 October 1774, *CMHS*, Series 4, IX: 716-717. Dartmouth pointed out to Gage that "This gentleman's general character cannot be unknown to you, and therefore, it will be very proper, that you should have attention to his conduct, and take every legal method to prevent his effecting any of those dangerous purposes, he is said to have in view."

[30] See George Washington, General Orders, 4 July 1775, *PGWDE*, Revolutionary, I: 54.

actions or words, as had Lee, to indicate his intentions or his loyalties. Likewise, unlike Lee, Rogers

still held his royal commission—not having exchanged it for an American, republican commission—

as the paper, documentary landscape around him was being transformed.

Major Rogers made landfall in Virginia near the beginning of September 1775 and quickly

turned his steps toward Philadelphia.[31] There he hoped to obtain from "the Gentlemen that

compose the Continental Congress…[their permit to set]tle my private Affairs, being much

[encumbered with de]bts."[32] Before he could obtain this instrument, however, he was arrested by

the Pennsylvania Committee of Safety.[33] Rogers had arrived in a country that was charged with

suspicion, anxiety, and insecurity. The invisible and mutable character of the political commitments

by which Americans were attempting to divide and identify themselves and each other meant that

Americans could well view with suspicion their friends, neighbors, and compatriots, let alone

transients. Besides the need to restore the basic social and institutional structures through which

identity normally functioned, the high-stakes of war and revolution meant that, even as it suddenly

became more difficult, it simultaneously became more essential to be able to tell who could be

trusted. Without letters of introduction and recommendation, Rogers lacked the key means or tools

---

[31] Having made landfall in Norfolk, Virginia near the beginning of September, Rogers was in Philadelphia within three weeks: *Pennsylvania Evening Post*, 12 September 1775, 1, reprinting a story from Williamsburg, VA, dated 2 September and reporting that "Major Rogers arrived at Norfolk a few days ago." *AHN*. Rogers wove a complex web of sobriquets as he traversed Revolutionary North America: Joseph Hewes to James Iredell, 28 June 1776, *LDC*, IV: 332-333 ("famous Major Rogers"); Jonathan Trumbull, Sr. to Henry Beekman Livingston, 13 October 1776, *AAO*, Series V, II: 1030 ("infamous"; "artful"); "Extract of a letter from a gentleman in the Army…," 1 November 1776, *AAO*, Series 5, III: 473 ("infamous"); Samuel Adams to Samuel Mather, 26 October 1776, *LDC*, V: 390 ("infamous"); Trumbull to George Washington, 13 October 1776, *PGWDE*, Revolutionary, VI: 559-561 ("Noted"); "Intelligence at Boston," 14 November 1776, *AAO*, Series V, III: 685 ("well-known"); Washington to Trumbull, 12 April 1777, *PGWDE*, Revolutionary, XI: 143 ("villain"); Nathanael Greene to George Washington, 24 October 1776, *PGWDE*, Revolutionary, VII: 23-24 ("vile Traytor").

[32] Rogers to Washington, 14 December 1775, *PGWDE*, Revolutionary, II: 550.

[33] Pennsylvania Committee of Safety, 22 September 1775, *AAO*, Series 4, III: 865.

by which the American opposition reconstructed networks of trust from the fragments of their old, disrupted social world (see Chapter 2).

As a native and a celebrity of the British North American colonies, who had, however, been long absent and was now far from his home colony of New Hampshire, Rogers fit into both of the two salient categories of dangerous individual, the "stranger" and the "suspected person." These categories had emerged during several cycles of protest—culminating in the enforcement of the Continental Association by local committees of observation in the autumn of 1774—as Americans on both sides attempted to distinguish opponents from allies and to enforce conformity with resistance strategies or Parliamentary authority. But the nature of such scrutiny shifted and the intensity grew as more or less peaceful opposition within the empire became armed insurgency.

From the perspective of many Patriots, once war had broken out, the "Tories" were now even more dangerous as potential enemy agents. Those who had not taken the part of open enemies to the American cause might now try to disguise their loyalties, even insinuate themselves into the councils and forces of the patriots, before ultimately betraying their compatriots. Those New Englanders and others who had committed their all to the American cause feared not only such subversion, but also that persons so unprincipled as they believed the Tories to be might dissimulate their allegiance and attempt to recover or secure the standing and the property that had been or would be justly taken from them.

Driven by such apprehensions, the company of volunteer infantry from Worcester who had made their way to the outskirts of Boston and incorporated themselves into a regiment of the Continental Army, addressed a memorial to the Provincial Congress—under the auspices of their colonel, Jonathan Ward—from Dorchester near the end of September 1775. The town and county of Worcester, they explained, had been "Intolerably infested with a Cruel and Merciless set of Tories." When the war had come, "then these Hardy Wretches trembled, some Confess'd and like

Vermin Crawl among the Roots of Vegitables endeavouring to secret themselves while they are a

Neusance to the Cause of Justice and Judgment." Worse still, others were, "in Sheeps Cloathing

secretly watching for prey to gratify their Voratious Appetites, or availing themselves of the good

Opinion of the Prudent ascend into places of Power, or Profit and Render'd Capable of acting their

predecessor Judas's part, when Opportunity favour their design betray the good Cause with, All Hail

and a Hypocritical Kiss." Those who had not disguised themselves for such purposes had "fled to

Boston" and taken an open part against their countrymen, by which they had forfeited their rights to

property and to life and had made themselves "Pirates." Now, even "some of those Vermin or

worse Emissaries of Tyranny" were "Crawling out of Boston to their forfeited seats at Worcester,"

to try to reclaim their property or belatedly insinuate themselves for purposes of future betrayal.

The Worcester volunteers petitioned the Congress that such Loyalists, "however humble and

Penitent they may appear," should not be allowed to return to Worcester and regain their standing

and property, but that they should be instead imprisoned or forced to return to Boston. [34]

The "Tories" were cast in this memorial (and in similar texts) as protean deceivers, masters

of disguise, so despicably changeable and mercenary that they could adapt their identities with each

change of circumstance. While the Worcester volunteers felt that they could clearly discern the

Tories' devious purposes and true selves underneath their "Sheeps Cloathing"—or at least possessed

a firm conviction that no second chances could be risked—they feared that the Congress and the

committee in Worcester might well be deceived. The civil war had made or revealed as enemies

friends, neighbors, and associates whose common origin with the Patriots made their Loyalism

traitorous, but who, for the same reason, could not be easily identified. Provincial congresses, soon

after Lexington and Concord, began to urge on county and local committees the need for a more

---

[34] Jonathan Ward, et al., to the Provincial Congress of Massachusetts, 27 September 1775, U.S. Revolution Collection, Box 2, Folder 2, AAS.

intense and systematic redoubling of their local efforts to identify and dispose appropriately of

"suspected persons" in their midst (see Chapter 4).

In Pennsylvania, to which Rogers would direct his course upon his return to America, the

Committee of Safety and the Continental Congress were on the lookout for suspect newcomers,

especially British officers. When, in June of 1775, Major Philip Skene arrived at Philadelphia from

London, he was arrested on shipboard and his papers seized by order of the Continental Congress.

It was known that Skene had been appointed governor of Ticonderoga (since captured by

Connecticut troops), and it was believed he had urged and helped plan military operations against

the rebellious colonists. After being held for a time in Philadelphia, Skene was sent as a prisoner to

Hartford, where he remained until exchanged in September of 1776.[35] In mid August of 1775, the

Committee of Safety ordered the arrest of a number of "Officers of the Ministerial Army," including

one Major French and his servants, of whose arrival as passengers at Gloucester from Cork they had

just been informed. These officers the Committee "enlarged upon their written Parole," dispatching

them to Washington's camp at Cambridge, under the direction and protection of "two respectable

Gentlemen" from Philadelphia.[36]

Major Rogers would not be taken up quite so immediately or, once examined, laid under

quite such narrow constraints as Skene or French, but his arrival was duly noted and his behavior

watched. On September 21, Richard Smith, in Philadelphia, would note in his diary that, "Major

---

[35] Messieurs Gibson & Aston to Messieurs John & Robert Barclay, 9 June 1775, APSED, Film 391, Reel 13, No. 1305, DLAR; Mordecai Lewis to Joseph Woods, 9 June 1775, APSED, Film 391, Reel 13, No. 1306, DLAR; Thomas Wharton to Samuel Wharton, 10 June 1775, APSED, Film 391, Reel 13, No. 1309, DLAR; Enoch Story to Messieurs John & Robert Barclay, 11 June 1775, APSED, Film 391, Reel 13, No. 1312, DLAR. "Skene, Philip," *ANB*.

[36] Pennsylvania Committee of Safety to George Washington, 17 August 1775, *PBFDE*. In September, [Alexander?] Pepperrell would write from Portsmouth to Lord Dartmouth in England to report his arrest. He had originally arrived at Boston and then made his way to Portsmouth. "[O]n my arrival there," he reported, "I was carried before a committee which is appointed to examine all Strangers whatever coming from England: I was made to declare I held no commission under the Crown, or any employment, and likewise that I had done nothing that was prejudicial to the Country." He was subsequently ordered confined to the town. Pepperrell to Dartmouth, 4 September 1775, APSED, Film 391, Reel 14, No. 1481, DLAR.

Robert Rogers was at the State House today; he is just come from England & is upon the Kings Halfpay."[37] Soon thereafter, Rogers was arrested by the Pennsylvania Committee of Safety. In consultation with the Continental Congress, the Committee determined that, having found nothing against him but his status as a half-pay officer, Rogers could be released, were he to give his parole "not to take up arms against the inhabitants of America, in the present controversy between Great Britain and America" or convey intelligence to the British.[38]

In requiring Rogers to give his parole, the Committee and the Congress identified him as belonging to a class of outsiders or disaffected persons who were to be set aside, placed outside the sphere of the civil war burgeoning around them. The parole, as such, took the place of and, in a sense, exempted Rogers and others of his stamp from taking an alternate form of oath used to distinguish adherents of each side. Such oaths of abjuration or allegiance, and the certificates issued to individuals to demonstrate that they had taken them, were successors to the less radical Continental Association. They would proliferate and gain importance as instruments of war and state building in the succeeding year and more of conflict, first within the more limited sphere of the military forces and certain high-level civil offices, but later encompassing the civil population as a whole (see Chapter 4).

Pre-war political fragmentation, the rise of local committees, and the institution of provisional independent governments led to the arrest or examination of Loyalists and royal officials, some of whom were subsequently released on their parole, bringing the figure of the parolee and the material embodiment of his identity, the parole certificate or pass, to the

---

[37] *LDC*, II: 39.

[38] *JCC*, 22 September 1775, III: 259. The next day Rogers came before the Committee of Safety, chaired by Benjamin Franklin—an admirer, correspondent, and patron of Rogers during their overlapping sojourns in London, who had returned to Philadelphia roughly five months ahead of the prisoner himself. Finding no reason to hold him longer, the Committee allowed Roger's to give his parole. Pennsylvania Committee of Safety, 23 September 1775, *AAO*, Series 4, III: 866.

communities of Revolutionary America. These initial examples prefigured a more salient population and regime of documentation to come during the course of the war. To the initial political parolees would be added paroled prisoners of war. Along with the individual parolees dispersed, lodged, or making their way through the American landscape, large bodies or groups of prisoners and parolees soon became a prominent and increasingly familiar feature of Revolutionary America.[39] In this context, parole certificates served to certify that the enemy officer encountered in friendly territory was permitted (or required) to be there, had given assurances that he would not work against the American cause, and had remained within the bounds prescribed for him. They likewise served to certify, to the officer's own superiors or countrymen, if the parolee was permitted to travel home or into territory held by his own army, that he could not honorably serve the cause—he was not shirking his duty.

In a typical parole, an individual gave his "Parole of Honor"—literally his "word of honor"—to abide by the terms of the parole (i.e., not work against the interests of the paroling authority until exchanged), and often explicitly bound himself on his faith or honor "as a gentleman." The parole certificate as a genre and the practice of parole more generally, embodied, documented, and put into practice a regime of identification in which individuals of differential social status played by different rules and were identified according to different standards, by different means, and under largely separate regimes, embodying and inscribing privilege in the material instruments and practices of identification and identity. Though common soldiers and seamen were sometimes allowed to give parole, the fundamental premise of the institution and the document was that soldiers and officers, and therefore prisoners, were divided broadly between

---

[39] In late September of 1776, for instance, Jedediah Huntington wrote to Jabez Huntington from the camp at King's Bridge, New York, reporting that about three hundred of "our men who were Prisoners at the Northward [Canada?]" were "arrived among us" and were "on Parole not to take up Arms until an Exchange of Prisoners is made." Jedediah Huntington to Jabez Huntington, 28 September 1776, Camp at King's Bridge, NY, Sol Feinstone Collection, Film 1, Reel 2, No. 594, DLAR.

gentlemen and commoners, those who were possessed of honor and could be trusted to keep their promises in order to preserve it, and those who were not and could not.[40]

Rogers, it seems, had hoped he might be able, if he were sufficiently circumspect and unobtrusive, to navigate the conflict-torn continent without offending or committing to either side—refusing to identify as either an American rebel or a British officer—and attend to his "private Affairs." He was, after all, famous for his cunning and resource. But Rogers was also sufficiently canny to recognize the opportunity these divisions offered, and, perhaps, desperate enough after a decade of setbacks to imagine they might offer the solution to his persistent troubles. Very nearly as soon as he had arrived in Philadelphia, "[t]he famous Partisan Major Rogers" paid a visit to John and Samuel Adams, delegates to the Continental Congress from Massachusetts. "He thinks We shall have hot Work, next Spring," John Adams would note later that day in his diary: "He told me an old half Pay Officer, such as himself, would sell well next Spring." On taking his leave Rogers made sure the two gentlemen from Massachusetts had taken his meaning, declaring that, "if you want me, next Spring for any Service, you know where I am, send for me. I am to be sold."[41]

His fellow Americans were not all so willing to tolerate such bold refusal to commit. "Patriot" authorities demanded to know whom they could or could not trust. By first arresting Rogers and then imposing the parole as a condition of his release, the Committee and the Congress foreclosed his suspension of identity, which he had hoped to preserve for the time being and turn to his advantage down the road. Though not quite requiring him to take an active part in upholding their cause, or even to declare a particular allegiance, they had formally fixed Rogers in a particular identity and thereby neutralized him as a potential threat.

---

[40] On the culture of honor in general and its relation to military hierarchy and command in particular, see Caroline Cox, *A Proper Sense of Honor: Service and Sacrifice in George Washington's Army*, (Chapel Hill, NC: University of North Carolina Press, 2004). On the culture of honor more generally, see Joanne B. Freeman, *Affairs of Honor: National Politics in the New Republic*, (New Haven, CT: Yale UP, 2001).

[41] John Adams, Diary, 21 Sept 1775, *PJADE*, II: 234.

In giving his parole, Rogers identified himself as both "Robert Rogers, Major on half pay in His Majesty's Army" and "a prisoner in the custody of the Committee of Safety for the Province of Pennsylvania." Being "enlarged on parole" he "solemnly promise[d] and engage[d], on the honour of a soldier and a gentleman" neither to take up arms against the "United Colonies" nor to convey intelligence "to General Gage, the British Ministry, or any other person or persons, of any matters relative to America."[42] Through both the substance and the fact of giving this parole, Rogers declared and acknowledged himself not only a soldier made prisoner but a particular class and character of prisoner—a gentleman capable of engaging "honour"—that is, possessing a character such that he was worthy to be trusted on his own recognizance. The Committee and the Congress by prescribing and accepting his parole, in this form, tacitly confirmed Rogers in this same character. They thus, in some measure—if in a backhanded manner—forwarded Rogers' efforts to renovate his reputation after the trials of the preceding decade and more. Rogers in turn by the substance and fact of his parole recognized "the United Colonies" as a legitimate political entity and authority (if not necessarily autonomous: Pennsylvania was still "the Province of Pennsylvania" and the British King was still simply "His Majesty") which could legitimately hold him prisoner, with which he could legitimately make such an agreement, and to which he could pledge his honor. In this way Rogers and the several layers of "American" authority implicated in the transaction contributed to the constitution of each other's identities, through a set of iterative acts of identification.

Rogers' parole was, of course, only words—a law of his own making that he bound himself to obey. But if he was to sustain and practice the identity he claimed as a gentleman and an officer, he had to abide by his word of honor (quite apart from any question of his principles or conscience). Even more immediately and more practically, he was aware that to pursue his private affairs he would need the Committee and the Congress's approval of his presence and movement within the

---

[42] Pennsylvania Committee of Safety, 23 September 1775, *AAO*, Series 4, III: 866.

colonies, as well as their certification of his identity as a person, who, if not an ally and adherent of the cause, was at least officially neutralized and harmless. Rogers' accordingly requested and received "a copy of his Parole, and the following Certificate, viz:"

> These are to certify to all persons to whom these presents may appear, that the above writing if a true copy of the parole of honour given by the bearer, Major Robert Rogers, to the Committee of Safety for the Province of Pennsylvania; it is therefore recommended to such persons that the said Major Rogers be permitted to pass where his business may lead him, without any hinderance or molestation.[43]

Rogers would thus leave Philadelphia with an instrument of identification, and of mobility, not unlike the "permit" that he would later tell Washington he had gone to request from Congress. But he left, by virtue of this same instrument, in a character that was both a step towards the restored standing he aimed at, and far different from the character in which he had hoped and expected to continue on his journey.

Having set out from Philadelphia,[44] Rogers soon came face to face with the fragility and contingency of his new paper identity and the Congressional authority that underwrote it. On his way through New Jersey, he lost his "Pockett Book," and with it "the Copy of my Parole with the Committees permission for my going to New Hampshire or where else I had Occasion."[45] Called before the New York Committee of Safety on his arrival in New York City, Rogers was forced to suspend his journey until a replacement pass and certificate of parole could be procured from Philadelphia and verified by the New York committee.[46] On the 29th of September, Rogers wrote accordingly to his old patron Benjamin Franklin, now chairman of the Pennsylvania Committee of

---

[43] Pennsylvania Committee of Safety, 23 September 1775, *AAO*, Series 4, III: 866.

[44] For his home in Portsmouth, by way of his brother James' home in far north New York (now Vermont): Rogers to Washington, 14 December 1775, *PGWDE*, Revolutionary, II: 540-551; John Sullivan to Washington, 17 December 1775, *PGWDE*, Revolutionary, II: 567-568.

[45] Rogers to Franklin, 29 September 1775, *PBFDE*.

[46] New York Committee of Safety, 27 September 1775, *AAO*, Series 4, III: 913.

Safety, to request a replacement.[47] In response to Rogers' letter to Franklin, the Committee

approved and dispatched a replacement certificate on October 3rd.[48] Rogers' papers were then, in

turn, read and recorded by the New York Provincial Congress, who added to his pass their minutes

to this effect and possibly a pass of their own, before sending Rogers on his way.[49]

Describing a wide arc north and west, through Albany, to his brother's house, and then back

east to New Hampshire, Rogers approached Portsmouth from the north. There he submitted his

"permit" to the New Hampshire Committee of Safety, which seems to have added its own visa and

approval, before he set off towards Boston.[50] Having made his way to the outskirts of Boston by

early December of 1775—three trying months after his return to America—Rogers had deliberately

brought himself to the epicenter of the American crisis, where he might be most suspect and most

in danger, but also where he might be best able to secure a new and sustainable identity. Writing to

his wife Elizabeth, at home in Portsmouth, Rogers would report, with a mixture of relief and

concern, that "it was luckey that I went to Medford and from thence wrote to General

washington—as many persons had given a Verey unfavorable Representation censerning My coming

to america." He had been told that "Some had wrote that I had been to Canada and if [not ...?] that

I was Second in comand to Genl Carleton," royal governor and commander in chief of Canada.[51]

These reports had preceded him in a letter to General Washington from Eleazar Wheelock,

the founder and president of Dartmouth College, to whom Rogers had paid a visit on his way

---

[47] Rogers to Franklin, 29 September 1775, *PBFDE*.

[48] Pennsylvania Committee of Safety, 3 October 1775, *AAO*, Series 4, III: 1812.

[49] New York Provincial Congress, 5 October 1775, *AAO*, Series 4, III: 1271-1272. Rogers to Elizabeth Rogers, 17 December 1775, Rogers-Roche Collection, Small Collections, Box 48, Folder 22, WLCL.

[50] Rogers to Elizabeth Rogers, 17 December 1775, Rogers-Roche Collection, Small Collections, Box 48, Folder 22, WLCL; Rogers to Washington, 14 December 1775, *PGWDE*, Revolutionary, II: 540-551; John Sullivan to Washington, 17 December 1775, *PGWDE*, Revolutionary, II: 567-568.

[51] Robert Rogers to Elizabeth Rogers, 17 December 1775, Rogers-Roche Collection, Small Collections, Box 48, Folder 22, WLCL.

through New Hampshire the previous month. Surprised and suspicious of the unexpected visit

from "the Famous Major Rogers"—whom he had "never before Seen" and who appeared "in but

ordinary Habit for one of his Character"—Wheelock had subsequently received third or fourth-

hand reports, through soldiers returning from the failed campaign to Canada, that Rogers had been

spotted to the northward. Along with speculation that he was secretly appointed to high command

in Canada, it was reported that Rogers, well in keeping with his famous exploits, "had lately been in

Indian Habit through Our Encampments at St Johns and had given a plan of them to the General."

Having evaded capture, or even detection, it was conjectured that Rogers, thus disguised, had "Made

his escape with the Indians which were at St Johns." Though expressing some uneasiness at

conveying reports of such a character, Wheelock considered that "If it Shall prove of any Service to

detect Such an Enemy I Shall be glad."[52]

In the course of his journey, Rogers had experienced the fragile and ephemeral nature of the

paper instruments of identification upon which he relied. But he had also experienced their

fundamental necessity as means to secure his claims to a stable and admissible identity and to make

that identity portable. He had, moreover, experienced the highly fragmented, multi-layered state of

governance and the corresponding regimes of identification symptomatic of a lack of centralized

authority. This entailed an iterative process of identification and re-identification by multiple

authorities, who had to review and recertify his papers. His identity became compound as he

journeyed through multiple, overlapping jurisdictions and his papers accreted new layers.

---

[52] Eleazar Wheelock to George Washington, 2 December 1775, *PGWDE*, Revolutionary Series, II: 473-475.

He had resolved, accordingly, "to lay My pass before general washington…[with] the different [Minutes?] made theron by the provinchal conresses of New York and newhampshire."[53] From Medford, Massachusetts, on the 14th of December, Rogers dispatched a letter to Washington in which he detailed his travel since his departure from England, and provided a transcription of "the passport I receivd at Philadelphia from the Committee of Safety…together with the Minutes made thereon by the Committees of safety at New York & New Hampshire." He petitioned Washington "for a continuance of that permission for me to go unmolested where my private Business may call me as it will take some Months from this time to settle with all my Creditors." Rogers assured Washington that, though an officer on half-pay, he expected never "to be call'd into the service again." He was indeed committed to the country, though he could not involve himself in the current war: "I love North America," he assured Washington, "it is my native Country & that of my Family's, and I intend to spend the Evening of my days in it."[54]

Though Rogers expressed to Washington a desire "to pay you my respects personally, the circumspect commander in chief instead dispatched General John Sullivan to take the measure of the famously cunning soldier, whose arrival had been preceded by such sinister reports. After two meetings with Rogers, Sullivan reported that he had "Strictly Examined him have Seen his Several permits and think them Genuine & in Every Respect agreeable to the Copy Sent you." Confronted with the rumors that had preceded him, Rogers admitted "Every thing in Mr Wheelocks Letter Except that of his having been in Canada which he warmly Denies & Says he can prove the Rout he Took and prove himself to have been in the Several Towns at or near the Days he has mentioned." Still suspicious of Rogers' presence so near the principal theatre of the war, Sullivan "asked him why

<hr>

[53] Rogers to Elizabeth Rogers, 17 December 1775, Rogers-Roche Collection, Small Collections, Box 48, Folder 22, WLCL.

[54] Rogers to Washington, 14 December 1775, *PGWDE*, Revolutionary, II: 550.

he came to the Camp as he had no Business with any particular person & had no Inclination to offer his Service in the American Cause." Rogers explained,

> that he had voluntarily waited upon the Committees of Several Colonies as he [thought] it a piece of Respect Due to them and would probably prevent his being Suspected and Treated as a person unfriendly to us—That he Likewise thought it his Duty to wait on your Excellencey & acquaint you with the Situation of his affairs and if he could to obtain your Licence to Travel unmolested.

Sullivan claimed to transmit a faithful report of "the Facts as handed to me" by Rogers, but professed that as to "what may be his Secret Designs I am unable to Say," suggesting that when it came to "what Steps are most proper to be taken Respecting him your Excellencey can best Judge." Nevertheless, Sullivan went on to offer the supposition that while he was "far from thinking that [Rogers] had been in Canada but as he was once Governor of Michalamackinack it is possible he may have a Commission to Take that Command & Stir up the Indians against us & only waits for an opportunity to get there." Sullivan advised Washington, accordingly, "Lest Some Blame might be Laid upon your Excellencey in future not to give him any other permit but Let him Avail himself of those he has & Should he prove a Traytor Let the Blame Centre upon those who Enlarged him."[55]

Thus, while Sullivan judged the identification and travel papers Rogers presented to be genuine and proper, Rogers' identity was shaped as much or more in Sullivan's judgment by an imagined instrument of identification: Rogers' possible, secret commission from the British to draw the Indians of the west into war against the colonies. Combined with the taint on his character conveyed by Wheelock's reports (containing similar speculation about a different commission altogether), this imagined commission might even poison the identities of those too closely associated with Rogers should it eventually come to light. It would be the better part of wisdom to take advantage of the decentralized and fragmented structures of identification that had already

---

[55] Sullivan to Washington, 17 December 1775, *PGWDE*, Revolutionary, II: 567-568.

shaped Rogers' new identity and his recent travels, by leaving him to fend for himself as he might, without risking the investment of any portion of Washington's own reputation.

The same day that Sullivan made his report, Rogers was able to write his wife that he had "this morning had the satisfaction to have my permit aproved." Rogers supposed that he had now "cleard up Every point—So that I shall have no further trouble Stay in america as long as I will"[56] Yet unbeknownst to him, the very next day Washington dispatched an inquiry to General Philip Schuyler at Albany, communicating the reports received from Wheelock and directing Schuyler "to have this Report examined into and acquaint me as to the Authenticity or probability of the Truth of it—if any Circumstances can be discovered to induce a Belief that he was there [at St. Johns] he should be apprehended, he is now in this Government."[57] Schuyler reported in response that,

> Since the Receipt of Your Excellency's of the 18th Major Rogers is come to this Town. I sent to him & amongst a Variety of Passes he produced a late one from the Committee of New Hampshire to pass unmolested to New York, for which Place he sets out to Day. I believe there is no Truth in the Intelligence sent by Mr Wheelock, for I find upon Enquiry, that Rogers arrived at this Place after St Johns was invested & that he went from hence to New England; I shall however make farther Enquiries.[58]

Though Washington now felt "apt to believe that the Intelligence given Doctor Wheelock, respecting Major Rogers was not true," he remained wary, advising Schuyler that as Rogers was "much suspected of unfriendly views to this Country, his Conduct should be attended to with some Degree of Vigilances & Circumspection."[59] Rogers himself was apparently undeterred by continuing suspicions and surveillance. By mid February of 1776 he was back in New York City and addressing a request to the Provincial Congress for yet another addition to his growing sheaf of papers, this

---

[56] Robert Rogers to Elizabeth Rogers, 17 December 1775, Rogers-Roche Collection, Small Collections, Box 48, Folder 22, WLCL.

[57] Washington to Schuyler, 18 December 1775, *PGWDE*, Revolutionary, II: 578-579.

[58] Schuyler to Washington, 5 January 1776, *PGWDE*, Revolutionary, III: 32-36.

[59] Washington to Schuyler, 16 January 1776, *PGWDE*, Revolutionary, III: 112-114.

time "a permit to go on board the Governour's ship, at any time when my business may require my attendance," ostensibly in pursuance of several land grants.[60]

Despite his apparent self-assurance and thickening patina of identifications, Rogers continued to gather new and increasingly anxious tangles of suspicion to himself as he circled through the colonies, orbiting the shifting center of conflict. By the end of June the Provincial Congress of his home colony, New Hampshire, had appointed a committee "to confer upon the expediency of seizing and securing Major Robert Rogers, in consequence of sundry informations against him, as inimical to the rights and liberties of this country."[61] At very nearly the same time, Rogers was arrested independently in South Amboy, New Jersey, on the orders of General Washington, and was then sent to Congress in Philadelphia.

When, after his escape from Philadelphia, the Revolutionaries found their next trace of Rogers, it was in the form of documents discovered on the body of a Loyalist soldier killed in New York at the end of August. In William Lounsbury's pocket book were found "a Commission sign'd by Genl Howe to Major Rogers empowering him to raise a Battalion of Rangers with the Rank of Lt Colo. Commandant...a Warrant to this Lounsberry sign'd by Major Rogers appointing him a Captain

---

[60] Rogers to Colonel Woodward, President of the Provincial Congress of New York, 19 February 1776, *AAO*, Series 4, IV: 1201. This letter, or another of the same substance, was read and filed by the Congress on the same day it was written (V: 291).

[61] Proceedings of the House of Representatives, Provincial Congress of New Hampshire, 25 June 1776, *AAO*, Series 5, I: 72. On the 2nd of July, several days after Rogers had already been seized in New Jersey, the House resolved that "Whereas it is strongly suspected that Major Robert Rogers, and one Samuel Dyer are inimical to the rights and liberties of Americans: Therefore, Voted, That it be, and hereby is, strongly recommended to the several Committees of Safety and of Correspondence in this Colony, or either or any of them, that they take effectual care to seize the bodies of the said Samuel Dyer and Robert Rogers, whenever or wherever found in this Colony, and to secure them, or either of them, under a proper guard; and convey them or either of them to this House, or Committee of Safety of this Colony, as soon as may be, for examination," ibid., Series 5, I: 79.

of one of these Companies…[and] a Muster Roll of the Men already enlisted."[62] A month later

General Washington would write to warn Governor Trumbull of Connecticut that "The influence of

their [the enemy's] money, and their artifices have already passed the Sound and several have been

detected of late who had enlisted to serve under their Banner and the particular command of Majr

Rogers."[63] Trumbull would in turn soon warn Colonel Livingston of his state's militia that "the

infamous Major Rogers…[was] now employed by General Howe" and had set about recruiting

soldiers. Trumbull did not doubt that Livingston knew Rogers "was a famous partisan or ranger in

the last war," and he presumed he had "no need to apprise you of the art of this Rogers. He has

been a famous scouter, or woods-hunter, skilled in waylaying, ambuscade, and sudden attacks…I

dare say you will guard against being surprised by him." Perhaps all the more for these reasons, "If

[Rogers] could be surprised and taken with one Captain Fairchild and some others, who have joined

him," Trumbull reminded Livingston, "it would be a notable stroke on the Tories at least."[64]

Over the course of the next several months, further paper traces of Rogers' travels and

nefarious activities continued to come to light in similar fashion. In the first days of January 1777, a

Loyalist named Strang was captured and "his Warrant from Rodgers to enlist men" was found

"secreted in the inside of his Breeches."[65] Through the discovery of Rogers' own commission from

---

[62] William Duer, in Committee of Safety, Harlem, NY, 30 August 1776, *PGWDE*, Revolutionary, VI: 164. Another captured muster roll of this sort, for a Loyalist company being raised in Dutchess County, NY, was used to identify and arrest those recorded as having enlisted. *PGWDE*, Revolutionary, VI: 440n1.

[63] Washington to Jonathan Trumbull, Sr., 30 September 1776, *PGWDE*, Revolutionary, VI: 440.

[64] Trumbull to Henry B. Livingston, 13 October 1776, *AAO*, Series 5, II: 1030. On the same day, Trumbull relayed new intelligence of Rogers back to Washington, detailing what were believed to be the plans of "the Noted Majr Rogers a famous Partisan or Ranger in the last Warr" to make nighttime raids on Connecticut coastal towns from his base on Long Island. Trumbull indicated that he had "inclosed the Copies of two Letters discover'd or forced from the possesior for your perusal but the most particular account of Rogers Intentions are from a Friendly woman of good Character who made her escape from Huntingdon a few Nights agoe where Rogers with his Party then was," *PGWDE*, Revolutionary, VI: 559-561. The following day Colonel Livingston himself reported to Washington that "Major Rogers is at Huntington tho' I cannot hear that he has the Command," 14 October 1776, *PGWDE*, Revolutionary, VI: 567.

[65] William Heath to Washington, 4 January 1777, *PGWDE*, Revolutionary VII: 514-515; Heath to Washington, 9 January 1777, *PGWDE*, Revolutionary, VIII: 26-28. Rogers, Orders to Daniel Strang, 30 December 1776, *AAO*, Series 5, III: 1490.

Howe and his subsequent commissions to Lounsbury, Strang, and others, it may have appeared, in a sense, that the supposititious commission as second-in-command in Canada or as an Indian leader in the West that it had been rumored and imagined he might be hiding when he first returned to America had been discovered as last. Though these newly uncovered instruments were clearly of much more recent date, they seemingly confirmed his long-suspected identity as an agent of British tyranny. But had Rogers always been a double agent or a spy, a Tory and an active British officer in disguise? Or had his suspicious compatriots in essence created him as such through a self-fulfilling identification? By their continual inquiries and refusals to accept his explanations, had they in essence driven him—whether a would-be Patriot or sincerely uncommitted—to seek employment, safety, and, very possibly, a vent for his resentment where he could find it?

Though unknown to Washington and his colleagues at the time, it is clear in historical perspective that Rogers had been at the very least disingenuous and had, at best, been shopping himself out (as he suggested to the Adams's), looking for his best opportunity. By the end of November 1775, before he had met with Sullivan or written to Washington, Rogers had dispatched a letter to the British commander-in-chief in Boston offering his services to the King's cause. In response, General Howe had "given encouragement, by desiring him to make his proposals, and by giving an assurance that I am well inclined to do every thing in my power to afford him an opportunity of recommending himself to His Majesty's future favour." Howe had heard from Governor Tryon of New York, indeed, "that the Rebels have made considerable overtures to [Rogers]."[66] Early in the new year, Howe would receive assurances from Lord Germain that "The King approves...your attention to Major Rogers, of whose firmness and fidelity we have received further testimony from Governour Tryon, and there is no doubt you will find the means of making

---

[66] Howe to the Earl of Dartmouth, 26 November 1775, *AAO*, Series 4, III: 1674.

him useful."[67] Tryon, it appears, had furnished Rogers with recommendations even as Rogers was seeking papers for very different purposes from rebel committees of safety and from Washington. Tryon may have, moreover, exaggerated the degree to which the rebels were eager to make use of Rogers' services, in order to make him appear more attractive to the British commanders and riskier for them to pass by. At the beginning of August 1776, Howe would be pleased to report to Germain that, "Major Rogers, having escaped to us from Philadelphia, is empowered to raise a battalion of Rangers, which, I hope, may be useful in the course of the campaign."[68]

Rogers and his new corps of rangers would harass and provoke the rebels for the next three years and more. The revolutionaries would rejoice, when they could, over every defeat of Rogers in battle or capture of members of his corps.[69] When Rogers himself was finally captured, it was only by happenstance: he was discovered among the passengers of a small schooner taken by an American captain near the Penobscot River. Reporting Rogers' capture and his arrival once more as a prisoner in Philadelphia to John Adams, James Lovell included little more than the bare facts of the event, except to comment laconically that "The Major looks much out of Place."[70]

The story of Major Rogers is one example of how the Revolutionary crisis of identification played out in the life of an individual "American." Many other and very different such stories could be told, varying with the individual's circumstances. All of these stories, however, would tell of how identities were fashioned and refashioned through instruments of identification. The following

---

[67] Germaine to Howe, 5 January 1776, *AAO*, Series 4, IV: 573.

[68] Howe to Germaine, 6 August 1776, *AAO*, Series 5, I: 788.

[69] Greene to Washington, 24 October 1776, *PGWDE*, Revolutionary, VII: 23-24; Samuel Adams to Samuel Mather, 26 October 1776, *LDC*, V: 390; 11 November 1776, *AAO*, Series 5, III: 471-474; 14 November 1776, *AAO*, Series 5, III: 685.

[70] Lovell to Adams, 8 January 1781, *PJADE*, XI: 18.

chapters consider in turn different facets of the crisis and different instruments of identification as they manifested in the lives of numerous "Americans" of all sorts.

Chapter 2

Letters

As revolution and civil war pulled their communities apart, the American Revolutionaries had to construct new networks of trust through which to forward the cause and reconstitute their social world. At the same time, they were driven to collaborate with the inhabitants of other colonies and the subjects of other empires to an unprecedented extent. To meet these challenges they tested the limits of established technologies of social identification and governance: letters of introduction and recommendation. Using these familiar instruments, the American Revolutionaries spun new webs from old relationships established to serve commerce, intellectual exchange, and social intercourse. As agents in the cause made their ways back and forth through the colonies and around the Atlantic, they bore and deployed letters of introduction and recommendation as attestations of their loyalty, service, credit, character, and ability.

Historians of the period are commonly familiar with the importance of letters of introduction and recommendation to the commerce and social intercourse of the time. And the historiography of letter writing in the early-modern and Enlightenment Atlantic World has grown in recent years.[1] But letters of introduction and recommendation have received little attention as distinct genres or as instruments of identification.[2] The historiography of identification, likewise, has

---

[1] See Konstantin Dierks, *In My Power: Letter Writing and Communications in Early America*, (Philadelphia: University of Pennsylvania Press, 2009); Sarah M.S. Pearsall, *Atlantic Families: Lives and Letters in the Later Eighteenth Century*, (New York: Oxford UP, 2008); Rebecca Earle ed., *Epistolary Selves: Letters and Letter-Writers, 1600-1945*, (Brookfield, VT: Ashgate, 1999); and William Merrill Decker, *Epistolary Practices: Letter Writing in America before Telecommunications*, (Chapel Hill, NC: University of North Carolina Press, 1998).

[2] Letters of introduction and recommendation often come most into focus in studies not focused primarily on letter writing. See Ditz's studies of mercantile self-presentation, trust and duplicity, secrecy and candor: "Secret Selves, Credible Personas: The Problematics of Trust and Public Display in the Writing of Eighteenth-Century Philadelphia Merchants," *Possible Pasts: Becoming Colonial in Early America*, Robert Blair St. George ed., (Ithaca, NY: Cornel UP, 2000),

largely excluded these letters, except as predecessors to early-modern or modern passports.[3] This chapter examines letters of introduction and recommendation as instruments of identification during the Revolution and as fundamental tools of Revolutionary collaboration and governance.

These instruments of identification, dealing in patronage and influence, were the currency of a system regulating access to positions of trust, sensitive information, valuable resources, and exclusive social circles that bridged the divide between the official and the unofficial, the public and the private. They could, likewise, facilitate access to other instruments of identification, including passports and certificates of loyalty. These letters were largely, however, socially exclusive instruments of privilege. They relied heavily on elitist concepts of honor, gentility, and character to identify their bearers, concepts that provided a shared vocabulary and culture among "gentlemen" (and their female social auxiliaries) while excluding members of the lower social orders, considered incapable of such moral refinements. As such, the Revolutionary community that these instruments enacted was a community that perpetuated disparities of power over identity. The letters reflected and embodied a hierarchical system of identity and identification that preceded, shaped, and in large measure survived the republican Revolution.

Letters of introduction and recommendation were instruments of a social order based on patronage. In the eighteenth-century British Empire, patronage—the grant of a social superior's influence in an inferior's social or professional favor—was the prime mechanism by which social access, appointive offices, and commissions were distributed among the upper middling classes, the

---

219-242; "Shipwrecked; or, Masculinity Imperiled: Mercantile Representations of Failure and the Gendered Self in Eighteenth-Century Philadelphia," *Journal of American History*, Vol. 81, No. 1 (Jun., 1994), 51-80; and Emma Rothschild, *The Inner Life of Empires: An Eighteenth-Century History*, (Princeton, NJ: Princeton UP, 2011), 26-29, 57, 193, 223, 248.

[3] See Valentin Groebner, *Who Are You?: Identification, Deception, and Surveillance in Early Modern Europe*, (Brooklyn, NY: Zone Books, 2007), 161-163, 165, 171, 174-176, 194, 214-215; Craig Robertson, *The Passport in America: The History of a Document*, (New York: Oxford UP, 2010), 11, 54, 96, 126-127, 129, 130-131, 133-134, 144, 149, 150.

gentry, and the aristocracy. It was also one of the few means by which persons of more humble

social origins and standing could ascend—raised by a patron—into the realms of gentility and the

social opportunities they offered. George Washington, as a young man in colonial Virginia, though

born into gentility and more than modest means, was elevated further—through appointments as a

surveyor and a militia officer—by the patronage of Colonel William Fairfax and his influential

family, including Thomas Fairfax, Sixth Lord Fairfax of Cameron.[4] Benjamin Franklin—who would

become in the eyes of nineteenth-century Americans the archetypal self-made man—though

industrious, ambitious, and talented, rose from being a runaway printer's apprentice and son of a

Boston tradesman to a wealthy and internationally famous gentleman scientist and statesman only

partly through his own efforts. He was aided along the way by the favor of senior printers, colonial

governors and assemblies, and the genteel and aristocratic natural philosophers of Europe.[5]

In this system (and more generally in the hierarchical social world within which it operated)

an individual's practical identity was defined in substantial measure by his or her location in the web

of social "connections" and "acquaintance"—mediated by wealth and "family"—and more

particularly by his or her position as client of a particular patron.[6] Letters of introduction and

recommendation might recommend the bearer on the basis of virtue, merit, general reputation, or

zeal for a shared cause, but these letters at least as frequently identified the bearer in terms of his

family, his social connections and standing, wealth, or a preceding chain of recommendations. Most

letters would specify—unless for individuals of the middling or lower sorts—that the bearer was a

---

[4] James Thomas Flexner, *George Washington: The Forge of Experience, 1732-1775*, (Boston: Little, Brown & Co., 1965), 26-56; Ron Chernow, *Washington: A Life*, (New York: Penguin, 2010), 15-28.

[5] Gordon S. Wood, *The Americanization of Benjamin Franklin*, (New York: Penguin, 2004), 25-27, ch. 1 passim; Joyce E. Chaplin, *The First Scientific American: Benjamin Franklin and the Pursuit of Genius*, (New York: Basic Books, 2006).

[6] Jack P. Greene, *Pursuits of Happiness: The Social Development of Early Modern British colonies and the Formation of American Culture*, (Chapel Hill, NC: University of North Carolina Press, 1988), 105-106; Rhys Isaac, *The Transformation of Virginia, 1740-1790*, (New York: Norton, 1988), 104-114, 132-133; Gordon S. Wood, *The Radicalism of the American Revolution*, (New York: Vintage, 1991), 57-77.

"gentleman," an educated, refined, and honorable member of the community of social elites who could be trusted to abide by certain codes of conduct and who could legitimately incur and reciprocate social debts and favors of honor and consideration among his fellow gentlemen.

Often such letters would make explicit that the bearer was a "friend" of the writer and typically they would assure the recipient that any consideration shown to the bearer would be considered by the writer as consideration to himself, laying him under an obligation or social debt to the recipient. Apart from numerous particular examples of such letters, this convention of the genre was reflected and reinforced in letter-writing guides of the period. Thus, J. Hill's 1750 *Young Secretary's Guide* defined "Letters of *Recommendation*, or Letters *Recommendatory*" as "those which one Friend sends to another, to prefer any Person or Business; and therein he insinuates the Honesty or Ability of the Person, and the Employments he is capable of undertaking; and the Reason why he recommends him, acknowledging what is done to the Party as done to himself."[7] In this manner, they performed the social economies that undergirded the system of introduction and recommendation. Thus, when President Hancock, in June of 1776, addressed a letter from Philadelphia to William Heath on behalf of "Col. Roberdeau of this city," he assured Heath that, "He is a Gentleman distinguished for his Benevolence towards all Men—; is a zealous American—; and a Friend of mine," and declared that, "Every Mark of Respect you are pleased to shew him, will be esteamed a Favour conferred on, Sir, your most obedt. & very hble Sert., John Hancock."[8] Similarly, in July of 1779, writing to Richard Peters on behalf of a Frenchman, Franklin recommended him "warmly to your Civilities and Counsels, and Those of my friends, who may with

---

[7] J. Hill, *Young secretary's guide*, (Boston: Thomas Fleet, 1750), *EAI*, Series 1, no. 6517 (filmed), 10.

[8] Hancock to Heath, 4 June 1776, *LDC*, XXV: 576. See, likewise, William Babcock to Horatio Gates, 2 April 1776, recommending "Mr Briendly" and assuring Gates that "any civility Shewn him, will be very thankfully acknowledged." Horatio Gates Papers, 1726-1828, Film 23, Reel 2 (Correspondence, Nov. 1769 - July 1776), DLAR.

you be assured of my considering them as done to myself, and of my Readiness to pay an equal

Regard to their Recommendations."[9]

Other letters appealed principally to the social connections shared by bearer and recipient.

In his letter of July 1774, introducing "Doctor Armstrong" to "Major [Horatio] Gates," Hugh

Mercer identified Armstrong as "Son to your old Acquaintance Col Armstrong of Carlisle." After

practicing in Virginia, the doctor was about to settle in Gates' "Neighbourhood" and Mercer begged

"leave to introduce him to your Notice & Good Offices." "His own Merit," Mercer supposed, "will

soon establish him in the good opinion of the People—but being altogether a Stranger Some

introduction to the principal familys is necessary."[10]

One of the most fundamental and common of the social favors solicited by these letters,

overlapping with the constitution of patronage relationships, was the introduction of the bearer to

the recipient's circle of "acquaintance" or "friendship." This was reflected in the standard formula

by which the writers of such letters "beg leave to introduce to your acquaintance" the bearer. In this

manner, John Adams wrote to Charles Lee in February of 1776 to "introduce to your acquaintance a

Country man of yours and a Citizen of the World, to whom a certain Heretical Pamphlet called

Common Sense, is imputed." "His Name is Paine," Adams told Lee, going on to explain that, "He is

travelling to N. York for his Curiosity and wishes to see a Gentl[ema]n, whose Character he so

---

[9] Franklin to Peters, 12 July 1779, *PBFDE*. See also, Samuel Rhoads to Franklin, 14 July 1781, recommending Samuel
Griffitts and declaring that "any Service done for him will be deemd as done to thy affectionate, & Constant Friend."
PBFDE. Similar appeals to reciprocity are found in passports of the period, as the issuing sovereign requests aid and
protection for its subject or citizen and promises to extend the like to the subjects or citizens of the other power in
similar circumstances.

[10] Mercer to Gates, 6 July 1774, Horatio Gates Papers, 1726-1828, Film 23, Reel 2 (Correspondence, Nov. 1769 - July
1776), DLAR. See also the letter of 30 August 1774 from Armstrong's father, John Armstrong, recommending his son
to Gates, concluding, "I shall only farther tell you that his Education has been as regular in the way of his profession as
our Metropolis wou'd permit, and in point of conduct for his years I believe he has been pritty happy in maintaining a
good Character, this last as it is a visible thing every man must soon be able to judge of it from his own observation. As
I learn that Doctor Mercer has wrote you, I shall not farther add but that I am with great respect...."

highly respects."[11] Likewise, John Jay wrote to Philip Schuyler the following May to "take the

Liberty of introducing to your Acquaintance" his brother-in-law Henry Brockhold Livingston. "I

can with great Truth assure You," Jay professed, "that this young Gentlemans Conduct has hitherto

been very satisfactory to his Family & Friends, and if he perseveres in it, I flatter myself he will

receive from you every Mark of that Attention, which, as a General, you so readily extend to [. . .]

and as a Friend, to your most obedt. Servt, John Jay."[12] By such means, social networks were

constructed and interwoven, continually reshaping the individuals' social identities in the process.

It was not uncommon for letters of introduction to identify the subject first and foremost in

terms of his inherited or privileged social status. Thus, when John Adams wrote a letter of

introduction for "Francis Dana Esqr. of Cambridge" to Washington in April of 1776, he described

him first as "a Gentleman of Family, Fortune and Education," before moving on to discuss his

circumstances, plans, and character.[13] The following day, William Babcock wrote to General

Horatio Gates a letter of introduction for "Mr Briendly," describing him as "a Gentleman of Family

& Fortune, a very particular Friend of mine."[14] In September of that year, James Caldwell of New

Jersey, in a letter of recommendation to William Patterson on behalf of a Mr. Hacket, expressed

himself "fond of introducing to the defence of the cause our young natives of property, & good

connections."[15]

---

[11] Adams to Lee, 19 February 1776, *LDC*, III: 277. See, likewise, Adams to Washington, 1 April 1776, recommending
Francis Dana and "introducing him to your Acquaintance." *PGWDE*, Revolutionary, IV: 1-3.

[12] Jay to Schuyler, 5 May 1776, *LDC*, III: 624.

[13] Adams to Washington, 1 April 1776, *PGWDE*, Revolutionary, IV: 1-3.

[14] Babcock to Gates, 2 April 1776, Horatio Gates Papers, 1726-1828, Film 23, Reel 2 (Correspondence, Nov. 1769 - July
1776), DLAR.

[15] Caldwell to Patterson, 29 September 1776, certified typescript copy, New Jersey. Revolutionary War. Numbered
Manuscripts, 1770's-1890's, Film 678, Reel 6 (Mss. Nos. 2211-2403), No. 2373, DLAR.

As compared to an individual's birth, rank, and wealth, his "character," reputation, and credit were more influenced by his own conduct. "Character," at this period and in this context carried a range of meanings, from the distinguishing mental and moral characteristics of an individual (akin to "personality"), to "the estimate formed of a person's qualities" (nearly synonymous with "reputation"), a third party's description of those qualities, a "formal testimony given by an employer as to the qualities and habits of one that has been in his employ" (equivalent to the present-day "recommendation" or "reference"), or a "recognized official rank, status, or position" (as in one who bears or assumes a "diplomatic character").[16] An individual's "character," as a facet of his identity, thus bridged the gap between and connected his internal self, independent of others, with the outward judgments and descriptions of others (essentially his reputation), interweaving elements of his identity largely under his control with those largely or entirely determined by others.

While credit was more particular to commercial or financial correspondence, an individual's "character" figured prominently in most introductions or recommendations, across a wide variety of contexts. Thus, when Hancock wrote to the Massachusetts Council in February of 1777 on behalf of John Wilcocks, the capture of whose vessel was soon to be tried in court, he informed them "that he is a Gentleman of the fairest Character; and a firm Friend to the American Cause." "The warm Recommendation I have received of Captain Wilcocks from Mr. Morris, and my own Knowledge of him," Hancock explained,

> induce me to request you will take a proper Notice of him, being well convinced, that your Attention cannot fail to place him in the fairest Light as a Gentleman of unsuspected Principles, and will of Course give him that Advantage which a Man engaged in a legal Controversy must always derive from possessing the Character of Honour and Integrity.[17]

---

[16] "Character, *n*." *Oxford English Dictionary*, (http://www.oed.com), 31 December 2011. Cf. Andrew S. Trees, *The Founding Fathers and the Politics of Character*, (Princeton, NJ: Princeton UP, 2004).

[17] Hancock to the Massachusetts Council, 25 February 1777, *LDC*, VI: 366.

When, likewise, Samuel Adams wrote a letter of introduction to Samuel Savage on behalf of Daniel

Clymer, in August of 1777, he described him as one "who is warmly attached to our great Cause"

and who "is besides Nephew to General Roberdeau whose Character is well known to the

Publick."[18] In September of 1779, responding to a recommendation that a lieutenant in the

Continental Navy be promoted, the Marine Committee of the Continental Congress expressed

themselves "pleased to find that the Character you give of Mr. Yeaton comports of our opinion of

his merit" and assured the recommender that "your recommendation of him shall have due weight

at a proper Opportunity."[19]

Some letters addressed the bearer's "honor." Honor was generally seen as an implicit

corollary of gentility—one of the requisite and exclusive characteristics of a gentleman.[20] It was

something one either possessed or did not. Some letters, nonetheless, appeared to recognize

degrees of honor, or evinced the necessity to vouch for this quality in particular. Thus, William

Duer, introducing Nathaniel Sackett to Washington in January of 1777, described him as "a member

of the Convention of the State, a Man of Honor, and of firm Attachment to the American Cause."[21]

In some cases the writer of a letter commended the bearer's "confidence"—his discretion or

trustworthiness. In elaborating his recommendation of Sackett, Duer characterized him as "a

Person of Intrigue, and Secrecy well calculated to prosecute such Measures as you shall think

conducive to give Success to your generous Exertions in the Cause of America."[22] Many letters

---

[18] Adams to Savage, 29 August 1777, *LDC*, VII: 568. Adams added assurances that, "Your friendly Notice of Mr
Clymer & Introducing him into the Circle of your Acquaintance will much oblige me."

[19] Marine Committee to Samuel Nicholson, 19 September 1779, *LDC*, XIII: 516.

[20] See Caroline Cox, *A Proper Sense of Honor: Service and Sacrifice in George Washington's Army*, (Chapel Hill, NC: University of
North Carolina Press, 2004). On the culture of honor more generally, see Joanne B. Freeman, *Affairs of Honor: National
Politics in the New Republic*, (New Haven, CT: Yale UP, 2001).

[21] Duer to Washington, 28 January 1777, *PGWDE*, Revolutionary, VIII: 170-172.

[22] Duer to Washington, 28 January 1777, *PGWDE*, Revolutionary, VIII: 170-172.

commended the bearer's abilities in a particular area, his previous experience or service in a profession or cause, his education, or other qualifications in general or for a particular profession or post. Still others, in the context of the Revolution, recommended the bearer because he had proven a particularly zealous Patriot or had suffered notably for his adherence to the cause of American liberty.[23]

Letters of introduction and recommendation often and easily blended the official and the unofficial, the public and the private. Such letters might identify the bearer by both his public and his private position or character. They might appeal to official or personal relationships between the writer and addressee. They might recommend the bearer to either or both private hospitality or public services, and might address the recipient in either a public or private capacity. Whether primarily official or unofficial, these letters were commonly carried as complements to, if not substitutes for, official instruments of identification such as passports, loyalty oath certificates, or diplomatic credentials. They were not uncommonly seen as instruments more basic, more essential for travellers and applicants than these official documents. They were often, moreover, an important part of applications for such official instruments.

Multiple facets of this intersection of public and private identification can be seen in a letter written by Richard Bache, in Philadelphia, to his father-in-law, Benjamin Franklin, in France, in November of 1779. In this letter, addressed to Franklin by his full diplomatic title, Bache, at the request of a friend, introduced to Franklin's "Civilities" Robert Carson and Robert Gray, "Gentlemen that have lived long in this State and have approved themselves good Citizens" and

---

[23] See William Livingston to Washington, 14 April 1778, *PGWDE*, Revolutionary, XIV: 514-515; Francis Barber to Washington, 13 July 1778, introducing and recommending the bearer John Hendricks as a source of intelligence, as a faithful patriot, and as one who, along with his brother, had "served much in this way & suffered much with I believe, little or no reward heretofore," *PGWDE*, Revolutionary, XVI: 61-62; James Bowdoin to Washington, 7 November 1778, introducing John Temple, *PGWDE*, Revolutionary, XVIII: 64-65; Henry Knox to Franklin, 28 November 1783, in favor of Jeremiah Platt, *PBFDE*. Regarding Platt, see also Washington to Lafayette and Franklin, 1 December 1783, in favor of Platt, *PBFDE*.

who were returning to Europe "upon a scheme of business." Bache supposed that the gentlemen "may probably stand in need of passports from France to Holland or elsewhere," and he expressed his obligation to Franklin for "any services you can render them in this, or any other line." Bache signed himself "Your affectionate son."[24] Written in his private, familial capacity, for friends of a friend, to his father-in-law, in the latter's private and public capacities, Bache's letter personally recommended private business men, identified by their public standing as citizens, for public protection and services. Less than a week later, again at the request of a friend, Bache wrote Franklin another letter in very nearly the same terms on behalf of John Rainey.[25] Likewise, when Washington, in January of 1781, wrote to Franklin to introduce John Laurens, he identified him first by his rank, his position as his aide de camp, and his commission from Congress to the French court. He then described him as a gentleman of character and a personal friend, before returning to his public standing as a worthy citizen and soldier. Washington recommended him as "a man of abilities," knowledgeable regarding American affairs, "and exemplary for his honor and candor." At the same time he felt he could assure Franklin of Laurens's "attachment to you personally," as well as, in his more official character, his "perfect disposition to conform to his instructions by availing himself of your advice & assistance upon all occasions." Washington closed by recommending Lauren's to Franklin's "friendship."[26] Letters issued to foreign officials or volunteers by American agents abroad could likewise blur the boundaries between the private and public spheres. Thus in his recommendation of Gerard, the new French ambassador to the Continental Congress, in March of 1778, Franklin, having cited Gerard's friendship toward America, concluded by recommending Gerard "warmly not only to all the civilities and respects that are due to his public character, but to

---

[24] Bache to Franklin, 2 November 1779, *PBFDE*.

[25] Bache to Franklin, 8 November 1779, *PBFDE*. For a similar example, see Joseph Wharton, Jr. to Franklin, 27 April 1780, introducing and recommending Dr. John Foulke, *PBFDE*.

[26] Washington to Franklin, 15 January 1781, *PBFDE*. See also, George Fox to William Temple Franklin, 1 November 1783, in favor of John Bleakley, *PBFDE*.

those tender regards and affectionate grateful attentions that friendship claims, and which are so proper to cultivate and strengthen it."[27]

Influence was the lifeblood and currency of this system. It was the form in which a portion of a patron's own social resources was mobilized in favor of a client, essentially mortgaging the patron's identity and extending a line of credit to the client. In this way, letters of introduction and recommendation were close cousins of bills of credit, which were likewise portable and, to some degree, transferable. These letters were, as such, basic adjuncts of individual identity, and their production and deployment a fundamental aspect of the education and social practice of individuals of the middling sorts and upper ranks of society.

Through the course of the century, indeed, educational primers, companions for youth, secretaries' handbooks, and guides to etiquette and writing had included instruction for writing proper letters of introduction and recommendation, as well as responses to such letters.[28] Likewise, in his much read, influential, and widely decried *Letters*, the redoubtable Lord Chesterfield repeatedly referenced letters of introduction and recommendation, by means of which his son was to make his way and secure his character among the aristocracy of Europe; certain editions, indeed, included a sample of one such letter at the end of the work.[29] In this classic English manual of social maneuvering, these letters were treated as such fundamental instruments of identification that they were conflated metaphorically with the very body of the social aspirant. Citing the authority of "My Lord Bacon," Chesterfield advised his son repeatedly "that a pleasing figure is a perpetual letter of

---

[27] Franklin to Laurens, 31 March 1778, Wharton, II: 529.

[28] See *The young secretary's guide,* (Boston: B. Green & J. Allen, 1703; B. Green, 1707); The *Young man's companion,* (New York, 1710; Philadelphia, 1718); *The Secretary's guide, or Young man's companion,* (Philadelphia, 1737); George Fisher, *The American instructor: or, Young man's best companion,* (Philadelphia, 1748; New York, 1760; Philadelphia, 1770). See also the apparent satire of this genre, *Polite epistolary correspondence. A collection of letters, on the most instructive and entertaining subjects,* (London, 1748 and 1751). *EAI.*

[29] See *Letters written by the late Right Honourable Phillip Dormer Stanhope, Earl of Chesterfield, to his son,* (New York, 1775), *EAI,* Series 1, no. 14471 (filmed), I: 115, II: 48, 52, 74, 101, III: 17, IV: 207.

recommendation." A more general conflation of the physical person with instruments of identification blurred the distinction between the voice (orality) and the document (paper and ink). Thus, the younger Chesterfield was advised to cultivate the favor of prominent women of society—for "their recommendation is a passport through all the realms of politeness"—and to "Remember *les attentions*: they must be your passports into good company"[30]

The colonial American opposition began reconstructing networks of trust across colonial borders well before the advent of the Revolutionary War, as committees corresponded and delegates met at provincial and continental congresses. An especially crucial stage of this process came as members of the New England opposition—rapidly becoming an "insurgency"—began preparations for possible military confrontation with the forces of British government.[31] These efforts were particularly sensitive—flirting, as they did, with what would surely be declared treason by King and Parliament—and required that those who coordinated these efforts be especially sure of the loyalties of collaborators. This required them to draw on the personal and local knowledge of their most trusted associates (who might offer their judgments of potential confederates based on previous acquaintance and connections) and to deploy the instruments and methods of peacetime society in the service of war. Thus in March of 1775 David Cheever wrote to James "Barrot" (Barret?) of Charlestown to inform him that "Mr John Austin the Barer of this Letter is the person Chose to Carry on our Millitary preperations and…more men the names of whome he will aquaint you with." Barret was asked to "furnish them with provision and a House to Carryon our military

---

[30] Chesterfield, *Letters*, II: 190, III: 182.

[31] On the idea of the American opposition and resistance as an "insurgency," see T.H. Breen, *American Insurgents, American Patriots: The Revolution of the People*, (New York: Hill & Wang, 2010).

preperations," until the following Wednesday, when "the Committee will be up…and Ease you of the Trouble."[32]

On a wider scale, the Revolutionary crisis of identification brought a continual flow of letters of introduction among the colonies, constructing and melding networks of trust and acquaintance and transplanting individual characters to new social settings. In late May of 1775, for instance, a little more than a month after Lexington and Concord, John Adams would write home to Massachusetts from Philadelphia to introduce to Joseph Palmer the southerners Aquilla Hall and Josias Carvill Hall. "They are," he explained, "two young military adventurers—Volunteers, joining the Army in the Massachusetts, to gain Experience & skill. They are of one of the first Families in Maryland and have independent Fortunes." "Their Letters," he pointed out, "will make Impressions on the Southern Colonies," and it was therefore "of Importance that they be treated with Respect." Adams concluded by requesting that Palmer "would introduce them to our Friends, &c &c."[33] In a similar manner, in July of 1775, Adams' cousin Samuel would write from Philadelphia, where he was a delegate to the Continental Congress, to James Warren back in Massachusetts to "recommend to your friendly Notice" and to "desire you would introduce into the Circle of our Friends Mr Hugh Hughes of New York," whom he described as "a worthy sensible man, whose Virtue has renderd him obnoxious to all the Torries of that City." "I know," Adams professed, "I cannot say more to you in favor of any Man. He is perhaps as poor as I am, but he 'goes about doing good.'"[34]

More officially, when George Washington left Philadelphia for Massachusetts, to take up his new post as commander in chief of the American forces, the Massachusetts delegates to the

---

[32] Cheever to Barret, 17 March 1775, U.S. Revolution Collection, Box 1, Folder 5, AAS.

[33] Adams to Palmer, 29 May 1775, *LDC*, I: 417.

[34] Adams to Warren, 12 July 1775, *LDC*, I: 623.

Continental Congress advised him regarding whom to trust and whose recommendations of others

he could receive with confidence. "There will be," they explained,

> three Committees, either of a Congress, or of an House of Representatives, which are and
> will be composed of our best Men; Such, whose Judgment and Integrity, may be most rely'd
> on; the Committee on the State of the Province, the Committee of Safety, and the
> Committee of Supplies. But least this Should be too general, We beg leave to mention
> particularly Messrs. Bowdoin, Sever, Dexter, Greenleaf, Derby, Pitts, Otis of the late
> Council—Hon. John Winthrop Esq. L.L.D. Joseph Hawley Esqr of Northampton, James
> Warren Esqr of Plymouth Coll Palmer of Braintree, Coll Orne and Elbridge Gerry Esqr of
> Marblehead, Dr Warren, Dr Church Mr John Pitts all of Boston, Dr Langdon President of
> Harvard Colledge, and Dr Chauncey and Dr Cooper of Boston. Coll Forster of Brookfield.

The delegates assured Washington that, "The Advice and Recommendations of these Gentlemen

and of Some others whom they may introduce to your Acquaintance may be depended on."[35]

At the same time, letters of recommendation played an important role in the processes of

choosing and commissioning officers and officials in the new provincial and Continental military

forces and civil governments. Provincial governments, the Continental Congress, and military

commanders like Washington received numerous recommendations of candidates, applications for

commissions, and letters of introduction applicants presented to further their case. When James Lea

applied in 1775 to the Pennsylvania Committee of Safety for a commission as lieutenant or captain

"in the Troops now to be raised in this Province," he presented a letter of recommendation, signed

by nine men, attesting to "his steady attachment to the Cause of Liberty, as well as constant and

unwearied attendance to Military Discipline."[36] In early August of 1775, Benjamin Franklin replied

to Ebenezer Hazard of New York, having received his "Application to be appointed Postmaster of

New York." Franklin had "seen a Recommendation" of Hazard by the New York Provincial

Congress, "to which" he promised to "pay due Respect by appointing you accordingly assoon [sic]

---

[35] Massachusetts Delegates to Washington, 22 June 1775, *LDC*, I: 534. Cf. *PGWDE*, Revolutionary, I: 25-27.

[36] Recommendation of James Lea, 1775, *PAA*, Series 1, IV: 686-687.

as Commissions and Instructions can be printed, & things got in Readiness to carry the Post

through."[37]

As positions were filled and newly commissioned officials and officers set out for their

posts, they often brought with them letters that would ease their reception. Thus when Dr. John

Morgan, newly appointed director general of the Continental Army hospital, set out from

Philadelphia late in 1775, he went as the bearer of a letter from Samuel Adams to James Warren in

which Adams remarked that Morgan "though not yet arrivd to the Age of forty has long sustaind

the Character of learned and is very eminent in the Profession of Physick and Surgery." "I dare

say," Adams concluded, "[he] will fill the place to which he is appointed with Dignity" and "You will

find him to be an agreable Acquaintance."[38] Through the course of the war, letters of introduction

and recommendation would ease the travels and transitions of military officers and civil officials.

Thus, in August of 1776, Brigadier General Hugh Mercer wrote a letter introducing Colonel Attlee

of the Pennsylvania line to General Washington, citing "His experience and Attention to every part

of the service entrusted to his direction" as sure to win Washington's "Regard."[39] The following

month, General Gates wrote to Washington an introduction to be handed him by Major Adam

Hubley, Jr., a former brigade major under the Baron De Wedtke, now going on leave to Philadelphia

to attend his "Private Affairs." "He is a Young Gentleman of Character in his Profession," Gates

explained, "and as such I introduce him to your Excellency."[40] When Washington, in March of

1777, sent General Greene to report to Congress on the present state of military affairs, he

recommended Greene both by declaring him very "much in my confidence" and "intimately

---

[37] Franklin to Hazard, 3 August 1775, H338, Ebenezer Hazard Papers, Item 3, APS.

[38] Adams to Warren, 14 November 1775, *LDC*, II: 345.

[39] Mercer to Washington, 12 August 1776, *PGWDE*, Revolutionary, V: 685-686.

[40] Gates to Washington, 3 September 1776, *PGWDE*, Revolutionary, VI: 205-206.

acquainted with my ideas" and with "everything respecting the army," and by suggesting that, "from the rank he holds as an able & good Officer in the estimation of all who know him, he deserves the greatest respect, and much regard is due to his Opinions in the line of his profession."[41]

On occasion, officers and others going on particular missions would be given general letters of introduction, addressed to no one in particular but requesting the favor of any reader for the bearer.[42] In other cases, officers on assignment or going on leave were given multiple letters to persons living along their intended route of travel. In October of 1778, for instance, Washington prepared for General Benjamin Lincoln, on his way to the Carolinas via Virginia, "a few introductory Letters (for you to some of the first Gentlemen in Carolina)," one to Mrs. Washington, and one to his brother-in-law in Fredericksburg, and considered furnishing others "to my friends in Virga if I knew what rout you would take."[43]

Occasionally, American revolutionaries found themselves in the awkward position of writing for former enemies, such as deserters or defectors from the Royal Army. Thus in December of 1777, Richard Caswell of North Carolina wrote to Washington a letter of introduction for Charles Forbes, a former ensign in the British service who, discontented with his treatment, left the army and made his way, via Bermuda, to North Carolina. He hoped now to serve in the American Army.

---

[41] Washington to Hancock, 18 March 1777, *PGWDE*, Revolutionary, VIII: 597-598. See also Benjamin Harrison to Washington, 21-24 July 1775, recommending Captain Thomas Price "of a Company of Rifle Men from Maryland," *PGWDE*, Revolutionary, I: 145-151; Charles Mynn Thruston to Washington, 2 June 1777, introducing John Byrn, a newly appointed adjutant going recruiting, *PGWDE*, Revolutionary, IX: 596; Christopher Gadsden to Washington, 4 July 1777, introducing Charles Cotesworth Pinckney, *PGWDE*, Revolutionary, X: 188. Cf. John Clark, Jr. to Washington, 18 November 1777, Washington to Clark, on the same date, and Clark to Washington, 30 December 1777, regarding Clark's request for a letter of recommendation to Congress when he went on leave. *PGWDE*, Revolutionary, XII: 301-303, 303-304, XIII: 63-64. For the resulting letter in Clark's favor, see Washington to Henry Laurens, 2 January 1778, *PGWDE*, Revolutionary, XIII: 118-119. See also Washington's somewhat qualified recommendation of Francis Wade, a deputy quartermaster general, addressed to General William Smallwood, 1 May 1778, *PGWDE*, Revolutionary, XV: 9; Richard Caswell to Washington, 14 September 1778, *PGWDE*, Revolutionary, XVI: 607-08, n3;

[42] See, regarding a general letter of introduction to the people of Virginia for an agent of the Quartermaster General going on a procurement mission, Nathanael Greene to Washington, 26 March 1778, *PGWDE*, Revolutionary, XIV: 318-320, n2.

[43] Washington to Lincoln, 9 October 1778, *PGWDE*, Revolutionary, XVII: 317.

Forbes had been allowed to take an oath of allegiance to the state, and Caswell had given him a pass

to Washington's camp. The letter Forbes was to bear was "merely to introduce" him to

Washington. "He is an entire Stranger," Caswell explained, "I know nothing more of him than what

is above."[44]

As the war got underway in the summer of 1775, Washington and other commanders found

that their armies attracted not only camp followers and others among the "lower sorts," but also

gentlemen visitors, some merely curious and others proposing to volunteer themselves as officers.

These visitors sometimes brought letters to help secure their reception in camp and to forward any

application they might make to the relevant commander. In mid July of 1775, for instance, Patrick

Henry, in Philadelphia, wrote a letter of introduction to General Washington on behalf of Benjamin

Ellery, of Rhode Island, who, Henry explained, "wishes to visit your Camp."[45] Two days later, John

Hancock wrote from Philadelphia a letter to Washington introducing Matthias Ogden and Aaron

Burr, who proposed to "Visit the Camp not as Spectators, but with a View of Joining the Army &

being Active during the Campaign."[46] By mid November of that year, Washington was convinced,

as he wrote to Colonel Alexander McDougall in response to a recommendation he had sent, that, "It

is exceedingly necessary for every person, appearing in the character of a Gentleman, & not

personally known, to bring Letters of Introduction from those that are, otherwise, a proper attention

cannot be paid to them. Indeed even common Civilities may be injudiciously bestowd as we have

---

[44] Caswell to Washington, 21 November 1777, *PGWDE*, Revolutionary, XII: 658.

[45] Henry to Washington, 17 July 1775, *PGWDE*, Revolutionary, I: 124. See also Charles Carroll to Washington, 26 September 1775, introducing to Washington's "notice & Countenance" "Mr Key" a "young gentleman" who "will endeavour to deserve your good opinion, & favour." *PGWDE*, Revolutionary, II: 45-46.

[46] Hancock to Washington, 19 July 1775, *PGWDE*, Revolutionary, I: 132-133. See also John Rutledge to Washington, 6 June 1777, introducing John Laurens, recently returned from abroad and wishing to join the service. *PGWDE*, Revolutionary, IX: 629-630.

some improper visitors."[47] Late the following month, Washington thanked Colonel Joseph Reed "for stopping visitors in search of preferment" and assured him that "it will give me pleasure to shew Civilities to others of your recommendation." "Indeed," he observed, as he had in similar terms to McDougall, "no Gentleman that is not well known, ought to come here with out Letters of Introduction, as it puts me in an aukward Situation with respect to my Conduct towards them."[48]

From the British side of the conflict, the war in America appeared to offer opportunities for advancement in both military and civilian spheres, and British commanders, like their American counterparts, were beset, if perhaps to a lesser degree, by those seeking preferment and bearing letters of introduction and recommendation. Thus British General James Grant, preparing to return to American from London in the spring of 1777, received several aspirants bearing such letters and seeking his favor. One man brought a letter by a friend of a friend recommending him to Grant's "Protection" as he himself returned to America as a doctor.[49] Another brought a recommendation from a friend of his father. The father had fallen on hard times and was now forced to send "his Son to America to get his Bread." The son hoped "to be in some civil Employment," and, the writer supposed, "tho' he brings Letters of Recommendation to the Howes, he will not be the worse for having a Friend to remind them of him." "This is a Favour," the writer concluded, "that I am no otherwise intitled to ask, than from a Consciousness, that I should be ready and happy to oblige you under similar Circumstances."[50] In July of 1780, Lord Shelburne wrote from London to

---

[47] Washington to McDougall, 10 November 1775, *PGWDE*, Revolutionary, II: 343-344.

[48] Washington to Reed, 25 December 1775, *PGWDE*, Revolutionary, II: 606-08.

[49] James Wemyss to James Grant, 8 April 1777, Papers of James Grant of Ballindalloch, 1740-1819, Army Career Series (1740-1805), Film 687, Reel 37, DLAR.

[50] [Archibald?] Saunders to James Grant, 22 April 1777, Papers of James Grant of Ballindalloch, 1740-1819, Army Career Series (1740-1805), Film 687, Reel 37, DLAR: "In casting my Eyes over a List of my American Friends, I saw none who I thought could have so much Weight and Influence as you. I have ventured to solicit the Favour of you, if you can do it with Ease, and without laying yourself under too great obligations to the General, to lend him every little Assistance in your Power, if an Openning offers of Employment. Tho' He is the Nephew of the Arch-Patriot (a Title

General Cornwallis in America, introducing a Dr. Trumbull as a man unjustly reduced to distress and as a skilled physician who might be of use to the army.[51] In other instances, American loyalists were recommended as possible resources to British commanders for their social standing and influence, knowledge of the country, or loyalty.[52]

Visitors, volunteers, and other gentlemen travellers through Revolutionary America often accumulated more and more letters of introduction as they travelled, sometimes building chains of letters, one given on the strength of another. Any given letter was apt to mention other such letters already in the bearer's possession as corroboration of the judgment given of the bearer. In July of 1775, Benjamin Harrison wrote to Washington from Philadelphia introducing Captain Thomas Price of Maryland, who came "with a high Character from thence" and bore "a Letter in his favor to Mr Flighman highly Commending him."[53] The Mr. Hacket introduced to William Patterson by James Caldwell in September of 1776, hoping to enter "the service of his country in this important crisis," already bore, when he received his letter from Caldwell, "letters to the Governor & some other Gentlemen."[54] In a similar manner, William Gordon wrote to Washington, in January of 1778, in favor of the Baron Von Steuben, who was "evidently the Gentleman, & a person of good understanding" and who "had the best of recommendations" already.[55]

---

more detestable than Rebel) yet I flatter myself he has none of his Principles, and am persuaded that his Conduct will not discredit my Recommendation."

[51] Shelburne to Cornwallis, 20 July 1780, Cornwallis Papers (microfilm), PRO 30/11/2, Reel 2, Page 335, DLAR.

[52] See Wemyss to Cornwallis, 28 July 1780, recommending a Mr. Gordon, a merchant, as "one of the Principal people, & a firm Friend to Government," and thus a reliable source of information. Cornwallis Papers (microfilm), PRO 30/11/2, Reel 1, Page 343, DLAR. See also Samuel Wells to William Smith, 21 March 1781, recommending Micah Townsend as a trustworthy loyalist and a reliable source of advice and information, Sir Henry Clinton Papers, Volume 152, Folder 9, WLCL.

[53] Harrison to Washington, 21-24 July 1775, *PGWDE*, Revolutionary, I: 145-151.

[54] Caldwell to Patterson, 29 September 1776, certified typescript copy, New Jersey. Revolutionary War. Numbered Manuscripts, 1770's-1890's, Film 678, Reel 6 (Mss. Nos. 2211-2403), No. 2373, DLAR.

[55] Gordon to Washington, 9 January 1778, *PGWDE*, Revolutionary, XIII: 187-188.

Letters of introduction and recommendation were so requisite for those travelling or seeking

positions as gentlemen, and the granting of such letters was so much an expected part of social life,

that the pressure to grant such letters (to avoid giving offense) could work powerfully against the

grantor's better judgment. This dynamic could create a kind of inflation of such letters, which

proliferated enormously, while at the same time the authority attached to them diminished. In some

cases the writers of such letters qualified their value themselves in the text of the instrument. And

some explicitly acknowledged the dilemma in which they found themselves. Thus William Fitzhugh,

in a letter to Washington of October 1776, hoped Washington would "forgive the trouble I have

Given, & may Hereafter Give you by recommendations, & Shew no more regard to them, than you

think, or may know they Deserve, As in my Scituation, I have many Applications, which might be

thought unfriendly to reject." At the same time, attempting to preserve the credit attached to his

recommendation, he assured Washington that, "I will not Name to you a man whom I do not know

or believe to be Worthy."[56]

Americans on both sides of the Atlantic had not only to evaluate their compatriots or

confederates from other colonies and elsewhere in the British Empire. They had also to distinguish

among "foreigners" who offered themselves to the American cause—or who claimed to represent

foreign powers wishing to treat with the new states. Some actually bore the characters they claimed

and could be trusted; others might be aligned with the enemy or might seek to take advantage of the

"Americans" for their own gain or advancement. Any of these individuals seeking the trust, aid, or

protection of the United States had to provide some documentation of the identities they claimed

---

[56] Fitzhugh to Washington, 13 October 1776, *PGWDE*, Revolutionary, VI: 553-557. In this same letter, Fitzhugh interceded on behalf of at least four different individuals.

(which they either bore already or wished to fashion), often in the form of some instrument of identification.

As the challenges and chaos of war set in, the new American governments, their military forces, and their agents abroad were desperate for assistance of any kind. But they had to be careful whose assistance they accepted. Their work took place not in well-defined places and stable networks of acquaintance, but in the swirl of multiple interconnected fields of mobility and correspondence. Merchants offered their procurement and shipping services to the governments in America and to their agents in Europe; French, Polish, Prussian, and other foreign military officers and experts—or those who claimed to be—offered themselves for commissions in the American military; persons claiming to be emissaries from any number of governments showed up on the doorsteps of the state governments, the Continental Congress, and their agents in Europe. Eager for aid but wary of exposing themselves to enemy agents or profiteers, the new governments and their agents had to decide how to determine whom to trust. To whom would they grant their own endorsements on behalf of the United Colonies or the new United States of America?

By the end of 1775, an increasing number of foreign visitors, largely French, arrived to seek commissions under or contracts with the new confederation and its army. They came with widely varying documentation of their identities. In December, Nicholas Cooke wrote to Washington from Providence, Rhode Island, a letter to be borne by Pierre Penet, who, with his companion Emmanuel de Pilarne, had recently arrived from Saint Domingue. Cooke assured Washington that "Mr Penet comes extremely well recommended to our Committee for providing Powder from a Merchant of Character at the Cape [François]." "I am informed," Cooke explained, "that the other Gentleman is a Person of some Consequence." He begged "Leave to introduce them to your Excellency."[57] Meanwhile, in Philadelphia, Franklin received two gentlemen lately arrived from France with letters

---

[57] Cooke to Washington, 11 December 1775, *PGWDE*, Revolutionary, II: 532.

from Franklin's correspondent C.G.F. Dumas.[58] In late February of 1776, Horatio Gates sent Franklin a letter by the hand of "Baron de Woedtkee," who, Gates wrote, "appears to be a Gentleman, and a Veteran." Gates supposed Franklin would "esteem him for he has with him other recommendations to your Notice, from some of your Paris acquaintance."[59] In June, Washington forwarded to the Congress at Philadelphia two French Gentlemen who had applied to be officers in the Continental Army and who bore "Letters to Dr Franklin and some other Gentlemen of the Congress."[60] The following month, the Congress granted a brevet commission as lieutenant colonel to another French gentleman, citing his knighthood in the order of St. Louis, his experience as an officer in the French service, and the fact that he was "well recommended in letters from abroad."[61]

Letters of recommendation, along with any formal credentials, helped American authorities distinguish those among the foreign applicants who had legitimate pretensions to be useful to the American cause. In July of 1776, Washington explained in a letter to the Baron de Calbiac that those of the Frenchman's countrymen who wished to enter the American service must see "the Propriety & Expediency of their furnishing some Testimonial and recommendation previous to any Appointment." "These would have been proper at any Time," he explained, "but the late Instance of Treachery & Ingratitude in Monsr —— in deserting and taking the Command of a Party of the Enemy in Canada, after he had been promoted to Office in the service of the United Colonies makes them indispensably necessary."[62] Without such letters, American authorities had little basis

---

[58] See Franklin to Dumas, 19 December 1775, Wharton, II: 64-67.

[59] Gates to Franklin, 23 February 1776, *PBFDE*.

[60] Washington to John Hancock, 21 June 1776, *PGWDE*, Revolutionary, V: 67-68. See also Horatio Gates to Franklin, 23 June 1776, regarding one of the two French gentlemen mentioned by Washington. *PBFDE*.

[61] *JCC*, 20 July 1776, V: 595. Cf. the grant of a commission to Jean Artur de Vermonet, "who appears to be a young gentleman of merit, and has held a lieutenant's commission in the service of France," as a brevet captain. *JCC*, 29 July 1776, V: 614-615.

[62] Washington to Calbiac, 23 July 1776, *PGWDE*, Revolutionary, V: 431-432.

on which to evaluate foreign applicants for commissions. Thus at the end of July, Washington

opened a letter to John Hancock by noting that, "This will be handed you by Captn Marquisie, with

whom I have no other acquaintance than what is derived from the Inclosed Letter from Genl

Schuyler." Schuyler himself, in his letter, had written that, "I do not know what his Abilities are as

an Engineer, he appears to be a Modest & Discreet Man."[63]

Even as they received numerous visitors from abroad, some bearing letters and others not,

the American revolutionaries deployed letters of introduction and recommendation to secure the

reception of the agents they dispatched abroad. Thus, in the instructions given to Silas Deane for

his mission to France, Deane was assured that "by delivering Dr. Franklin's letters to Monsieur Le

Roy, at the Louvre, and M. Dubourg, you will be introduced to a set of acquaintance, all friends to

the Americans."[64] American agents abroad in turn issued or sought letters for their own agents. In

December of 1776, Deane wrote home that he had had "overtures from the King of Prussia in the

commercial way," and had "sent a person of great confidence to his court, with letters of

introduction from his agent here, with whom I am on the best terms."[65] American agents, likewise,

often wrote letters of recommendation (or testimonials of service) for colleagues and subordinates

returning to America.[66]

---

[63] See Washington to Hancock, 31 July 1776, *PGWDE*, Revolutionary, V: 525-526. For Schuyler's letter, see n1.

[64] Instructions to Silas Deane, 3 March 1776, Wharton, II: 78-80.

[65] Deane to John Jay, 3 December 1776, Wharton, II: 212-216.

[66] See Franklin, Lee, and Adams to the President of Congress, 22 September 1778, on behalf of courier Jonathan Loring Austin, Wharton, II: 735; Franklin to the President of Congress, 1 June 1780, recommending John Paul Jones, Wharton, III: 751-752; Adams to the President of Congress, 1 September 1783, recommending Thaxter, Wharton, VI: 668-669. Americans also sometimes wrote letters of introduction or recommendation to their compatriots abroad for foreign volunteers in the American service now returning to Europe. See Washington to Franklin, 28 December 1778, introducing and recommending Lafayette, on his return to Europe, *PGWDE*, Revolutionary, XVIII: 521-522; Franklin to the Council of Massachusetts Bay, 4 June 1779, regarding their recommendation of Lafayette, Wharton, III: 207-208. See also Franklin to John Jay, 9 June 1779, on Colonel S. Duicks, returned from America with a "recommendatory letter from Governor Trumbull" of Connecticut, Wharton, III: 215.

Almost as soon as they arrived in Europe, American agents were overwhelmed with applicants seeking recommendations to the American governments or military commissions and commercial contracts.[67] The American agents found it difficult to refuse the applicants and more difficult still to distinguish those who might in fact be of service to the American cause from those who merely sought titles or wealth. There was a real need for certain types of experienced military officers—notably engineers—and others to serve the cause, and the American agents in Europe were in some instances directed to seek them out. But the volume of applicants and the difficulty of distinguishing the desirable from the undesirable undermined the effectiveness of these efforts and quickly made the task an endless one. In early February 1777—less than two months after Franklin's arrival in France—Franklin, Lee, and Deane were able to report to the Committee of Secret Correspondence that they had already sent over some "excellent engineers," as well as a few cavalry officers. But their report lapsed into a lament and a warning:

> Officers of infantry, of all ranks, have offered themselves without number. It is quite a business to receive the applications and refuse them. Many have gone over at their own expense, contrary to our advice. To some few of those, who were well recommended, we have given letters of introduction.[68]

These letters would help the Congress select those among the French officers bearing down on them who deserved their confidence from those who had set off for America against the advice of the American commissioners at Paris. But it soon became clear that far too many applicants were

---

[67] On these applicants and the many who were denied recommendations by American agents, cf. Catherine M. Prelinger, "Less Lucky than Lafayette: A Note on French Applicants to Benjamin Franklin for Commissions in the American Army, 1776-1785," *Proceedings of the Fourth Annual Meeting of the Western Society for French History*, Joyce Duncan Falk ed., (Santa Barbara, CA: Western Society for French History, 1977), 263-271.

[68] Franklin, Lee, and Deane to the Committee of Secret Correspondence, 6 February 1777, Wharton, II: 262. For one of these recommendations, see Franklin to the President of Congress, 20 January 1777, recommending Captain Balm as a cavalry officer, Wharton, II: 251. See also Franklin and Deane to the President of Congress, 6 February 1777, recommending Monsieur de Coudray as "an officer of great reputation here for his talents in general, and particularly for skill and abilities in his profession," Wharton, II: 265. For a subsequent recommendation, see Franklin to Peters, 12 September 1777, recommending Monsieur Gerard, recommended to him by Dubourg, "a gentleman of distinction here, and a hearty friend to our cause," Wharton, II: 393.

"well recommended" and that the testimonials they brought to bear in their applications could not serve as a sufficient index to their abilities, character, or motives.

Back home, by late February of 1777, General Washington was complaining that, "The French Gentl. come to me in such Shoals, many of them with nothing more than introductory Letters, that I am under the most disagreeable Dilemma what to do with them." He recognized that, "Policy might dictate the Propriety of paying some attention to them," but insisted that it was "entirely out of my Power to comply with their requests," having no places in which to employ them.[69] In April, General William Heath wrote to Washington from Boston that, "We Swarm with French Officers at this Place." Two had recently arrived with whom Heath was favorably impressed as "Gentlemen of Education, Sense and Genius," and one of them had "Letters to Congress, to your Excellency, and to Some Private Gentlemen from Dr Franklin & Mr Dean, who have wrote to have the officers forwarded wherever they may arrive, which will be done as Soon as Possible."[70] The following month, Washington wrote to Richard Henry Lee that, while he still believed he could make good use of foreign artillery officers and engineers, the latter in particular had to be chosen carefully, based on proper credentials. The many persons arriving from abroad who claimed such skills could not simply be taken at their word. "Gentn of this profession," Washington insisted, "ought to produce sufficient and authentic testimonials of their skill & knowledge, and not expect that a pompous narrative of their Services, and loss of Papers (the usual excuse) can be a proper Introduction into our Army."[71]

---

[69] Washington to Artemas Ward, 20 February 1777, *PGWDE*, Revolutionary, VIII: 390-391. Having recently received two French gentlemen with letters of introduction from Ward, Washington begged Ward "to ease me of this Load by making some Provision for the meritorious among them in your State—or endeavour to convince them, that 'till Congress shall adopt some general Mode of providing for them, they will incur Expence by waiting upon me, without any Prospect of having their Wishes gratified."

[70] Heath to Washington, 23 April 1777, *PGWDE*, Revolutionary, IX: 244-246.

[71] Washington to Lee, 17 May 1777, *PGWDE*, Revolutionary, IX: 453-454.

Washington recognized the pressures under which the agents abroad labored, but at the same time he saw the dangers in too freely granting letters to those hoping to find preferment in America. That August, Washington wrote to Deane explaining the difficulties he faced finding proper employment in the army for all of the foreign officers arriving with recommendations, including from Deane himself. "I make no doubt but you are sufficiently importuned for Letters of recommendation," Washington acknowledged, "which I am confident you grant to none but those whom you think worthy of them." Nonetheless, Washington hoped that Deane would "in future let the Gentlemen who apply for them, into a true State of the nature of our Service and of the difficulty of getting into it, in any but an inferior Station; if, after that, they choose to come over upon a Risque, they cannot complain if their expectations are not answered." He pointed out to Deane that, "Altho letters of recommendation are not binding, yet if the parties that bring them have not their wishes fully complyed with, they are apt to attribute their disappointment to slight of them and want of attention to the Gentlemen recommending."[72] For the sake of the American relationship with France, it seemed, Deane might be more circumspect. A few days after writing to Deane, Washington wrote in similar terms to Franklin, acknowledging "that it is a delicate and perplexing task to refuse applications of persons patronised (as I suppose often happens) by some of the first characters in the Kingdom where you are, and whose favour it is of importance to conciliate." "[B]ut I beg leave to suggest," Washington went on, "whether it would not be better to do that, than by compliance, to expose them to those mortifications which they must unavoidably experience, and which they are too apt to impute to other causes than the true, and may represent under very disadvantageous colors." Moreover, Washington observed, even when Franklin carefully promised nothing when he issued letters of recommendation, still the bearers tended to "draw as

---

[72] Washington to Deane, 13 August 1777, *PGWDE*, Revolutionary, X: 600-601.

strong an assurance of success from that, as from a positive engagement and estimate the hardship

of a disappointment nearly the same in one case as another."[73]

In mid October of that same year, Franklin wrote to James Lovell of the Committee of

Secret Correspondence to explain the flood of Frenchmen arriving in America, whose numbers and

conduct were already exasperating Congress, and to justify the commissioners' recommendations of

some who had put them in an awkward position. "You can have no conception," Franklin

contended, "of the arts and interest made use of to recommend and engage us to recommend very

indifferent persons.

> The importunity is boundless. The numbers we refuse incredible. Which if you knew you
> would applaud us for, and on that account excuse the few we have been prevailed on to
> introduce to you. But, as somebody says,
>
> > "Poets lose half the prase they would have got
> > Were it but known what they discreetly blot."
>
> I wish we had an absolute order to give no letter of recommendation, or even introduction,
> for the future, to any foreign officer whatever.[74]

Franklin assured Lovell that he "was very sensible, before I left America, of the inconveniences

attending the employment of foreign officers," and that "therefore immediately on my arrival here I

gave all the discouragement in my power to their going over." But "numbers had been previously

engaged by Mr. Deane, who could not resist the applications made to him."[75]

---

[73] Washington to Franklin, 17 August 1777, *PGWDE*, Revolutionary, X: 647-648.

[74] Franklin to James Lovell, 17 October 1777, Wharton, II: 411-412.

[75] Franklin to James Lovell, 17 October 1777, Wharton, II: 411-412. Franklin admitted that, "I was concerned in
sending the four engineers, and in making the contract with them; but before they went I had reason to dislike one of
them, and to wish the agreement had not been made, for I foresaw the discontent that man was capable of producing
among his companions, and I fancy that if, instead of America, they had gone to heaven, it would have been the same
thing." Franklin informed Lovell that the commissioners had in fact seen that even Congress's efforts to discourage
further emigrations of French officers to America would likely do nothing but multiply their numbers, and so, "As to the
instruction passed in Congress, respecting French officers who do not understand English, we never made it known
here, from the same apprehension that you express. All that understood a little English would have thought themselves
entitled to a commission, and the rest would have undertaken to learn it in the passage."

Franklin did not mean to blame Deane, and when he was informed that Congress had disavowed some of Deane's agreements with French Officers, he wrote Lovell again, in defense of Deane. "I, who am upon the spot," he wrote,

> and know the infinite difficulty of resisting the powerful solicitations of great men, who, if disobliged, might have it in their power to obstruct the supplies he [Deane] was then obtaining, do not wonder that, being then a stranger to the people and unacquainted with the language, he was at first prevailed on to make some such agreements, when all were recommended, as they always are, as *officiers expérimentés, braves comme leurs épées, pleins de courage, des talents, et de zèle, pour notre causes*, etc., etc.; in short, mere Caesars, each of whom would have been an invaluable acquisition to America.

Again, he insisted to Lovell, "You can have no conception how we are still besieged and worried on this head, our time cut to pieces by personal applications, besides those contained in dozens of letters by every post." These, he emphasized, "are so generally refused that scarce one in a hundred obtains from us a simple recommendation to civilities."[76] Even those who were unsuccessful in their initial ventures to America might return to American agents abroad to apply for still more letters. Thus, in August of 1778, Claude-Valentin Millin de la Brosse, having earlier failed to secure a place in the American army despite "Mr. Deane's sponsorship," wrote to Franklin seeking encouragement now to return to America "not as an officer but as an eager citizen." He hoped the encouragement would take the form of a grant of land, passage for himself and a servant, and "some letters of recommendation."[77]

Franklin's protests to Lovell bring out the abnormal situation in which the commissioners were solicited for letters of recommendation. They were themselves strangers in Europe, and so had little knowledge on which to rely in determining the character of applicants. Nor could they trust the recommendations the applicants presented. Franklin, indeed, wrote to a French acquaintance his opinion that,

---

[76] Franklin to Lovell, 21 December 1777, Wharton, II: 457.

[77] de la Brosse to Franklin, 19 August 1778, *PBFDE*.

the natural Complacence of this Country often carries People too far in the Article of Recommendations. You give them with too much Facility to Persons of whose real Characters you know nothing, and sometimes at the request of others of whom you know as little. Frequently if a Man has no useful Talents, is good for nothing, and burthensome to his Relations, or is indiscreet, profligate and extravagant, they are glad to get rid of him by sending him to the other End of the World; and for that purpose scruple not to recommend him to those they wish should recommend him to others, as a bon sujet plein de merite, &c. &c.

"In consequence of my crediting such Recommendations," Franklin judged, "my own are out of Credit, and I cannot advise any body to have the least Dependance on them."[78] The American agents were writing letters for strangers (those from whom they would normally and were now receiving letters of recommendation, rather than writing them); and while they might claim the dignity of foreign ministers, they were, as Franklin made clear to Lovell, in a real sense inferiors to, or at least dependent on those they were writing for.[79] This was quite the reverse, or at least a significant unbalancing of the typical situation—the disparity of social resources on which the system of introduction and recommendation was premised.

Not all foreign applicants sought commissions in the American military. Some, like de la Brosse in his second application, sought civil posts, contracts, sinecures, special favors, or subsidies and other "encouragement" to resettle in America, either as gentlemen landholders, or as practitioners of a particular craft or profession. Franklin, especially, sought to make clear that the American states were far from desperate for new settlers, and had no place for aristocrats and little use for the refined crafts and accomplishments many of these applicants offered. When, however,

---

[78] Franklin to [Barbeu-Dubourg?], [After October 2, 1777?], *PBFDE.*

[79] On 2 April 1777, Franklin prepared the, "Model of a Letter of Recommendation of a Person You Are Unacquainted with," in which he satirized the position in which the commissioners so often found themselves when applied to for letters of recommendation: "The Bearer of this who is going to America, presses me to give him a Letter of Recommendation, tho' I know nothing of him, not even his Name. This may seem extraordinary, but I assure you it is not uncommon here. Sometimes indeed one unknown Person brings me another equally unknown, to recommend him; and sometimes they recommend one another! As to this Gentleman, I must refer you to himself for his Character and Merits, with which he is certainly better acquainted than I can possibly be; I recommend him however to those Civilities which every Stranger, of whom one knows no Harm, has a Right to, and I request you will do him all the good Offices and show him all the Favour that on further Acquaintance you shall find him to deserve. I have the honour to be, &c." *PBFDE.*

those who applied were of respectable character and sought no remuneration or special favors, but only letters of introduction and recommendation as travellers or as would-be American citizens, Franklin was sometimes happy to comply. Thus, in July of 1779, he wrote to Richard Peters a letter introducing a Monsieur Vatteville, going to America "with a View of settling in Pennsylvania." "He is recommended to me," Franklin explained, "as a Gentleman of good family & excellent Character by several respectable Persons." Though he was also recommended as "a valuable Acquisition to our Military," Franklin was careful to make clear "that I could give him no promises nor even Expectations of Employment in our Armies, which were full." Franklin felt free to assure him, however, that "there was no doubt of his meeting a hospitable favourable Reception in our Country as a stranger of Merit who desired to become our fellow Citizen," and recommended him accordingly to his friends' "Civilities and Counsels."[80] In November of the same year, Franklin wrote to Joseph Reed to recommend a Monsieur Van Noemer of Holland, who wished to settle in Pennsylvania and was "well recommended to me, as a Person of Character, for Learning & Virtue, & likely to make a good & useful Citizen." Franklin, as such, commended him to "those Civilities & that Protection which you have a Pleasure in affording to Strangers of Merit."[81]

/

---

[80] Franklin to Peters, 12 July 1779, *PBFDE*. See also his recommendation of Vatteville addressed to Richard Bache, 15 July 1779, *PBFDE*.

[81] Franklin to Reed, 1 November 1779, *PBFDE*. Franklin was very conscious of the benefits that would accrue to Pennsylvania and the United States more generally from wealthy families relocating to the state and hoped that hospitality extended to gentlemen like Van Noemer would encourage others: "The Lovers of Liberty in all Parts of Europe, begin to cast their Eyes on our State, whose Constitution they admire, and meditate a Removal thither as soon as Peace shall render a Passage more safe for themselves & Families, & the Conveyance of their Substance more secure. I am persuaded, by the Number of Letters I have received on this Subject, that we shall have a great Number of wealthy People, with their Circles of Acquaintance, & Relations. The Hospitality & Friendly Reception reputable Settlers from any Country meet with among us, will have its usual Effect in encouraging others to follow: And I therefore, as well as upon his own Account, hope that our Country will be made agreeable to this Gentleman." See also Franklin to Jefferson, 6 May 1781, recommending a Mr. Grieve, going to settle in Virginia, *PBFDE*; Henry Harford to Franklin, [August 1782?], proposing to settle in America and become a citizen, *PBFDE*; Franklin to Robert R. Livingston, 7 November 1782, recommending the Baron de Kermelin, of Sweden, who proposed to travel through the U.S. to familiarize himself with the country, *PBFDE*; Franklin to John Ewing, 4 April 1783, in favor of a Mr. Redford of Ireland, going to settle in America, *PBFDE*; Franklin to Livingston, 27 April 1783, in favor of the Count del Veome, an Italian traveller, Wharton, VI: 396.

Besides the letters they granted to foreign officers and others wishing to find preferment or settle in America, the American agents abroad also sometimes gave letters to agents of foreign governments going to the United States. Thus, in March of 1778, Franklin wrote a letter of introduction to Henry Laurens on behalf of Gerard, who had just recently negotiated the Franco-American treaties with Franklin and his colleagues and who was now going to America as the French ambassador to the Continental Congress.[82] In June of 1779, Franklin wrote to John Jay a letter recommending the Chevalier de la Luzerne, the new French minister to the United States, on his way to America.[83] John Adams, back home in Braintree, likewise wrote to Congress in August recommending Luzerne for both his "connections" and his "personal character."[84]

As in some of the cases above, it was common for applicants arriving in America to attempt to gain new letters from prominent Americans—sometimes on the basis of recommendations brought with them, and sometimes merely on the strength of their own self-identification. In a letter to Nathaniel Shaw, Jr., for instance, in August of 1776, Washington explained that the missive would be "accompanied by four french Gentn from the Island of Guadaloup, who arrived from thence at Newburypt with a view of engaging in the Continental Service." They had come to him six weeks earlier, bearing a letter from General Ward, in Boston. This letter Washington "inclosed to the President of the Congress intending to forward it by them, that it might serve as some sort of introduction." However, "for want of proper Credentials added to the unsuccessfullness of some of their Countrymen on that same Accot," the four men had subsequently decided not to apply to Congress after all.[85] Later that month, Washington wrote to John Hancock a letter of introduction

---

[82] Franklin to Laurens, 31 March 1778, Wharton, II: 529.

[83] Franklin to Jay, 9 June 1779, Wharton, III: 215.

[84] Adams to the President of Congress, 3 August 1779, Wharton, III: 277-278.

[85] Washington to Shaw, 5 August 1776, *PGWDE*, Revolutionary, V: 571-572.

for Captain Nicholas George Moeballe, "a Dutch Gentleman from Surinam" who had "come to the Continent with a view of Entering into the Service of the States." Moeballe bore "the Inclosed Letters from Mr Brown of Providence and General Greene." "What other Letters & Credentials" he might have Washington did not know, but he had, at Moeballe's request, given him "this Line to Congress to whom he wishes to be Introduced, and where he will make his pretensions known."[86] In May of 1777, Washington wrote a letter to be handed to Hancock by Colonel Conway, "an Irish Gentleman, in the service of France" and whom, Washington explained, "was introduced to me Yesterday, by a Letter from Mr Deane & One from Genl Heath, Copies of which are transmitted."[87]

Often those writing letters for newly arrived foreigners did little more than state who the bearers were and cite any letters of recommendation they had brought from abroad. Some were explicitly guarded about the import that was to be attached to the letters they wrote for new arrivals. Thus in May of 1777, in a letter of introduction to Richard Henry Lee for the Chevalier D'Annmours, Washington expressed his highly favorable impression of the bearer, besides citing his "Letters of recommendation from Doctr Franklin," but he was careful to declare in conclusion that, "I mean this as a Letter of Introduction only"—it was not to be read as a recommendation by Washington himself.[88] That August, in a similar manner, Washington forwarded to John Hancock the Polish Count Pulaski, inclosing a copy of Franklin's letter of recommendation in his favor, and citing another previously received from Deane. "How he can with propriety be provided for," Washington told Hancock, "you will be best able to determine—he takes this from me, as an

---

[86] Washington to Hancock, 14 August 1776, *PGWDE*, Revolutionary, VI: 25-26.

[87] Washington to Hancock, 9 May 1777, *PGWDE*, Revolutionary, IX: 370-371. See also *PGWDE*, Revolutionary, XVI: 87-88n1; Washington to Lafayette, 19 August 1778, *PGWDE*, Revolutionary, XVI: 329, n1; William Heath to Washington, 30 October 1778, *PGWDE*, Revolutionary, XVII: 645-646, n.

[88] Washington to Lee, 10 May 1777, *PGWDE*, Revolutionary, IX: 377-378.

introductory Letter at his own request."[89] Others likely refused altogether to write introductions for

individuals entirely unknown to them.

But letters applicants brought could exert uncomfortable pressure on those Americans to

whom they were addressed. A letter from Robert Morris to Washington in May of 1777 made these

pressures and the dilemma they raised explicit. "The bearear of this the Marquis Armand de la

Rouerie," Morris wrote, "is entitled to my Warmest recommendations because he brought from his

own Country letters to me that I am obliged to attend to & put great faith in as they come from

persons Worthy of the utmost Credit." One of the letters was "from Mr Deane who not only

mentions him as a Gentn of Rank, good Family & Fortune but also as a Man of great Merit desiring

my particular attention to him & that I should supply him with Money which will be repaid in

France by a Gentn to whom America is under the most important obligations." "You will

therefore," Morris concluded, "excuse & oblige me at the same time by your favourable attention to

Monsr Armand."[90]

While numerous foreigners ventured to America, many Americans were themselves overseas

when the war began or went abroad during its course. These latter included many loyalist refugees,

who sometimes carried letters of introduction to potential patrons in England or elsewhere. But

they also included many adherents of the Revolution, and those of more ambiguous loyalties,

travelling on private business. Merchants and members of the middling and upper ranks of society

in particular often bore letters of introduction or recommendation addressed to American agents

abroad or to other prominent figures.[91]

---

[89] Washington to Hancock, 21 August 1777, *PGWDE*, Revolutionary, XI: 27.

[90] Morris to Washington, 10 May 1777, *PGWDE*, Revolutionary, IX: 380-381.

[91] See Arthur and William Bryan, Jr. to Franklin, 25 May 1778, *PBF*, XXVI: 528. John Bondfield to the American
Commissioners, 14 June 1778, *PBF*, XXVI: 617; William Castle: Petition to the American Commissioners, before 22

The letters they presented came both from persons back home in America and from acquaintances abroad. Thus, in May of 1778, Arthur and William Bryan, Jr. wrote a letter of introduction to Franklin—appealing to "Our acquaintance with you when you were here [in Dublin]"—for "our friend Captain Joy Castle," who, with his family, was "driven from Philadelphia by the war" but now hoped to return. "He is a fair and honest man," they wrote, "and connected with some of the leading citizens of Philadelphia."[92] In September of 1779, Edward Bridgen, in London, wrote to Franklin a letter introducing the bearer, a Mr. Story, as "an honest tryed Citizen and one in whom I can confide."[93] In November, Franklin's son-in-law, Richard Bache, wrote to him from Philadelphia to recommend three Pennsylvania men going to Europe on business who might need passports.[94] The following March, Thomas Digges, in England, wrote to Franklin the most recent of a series of introductions and recommendations he had sent his way, in this case for Captain Jonathan Snelling of Boston, long in Europe but now returning home.[95] In May of 1781, James Lovell wrote from Philadelphia to recommend to Franklin a Dr. Putnam who, "by the uniformity of his attachment to our public cause merits your patronage."[96] The following July, Samuel Rhoads, in Philadelphia, introduced Franklin to Samuel Griffitts, "Son of our late fellow Citizen William Griffitts decd.," a "virtuous youth in pursuit of Medical, & Chirugical Knowledge, who was "in high Esteem amongst his Acquaintance here" and Rhoads's "Kinsman" besides. Since he was "an utter Stranger in Europe," Rhoads recommended him to Franklin's "friendly Notice, &

June 1778, *PBF*, XXVI: 669, 669n; Christopher Gadsden to Franklin (and preceding editorial notes), 14 May 1778, *PBF*, XXVI: 454-457; Richard Bache to Franklin, 2 November 1779, 8 November 1779, *PBFDE*; Jonathan Nesbitt to Franklin, 20 October 1780, *PBFDE*; Jonathan Williams, Jr., to Franklin, 8 March 1782, 4 January 1783, *PBFDE*.

[92] Arthur and William Bryan, Jr. to Franklin, 25 May 1778, *PBFDE*.

[93] Bridgen to Franklin, 6 September 1779, *PBFDE*.

[94] Bache to Franklin, 2 November 1779, *PBFDE*. Bache to Franklin, 8 November 1779, *PBFDE*.

[95] Digges to Franklin, 17 March 1780, *PBFDE*. See also Digges to Franklin, 30 May 1780, introducing and recommending Dr. Upton Scott, *PBFDE*.

[96] Lovell to Franklin, 17 May 1781, Wharton, IV: 421.

advice."[97] That October, Thomas Jefferson wrote from Virginia to Franklin to recommend the bearer, Colonel James Monroe. Jefferson identified him as a distinguished officer in the American army, now going to Europe to complete his previously suspended studies, and recommended him as "a citizen of this state, of abilities, merit & fortune, and my particular friend."[98] In December, John Adams wrote from Amsterdam to introduce and recommend William Cheever, "a Citizen of Boston who proposes to Spend Sometime in France."[99]

Often those who brought letters of introduction to Americans in Europe sought additional letters, either to other Americans abroad or to European figures, in essence transposing their recommendations from America into the European sphere. Thus in April of 1780, Joseph Wharton, Jr. of Philadelphia wrote an introduction to Franklin on behalf of Dr. John Foulke, a Quaker physician going to Europe to pursue further training who, "being a perfect Stranger in Paris," would, Wharton explained, "stand in need of recommendations" from Franklin "to the most eminent in the Medical branches as well as for favorable introductions into the Hospitals."[100] In October, Franklin gave to a Mr. Searle, arrived from Pennsylvania, a recommendation to John Adams as "a member of Congress for Pennsylvania, with whose conversation you will be pleased, as he can give you good information of the state of our affairs when he left America."[101]

In many instances, both established and would-be U.S. citizens abroad were as eager to refashion their "private" identities as they were to secure official certification of—or protection founded on—their "public" identities. In the process, letters served to both distinguish and bind

---

[97] Rhoads to Franklin, 14 July 1781, *PBFDE*.

[98] Jefferson to Franklin, 5 October 1781, *PBFDE*.

[99] Adams to Franklin, 28 December 1781, *PBFDE*. See also Washington to Franklin, 9 December 1783, in favor of a Dr. Witherspoon, *PBFDE*.

[100] Wharton to Franklin, 27 April 1780, *PBFDE*.

[101] Franklin to Adams, 8 October 1780, Wharton, IV: 87. See also Franklin to Dumas, 9 October 1780, recommending Searle, Wharton, IV: 87-88.

together official and unofficial capacities. U.S. agents in fact furnished many applicants, both citizens and otherwise, who made no application for official instruments of identification, with letters in regard to their social standing and connections. And they often supplemented the official certificates and passports they issued with personal letters of this sort. These addressed, as it were, the dimensions of personal identity that intersected with the official—especially in a culture that assumed a close correlation between social rank and the public "quality" of the person.

While John Vaughan, for instance, had hoped to set off for America already having taken the oath of allegiance and hence with the beginnings of a character as an American, he also set off with the means of entry into American society in the form of one or more letters of introduction and recommendation. (On Vaughan see also Chapter 8.) Franklin himself supplied Vaughan with a letter of introduction and recommendation to Franklin's daughter and son-in-law—Sarah and Richard Bache of Philadelphia—in which he described Vaughan as the "son of a worthy friend of mine, and a very amiable and good young man." He explained that Vaughan "has been some years in France and Spain studying the two languages and acquiring commercial knowledge, and assured the Baches that "His establishment in America has ever been the intention of his parents as well as his desire. For which reason he left England soon after my arrival here and has remained on the continent, as I before mentioned." Franklin recommended Vaughan "in the most particular manner to your civilities and kind attention, and request for him your counsel and protection, which may be useful to him as a stranger."[102]

Besides the usual tasks of introduction and explicit recommendation, Franklin seemed intent, even in this brief letter to family members, to insist on Vaughan's long-standing intention to become an American, the fact that this intention (and hence, presumably, the affection for America) was shared by Vaughan's family, and, perhaps most importantly, that Vaughan had been,

---

[102] Franklin to Sarah and Richard Bache, 19 January 1782, Wharton, V: 119.

deliberately, out of Britain and British territory for most of the war to date. This latter fact may have been of particular importance as it suggested Vaughan was detached from British affairs, therefore unlikely to be a British agent or spy. It also implied that he had already undertaken a kind of expatriation, in preparation for his rebirth as an American. These bases for trusting Vaughan were reinforced by Franklin's implied judgment of his credibility and by his drawing attention to Vaughan's lineage as the son of one of Franklin's friends. In these ways, Franklin can be seen as building up the case, even in this unofficial form, for Vaughan's naturalization or denization, both in relation to any formal process thereof and in the social realm.

The letter of introduction to the Baches was not the only one that Vaughan carried. Vaughan had been, as William Carmichael wrote, "strongly recommended" to him in a letter from Franklin that Vaughan presented upon his arrival in Spain from France.[103] Carmichael in turn mentioned this recommendation from Franklin in a letter to Robert R. Livingston in which, besides praising the service and abilities of a Colonel Livingston, introduced and recommended Vaughan to Livingston by mentioning Franklin's letter and assuring Livingston that "I have found him every way worthy of his recommendation."[104] The chain of introduction and recommendation was thus continued, with Carmichael verifying Franklin's testimony and adding to it the force of his own judgment, continuing the construction of Vaughan's reputation in American society (extended overseas through networks of correspondence and expatriate communities) and his connections to the social and political networks of the United States. These two links in the chain each made use of the writer's social connections and personal character, but within exchanges that melded the official and the unofficial. Franklin, the U.S. minister plenipotentiary, recommended Vaughan to his

---

[103] Jay to Franklin, 31 May 1781, Wharton, V: 462-463. Carmichael to Robert R. Livingston, 27 February 1782, Wharton, V: 204-205.

[104] Carmichael to Livingston, 27 February 1782, Wharton, V: 204-205.

acquaintance Carmichael, secretary to Jay, the U.S. envoy to Spain. And Carmichael in turn passed

on and amplified the recommendation in a report to the Secretary of Foreign Affairs that

nonetheless maintained a personal tone (noting, among other things, the "pleasure…of [Colonel

Livingston's] acquaintance") and implicitly relied on the personal judgment and reputation of the

writer.

Both at home and abroad, negative or monitory identification of individuals who appeared

suspect and might impose themselves on others was an important counterpart to letters of

introduction and recommendation. Those who had their suspicions of particular individuals often

wrote ahead to warn their compatriots to beware if the suspect persons came calling. In May of

1777, for instance, in a letter to Richard Henry Lee, Washington warned that,

> By the time, Or before this Letter can reach you, Congress will be visited by a person who
> calls himself Colo. Michael Fabricy a Kovats who according to his own Account is a most
> valuable Officer from Prussia. What his Credentials are, I know not, but from what little I
> have seen of him, they ought to be strong to convince me of his real Importance for if his
> conversations have been faithfully Interpreted he has been caught tripping several times.[105]

In other cases, more than suspicion underlay such warnings. Thomas Digges, living in

London and known to the American commissioners in France as a merchant from Maryland, had

gained their good opinion early on.[106] Digges had "pretended to be a zealous American" Franklin

explained to John Jay, in the fall of 1781. He had expressed "much concern for our poor people

[sailors] in the English prisons" and had drawn on Franklin for nearly five hundred pounds sterling

the previous winter, supposedly to provide for the relief of the prisoners. But Franklin had now

---

[105] Washington to Lee, 17 May 1777, *PGWDE*, Revolutionary, IX: 453-454.

[106] By December of 1777, Arthur Lee, recommending persons in England to whom the Committee for Foreign Affairs could confide information and tasks, was able to write to the Committee from Paris that (presumably during Lee's earlier time in London) it had "fallen very particularly within my knowledge" that Digges had "exerted himself with great assiduity and address in gaining intelligence and doing other services in England." Lee to the Committee for Foreign Affairs, 8 December 1778, Wharton, II: 447.

discovered that "the villain" Digges had used only thirty pounds for that purpose and had since

"failed and absconded."[107] By February of the following year, Franklin would express to [Captain?]

Cunningham his conviction that Digges was in fact "the greatest villain I ever met with."[108] Digges

reappeared that same spring, acting supposedly on behalf of the British ministry, when he arrived in

Holland to inquire of John Adams whether there were in fact Americans in Europe commissioned

to treat for peace. Digges at the same period wrote to Franklin indicating that he hoped to meet

with him in person to give his explanations.[109]

But Franklin, even as he wrote to his friend Hartley regarding how peace negotiations might

be initiated, informed him that

> As to Digges, I have no confidence in him, nor in anything he says, or may say, of his being
> sent by ministers. Nor will I have any communication with him, except in receiving and
> considering the justification of himself which he pretends he shall be able and intends to
> make for his excessive drafts on me, on account of the relief I have ordered to the prisoners,
> and his embezzlement of the money.[110]

Franklin's opinion spread quickly, and as the negotiations for peace neared, the new British ministry

distanced itself from Digges, to avoid having the damage to his reputation and his diplomatic

resources erode their own, and therefore undermine the efforts to negotiate a treaty with the

Americans. As preparations for the peace negotiations moved forward, Shelburne instructed

Oswald that,

> In regard to Mr. Digges, you may assure Dr. Franklin that he need be under no uneasiness
> about his connection with or attendance upon sir Guy Carleton. He is now in London, and
> my knowledge of him is merely this—he had been, it seems, employed by the late

---

[107] Franklin to Jay, 20 August 1781, Wharton, IV: 643-647.

[108] Franklin to Cunningham, 6 February 1782, Wharton, V: 149. Franklin told Cunningham that he had never been able
to get from Digges a formal account of what Digges had done with the money he had been given. Digges had,
apparently, sought from Cunningham repayment for fifty or sixty pounds he had supposedly advanced. But Franklin
assured Cunningham that he owed Digges nothing, since Digges had in fact originally received the money he had
supposedly advanced from Franklin.

[109] Franklin to Cunningham, Wharton, V: 148-149; Digges to Franklin, 22-26 March 1782, *PBFDE*.

[110] Franklin to Hartley, 5 April 1782, Wharton, V: 293-294.

administration in an indirect commission to sound Mr. Adams, which scheme appears to have had no consequences. The man was afterwards recommended to me, but having heard by accident a very indifferent account of his character, and particularly that Mr. Franklin had a bad opinion of him, I from that moment resolved to have nothing to do with him.[111]

This message, intended for Franklin, was no doubt intended to reassure him, and so may give more weight to the actual play of counter-recommendations than they deserved (if they existed at all). But Shelburne's account suggests the multiple streams of influence—recommendation and counter-recommendation—and the fortuitous events and information that could play into an attempt to verify the character of an unfamiliar individual. It likewise illustrates—in the rapid oscillation and multiple faces of Digges's "character"—the vulnerabilities of this system of identification and portable identity.

But the incident also gives some sense of how the system worked to communicate negative as much as positive character, and to extend the reach of local knowledge beyond the bounds of orality. The Digges incident illustrates the propagation of disrepute, the active counterpart to the reactive sanctions imposed by the system on persons who simply lacked instruments of recommendation and identification. It illustrates—along with, for example, public advertisement of fugitives, debtors, and confidence men (quite apart from slave pass laws or physical branding of slaves and criminals)—one facet of the systemic effort to regulate identity in ways that would follow the individual in his or her travels.

An inability to command letters of recommendation could be held against an individual as more than a simple lack of substantiating evidence. Such a lack could be viewed as positive evidence of an individual's disreputable character and lack of social standing or credit, and, hence, as evidence against the likely veracity of any of the individual's claims. A person's character was constituted by the number and standing of the persons who were willing to vouch for him or her and thereby put

---

[111] Shelburne to Oswald, 20 June 1782, Wharton, I: 658.

their own reputation and credit at stake. Likewise, when an individual's travels resulted in or were accompanied by an apparent severing of connections (if correspondence was not maintained) it could be seen as a symptom of unsettledness, flight, or dishonor—a likely indication that the individual had fled a previous home to escape debts, justice, dishonor, or a deservedly bad character. Those who needed to travel without letters of introduction and recommendation (perhaps to escape disrepute or debt) were—as part of the proper functioning of the social regulation of identity— forced into the lower ranks of society unless they could mobilize other social and cultural resources (e.g. manners, education) persuasively to establish, at least, their basic social rank. The system worked to mitigate or correct for the ways mobility undermined the regulation and stabilization of identity. It was developed, in large part, to prevent precisely the escape from a deservedly poor character that mobility could allow, and to prevent attempts at unsanctioned social mobility or fraud through the mutability of identity made possible by the disjunctions between different spheres of local knowledge. In so far as letters of introduction and recommendation were made necessities for social access and securing aid, continually re-securing these instruments was a necessity forced on anyone who wished to travel and function at any sort of respectable social level—unless they were bold enough to resort to forgery or false personation.

Franklin was, in fact, concerned that his compatriots in the Continental Congress were not sufficiently wary of the potential for deception. He was likewise worried they might not be sufficiently conscious that their decisions actually created new and possibly spurious characters. In adopting agents as their representatives, they recreated these persons in new identities certified or conferred by the United States. This influence would be a product both of their future behavior as their agents, and of the public's or other states' awareness of those agents' previous character. It would be all too easy for the new states to associate themselves with persons concerning whose standing they at best misunderstood or found themselves misinformed, and at worst in which they had been deceived. The risks of misinformation or deception were amplified by the potential for the states to misunderstand the nature of particular statuses in European states and other contexts.

The nascent states, Franklin would warn, must be wary of employing strangers of little or questionable reputation or public character. In May of 1779 he wrote to the Congress that,

> we have in America too readily, in various instances, given faith to the pretensions of strangers from Europe, and who offer their services as persons who have powerful friends and great interest in their own country, and by that means obtain contracts, orders, or commissions to procure what we want, and who, when they come here, are totally unknown, and have no other credit but what such commissions give them; or, if known, the commissions do not add so much to their credit as they diminish that of their employers.[112]

Not only would the actions of these agents reflect on the Congress, but their choice of whom to employ would reflect on them as well. If their chosen agents lacked previous public reputation or character, they could exercise very little influence in European affairs and would make the states themselves appear inconsequential. An agent with a poor reputation or character, chosen in ignorance, for lack of proper vetting and identification, could be still more damaging.

Worse still, neglect of due diligence in the identification of those who presented themselves as would-be agents laid the states open to the impositions of opportunists. Franklin gave as a cautionary example his own encounter with a correspondent who sought to take advantage of what he believed to be Franklin's insufficient canniness and political experience. The correspondent thought Franklin to be unfamiliar with European politics, foreign affairs, and the workings and networks of official diplomacy and statecraft. Franklin recounted how

> I have received two letters from a Frenchman, settled in one of the ports of Barbary, offering himself to act as our minister with the emperor, with whom he pretended to be intimate, and acquainting me that his imperial majesty wondered we had never sent to thank him for being the first power on this side of the Atlantic that had acknowledged out independence and opened his ports to us; advising that we should send the emperor a present.

____

[112] Frank to the Committee of Foreign Affairs, 26 May 1779, Wharton, III: 192

But, Franklin reported, "On inquiry at the office in whose department Africa is included" he "learned the character of this man to be such that it was not safe to have any correspondence with him, and therefore I did not answer his letters."[113]

Franklin was all too familiar with the efforts of the ambitious to take advantage of what they perceived as the desperation, ignorance, or pliability of the American governments. He reported to Congress that, the Congress's agents having had only limited success securing loans in Holland, "A Mr. Neufville came from thence to me last spring, proposing to procure great sums, if he might be employed for that purpose, and the business taken away from the house that had commenced it." But Neufville's terms, he said, proved "very extravagant": mortgages on all American estates, large guaranteed consignments of goods, etc. Only when he had agreed to the terms enjoyed by the previous agents did Franklin agree to consider his proposals, if he could provide a list of subscribers proving he could raise the sums he claimed. Neufville, Franklin reported, had put him off for three months, and in the end

> I received, instead of the subscription, a new set of propositions, among the terms of which were an additional *one per cent.*, and a patent from Congress appointing him and his sons *"commissioners for trade and navigation and treasurers of the general Congress and of every private State of the thirteen United States of North America through the seven United Provinces,"* with other extravagancies

Franklin had refused the new terms, but was informed that Neufville planned to petition Congress directly, with the support of friends who charged Franklin with negligence of the interests of the United States for refusing Neufville. Franklin reported these transactions to Congress "that it may be understood why I have dropped a correspondence on this subject with a man who seemed to me a vain promiser, extremely self-interested, and aiming chiefly to make an appearance without solidity."[114] Neufville apparently saw in the United States and their plight an opportunity to secure

---

[113] Frank to the Committee of Foreign Affairs, 26 May 1779, Wharton, III: 192.

[114] Franklin to the President of Congress, 4 October 1779, Wharton, III: 361-362.

not only lucrative commercial and financial commissions but also new titles—hence public character and status—for not only himself but his family as well, all to be embodied in a "patent" or commission.

The American Revolutionaries would throughout the war use letters of introduction and recommendation to build networks of trust. By these means, they could identify persons worthy of confidence and likely to be useful to the republican cause. At the same time, such instruments belonged, by their basic assumptions, to "gentlemen," and therefore marked off a privileged sphere of access among the "Americans" struggling mutually for independence. The same exclusivity extended further, into another and explicitly public set of identification papers, the commissions used to mark authority in both the civil and military spheres. Men who bore commissions served the cause, but they were almost exclusively "gentlemen." Commission thus served, in a sense, to identify the bearers of official authority among the ranks of social power. They were, at the same time, the familiar, fundamental instruments of sovereign governance. In both respects they were central to the constitution of the new republican states and confederation as both emblematic and practical sovereigns in opposition to the British Empire from which they sprang. The following chapter examines how the Revolutionary contest for sovereignty was enacted by replacing British imperial commissions with new American instruments, a process through which the American states both rejected and imitated the social and political distinctions of the imperial regime they cast off.

Chapter 3

Commissions

On a Sunday morning in the late summer of 1776, two French Canadian men arrived at Fort Ticonderoga, then held by Continental Army forces under Major General Horatio Gates. The two men had been captains in a British regiment of Canadian Provincials, but they had deserted and fled to the rebel army from their station near St. John's, Newfoundland. They brought encouraging reports that Royal Governor Guy Carleton was rapidly alienating even Loyalist Canadians by exacting burdensome quotas of cattle to supply the army, offering only paper notes payable in return, and offending "the sensibility of the Canadians" with demonstrations of unnecessary cruelty toward adherents to the rebel cause and prisoners in his power. Most strikingly, they told of a "diversion" Carleton had "exhibited" for the amusement of his soldiers, in which officers who had served in rebel militia companies or the Continental forces "were forced to burn their commissions, to the very minutest particle—an operation which, as was expected by the beholders, singed the fingers of such of the criminals who were not very dexterous in disappointing that most humane General." The Continental officers, the two reported, were then imprisoned on men-of-war destined for the West Indies.[1]

A little more than a week earlier, Ambrose Serle, aboard a British ship in New York Harbor, had written home to Lord Dartmouth reports of American commissions in flames. "The Congress

____

[1] Particulars collected from the verbal examination and the conversation of two Canadian Captains, August 1776, Ms. and Transcription, Horatio Gates Papers, 1726-1828, Film 23, Reel 3, DLAR. The examination is not dated and the precise date of the arrival of the two men (L'Oiseau and Allain) is not given, but the examination was enclosed in and referenced by Gates's letter to George Washington, 7 August 1776. The preceding Sunday, probably the "Sunday morning" noted in the heading of the examination as the day of the two men's arrival, was the 4th of August. The report of the examination notes that another examinee, apparently another French Canadian man, named Mesnard, "confirmes what L'Oiseau says respecting the commissions given to the Canadians under the authority of the Congress."

sent commissions to Judges and other Officers for the Execution of Justice" in Berkshire County,

Massachusetts, Serle reported, "[but] [t]he Multitude burnt the Commissions, and declared they

would have no Law but the Law of Moses." "The People," he emphasized, "have opposed the

Decrees of the Congress, not from Principles of Loyalty, but from a thorough Hatred of all

Subjection and Order." After all, he reminded Dartmouth, "This was the County, which first

opposed the Administration of Justice under lawful Authority."[2] For Serle, the burning of the

Congressional commissions by the Berkshire "Multitude" was emblematic of the immolation of

social order and the rule of law, proof that the deluded people wanted not new and better

government but anarchy.

By forcing his prisoners to burn their rebel commissions in their own hands, Carleton had

made a public spectacle of his and his sovereign's contempt for the rebels and their pretensions to

---

[2] Serle to Dartmouth, 25 July 1776, APSED, Film 391, Reel 15, No. 1694, DLAR. It is unclear to which events precisely the reports Serle had received referred, and to what degree these reports were accurate. According to a petition made by John Ashley and others from Berkshire County to the Massachusetts Provincial Congress in April of 1776, in February and extralegal Committee of Inspection and attendant crowds, organized, lead, and incited by Reverend Thomas Allen and his associates, had publicly denied the legitimacy of the present Massachusetts "Constitution," sanctioned by the Continental Congress, and the authority of the Provincial Congress, and had subsequently prevented the appointed sitting of the Court of Sessions at Pittsfield on the last Tuesday of the month and "immediately took away such commissions from the civil officers of the County on which they could lay their hands," as a consequence of which, the petitioners claimed, "we are reduced to a state of anarchy and confusion." No references is made in the petition or in other extant sources thus far identified to the "Law of Moses" declaration mentioned by Serle, or to the commissions of the magistrates being burned, though precisely what was done with them is not made clear. The petition makes pervasive use of fire metaphors, referring to Allen and his associates as "incendiaries," who had "blazed abroad" reports injurious to the petitioners, and had "inflamed" the people, who, "being inflamed," subsequently prevented the sitting of the court and seized the commissions. It is possible, if the commissions were not actually burned, that Serle received garbled versions of reports in these terms that made it appear or actually claimed that the commissions had been burned. Petition of John Ashley et al., 12 April 1776, *AAO*, Series 4, V: 1275-1276. See also, *History of Berkshire County, Massachusetts, with Biographical Sketches of its Prominent Men*, (New York: J.B. Beers & Co., 1885), II: 299-300. At least as late as September of 1776, the Committee of Pittsfield, in Berkshire County, had refused to recognize the legitimacy of a commission as Justice of the Peace issued to Charles Goodrich by the "major part of the Council of this Colony"— characterizing Goodrich as having "procured to himself a commission in the King's name." The Committee had, apparently, prevented him from exercising his commission, and had, on the basis of the above charge and a charge of having refused to submit to be drafted for the expedition against Canada, advertised him in the papers as a enemy of the country, calling for his ostracism. Goodrich in turn had, on petition, secured from the Massachusetts Assembly resolves, including the declaration that, "Mr. Goodrich received a commission from the major part of the Council of this Colony, of such tenure and form as they judged it proper to adopt, and such, as far as they could learn, as was agreeable to the practice of the other Colonies, and agreeable to the sentiments of the Congress. The said Committee, therefore, in exhibiting this charge, have discovered an entire ignorance of the line of their duty, and great Indecency towards the constitutional authority of this State." Goodrich to the Printer of the Connecticut Courant, 18 September 1776, *AAO*, Series 5, II: 388-389; Massachusetts Council, 16 September 1776, *AAO*, Series 5, II: 742.

authority, as embodied in the commissions. The people of Berkshire county, in Serle's recounting, had defied those who would presume to set authorities over them. In both instances, the commissions served as effigies of the pretended authority to issue them. At the same time, they were the instruments of identification that the appointed officers and officials needed to lawfully exercise their commissioned authority. In many ways similar to colonists' seizure and destruction of stamped paper and documents (as well as royalist pamphlets) during the Stamp Act protests—measures that were both symbolic rejections of the tax legislation and pragmatic attacks on the stamp commissioners' ability to execute the Act—so the burning of commissions served to destroy both symbolic and practical sovereignty.[3]

Both episodes were evocative of the longstanding practice by European states and colonial governments of ordering condemned writings to be burned in public "by the common hangman"—a ceremony that expressed the sovereign's disdain of the work and its author and destroyed the text (though rarely were all extant copies accounted for).[4] As recently as the spring of 1775, Parliament had ordered the public burning of pamphlets that voiced support for the American opposition, while members of Parliament sympathetic to the Americans suggested that the proposed acts for

---

[3] See, e.g., Edmund S. and Helen M. Morgan, *The Stamp Act Crisis: Prologue to Revolution*, (Chapel Hill, NC: University of North Carolina Press, 1962), 202, 203; Merrill Jensen, *The Founding of a Nation: A History of the American Revolution, 1763-1776*, (Indianapolis, IN: Hackett, 1968), 132, 138-139, 149, 152.

[4] Most famously, perhaps, in the context of the eighteenth-century British Empire, Parliament had, in 1763, ordered the burning of John Wilkes' *North Britain No. 45*, as a seditious libel. Jensen, *The Founding of a Nation*, 156-157. On the practice of ordering condemned or "forbidden" books burned by the public hangman in France during the eighteenth century, see Robert Darnton, *The Forbidden Best-Sellers of Pre-Revolutionary France*, (New York: Norton, 1996), 3, 35-36, 49. Darnton emphasizes that the French magistrates only rarely ordered such burnings; that when they did they often had "dummy copies" burned for the purpose of the spectacle, retaining the originals themselves; and that, "[k]nowing that nothing promoted sales better than a good bonfire, they preferred to impound books and imprison booksellers with as little fuss as possible (3)." On the burning of blasphemous, seditious, or otherwise condemned books on order of the government during the colonial period, see, e.g., Lawrence C. Wroth, *The Colonial Printer*, (Charlottesville, VA: Dominion Books, 1964), 23, 175; Hugh Amory and David D. Hall eds., *A History of the Book in America, Volume I: The Colonial Book in the Atlantic World*, (Cambridge: Cambridge UP, 2000), 457; David S. Shields, *Oracles of Empire: Poetry, Politics, and Commerce in British America, 1690-1750*, (Chicago: University of Chicago Press, 1990), 162, 165-166. In 1770, students at Princeton reportedly hired a hangman themselves and held a public burning of a letter from New York merchants to the merchants of Philadelphia announcing their intention to break the non-importation agreement they had previously committed to: *New York Journal*, 19 July 1770, *AHN*.

restraining the commerce of the colonies were so "treasonable against the community" that they "ought to be burnt by the common hangman."[5] In the colonies, from at least the winter of 1774, when the freeholders of Elizabethtown, New Jersey, had ordered and executed the public burning of two Loyalist pamphlets, the American rebels, from local committees to provincial governments, condemned and burned the writings of their enemies.[6]

Meanwhile, some among the American opposition who had been commissioned as civil or military officers under the crown publicly burned their commissions to mark their break with British authority—in some cases as a prelude to taking up American commissions. In January of 1775, Patriots in Boston published reports that in Greenwich, New Hampshire, zealous Patriot and former Deputy Sheriff Thomas Weeks had resigned his commission and had it publicly burned to mark "his firm Attachment to the Liberty of his Country, and Abhorrence of keeping a Commission confirm'd under an unconstitutional Government [the Massachusetts Government Act]."[7] Early that same year, according to a later account, Major John Sullivan "and other citizens of Durham," New

---

[5] See, e.g., the Parliamentary order for the burning of *The Crisis, No. III*, 7 [27?] February 1775, *AAO*, Series 4, II: 56. For an account of the burning of this pamphlet, and of popular reaction against it, see "Extract of a Letter from London," 7 March 1775, *AAO*, Series 4, II: 55. On the burning of *The Crisis*, the pamphlet's subsequent success in America, and its role as a kind of predecessor to Paine's *Common Sense*, see also T.H. Breen, *American Insurgents, American Patriots: The Revolution of the People*, (New York: Hill & Wang, 2010), 262-274. Breen, in writing of the decision to burn *The Crisis*, refers to Parliament having "settled for a bizarre punishment (265)." Given the long-standing practice of burning seditious or otherwise condemned writings by the hand of the common hangman, it seems likely that this order is only bizarre in retrospect. The preceding attempt by Parliament to try the pamphlet itself for treason may have been more so by the standards of the time. See also a reference to the Parliament's order for the burning of an "inflammatory pamphlet" (possibly the same pamphlet as above), in the extract of a letter from London, 24 February 1775, in *The Journals of Each Provincial Congress of Massachusetts in 1774 and 1775...*, (Boston: Dutton & Wentworth, 1838), 744-747. For the suggestion that the restraining acts should be publicly burnt, see the minutes of a debate in the House of Commons, 17 March 1775, *AAO*, Series 4, I: 1703-1704.

[6] 1 December 1774, *AAO*, Series 4, I: 1012-1013. For examples of burnings of the same pamphlets and examples of the ongoing practice of the public burning of Loyalist tracts, see Freeholders of Ulster County, NY, 6 January 1775; Precinct of Shawangunk, Ulster County, NY, 26 January 1775; Committee of Hanover, NY, 27 January 1775; Committee of Walkill, NY, 30 January 1775: *AAO*, Series 4, I: 1100, 1183, 1191, 1201; Freeholders of New Windsor, Ulster County, NY, 14 March 1775, *AAO*, Series 4, II: 131-133. See also Jensen, *The Founding of a Nation*, 523. For an instance of the use of such public burnings of offensive writings in inter-colonial dispute during this same period, see Pauline Maier, *From Resistance to Revolution: Colonial Radicals and the Development of American Opposition to Britain, 1765-1776*, (New York: Norton, 1991), 197.

[7] "Hardwick, December 19, 1774," *Boston Evening Post*, 16 January 1775, *AHN*.

Hampshire, "holding civil or military commissions from the King" built a bonfire on Durham common and, "in the presence of a large number of persons, burned their commissions, uniforms, and all other insignia which in any way connected them with the Royal Government."[8]

The crisis of identification brought on by the American Revolution was tightly bound up with the contest for authority and sovereignty at the heart of the Revolution itself. The instruments of British imperial sovereignty had to be replaced with those of the new republican states. And the demands of governance and war required practical, material instruments that allowed those on both sides to know who held legitimate authority, under whose auspices, and in what character. In both the civilian and military contexts, the most fundamental of such instruments was the commission. This chapter examines the development, deployment, and significance of Revolutionary commissions as instruments of identification central to the Revolutionary contest for authority and sovereignty.

Commissions had been fundamental to the government of the empire and colonies. Colonial governance (civil and military) had been constructed through chains of commissions, which simultaneously served as instruments of patronage in the distribution of places of profit and honor. In his *Military Guide for Young Officers* (1776), Thomas Simes defined a commission as "the authority granted by a Prince, or his General, to Officers, by which he invests them with command, agreeable to his pleasure and their abilities."[9] The Crown or the proprietor of a colony granted commissions to the governor and other selected executive and military officials under the royal seal ("the Great

---

[8] Thomas Coffin Amory, *General John Sullivan: A Vindication of his Character as a Soldier and a Patriot*, (Morrisania, NY: 1867), 3-4. See also Amory, *The Military Services and Public Life of Major-General John Sullivan, of the American Revolutionary Army*, (Boston: Wiggin and Lunt; Albany, NY: J. Munsell, 1868), 14.

[9] Simes, *The Military Guide for Young Officers*, (London: reprinted Philadelphia: J. Humphreys, R. Bell, and R. Aitken Printers, 1776), *EAI*, Series 1, no. 15083 (filmed).

Seal of England"), the seal of the Privy Council, or the proprietor's seal.[10] The governors in turn—

sometimes in consultation with the assembly of the colony—granted commissions to militia officers,

judges, justices of the peace, and subordinate judicial and executive officials under the seal of the

colony. The officials of the imperial bureaucracy who were not integrated with provincial

governments—such as customs officials and officers of Royal Army garrisons (which became more

familiar and objectionable to the colonists in the decade after the French and Indian War)—

operated under royal commissions of their own. Magistrates, officials, and officers themselves

issued deputy commissions, warrants, certificates, judgments, letters of administration, and

numerous other documents, under their seals of office, through which the authority flowing from

their own commissions (which authorized them to issue these subordinate instruments) was

channeled to turn the wheels of imperial, provincial, and local governance.[11]

Commissions were, from this perspective, both the emblems and the material instruments of

imperial and provincial authority. They were the means through which local authorities governed an

extended, decentralized empire in spite of great distances, limited governmental capacity, difficult

travel, and communications that were often slow or unreliable. Militia commissions were archetypal

---

[10] See *Massachusetts Royal Commissions, 1681-1774, Publications of the Colonial Society of Massachusetts, II: Collections*, (Boston, 1913).

[11] On commissions and colonial governance see *Massachusetts Royal Commissions*; Leonard Woods Labaree, *Royal Government in America: A Study of the British Colonial System before 1783*, (New Haven, CT: Yale UP, 1930), 8-11, 19-21, 30, 51-52, 87, 421, 423, 442; Evarts Boutell Greene, *The Provincial Governor in the English Colonies of North America*, (New York: Longmans, Green, & Co., 1898), 47, 49, 50, 93-96. On structures of imperial and colonial governance more generally, see A.J.R. Russell-Wood ed, *Government and Governance of European Empires, 1450-1800: Part II*, (Burlington, VT: Ashgate, 2000), and Russell-Wood ed., *Local Government in European Overseas Empires, 1450-1800: Parts I & II*, (Burlington, VT: Ashgate, 1999); Mark A. Burkholder ed., *Administrators of Empire*, (Burlington, VT: Ashgate, 1998). For the English background of these structures of governance and commission, see, esp., Michael J. Braddick, *State Formation in Early Modern England, c. 1550-1700*, (Cambridge: Cambridge UP, 2000). Contemporary manuals, guides, and digests for the use of civil and judicial officers offered forms of a wide variety of commissions and related instruments for governance at the provincial, county, and local levels. See, e.g., Elie Vallette, *The deputy commissary's guide within the Province of Maryland...*, (Annapolis, MD: Ann Catherine Green and Son, Printers, 1774), *EAI*, Series 1, no. 13742 (filmed), 163 ("A Deputy Commissary's Commission"), 198 ("An Especial Commission to pass account"), 203 ("A Commission of Rebellion"), 213 ("A Commission to examine Evidence"), 214 ("Commissioner's Oath"). For the variety and importance of commissions in colonial governance, see, esp., James Davis, *The office and authority of a justice of the peace...*, (Newbern, NC: James Davis, Printer, 1774), *EAI*, Series 1, no. 13236 (filmed).

in this respect. Officers were often elected or nominated on the local level, sometimes by the members of the units they would command. But their commissions were issued at the provincial level, typically by the governor, whose own royal or proprietary commission ordinarily made him commander in chief of the militia.[12] The militia was in turn a pervasive and fundamental institution of colonial order, comprising most adult white men of the colony. It reinforced social structures of authority at local levels, while constituting an integral component of the identities of the gentry and other provincial elites.[13]

As part of this same process of constituting imperial governance, commissions were likewise deployed to extend and secure the military, governmental, diplomatic, and physical frontiers of the North American empire. In these borderlands, commissions were one of several instruments of identification by which British imperial and colonial regimes attempted to forge alliances with (and co-opt the authority of) Native American leaders by identifying them in documentary forms as subordinate agents of the British Empire. Thus, in composing their "Plan for the Future Management of Indian Affairs" in 1764, in the wake of the Seven Years War, the Lords of Trade provided that the two Superintendents of Indian Affairs should "have power to confer such honors and rewards on the Indians as shall be necessary, and of granting Commissions to principal Indians in their respective Districts, to be War Captains or Officers of other Military Distinctions."[14] The following year, in a treaty with the Chickasaw and Choctaw at Mobile, the representatives of the two

---

[12] Jerrilyn Greene Marston, *King and Congress: The Transfer of Political Legitimacy, 1774-1776*, (Princeton, NJ: Princeton UP, 1987), 135; Don Higginbotham, *The War of American Independence: Military Attitudes, Policies, and Practices, 1763-1789*, (Boston: Northeastern UP, 1983), 17-18.

[13] Rhys Isaac, *The Transformation of Virginia, 1740-1790*, (New York: Norton, 1988), 104-110; Gordon S. Wood, *The Radicalism of the American Revolution*, (New York: Vintage, 1993), 74, 88; John Wood Sweet, *Bodies Politic: Negotiating Race in the American North, 1730-1830*, (Philadelphia: University of Pennsylvania Press, 2006), 197-200; Fred Anderson, *A People's Army: Massachusetts Soldiers and Society in the Seven Years' War*, (Chapel Hill, NC: University of North Carolina Press, 1984), 26-27; Sally E. Hadden, *Slave Patrols: Law and Violence in Virginia and the Carolinas*, (Cambridge, MA: Harvard UP, 2001), 42-47.

[14] *PAA*, Series 1, IV: 182-188.

Native American nations—whether by their own words or in a ventriloquized imposition of the categories through which British authorities hoped to identify and understand them—described themselves as "We, the Chiefs and Head Warriors, distinguished by great and small Medals and Gorgets, and bearing his Majesty's Commissions as Chiefs and Leaders of our respective Nations."[15]

For British Americans, as for the commissioned "War Captains" of Britain's extended empire, commissions and associated instruments constituted fundamental loci of the material experience and practice of empire. Whether military, judicial, or civil, commissions were closely intertwined with the identity and honor of those who bore them, not only in their legal and symbolic qualities but also in their materiality as documents.[16] Thus, in the autumn of 1774, John Temple, onetime Surveyor General of the Customs and Lieutenant Governor of New Hampshire, writing to Lord Dartmouth to protest his dismissal from the latter post, explained that while he had never "benefited a single shilling" from the office in his fourteen-year tenure, "I however highly valued it as an honor done me by my sovereign, and as an office that was created purposely by Mr Pitt to give me rank in that country, there never having been a Lieut. Governor to that province before." The commission, as a document, was particularly meaningful in his eyes, as "it was the first new

---

[15] *PAA*, Series 1, IV: 320-321. On the British, French, and American use of medals, badges, and such to distinguish allied chiefs, cf. Eric Hinderaker, *Elusive Empires: Constructing Colonialism in the Ohio Valley, 1673-1800*, (Cambridge: Cambridge UP, 1997), 73-75; Collin G. Calloway, *The American Revolution in Indian Country: Crisis and Diversity in Native American Communities*, (Cambrige: Cambridge UP, 1995), 7, 8, 28, 40, 42, 44, 60, 76, 139, 224, 236, 250, 251, 280n25; Richard White, *The Middle Ground: Indians, Empires, and Republics in the Great Lakes Region, 1650-1815*, (Cambridge: Cambridge UP, 1991), 177, 179, 209.

[16] In *The Military Medley*, (Dublin: S. Powell, 1767), a primer, compendium, and reference for officers, Thomas Simes defined an "Officer," in the several possible degrees, by the type of commission or other instrument he bore (or lacked): "OFFICER in the army, is a person, having a commission in the army; those having commissions from the king, are called commissioned officers. Such as have no commission, but only warrants from their colonels, are called warrant officers. Those that have no commissions nor warrants, are called non-commissioned officers." *ECCO*. Significantly, in the Anglo-American military, the lowest class of officers in the army were labeled not according to some positive quality or category, but by their lack of a commission: "non-commissioned officers." In practice commissioned officers were sometimes referred to simply as "commission officers": see *JCC*, 12 October 1775, III: 289: "Resolved, That each captain and other commission officer, while in the recruiting service of this Continent, or on their march to join the army, shall be allowed two dollars and two thirds [of a dollar] per week, for their subsistence."

commission his present Majesty ever signed."[17] The preceding spring, near the other extreme of the

imperial chain of commissions, and on the far frontier of the British North American empire,

Pennsylvania Justice of the Peace Andrew McFarlane had written to his colony's governor, John

Penn, to assure him that though he had been arrested and imprisoned by refractory frontier

dissidents, and his business was suffering in his absence, nevertheless "I am willing to suffer a great

Deal more rather than Bring a Disgrace on the Commission"—the instrument authenticated by

Penn's signature and seal—"which I bear under your Honour."[18]

Yet the commission, as a document, bore a dual character. On the one hand it was a highly

individual adjunct to the bearer's identity. On the other it was fundamentally material and

impersonal, separable from the individual as a standardized legal text or a blank form (especially

when printed), before it was filled up (by hand) with the individual information that would animate

it as an instrument of identification. In this latter dimension, indeed, it partook of the character of a

commercial good or commodity. Royal governors of the colonies often "purchased" their

commissions at great expense.[19] Commissioned military officers of the rank of colonel and below

purchased, and sometimes sold, their commissions.[20] Commissions themselves, as documents

composed of paper (or parchment), ink, wax, and sometimes ribbons or other embellishments, were

composed of commodities that were produced by private manufacturers and artisans; distributed

through merchants and purveyors; purchased by the state; and familiar to everyone as items of

---

[17] Temple to Dartmouth, 13 October 1774, *CMHS*, Series 6, IV: 376-379.

[18] McFarlane to Penn, 9 April 1774, *PAA*, Series 1, IV: 487-488.

[19] Greene, *Provincial Governor*, 47.

[20] Higginbotham, *War of American Independence*, 124; "commission," *Oxford Companion to Military History*, Richard Holmes ed., (New York: Oxford UP, 2001). The purchase of commissions was a requirement of long standing meant to ensure that only men of a certain social station might become officers

expense.[21] Commissions composed using printed blank forms were, moreover, the product of the

labor and craft of a printing house. In these respects, commissions (like instruments of

identification more generally) bore a complex character very similar to that borne by financial

instruments such as paper currency, bills of exchange, and commercial powers of attorney. They

particularly resembled bills of credit. Commissions drew credit on the authority of the sovereign (or

his deputies) to certify the bearer's authority on the move and at a distance, and they drew on

treasury funds as instruments through which a bearer was authorized to incur expenses to the public,

including his salary.

In fact, such material instruments of authority bore likewise the character of a commodity in

that they were subject to the customs duties and other taxes of the empire, both in the taxation of

their constituent commodities and in the taxation of the commissions themselves as composite legal

documents.[22] The Stamp Act of 1765, though it exempted most military commissions and the

commissions of judges and justices of the peace, levied stamp duties on "every skin or piece of

vellum or parchment, or sheet or piece of paper, on which shall be ingrossed, written, or printed"

---

[21] Though officers would not pay the expenses of the materials that composed their own commissions, they might well
bear the expense of ink, wax, and pens used in the issuing of commissions, warrants, passes, and other documents to
others. In any event, officers were intimately familiar with the expense, materiality, and material limits of writing
supplies through their own expenditures in support of their correspondence, diaries, and paperwork and record keeping
of many varieties. Simes (*Military Medley*, Dublin: 1767) advised the "young Gentleman...upon obtaining his first
Commission in the Infantry" that among the necessary supplies with which he must furnish himself—including
substantial supplies of clothing and bedding—were "a travelling Letter-Case, to contain Pens, Ink, Paper, Wax, and
Wafer," as well as a case of drawing instruments (150-151). In his "Scheme of an Ensign's constant Expences," he
identified among the regular expenses of the young officer—including meals, drink, linen, and barbering—"Hair
Powder, Pomatum, Soap, Blackball, Pens, Paper, Ink, Wax, and Wafers" as a single line-item amounting to more than
three pounds in expenses a year (152). *ECCO.*

[22] The "Townshend Act" of 1767, for instance, had imposed duties on more than sixty different descriptions or
categories of paper. Parliament of Great Britain, 20 November 1767, "An act for granting certain duties in the British
colonies and plantations in America; for allowing a drawback of the duties of customs upon the exportation, from this
kingdom, of coffee and cocoa nuts of the produce of the said colonies or plantations; for discontinuing the drawbacks
payable on china earthen ware exported to America; and for more effectually preventing the clandestine running of
goods in the colonies and plantations," *The statutes at large* ... [from 1225 to 1867], Danby Pickering ed., (Cambridge :
Printed by Benthem, for C. Bathhurst ; London, 1762-1869), reproduced by *The Avalon Project: Documents in Law, History
and Diplomacy* (http://avalon.law.yale.edu/18th_century/townsend_act_1767.asp), Yale University Law School.

commissions of all other civil and judicial offices in the colonies.[23] Yet the architects of the Act responded to reports that it would provoke discontent in the North American colonies by pointing out that the duties the act imposed on North America were, in general, lower than those imposed on the island colonies of the West Indies and those already paid in England. Thus, Thomas Whately pointed out to John Temple that "Commissions & appointments to offices are also charged as high in the Islands as they are here; but on the continent at no more than two thirds; & all commissions of the army, navy, militia, & justices of the peace are entirely excepted. Your annual offices too are lightly taxed. It is not so in England."[24] The ensuing controversy, however, focused not on the relative burden of duties but on the colonists' complaints of "taxation without representation." A commission could now mark out its bearer as a local enemy precisely because of the taxation of the document itself and the commodities that composed it.

In their legal and constitutional character as instruments through which imperial authority was distributed and practiced, commissions had long been key focuses of intra-imperial contest over the distribution of sovereignty in the governance of the colonies. As the embodiments of royal or proprietary authority, they were central to disputes over constitutional primacy in the governance of the colonies between these outside powers and local assemblies or elites.[25] During the Stamp Act crisis and the Imperial Crisis more generally, commissions under particular acts of Parliament became emblems of the contested policies and the disputed sovereignty of Parliament over the

---

[23] Parliament of Great Britain, 22 March 1765, "An act for granting and applying certain stamp duties, and other duties, in the British colonies and plantations in America, towards further defraying the expences of defending, protecting, and securing the same; and for amending such parts of the several acts of parliament relating to the trade and revenues of the said colonies and plantations, as direct the manner of determining and recovering the penalties and forfeitures therein mentioned," *The statutes at large* ... [from 1225 to 1867], Danby Pickering ed., (Cambridge : Printed by Benthem, for C. Bathhurst ; London, 1762-1869), reproduced by *The Avalon Project: Documents in Law, History and Diplomacy* (http://avalon.law.yale.edu/18th_century/townsend_act_1767.asp), Yale University Law School.

[24] Whately to Temple, February 1765, *CMHS*, Series 6, IX: 49-51.

[25] Jack P. Greene, *Peripheries and Center: Constitutional Development in the Extended Polities of the British Empire and the United States, 1607-1788*, (New York: Norton, 1990), 28-37, 50-51, 73.

colonies. Less fundamentally, the choice of individuals to receive various commissions and the powers they embodied was frequently the subject of conflict among contesting interests. Commissions served likewise as vectors of conflict and contested authority among and within the colonies themselves. Particularly on the frontiers of the colonies, distant from the centers of authority that could verify claims to authority, the use of false or misappropriated instruments to fraudulently claim authority was not unknown.[26]

More substantive and threatening were the conflicts embodied in the authentic commissions issued by distinct authorities with contesting claims to the same jurisdiction or authority. Among the most intense of such inter-colonial contests was that between Virginia and Pennsylvania in the wake of the French and Indian War over their competing claims to lands west of the Appalachians, around the forks of the Ohio River. As each colony attempted to claim and to exercise sovereignty over the district, it dispatched commissioned agents, who in turn distributed commissions for new militia officers, local magistrates, and the like. Representatives of each of the competing regimes identified one another by these commissions and denied the legitimacy of each other's instruments.[27] Well before this crisis in the western district had reached its conclusion, however, an analogous but yet more fundamental and far-reaching contest for sovereignty had begun in New England, bringing

---

[26] Thus Arthur St. Clair, serving as a magistrate in western Pennsylvania in 1773, wrote to authorities in Philadelphia seeking confirmation or refutation of reports that had reached him of the distribution or circulation of blank "warrants" (commissions) from the Governor. Joseph Shippen assured St. Clair that, "The reports you mention about blank warrants are absolutely false, and the person who first propagated the story by pretending he was possessed of a number of them, has confessed before witnesses that he never had any, either with the Governor's name or his seal; tho' he had made some few ignorant people believe so, by producing to them blank copies, such as the Surveyor General fills up and directs to the deputies," Shippen to St. Clair, 3 August 1773, *The St. Clair Papers*, William Henry Smith ed., (Cincinnati, R. Clarke, 1882), I: 271.

[27] John Connolly to Washington, 1 February 1774, *PGWDE*, Revolutionary, IX: 464-466; St. Clair to Penn, 2 February 1774, *PAA*, Series 1, IV: 476-478; Aeneas Mackay to Penn, 4 April 1774, *PAA*, Series 1, IV: 484-486; St. Clair to Penn, 16 June 1774, *PAA*, Series 1, IV: 519-521; Dunmore to [Connolly?], 20 June 1774, *PAA*, Series 1, IV: 522-523; St. Clair to Penn, 12 July 1774, *PAA*, Series 1, IV: 542-543; St. Clair to Penn, 8 August 1774, *PAA*, Series 1, IV: 558-560; Dartmouth to Dunmore, 8 September 1774, *PAA*, Series 1, IV: 577-578; St. Clair to Penn, 4 December 1774, *PAA*, Series 1, IV: 586-588; Robert Hanna, J.A. Cavet, and Thomas Scott to Penn, 23 May 1775, *PAA*, Series 1, IV: 627-628.

with it a destabilizing transformation of the documentary landscape of authority—as embodied, in large measure, by commissions.

As opposition to the Boston Port Bill and the Massachusetts Government Act became more organized during the spring and summer of 1774, opposition groups coerced those who had accepted or had been selected for commissions under the latter law—especially the despised "mandamus councilors"—to either resign or refuse their commissions, or else flee to Boston to seek protection under Governor Gage. In New England and, soon, throughout the colonies, the loosely organized opposition groups that effected these measures soon gave way to a pervasive regime made up of local committees of correspondence, observation, and safety, provincial congresses, and the Continental Congress. As part of this same process, the opposition began to shift its focus from expelling or neutralizing the agents of the new imperial policies to creating their own structures of authority, including new chains of commission, as they worked to reconstitute law and order.[28]

Militia officers accordingly, in rapidly increasing numbers, refused new commissions or resigned their current commissions under the colonial governments, often only to continue in their commands under local auspices or the authority of the provincial congresses.[29] On the 9th of September 1774, delegates from the towns of Suffolk County, Massachusetts, adopted a series of resolves expressing their determination to resist the Coercive Acts, resolves that included advising their fellow countrymen, "to take away all commissions from the officers of the militia," and recommending "that those who now hold commissions, or such other persons, be elected in each

---

[28] On these developments, see Maier, *Resistance to Revolution*; Breen, *American Insurgents*; David Ammerman, *In the Common Cause: American Responses to the Coercive Acts of 1774*, (Charlottesville, VA: UP of Virginia, 1974); Harry Alonzo Cushing, *History of the Transition from Provincial to Commonwealth Government in Massachusetts*, PhD Diss., (New York: Columbia University, 1896).

[29] Charles Neimeyer, "'Town Born, Turn Out': Town Militias, Tories, and the Struggle for Control of the Massachusetts Backcountry," *War and Society in the American Revolution: Mobilization and Home Fronts*, John Resch and Walter Sargent eds., (DeKalb, IL: Northern Illinois UP, 2007), esp. 30-32.

town as officers in the militia, as shall be judged of sufficient capacity for that purpose, and who

have evidenced themselves the inflexible friends to the rights of the people." On the 17th, the First

Continental Congress, in Philadelphia, adopted these same resolves.[30] The militia in New England

and, increasingly, throughout the colonies, would soon be further reshaped for resistance as new

companies of "minutemen" were chosen and trained.[31] Opposition institutions at every level began

to assume to themselves, if only with temporary views in mind, the de facto powers of quotidian

sovereignty.[32] These included some measure of authority to originate new instruments and

structures of authority distinct from and, in a sense, mutually inconsistent with the standing paper

regimes of colony and empire—regimes which they had already begun to dismantle, as they

repopulated the landscape with instruments of a new lineage.

In New England, by the autumn of 1774, a commission under the Coercive Acts or the

administration of Governor Gage marked its bearer as an "enemy of the country." By October

representatives of the American opposition had declared as much on a broader, continental scale,

resolving unanimously in the recently formed Continental Congress,

> That every person and persons whatsoever, who shall take, accept, or act under any
> commission or authority, in any wise derived from the act passed in the last session of
> parliament, changing the form of government, and violating the charter of the province of
> Massachusetts-bay, ought to be held in detestation and abhorrence by all good men, and
> considered as the wicked tools of that despotism, which is preparing to destroy those rights,
> which God, nature, and compact, have given to America.[33]

---

[30] *JCC*, I: 31-37.

[31] Breen, *American Insurgents*, 22-23; Higginbotham, *War of American Independence*, 47-48, 94.

[32] See Breen, *American Insurgents*, chs. 6-8.

[33] Thus when, in early June of 1775, the Continental Congress learned of the recent arrival and arrest by Pennsylvania authorities of Major Philip Skeene, "lately appointed governor of the forts of Ticonderoga, and Crown Point," and a Lieutenant bearing a "commission in the regular troops, now in the province of Quebec," they immediately resolved to appoint a committee to investigate their suspicions that Skeene was "a dangerous partizan of Administration," bearing papers that might "contain intelligence of Ministerial designs against America." *JCC*, 8 June 1775, II: 82. (Cf. discussion of Rogers, Skene, French, and Pepperell in Chapter 1.)

This Congress itself had begun, a month before, with the presentation and reading of the delegates'

own commissions from the provincial assemblies and extralegal provincial congresses that had

chosen them.[34] Increasingly over the succeeding months, and even more so following Lexington

and Concord the following spring, any sort of British commission identified its bearer as a

"suspected person" or "suspicious character"—a potential agent of imperial tyranny to be examined

and neutralized.[35] The Revolutionary governments were on the lookout, in particular, for arrivals

from abroad, like Major Rogers, who might bear commissions, openly or in secret, as agents of

imperial reaction. Those known or suspected of bearing such instruments were detained, searched,

and either paroled or imprisoned.[36] Before long, British authorities in America were issuing

commissions to Loyalists to raise and command troops to fight the rebels, adding a new dimension

to the contest for sovereignty embodied in opposed commissions.[37]

---

[34] John Adams, Diary, 4 September 1774, *PJADE*, II: 144.

[35] *JCC*, 8 June 1775, II: 82. (Cf. discussion of "strangers" and "suspected persons" in Chapters 1 and 4.) In a petition to the New Jersey Provincial Congress, 10 July 1776, John Hicks explained that his commission as a half-pay officer in the British army (like Rogers) and his decision to remain neutral in the dispute with Great Britain, in order to retain his half pay for the support of his large family, had made him suspected as a Tory. He professed he now saw the need for unity among the colonies and was "determined his allowance of half-pay shall not be any restraint upon his future conduct," asking that he be restored to public favor and be allowed to sign the Continental Association. Records of the States of the United States, New Jersey, 1681-1786, Film 281, Reel 1, DLAR. In a letter to President Hancock of the Continental Congress in October of 1776, John Foxcroft, former Co-Deputy Postmaster (with Benjamin Franklin) for North America, requesting permission to rejoin and relocate his family, who had remained in the environs of New York City, he explained that, "I left New York not from any charge against me, but because the Council of Safety then thought it improper when an Enemy every Moment Expected to land in that City that I should be there in a Kings Commission." Foxcroft to Hancock, 15 October 1776, Papers of Elias Boudinot, 1773-1812, Library of Congress, Film 732, Reel 1, DLAR.

[36] See the discussion of Rogers, Skene, French, and Pepperell, among others, in Chapter 1. In some cases, their commissions had already been rendered principally tokens of allegiance or instruments of identification (but not authority), their practical power having been negated by de facto shifts in power on the ground during the early stages of the war. Major Philip Skene, arriving at Philadelphia in June of 1775, bearing commission as the Governor of Fort Ticonderoga, Crown Point, & the Lakes, found, as a Philadelphia merchant relayed to his correspondent in London, that he "has no Government to go to, the New England Men having some time since taken possession of those important Places." Jonathan Morton to Thomas Powell, 8 June 1775, APSED, Film 391, Reel 13, No. 1302, DLAR.

[37] Cf. Harry M. Ward, *The War for Independence and the Transformation of American Society*, (London: University College London Press, 1999), 66 (James DeLancey commission from Tryon, 1777), 75 (Josiah Philips commission from Dunmore, 1775). See also Chapter 1 on commissions issued to and by Rogers in this capacity.

The outbreak of war at Lexington and Concord spurred further and increasingly rapid destabilization of royal authority at the local level, as embodied in royal and provincial commissions. It happened so quickly and thoroughly that even sympathetic observers feared an entire dissolution of civil order. Dr. Eleazar Wheelock, president of Dartmouth College would soon report to Governor Trumbull of Connecticut that,

> we are many of us...alarmed by the rash, precipitant, and headlong conduct of a number among us who have been honoured with His Majesty' s commissions, civil and military, but have of late openly and publickly given them up, and that only upon this principle, viz: that His Majesty has forfeited his Crown, and that all commissions from him are therefore vacated of course; and have accordingly appointed a set of officers of their own choosing, and appear to be plunging themselves and their dependants as far and as fast as they can into a state of anarchy.[38]

The documentary landscape of civil and judicial authority, even in Massachusetts, did not change as rapidly as Wheelock feared, though de facto power shifted somewhat in advance of the changes on paper. Nearly five months after Lexington and Concord, the Massachusetts Council was still issuing commissions to Justices of the Peace using printed forms in the name of "GEORGE the THIRD, By the Grace of GOD, of *Great-Britain, France* and *Ireland*, KING, Defender of the Faith, &c," and dated, in manuscript, "In the fifteenth Year of his Majesty's Reign."[39] Independence, after all, had not been declared, and the provincial governments sought to balance between submission to Parliamentary policy and breaking with their allegiance to the Crown itself.

The fragmented and contested state of government in Massachusetts was reflected in the fact that these same commissions were witnessed by what was termed, in manuscript, "the Major Part of the Council of the said Province met at Watertown,"—not Boston, now the citadel of imperial occupation under Governor Gage—and signed ("By Command of the Major Part of the

---

[38] Wheelock to Trumbull, 13 May 1775, *AAO*, Series 4, II: 582-583.

[39] See, e.g., Council of Massachusetts, Commission of Jonathan Grout as Justice of the Peace, 6 September 1775, Collections of Ira & Larry Goldberg Auctioneers, (http://www.goldbergauctions.com), Sale 33, Lot 340, 9 July 2013.

Council, with the advice and Consent of Council") by the Deputy Secretary. Using the material and verbal forms of royal authority, they struggled to find a logic of legitimacy in alienation from the governor and in exile from the legal seat of government, as they advised and consented to their own commissions.[40] As late as September of 1776, such documents still used the same printed form, though now, in some cases, the name of the King was crossed out and "The Government & People of the Massachusetts Bay in New England" inserted at the head of the document, in manuscript; Massachusetts was now referred to, again in manuscript, as a "State" (though still a *"Province"* in the printed conclusion); and the date was now given in terms of "the Year of our Lord."[41]

Military commissions changed much more rapidly than their civil counterparts. The new provincial armies urgently required instruments of identification that were independent of the structures of royal authority against which they were now contending in arms. By the nineteenth of May, exactly a month after Lexington and Concord, the Provincial Congress of Massachusetts commissioned Artemas Ward "General and Commander in Chief of all the Forces raised by the Congress...for the Defence of this and the other American Colonies." Ward's commission was issued entirely in manuscript, and without reference to the King or to the empire, with the exception of the implicit reference to Massachusetts' dependent status in the name under which the document was issued: "The Congress of the Colony of the Massachusetts Bay."[42] By the same day Ward's commission was issued, the Congress, under the same heading, had begun issuing commissions to subordinate officers as far down the chain of command as ensigns, using printed blank forms completed in manuscript and signed by Joseph Warren, President Pro Tem of the Congress. Less

---

[40] See, e.g., Council of Massachusetts, Commission of Jonathan Grout as Justice of the Peace, 6 September 1775, Collections of Ira & Larry Goldberg Auctioneers, (http://www.goldbergauctions.com), Sale 33, Lot 340, 9 July 2013.

[41] See, e.g., Council of Massachusetts Bay, Commission of Henry Bromfield as Justice of the Peace, Suffolk County, 19 September 1776, Collections of Legendary Auctions, Inc., (http://www.legendaryauctions.com), Lot 1637, 9 July 2013.

[42] Provincial Congress of Massachusetts, Commission of Artemas Ward to be General and Commander in Chief, 19 May 1775, Ward Family Papers, 1661-1919, Box 1, Folder 3, Item 31, AAS.

than a month later, "The Congress of the Colony of New-Hampshire" had followed suit.[43] By early autumn, the committees of safety in New York and Virginia had begun issuing commissions, on behalf of the provincial congresses of which they formed part, using their own printed forms. The Pennsylvania Committee of Safety, meanwhile, had begun receiving requests from local militia units that they commission their newly selected officers.[44]

The uncertainty over the authority and identities embodied in these provincial documents was suggested by a new series of printed commission forms, in several variants, employed by the Massachusetts General Court during the winter and spring of the following year. In contrast to the first generation of Massachusetts Provincial Army commissions, which omitted all explicit references to the King or to imperial authority (except the word "colony")—issued simply in the name of the Congress, and dated "A.D"—a printed form in use as early as February of 1776 for the Massachusetts militia commissioned their recipients under the name and "By the Command of the Major Part of the Council" of the colony of Massachusetts Bay and were dated in print "in the Sixteenth Year of the Reign of his Majesty King George the Third, Anno Domini, 1776." By the following month, and onward to at least May, a typographical variant of the same form was

---

[43] Provincial Congress of Massachusetts, Commission of James Brickett as Lieutenant Colonel, and Commission of Zaccheus Crocker as Lieutenant, 19 May 1775, Sol Feinstone Collection, Film 1, Reel 2, Nos. 888 and 889, DLAR. Provincial Congress of Massachusetts, Commission of Gamalial Whiting as Lieutenant, 19 May 1775, Miscellaneous Bound Manuscripts, MHS. Provincial Congress of Massachusetts, Commission of Jonas Proctor as Ensign, 19 May 1775, and Provincial Congress of New Hampshire, Commission of Levi Spaulding as Captain, 3rd Company, 3rd Regiment of Foot, 6 June 1775, George Washington Papers, 1741-1799, Series 4: General Correspondence, 1697-1799, Library of Congress, AM. Cf. Provincial Congress of Massachusetts, Form of a Commission, (Watertown, MA: Benjamin Edes, 1775), *EAI*, Series 1, no. 14242 (filmed), taking much the same form as the commissions above, but appointing the bearer to be an officer in a company raised for "the Protection and Defence of the Sea-Coast in this Colony."

[44] New York Committee of Safety, Commission of [blank], signed by John Haring (Chairman) and John McKesson (Secretary), after 22 August 1775, *EAI*, Series 1, no. 42901 (filmed); Virginia Committee of Safety, Commission of Thomas Jefferson as Lieutenant and Commander in Chief, Militia, Albemarle County, 26 September 1775, Thomas Jefferson Papers, Series 1: General Correspondence, 1651-1827, Library of Congress, AM. Michael Swoope to the Pennsylvania Committee of Safety, 2 August 1775, *PAA*, Series 1, IV: 642. Swoope noted that "the Congress have directed the Committee of Safety, in case of the recess of the Assembly, to commission the Field Officers." See also Inhabitants of York County, PA, to the Pennsylvania Committee of Safety, 14 September 1775, *PAA*, Series 1, IV: 656-657; Lund Washington to George Washington, 29 September 1775, *PGWDE*, Revolutionary, II: 64-66.

employed, but with the reference to the year of the King's reign crossed out and "In the Year of our Lord" substituted in manuscript.[45] Several years after independence had been declared, Massachusetts militia commissions took much the same form, though with a few small, important changes. Still issued by "the Major Part of the Council" of Massachusetts-Bay, they now omitted "the colony of." They were "GIVEN under…the Seal of the said State" and the year was framed, in print now, as "in the Year of our LORD."[46]

The crisis of both formal and practical sovereignty quickly became more general throughout the colonies. On the 4th of May 1776, the General Assembly of Rhode Island passed *An Act repealing an act, entitled "An act for the more effectually securing to His Majesty, the allegiance of his subjects, in this his colony and dominion of Rhode Island and Providence Plantations;" and altering the forms of commissions, of all writs and processes in the courts, and of the oaths prescribed by law.* At the core of the new law—after asserting the reciprocal nature of the compact of a people with a sovereign, detailing how the King had violated his obligations of protection and attempted to impose tyranny, and repealing the old Act—the Assembly enacted,

> that in all commissions for offices, civil and military; and in all writs and proceses in law, whether original, judicial or executory, civil or criminal, wherever the name and authority of the said King is made use of, the same shall be omitted; and in the room thereof, the name and authority of the Governor and Company of this colony shall be substituted, in the

---

[45] Council of Massachusetts, Commission of Jonathan Grout as Lieutenant Colonel, 7th Regiment, Militia, Worcester County, 14 February 1776, Collections of Ira & Larry Goldberg Auctioneers, (http://www.goldbergauctions.com), Sale 33, Lot 341, 9 July 2013; Council of Massachusetts, Commission of Noah Whitman as Lieutenant, 23 March 1776, Collections of University Archives, (http://www.universityarchives.com), No. 39645, 11 July 2013; Commission of William Foster as a Second Lieutenant in the Massachusetts Militia, by the Major Part of the Council of the Massachusetts-Bay, 10 May 1776, Sol Feinstone Collection, Film 1, Reel 2, No. 889, DLAR. Cf. Council of Massachusetts, Form of a Commission, (Watertown, MA: Benjamin Edes, 1775), *EAI*, Series 1, no. 14201 (filmed). This variant invokes the authority granted to the Council in the absence of the Governor and Lieutenant Governor by the royal charter that the opposition government had declared restored by the autumn of 1775.

[46] Council of the Massachusetts-Bay, Commission of Abel Parker as Second Lieutenant, Massachusetts Militia, 28 October 1779, Ms. N-659 1779 Oct. 28, Joel Parker Papers, Box 1, MHS.

following words, to wit: "The Governor and Company of the English Colony of Rhode Island and Providence Plantations."[47]

In parallel to evolving practice in Massachusetts, the Act provided likewise, "that no instrument in writing, of any nature or kind, whether public or private, shall, in the date thereof, mention the year of the said King's reign." Along with corresponding changes to oaths of office, civil and military, the Rhode Island Assembly by these measures marked a break with the British sovereign and implicitly claimed a kind of provisional autonomy. As in Massachusetts, however, the break was ambiguous and halting: Rhode Island was still an "English Colony" and made no overt declaration of independence, despite striding boldly to the brink, and despite the portentous emendations to the colony's official emblems and instruments. In the wake of the Declaration of Independence, new state constitutions and legislative enactments would similarly mark, though more definitely, the break with Britain by recasting their forms of commissions for governance and military command. The constitution published by the Delaware convention in the autumn of 1776, thus, provided in Article XX that, "Commissions shall run in the Name of The Delaware State."[48]

Even as the provincial governments worked to create or adapt documentary forms of authority for their military officers, the Continental Congress in Philadelphia had begun to develop analogous instruments for the new Continental Army.[49] By mid June of 1775, John Hancock,

---

[47] John Russell Bartlett ed., *Records of the Colony of Rhode Island and Providence Plantations in New England*, (New York: AMS, 1968), VII: 522-526. The Act also directed "That the courts of law be no longer entitled, nor considered, as the King's courts."

[48] *Proceedings of the Convention of the Delaware state, held at New-Castle on Tuesday the twenty-seventh of August, 1776*, (Wilmington, DE: James Adams, Printer, 1776), *EAI*, Series 1, no. 43018 (filmed), 26: "Commissions shall run in the Name of The Delaware State, and bear Test by the President. Writs shall run in the same Manner, and bear Test in the Name of the Chief-Justice or Justice first named in the Commissions for the several Courts, and be sealed with the Public Seals of such Courts. Indictments shall conclude, against the Peace and Dignity of the State."

[49] This continental regime would, indeed, begin partially to displace and replace the provincial regimes—as provincial units were adopted into the Continental Army—even as the new provincial regimes were still in the process of replacing their colonial, imperial predecessors and adversaries.

President of the Continental Congress, would write to Joseph Warren, President of the

Massachusetts Provincial Congress, that "The Congress have appointed George Washington, Esqr.,

General and Commander in Chief of the Continental Army. His Commission is made out and I shall

Sign it to morrow."[50] The previous day Congress had agreed on the text of Washington's

commission and ordered, "That the same be fairly transcribed, to be signed by the president, and

attested by the secretary, and delivered to the General."[51] The day following Hancock's letter to

Warren, Washington was issued his commission by "The delegates of the United Colonies."[52]

By his instructions from the Congress, Washington was himself constituted a mobile locus

of authority, an anchor of the Continental chain of commission. He was empowered to issue and

regulate commissions in the field, under the pressure of circumstances and at a distance from the

Congress that made it impossible for them to respond to the Army's immediate needs. He was

likewise delegated to act in the stead of provincial authorities in cases where officers and

commissions were requisite but the legislature could not respond quickly enough. "In all cases of

vacancy [in the berth] of a Colonel or other inferior officer," he was instructed, "you are by Brevet

or Warrant under your seal" to appoint a replacement to serve until the relevant provincial

government ruled otherwise. "The Officers now in the army," the Congress directed, were to

"receive their commissions from the Genl & commander in Chief."[53]

---

[50] Hancock to Warren, 18 June 1775, *CMHS*, LXXII: 57-58.

[51] *JCC*, 17 June 1775, II: 96-97.

[52] Hancock to Warren, 18 June 1775, *CMHS*, LXXII: 57-58: "By all means have his Commission read at the head of the whole Forces." For Washington's commission, see *JCC*, II: 96-97, and *PGWDE*, Revolutionary, I: 6-8. Washington reported to his brother John Augustine on the 20th that "I am now Commissioned a Generl & Commander in Chief of all the Forces now raisd, or to be raisd, for the defence of the United Colonies," *PGWDE*, Revolutionary, I: 19-20. John Adams would soon write from Philadelphia to James Warren, back in war-beset Massachusetts, assuring him that "You will soon find that the Continental Congress are in, deep enough. The Commissions to the officers of the Army; the Vote for your Government; the Votes about North Carolina; and a Multitude of other Votes which you will soon hear of will convince you," Adams to Warren, 27 June 1775, *PJADE*, III: 34.

[53] Continental Congress to George Washington, 22 June 1775, *PGWDE*, Revolutionary, I: 21-23.

The resulting instruments evinced in their language their place in the chain of commission and bore in their material form their ad hoc character. These commissions were issued "By his Excellency George Washington, Esquire, Commander in Chief of the Army of the United Colonies in North America...By Virtue of the Powers and Authorities to me granted by the honourable Continental Congress." The commissions would "constitute and appoint" the recipient as an officer of a particular rank, in a particular unit. They were tenable "until farther order" from the Congress, the Massachusetts General Court (or other provincial legislature, depending on the case), Washington himself, or a future commander in chief. The documents were formal and conventional in their language and form (consisting of a heading indicating the issuing authority, a salutation, the body of the commission, a paragraph giving the place and date of signature and seal, the signature, the countersignature, and a seal). But they were issued in manuscript, rather than on a printed form. And the manuscript was not typically in the fair hand of an engrossed instrument—such as Washington's own commission, or the Massachusetts commission to General Ward—but simply the official, or even the informal, hand of Washington's secretary or one of his aides de camp. Washington's own handwriting appeared only in the signature.[54]

The language and the physical forms of the commissions Washington would assign or distribute on behalf of Congress would, on the other hand, be shaped by the Congress and printed (or otherwise produced) under their direction. Two days after commissioning Washington as commander in chief, the Congress appointed Richard Henry Lee, Edward Rutledge, and John Adams "a committee to prepare the form of a commission for the Major generals, and also for the brigadier generals, and other officers in the army." The same day, the forms of commission for the

---

[54] See Washington, Commission to Benjamin Wormwell as Lieutenant, Captain Martindale's company, 24 October 1775, Cambridge, MA, George Washington Papers, Series 4: General Correspondence, 1697-1799, Library of Congress, AM.

major and brigadier generals of the army were established.[55] The Congress had chosen the generals

themselves, and their commissions, though uniform in language and form, were to be issued in fair

copy manuscript ("engrossed"), as essentially individual documents. At the same time, it was

ordered "That the secretary get a number of commissions printed, with proper blanks, for the other

officers."[56]

The standardized, printed commissions for inferior officers produced on the order of

Congress were printed, in landscape, on what appear to be half sheets. Lacking any ornamentation

or notable typographical flourishes, they were headed simply "In CONGRESS," and issued in the

name of "The DELEGATES of the United Colonies," each of whom was then listed separately.

The printed form left blanks for the insertion of the recipient's name and appointed rank and for the

signature of the President, *By Order of the Congress.* Perhaps in order to avoid the difficult question

of how to formulate the date (whether in terms of the year of His Majesty's reign), no form was

included, as on many such instruments. Instead, the date would be inserted, entirely in manuscript,

beneath the countersignature of the Secretary of the Congress.[57]

Soon, streams of commissions were flowing northward from the newly opened wellspring at

Philadelphia, to carve new channels of identity and authority across the American landscape. "I

Send you the Remained of the Commissions Sign'd," President Hancock informed General

Washington by the end of June. "[S]hould you have Occasion for more," he reminded him, "please

to Acquaint me, & they shall be immediately Transmitted you"—a reminder Hancock would make

---

[55] *JCC*, 19 June 1775, II: 99-100.

[56] *JCC*, 19 June 1775, II: 99-100.

[57] See Continental Congress, Commission to John Crane as First Major, 1 January 1776, George Washington Papers, Series 4: General Correspondence, 1697-1799, Library of Congress, AM; Continental Congress, Commission to John Paul Jones as Captain in the Navy of the United States of North America, 8 October 1776, *EAI*, Series 1, no. 15180 (filmed).

frequently in the coming months.[58] Large numbers of commissions, both blank and completed, flowed back and forth continually in crisscrossing streams, as the theatre of war shifted and fragmented. Over time, as the recruiting of new units or additional soldiers was authorized, and when the Articles of War were revised by Congress—"a new Plan of an Army," as John Adams put it—new waves of commissions would be dispatched across the states.[59] Nevertheless, the supply of blank commissions in the hands of any particular commander or at any given station was often insufficient to satisfy the demand. In other cases the awaited commissions were dispatched to or arrived at the wrong place.[60] Even Washington was repeatedly driven to remind the President of Congress or compelled to explain to his frustrated officers that he still (or yet again) had too few commissions to meet the needs of the service.[61] On the other hand, as the Congress addressed

---

[58] As the senior officers chosen to serve under Washington gathered and made their way toward the camps outside Boston, they collected their commissions as the instruments of their new rank and authority. "Brigr Genl Gates [has] not yet Arriv'd in the City [Philadelphia]," Hancock informed Washington, "[but] I expect him to morrow, and shall Deliver him his Commission, and promote his Joining you as soon as possible." Hancock to Washington, 28 June 1775, *PGWDE*, Revolutionary, I: 42-44. "Should you have Occasion for a further Supply of Commissions, please to Inform me & they shall be immediately Transmitted you." Hancock to Washington, 5 July 1775, *PGWDE*, Revolutionary, I: 64.

[59] See John Adams to James Warren, 25 September 1776, *PJADE*, V: 22: "This Express carries a new Plan of an Army. I hope the General Court without one Moments delay will Send Commissions to whole Corps of their Officers, either by Expresses or Committees to New York and Ticonderoga, that as many Men may be inlisted without delay as possible. It may be best to send a Committee with full Powers to each Place. There is no Time to be lost. I inclose you a sett of Articles as lately amended. Discipline I hope will be introduced at last."

[60] As Washington was still on his way to his new command in Massachusetts, newly created Major General Philip Schuyler would write to inform him that "I beleive the Commissions for this Department were already forwarded to You before my Letter (In Obedience to Your Order) to the Congress on that Subject arrived." "If they are to be sent back," Schuyler continued, "I beg of You to Order them to be directed to the President of the Provincial Convention here." Schuyler to Washington, 1 July 1775, *PGWDE*, Revolutionary, I: 47-49.

[61] Thus, having informed Washington of the several appointments made on his recommendation and those left to his discretion by Congress in late July of 1775, President Hancock noted in closing that "Mr Thomas & Mr Trumbull's Commission[s] are Inclos'd in unseal'd Letters to them" and that he had "Sent five Bundles of Commissions [numbering] 284 the rest shall follow." Hancock to Washington, 24 July 1775, *PGWDE*, Revolutionary, I: 164-168. Having received these commissions, Washington would remind Hancock that these were "yet much short of the necessary Number." Washington Hancock, 4-5 August 1775, *PGWDE*, Revolutionary, I: 223. In the meantime, Washington had written to Major General Schuyler, commanding in the New York department, that, "The Commissions which have been forwarded to me, are not sufficient to answer the Demand I have for them there being at least 1000 Officers in this Department & not more than 500 Commissions in my Possession." He directed Schuyler accordingly that, "As you are so much nearer to Philada than I am I request you to apply to Congress for as many as you are like to Want." Washington to Schuyler, 10-11 July 1775, *PGWDE*, Revolutionary, I: 101-102. By the end of September, Hancock would send Washington another 550 commissions in eleven bundles. Hancock to Washington, 26 September 1775, *PGWDE*, Revolutionary, II: 48-50. A week later he would once again assure Washington that were the most

particular vacancies in the corps of senior officers and issued commissions on an ad hoc basis, they

would sometimes dispatch the individual commission directly to its intended bearer.[62]

Because the state governments typically retained authority to appoint field officers in their

state's regiments in the Continental service, the process of commissioning became increasingly

complex and prone to confusion, particularly as the sphere of military organization spread rapidly

beyond New England. In early August of 1775 the president of the New York Provincial Congress

would write Washington that, "We are informed in a Letter from the Continental Congress that the

General would make out the Commissions for our Regiments to such Persons as this Congress

should recommend; but are at a loss to know whether You, or General Schuyler are to issue the

Commissions."[63] The New York Congress had been informed that the commissions had been sent

to Washington. "If this should be the Case, and the Commissions are to be filled up by General

Schuyler," President Livingston went on, "we beg you will send them to him or us without Delay."

On the other hand, he wrote, "If they are to be filled up by Your Excellency, we submit it, whether,

to prevent Delay, it would not be proper to send them in blank to General Schuyler, or to us; that

the Names may be filled up agreable to the Arrangement made by this Congress."[64] In cases where

---

recent batch of commissions not sufficient, "upon the first Notice I will forward the Number your Require," Hancock to Washington, 3 October 1775, *PGWDE*, Revolutionary, II: 88-89.

[62] Thus in June of 1776 they would resolve, "That an express be sent to Hugh Mercer, Esqr. who was yesterday appointed a brigadier general, with his commission, and that he be desired immediately to repair to head quarters, at New York." *JCC*, 6 June 1776, V: 424.

[63] Peter Van Brugh Livingston to Washington, 3 August 1775, *PGWDE*, Revolutionary, I: 217.

[64] In total, Livingston estimated, "The Number of Commissions wanted will be about two hundred." Peter Van Brugh Livingston to Washington, 3 August 1775, *PGWDE*, Revolutionary, I: 217. Within a little over two weeks, Livingston would inform Washington that the New York Provincial Congress had, apparently having received an answer from Washington to their previous inquiries on this head, written "to Mr Thompson Secretary to the Continental Congress for Blank Commissions," Livingston to Washington, 21 August 1775, *PGWDE*, Revolutionary, I: 342-343. A little less than a month later, the Continental Congress would order "That the President forward to General Schuyler four hundred blank Commissions for the officers in his Army, to be by him filled up, agreeable to the order of Congress." *JCC*, 14 September 1775, II: 249. A week later, Congress resolved, "that General Schuyler be empowered to nominate and appoint a proper person to the office of Brigade Major in the army under his command and to issue a commission accordingly," *JCC*, 21 September 1775, II: 257.

commissions were actually completed by state legislatures themselves, any anxiety was compounded

by the possibility that the commissions themselves would be delayed, damaged, or stolen on their

way from the legislature to the commander in the field, or that they would be sent to what was by

that time the wrong location.[65] (Meanwhile, provincial governments had to manage the commissions

for officers in their respective militias, with all the attendant administrative challenges.[66])

To avoid confusion or miscarriage, as well as potentially fatal delays, Continental Authorities

turned in some crucial cases to still more pragmatic expedients. To recruit forces for the assault on

Quebec that would be made in early 1776, the Continental Congress resolved, "That, from the

necessity of the case, and to prevent delays, blank commissions be issued by the president for the

field officers, captains, and subalterns, who are to command the battalions ordered to be raised for

Canada, in New Hampshire, and Connecticut," which commissions were "to be filled up with the

names of such gentlemen as shall be judged most proper by the convention or committee of safety

of New Hampshire, and by the Governor and council of Connecticut." Perhaps anxious not to

compromise their authority by exercising too loose a command, the Congress was careful to

stipulate "That the foregoing resolution be not drawn into a precedent."[67] In other circumstances,

Congress or its commanders in the field made similar arrangements with local committees and

---

[65] See the resolve of the Rhode Island General Assembly, 28 October 1776, dispatching two couriers, "with the greatest despatch," to Washington, with a letter from the state government "and the commissions for the officers appointed by this Assembly." Bartlett ed., *Records of the State of Rhode Island*, VIII: 21.

[66] See John Augustine Washington's letter from Bushfield, Virginia, under orders from the Virginia Committee of Safety, in November of 1775, conveying commissions to the senior officers in local militia or minute companies, providing provisional lists of the men assigned to each unit, directing the commissioned officers to select their sergeants from among these men, while expecting that their rosters would change once the raising and reorganizing of the militia and minutemen had been completed, and directing them to forward to him the names of any "Patrolers" to be appointed in the district, "that I may issue Commissions immediately." Sol Feinstone Collection, Film 1, Reel 5, No. 2288, DLAR. See also the Rhode Island Assembly's resolve, 14 June 1779, appointing Colonel William Barton to command a corps of Light Infantry and providing that, "whereas, for rendering the said corps as useful as possible, it is expedienct that the officers be peculiarly calculated for this kind of war, placing entire confidence in each other,-- It is further voted and resolved, that Col. Barton nominate from time to time such candidates as he shall judge proper; who, upon being approved by this General Assembly, or the council of war, shall be appointed and commissioned accordingly." Bartlett ed., *Records of the State of Rhode Island*, VIII: 561-562.

[67] *JCC*, 20 January 1776, IV: 74-75.

governments—drawing on stocks of blank commissions, completing them according to recommendations from local authorities, and dispatching them to be delivered to the officers of, for instance, companies raised for local defense.[68]

Supplies of Continental commissions for both the land and sea forces—in the hands of commanders or of state governments—continually ran low well into the war, however, encouraging new iterations of pragmatic adaptation. In June of 1778, the Rhode Island Council of War was driven to resolve "that his Excellency ye Governor where no Continental Commissions are in the State" should "grant Commissions or Letters of Marque & Reprisal to Armed Vessels to Cruise on ye Coasts of this [&] the Neighbouring States, of ye Same Terms of those Issued by Congress Mutatis Mutandis."[69] This resolve came after the Council had, the previous year, requested from the Continental Congress "a Supply" of such commissions, and after the Council had earlier the same month asked the Governor to borrow from the Governor of Connecticut "Eight Continental Commissions and Letters of Marque & Reprisal; to be repaid out of those we have Written to Congress for when they Arrive"—a request that apparently was unsuccessful.[70]

The confusion endemic to collaborations in the administration of commissions across great distances and under pressing circumstances was further complicated by the limits of the commission as a material document. These paper or parchment instruments were vulnerable to damage, loss, and theft. When joined with the imperfect distribution of the knowledge of officers' identities and authority across space and among governments—the circumstance that necessitated commissions in

---

[68] See General Horatio Gates to the Committee of Manchester, NH, 20 July 1776, enclosing eighteen commissions "filled up" as requested and according to the recommendation of the committee, for officers in local defense forces. Horatio Gates Papers, 1726-1828, Film 23, Reel 3 (Correspondence, July 1776 - October 1776), DLAR.

[69] Rhode Island Council of War, 17 June 1778, Records of the States of the United States, Rhode Island, 1775-1818, Film 285, E4, Reel 1, Minutes of the Council of War, DLAR. The Council directed, concerning these commissions to be issued by the Governor, "that ye Same be Authenticated under ye Seal of the State and Countersigned by the Secretary; and that Bond be taken & Instructions given in the Usual Manner."

[70] Rhode Island Council of War, 24 April 1777, 12 June 1778, Records of the States of the United States, Rhode Island, 1775-1818, Film 285, E4, Reel 1, Minutes of the Council of War, DLAR.

the first place—such eventualities could render a person's official identity and authority inoperative until the commission could be replaced. Thus, in the autumn of 1776, Bernard Mousac, who had served in the Canada campaign as a captain and an engineer under a commission granted him by the commissioners to Canada, was forced to petition the Continental Congress for a new commission, having "lost his commission, with his baggage, at Chambly." Upon attestation of the truth of these claims by former commissioner to Canada Benjamin Franklin, the Congress resolved, "That a new commission be granted to him."[71] In April of 1777, Captain John Flahaven of the 1st New Jersey Regiment was taken prisoner by the British during an unauthorized attack on the enemy sentries. It was not discovered until August that "he had [his commission] not with him." Commissary General for Prisoners of War, Elias Boudinot, forwarded the captive Captain's commission to him in prison, "in Case it may be of any Service to him."[72]

The creation of a new Continental landscape of documentary authority was, simultaneously, a process of partially papering over provincial regimes. As such, it brought with it many contentions. These disputes were complicated by the fact that the commissioning process was, in the end, a process of distributing the material instruments of authority and identification. Once a commission was delivered and accepted, retracting the document or altering its terms was likely to cause as great offense to the recipient as the original commissioning may have caused to other officers.

The most troubling case during the early months of this process concerned the choice of general officers by the Continental Congress from among those commissioned in the Massachusetts

---

[71] *JCC*, 29 August 1776, V: 715.

[72] Boudinot to Lewis Pintard, 16 August 1777, Elias Boudinot, Letter Book, 1777-1778, Film 567, Reel 1, Pages 36-37, DLAR.

provincial army. In one of his first reports to Congress from his new command at Cambridge,

Washington informed them that, "the Appointments of the General Officers in the Province of

Massachusetts Bay—have by no Means corresponded with the Judgment & Wishes of either the

civil or Military." Made wary by "The great Dissatisfaction expressed on this Subject & the apparent

Danger of throwing the Army into the utmost Disorder, together with the strong Representations of

the Provincial Congress," he had determined "to retain the Commissions in my Hands untill the

Pleasure of the Congress should be farther known." Unfortunately, Washington had delivered

General Israel Putnam's commission "the Day I cam into Camp & before I was apprized of these

Uneasinesses." The choice of Putnam over General Spencer had "so much disgusted" the latter that

he had left his command and the camp without notifying Washington.[73] Congress appreciated the

difficulty of Washington's situation and approved his discretion in not recalling Putnam's

commission, judging that, "as Putnams Commission was delivered, it would perhaps have offended

the old Gentleman to have superceded him."[74]

Members of Congress, however, were incensed by the disrespectful behavior of Spencer and

other Massachusetts officers, given the threat it posed to the structures of Continental authority

essential to the collective cause. "Gentlemen here," John Adams insisted to James Warren, "had no

private Friendships Connections, or Interests which prompted them to vote for the arrangement

they made but were influenced only by a Regard to the Service; and they are determined that their

---

[73] Washington to the Continental Congress, 10-11 July 1775, *PGWDE*, Revolutionary, I: 89-90. Conscious of the tensions and suspicions among the colonies, and anxious to create and preserve a character as an impartial, virtuous, and continental officer, Washington made sure to assure Congress of the integrity of his motives in retaining the commissions: "In such a Step I must beg the Congress will do me the Justice I believe, that I have been actuated solely by a Regard to the publick Good: I have not, nor could have any private Attachments; every Gentleman in Appointment, was an entire Stranger to me but from Character. I must therefore rely upon the Candour of the Congress for their favourable Construction of my Conduct in this Particular."

[74] Harrison to Washington, 21-24 July 1775, *PGWDE*, Revolutionary, I: 145.

Commissions shall not be despised."[75] Warren was able to respond with reports of easing tensions and Spencer's return to camp and his duty. But he nonetheless affirmed his approval of the Congress's broader determination. "I am Convinced," he wrote, "of the Necessity of supporting your own dignity, and the Importance of your Commissions. If you suffer them to be despised they will soon depreciate, and become of little value."[76] Commissions were analogous to the currency that would convey the continental confederation's authority and power. As would in fact be the case with the Continental paper currency, if the commissions were not properly backed and their authority credited, they would cease to carry any practical value and would sink in the public estimation, discrediting in the process the government that issued them.

As was standard practice for the period, Washington announced the new commissions to the army, giving public recognition to the authority of new commanders, promoting general knowledge in the ranks of the hierarchy of command, and, by these means, supporting the authority of the commissions themselves as practical instruments of identification. In his general orders to the army the day after he took command, Washington announced that "The Hon: Artemus Ward, Charles Lee, Philip Schuyler, and Israel Putnam Esquires, are appointed Major Generals of the American Army and due Obedience is to be paid them as such." Likewise "Thomas Mifflin Esqr." was "appointed by the General one of his Aid-de-Camps. Joseph Reed Esqr. is in like manner appointed Secretary to the General, and they are in future to be consider'd and regarded as such."[77] The practical operation of these identities, however, depended on their commissions, the material instruments of their authority. "The Continental Congress not having compleated the appointments of the other officers in said army, nor had sufficient time to prepare and forward their

---

[75] Adams to Warren, 23 July 1775, *CMHS*, LXXII: 85-88.

[76] Warren to Adams, 31 July 1775, *PJADE*, III: 66.

[77] Washington, General Orders, 4 July 1775, *PGWDE*, Revolutionary, I: 54-58.

Commissions," Washington explained, "every Officer is to continue to do duty in the Rank and Station he at present holds untill further orders."[78]

Commissions—perhaps especially in the military context—were not simply symbols of an abstract appointment, but were meant to be deployed in practice. Apart from their function in the exercise of authority, and as in European warfare and inter-imperial relations, commissions distinguished the legitimate military surrogates of a sovereign—whether military officers or licensed privateers—from pirates, bandits, brigands, and rebels. Not simply having been granted a commission, but having a commission in one's immediate possession could make the difference, if taken prisoner, between being treated as a prisoner of war and being hanged as an outlaw. (The sovereign against whom revolutionaries rebelled was not likely to recognize the legitimacy of their commissions: the British did not recognize American commissions in practice for the first several years of the war, or formally until the Peace of 1783 was signed, but they did not generally punish captured rebels as traitors or outlaws.[79]) Openly bearing a commission (as well as wearing a uniform) could save an officer captured behind enemy lines from being treated (and executed) as a spy. Late in the war, Washington would actually lament to Governor Livingston of New Jersey that it was "a pity" that a certain "Villain" recently captured could not have been "apprehended lurking in the Country in a manner that would bring him under the discipline of a Spy." But unfortunately, "[w]hen he was taken before he was in Arms in his proper uniform with a party—and had his

---

[78] Washington, General Orders, 4 July 1775, *PGWDE*, Revolutionary, I: 54-58.

[79] It was recognized that this custom and related legal provisions were subject to abuse. One British naval officer, having captured a ship of smugglers and pirates off the coast of England in 1779, subsequently wrote to Lord Dartmouth that, "tho' he says he is an American born & produces a Coms signed by Franklyn, yet I must suspend my Belief. I find tis not an uncommon Thing for these Cutters to have 3 Commissions one from Franklyn, another from France, and a third from England. By this Means infinite Mischief is done & the Villains have hitherto escaped with Impunity." W. Rawlings to Dartmouth, [June or July] 1779, APSED, Film 391, Reel 16, No. 1888, DLAR.

Commission in his pocket—It was, therefore a matter of great doubt whether he could be considered otherwise than a prisoner of War."[80]

Accordingly, when the Declaration of Independence changed the terms of the war, General Horatio Gates would write anxiously to the Continental Congress of the need for officers' commissions to keep pace: the instruments should be made consistent with a new oath of allegiance "and be made subordinate to the Supreme Power of the Congress, under the new System." "Otherwise," he pointed out, "an Inconsistency, which the Multiplicity of Business alone must have occasioned, may turn to the Prejudice of those, whom the Fate of War may put into the Hands of the Enemy."[81] Inattention to the terms of commissions could render their legitimacy dubious in the new context and leave the officers who bore them vulnerable to suspicion as armed outlaws.

At a minimum, the lack of a legitimate commission—or any commission at all—if captured would likely mean that the prisoner would not be accorded the consideration normally shown to officers: he would not be allowed to give his parole and go at large (within prescribed limits), and would instead be confined in a jail or prison ship, like a common soldier or a criminal, exposing him to the attendant suffering and serious threats to his health this entailed. Thus, in February of 1777, British General William Howe informed his commander in New Jersey, James Grant, that, "Your Prisoner Randolph came here the other morning without any [certificate] of coming from any officer & having acknowledged under his hand he had no proper commission as an officer [duly] acting per Sullivan's direction." In consequence, Howe noted, "I have not admitted him to his parole & he is confined at the Provost's."[82]

---

[80] Washington to Livingston, 12 January 1782, Sol Feinstone Collection, Film 1, Reel 5, No. 2206, DLAR.

[81] Gates to the President of the Continental Congress, 23 September 1776, Horatio Gates Papers, 1726-1828, Film 23, Reel 3 (Correspondence, July 1776 - October 1776), DLAR.

[82] Howe to Grant, 7 February 1777, Papers of James Grant of Ballindalloch, 1740-1819, Army Career Series (1740-1805), Film 687, Reel 37, DLAR.

By the same token—and in much the same way that royal commissions had been used to identify enemies from the latter years of the Imperial Crisis onward—commissions distinguished between friends and enemies. When, in the summer of 1776, a Monsieur Traversé arrived unexpectedly from Canada at Haverhill, New Hampshire, claiming to be a refugee from persecution as a friend to the American cause, the local Patriot committee judged him "an honest Man" and accepted his claim to have served as "a Captain of Militia" in the American invasion of Canada "under Commission of Captain Goforth" at Trois Riviers, after having heard his account of himself and examined "his papers"—apparently including his commission—which seemed to substantiate his claims.[83]

The immediate embodiment of the bearer's authority in the commission itself as a material instrument was centered in a standard clause, with slight variations, which declared that by the commission itself those properly subordinate to the individual thereby commissioned were to obey him according to the rank and authority thus conferred. The early standardized commissions for the Massachusetts Provincial Army, and commissions issued in 1776 for the Massachusetts militia, declared that those under the officer's command "are *hereby* commanded to obey you as their [officer of a particular rank: e.g. Lieutenant Colonel]."[84] In their commission to Washington as commander in chief, the Continental Congress declared that, "we do *hereby* strictly charge and require all officers and soldiers under your command to be obedient to your orders & diligent in the exercise of their several duties."[85] The brevet and warrant commissions Washington issued under congressional

---

[83] Reuben Foster et al. to General John Sullivan, 22 July 1776, Horatio Gates Papers, 1726-1828, Film 23, Reel 3 (Correspondence, July 1776 - October 1776), DLAR.

[84] (Emphasis added.) See Provincial Congress of Massachusetts, Commission of James Brickett as Lieutenant Colonel, and Commission of Zaccheus Crocker as Lieutenant, 19 May 1775, Sol Feinstone Collection, Film 1, Reel 2, Nos. 888 and 889, DLAR; Commission of William Foster as a Second Lieutenant in the Massachusetts Militia, by the Major Part of the Council of the Massachusetts-Bay, 10 May 1776, Sol Feinstone Collection, Film 1, Reel 2, No. 889, DLAR.

[85] (Emphasis added.) 19 June 1775, *PGWDE*, I: 6-8.

authority declared that, "I do *hereby* constitute and appoint you...Willing and commanding all Persons whatsoever, any way concerned to be obedient to you & assisting in the due Execution of the Premisses."[86] The Continental Congress' standardized commissions used a printed form and declared in a similar manner that, "We...Do *by these presents*...strictly charge and require all officers and soldiers under your command, to be obedient to your orders, as [e.g. first Major]."[87] State commissions followed much the same pattern. Thus, Abel Parker's commission as a Second Lieutenant in the Massachusetts militia provided that the soldiers of the company he was to command "are *hereby* commanded to obey you as their 'Second Lieut'."[88]

It took considerable effort to keep track of the state of army commissions. Before the end of his first month in command of the forces outside Boston, Washington ordered the preparation of "A Return signed by the Commanding Officers of regiments and Corps, to be delivered to the Adjutant General...of the Names, Ranks & Dates of the Officer's Commissions, in their respective Regiments and Corps, mentioning also the Vacancies, and how occasioned."[89] Washington would in turn seek equivalent information from the Massachusetts Provincial Congress. By early August, Warren would send Washington "Agreable to your Excellencys desire a List of Such Officers in the

---

[86] (Emphasis added.) See Washington, Commission to Benjamin Wormwell as Lieutenant, Captain Martindale's company, 24 October 1775, Cambridge, MA, and Washington, Commission to William Marony as Provost Marshall (draft), 10 January 1776, George Washington Papers, Series 4: General Correspondence, 1697-1799, Library of Congress, AM.

[87] (Emphasis added.) See Continental Congress, Commission to John Crane as First Major, Regiment of Artillery, Henry Knox commanding, 1 January 1776; Continental Congress, Commission to Antoine F. Wuibert as Engineer and Lieutenant Colonel, 24 June 1776, George Washington Papers, Series 4: General Correspondence, 1697-1799, Library of Congress, AM.

[88] (Emphasis added.) Council of the Massachusetts-Bay, Commission of Abel Parker as Second Lieutenant, Massachusetts Militia, 28 October 1779, Ms. N-659 1779 Oct. 28, Joel Parker Papers, Box 1, MHS.

[89] Washington, General Orders, 31 July 1775, *PGWDE*, Revolutionary, I: 197-198. Nearly the same order was repeated the following month, General Orders, 25 August 1775, *PGWDE*, Revolutionary, I: 360-361: "A Return signed by the Commanding Officer of each regiment, of the Commission'd Officers vacant, distinguishing their names, rank, and by what means vacant; this must be delivered to the Adjutant Genl at orderly time to morrow."

army as have received Commissions from the Congress of this Colony."[90] Other American

commanders would conduct similar inventories, each effort an attempt to manage physical

instruments that were in constant dispute.[91]

Regulation of commissions required that the bearers be properly integrated with several

structures of discipline that, along with the commission regime itself, reinforced order among the

officer corps and the army as a whole. Officially, discipline was founded upon the Articles of War

established by the Continental Congress. The Articles would be enforced by courts martial, while

individual officers would be preventatively bound to the Articles by their acknowledgment of having

read (or heard) and accepted them. By the end of August 1775, Washington had ordered that "the

Rules and Regulations of war (as established by the Continental Congress) [be] returned to him

signed, as he will thereupon proceed to distribute the Continental Commissions, agreeable to the

Ranks lately settled."[92] From the first institution of the Continental Army, those receiving

commissions as officers were required to swear to serve faithfully in their appointed capacities—

though the requirement was not enforced with complete uniformity or consistency, especially in the

---

[90] With the list of officers Warren sent "Also the Resolves of the Congress: which though Inaccurate may serve to Shew
in what manner the Congress Intended to Rank the several Regiments raised in this Colony." Warren to Washington, 3
August 1775, *PGWDE*, Revolutionary, I: 218.

[91] See General Horatio Gates's order as commander of the Northern Army in August of 1776: "The Commanding
Officers of the Old-Corps, will at orderly Time, next Saturday, give in to the Depy: Adjt: General, a signed Return of the
Names, Rank, and Dates of Commissions, of the Field Commissioned and Staff Officers in their respective Corps; The
Majors of Brigade will receive the Form in which these Returns are to be made." 29 August 1776, Orderly Book,
Northern Army, 10 July 1776 – 3 June 1777, Horatio Gates Papers, 1726-1828, Film 23, Reel 18 (Orderly Books, August
1758 - February 1783; Returns, January 1756 - November 1778), DLAR.

[92] Washington, General Orders, 24 August 1775, *PGWDE*, Revolutionary, I: 356-358. In a similar manner, the form of
enlistment for soldiers recruited into the Continental Army, as stipulated by the Continental Congress in October of
1775, required that the recruit attest in writing (or by marking or signing a form in which their name was inserted) not
only that he had voluntarily enlisted for the particular term, but that "[I] do bind myself to conform in all instances to
such rules and regulations as are or shall be established for the government of the said army," *JCC*, 12 October 1775, III:
289.

early, chaotic months of the war. The provincial armies and reconstituted provincial and state

militias imposed similar requirements.[93]

It was expected that a sense of honor would bind officers—expected and assumed to be

gentlemen—both to fulfill their oaths of office and to maintain the dignity of the commission,

issued to them in confidence that they would not abuse their authority or depart from the prescribed

discipline. Continental commissions thus typically began: "reposing especial Trust and Confidence

in your Patriotism, Valour, Conduct and Fidelity, DO by these Presents, constitute and appoint you

to be..."[94] Officers who violated this trust were not simply judged culpable and punished, but were

deemed unworthy of the commission they had dishonored. When, for instance, in August of 1775,

Captain Eleazer Lindsey was "tried by a General Court Martial, for 'absenting himself from his post,

which was attacked and abandoned to the enemy'," the court ruled that Lindsey should be

"'discharged [from] the service, as a person improper to sustain a Commission'."[95]

The integrity of the chain of commission required that Washington and others guard against

not only misjudgment of the characters of candidates but also against fraud or errors in applications.

Conscious of such risks, Washington wrote to the Massachusetts Council (the General Court's

upper house) in early September to request verification of the identity of a claimant to a Continental

---

[93] See Chapter 4.

[94] See Continental Congress, Commission in the Continental Army (blank), *EAI*, Series 1, no. 15129 (filmed);
Continental Congress, Commission of Henry Knox as Brigade General of Artillery, Continental Army, December 1776,
and Commission of John Harper as Quarter Master, Fourth Battalion, Pennsylvania Troops, 9 February 1776, GLC
2437.00500 and GLC 184.15, Gilder-Lehrman Institute, New York, NY.

[95] Washington, General Orders, 16 August 1775, *PGWDE*, Revolutionary, I: 312. Though officers' official and private
identities overlapped and informed one another, the disjunction between the official character of an officer, as embodied
in and certified by his commission, and the private character of a civilian fostered ambiguities and contentions. It
encouraged some individuals, for instance, to attempt to exploit the same to escape the liabilities that they accrued to
one identity, or one aspect thereof. This was particularly problematic along the legal frontier between those subject to
military law under a court martial and those outside its jurisdiction. In the early summer of 1776, therefore, in the face
of reports of "plundering, embezzlement of public monies, and other misdemeanors" by continental officers during the
Canada campaign, the Continental Congress was driven to declare that though "an opinion has prevailed that officers
resigning their commissions are not subject to trial by a court martial for offences committed previous to such
resignation," and though under such opinion "some have evaded the punishments to which they were liable...such
opinion is not just." *JCC*, 21 June 1776, V: 472.

commission. "Col. Sergeant," he explained, "has applied to me for his Commission in the

Continental Army, & I have no Objection to comply with his Request but his not having received

one under the Legislature of this Province." Washington was willing to overlook this, "as I do not

mean to confine myself to Forms," as long as "he has been considered by this Governmt as an

Officer authorized to raise a Regiment, & would have received a Commission on the Provincial

Establishment." Washington requested that the Council would "signify this to me for my

Government & Security"—he would then "make no Difficulty to grant a Commission to him on the

same Terms as are prescribed to other Officers."[96]

Washington attempted to further ensure the integrity of the new Continental instruments of

identification by requiring (in general practice) provincial documents as necessary (though not

sufficient) proof of legitimate claims to Continental commissions. In his General Orders of

September 20th he announced that "As the Commissions are ready to be delivered to the Officers

serving in the Army of the United Colonies; The General recommends it to them, to apply (as soon

as it is convenient) to him at Head Quarters, for the same." However, he stipulated that "No

Person is to presume to demand a Continental Commission, who is not in actual possession of the

like Commission, from the proper Authority of the Colony he is at present engaged to serve, which

must be produced, at the time application is made for a Continental Commission." Each officer was

to deliver "his present Commission, or Claim to a Commission; to his Colonel, or Officer

commanding the Regiment; and each Col. or Officer commanding a Regt is forthwith to apply to

the General for the Commissions, for the Officers of his respective Regt." This would be carried

---

[96] Washington to the Council of Massachusetts, 4 September 1775, *PGWDE*, Revolutionary, I: 413.

out at a rate of three regiments a day, in order of the regiments' rank, "until the whole are

supplied."[97]

Especially at the margins of institutional oversight, where verification of the legitimacy of

commissions was difficult, fraud—through the forgery or, more commonly, misappropriation of

commissions—like the issuing of commissions to improper persons, was a serious concern. The

possibilities for fraud ranged from relatively minor internal usurpations of low-level commands, to

imposition on American troops by an enemy agent bearing a false or purloined commission. From

the northern frontier of the war, at Fort George, in July of 1776, the Baron de Woedtkee wrote to

warn General Gates of the need to recall a Mr. Hare, recently gone to Albany with some recent

arrivals from Canada, and to place him under arrest. Hare, he explained, "has assumed to himself

the Title of Major," but, once taken, should be "deprived of that Commission he has Assumed to

himself which I assure you I never authorized [him] to take."[98]

As new campaigns were launched and rebel governance further extended over the

succeeding years of war, the regulation of commissions would be integral to the practice of

sovereignty—including maintaining the preeminence of civilian over military authority. When in the

spring of 1776 the Continental Congress dispatched commissioners to Canada—Franklin and

---

[97] Washington, General Orders, 20 September 1775, *PGWDE*, Revolutionary, II: 16: To account for anomalies and gaps
in the provincial landscape of documentary authority and identity, Washington qualified his requirement by stipulating
that, "If, from unavoidable circumstances, any Gentleman has served from the beginning of the Campaign, in the Rank
of a Commissioned Officer, & has not yet received a Commission, being justly entitled thereto; such Officer's
pretensions will be duly weighed and consider'd; and upon sufficient proof of the Justice of his claim, a Commission will
issue accordingly." Less than a week later Washington would have to re-initiate this process of distribution, which had
apparently been halted by a dispute over rank between two colonels. Washington, General Orders, 25 September 1775,
PGWDE, Revolutionary, II: 39: "As the Committee have settled the Rank between Col. Stark and Col. Jonathan Brewer;
The General desires the Colonels of the regiments, No. 6, 7 & 8 will apply immediately for Continental Commissions for
the Officers of their respective Corps; and that the three next Regiments in Sucession will apply to morrow morning,
and so three every morning afterwards, until the whole are served."

[98] Woedtkee to Gates, 20 July 1776, Horatio Gates Papers, 1726-1828, Film 23, Reel 3 (Correspondence, July 1776 -
October 1776), DLAR.

Adams among them—they conferred on the commissioners, as an essential tool of their mission, power over commissions.[99] "In reforming any abuses you may observe in *Canada*," the commissioners were instructed, "establishing and enforcing regulations for preservation of Peace and good Order there, and composing differences between the Troops of the United Colonies and the *Canadians*, all Officers and Soldiers are required to yield Obedience to you." As the means "to enforce the decisions that you or any two of you may make," they were "impowered to suspend any Military Officer from the exercise of his Commission, till the pleasure of the Congress shall be known, if you or any two of you shall think it expedient." In case former provisions had not been properly carried into effect, and it were necessary to establish new or reauthorize existing units on the Canadian front, the Commissioners were instructed to form a battalion from the New York soldiers already there and were empowered "to appoint the Field and other Officers out of the Gentlemen who have continued there during the Campaign, according to their respective ranks and merit." "To enable you to carry this resolution into effect," the Congress noted, "you are furnished with Blank Commissions signed by the President." These powers accompanied the authority to issue and regulate other emblems of sovereignty: the commissioners were empowered "to grant Passports" for the trade with Native Americans of the region, and "to use every wise and prudent measure to introduce and give credit and circulation to the Continental Money in *Canada*."[100]

In the contest for sovereignty in British North America, moreover, both the royal and rebel authorities adapted the British imperial tactic, renewed during the Imperial Crisis, of deploying commissions and allied instruments in contested borderlands: using the grant of commissions to co-opt the authority of Native American leaders and thereby, they supposed, cementing alliances and

---

[99] On 19 March 1776, a draft of the commission and instructions of the commissioners was presented to Congress. *JCC*, IV: 213.

[100] *The journals of the proceedings of Congress. Held at Philadelphia, from January to May, 1776*, (Philadelphia: R. Aitken, 1776), *EAI*, Series 1, no. 15145 (filmed): 117-118.

securing the frontiers of the provinces. The Continental Congress thus resolved on January 27th, 1776, "That a commission issue to Cayashota, giving him the rank of a colonel, and that a silver gorget be presented to him."[101] American military leaders through the course of the war used such grants of commissions to Native American leaders as a negotiating tool to smooth the path of their military operations in Native American territory.[102]

On the British side, in August of 1779, Lieutenant Governor of Nova Scotia Michael Francklin reported to Sir Henry Clinton his success in reversing such efforts by the rebels among the Indians of Nova Scotia. The previous year, he explained, "the Americans prevailed on the Indians of St. John's River, to return the British flag to Fort Howe," declare war, and commence hostilities. Francklin had been dispatched to the area to effect reconciliation. As part of the successful peace negotiations, Francklin had persuaded the Native American belligerents "to deliver up the treaty they had entered into with the Massachusetts to give me some of their commissions, and medals, they had received from the Americans, and to take an oath to remain quiet."[103] The following year, British Indian Agent Alexander Cameron wrote Clinton from Pensacola of the need for funds to counteract the efforts of the Spanish to win to their side the "Indians of this Department," who were otherwise "well disposed to support the English at present." The Spanish, he reported, "take every method to alienate their affections from us by flattering talks, what presents they can spare, as well as medals, gorgets & commissions, &c."[104]

---

[101] *JCC*, 27 January 1776, IV: 95.

[102] See the grant of a colonel's commission, among other inducements used by McIntosh to convince Lenni Lenape leader White Eyes to allow the American attack on Detroit, discussed in Charles Patrick Neimeyer, *America Goes to War: A Social History of the Continental Army*, (New York: New York UP, 1996), 106-107.

[103] Francklin to Clinton, 2 August 1779, Royal Commission on Historical Manuscripts, *Report on American Manuscripts in the Royal Institution of Great Britain*, (London: Mackie & Co., 1904-1909), II: 1-2.

[104] Cameron to Clinton, 18 July 1780, *Report on American Manuscripts in the Royal Institution of Great Britain*, II: 159-160.

Familiar, fundamental, and integral instruments of identification, commissions became basic foci of the Revolutionary remaking of sovereignty. They served to constitute the cadres of officials and officers through which revolution, a war for independence, and governance were put into practice. As resistance to the Coercive Acts and Parliamentary authority more generally reached a crisis in the summer and fall of 1774, and as fighting began in the spring of 1775, the processes of resigning commissions under the disputed acts and, soon, under the crown more generally, and of taking up new and ostensibly temporary provincial commissions, became an emblematic ritual of allegiance to the "liberties of America." It was also, by the same token, a key means of distinguishing adherents on each side, a way to test and secure the loyalties of those entrusted with authority, information, and munitions. The promulgation of new state constitutions, the institution of independent state governments, and the collective Declaration of Independence by the United States of America amplified both the emblematic and the practical roles of commissions in Revolutionary America as instruments of sovereignty and individual identification.

As emblems of the sovereignty of the aspirant new republics, the new commissions—signed, sealed, and delivered—had to be deployed to displace those of the British imperial regime. In the day-to-day practice of governance and warfare, individual officials and officers needed commissions to prove or certify their authority, both in the eyes of their own governments and compatriots and in the eyes of the enemy and the international community. Commissions identified the official leaders and agents of the Revolution—almost exclusively "gentlemen." But "Americans" also had to identify the adherents of the cause and members of the citizenry more generally, by parsing one another's loyalties. Both sides of the conflict, indeed, instituted repeated loyalty testing and issued loyalty certificates to distinguish supporters from enemies. The following chapter examines how these certificates were used to make political loyalties legible and portable.

Chapter 4

Certificates

Early in August of 1777, Philip Skene, "by the Request of General Burgoyne…sett out" into upstate New York with a detachment of Burgoyne's army "to try the affections of the Country." Skene, a dedicated Loyalist, was a former major in the British army, a large landholder in New York, a militia colonel, and a county judge who, having travelled to Britain, had in 1775 been named lieutenant governor of Ticonderoga and Crown point. Having returned to America in June of 1775 with his new appointment, Skene had spent more than a year in Hartford, Connecticut, as a prisoner of the rebels. Exchanged at last, he had travelled again to England, only to return once more to America to aid General Burgoyne's expedition. Burgoyne was leading the British south along the valley of the Hudson, in an attempt to sever New England from the rest of the rebellious colonies. He and Skene hoped that the inhabitants of upstate New York would reveal themselves as loyal subjects of the King once the British army arrived to protect them from retribution by the rebels. Until these provincials were put to the test, however, Burgoyne and Skene could do little more than hope—to distinguish Loyalist from rebel, true friend from deceitful enemy, or even one army from another was no easy task. A little less than a week after setting out, Skene received a bracing reminder of the challenges of identification. Just south of the Mills at Sancoick, Skene spotted a party of soldiers "at the end of a Worms fence Extending to the Eastward." "I was in doubt," he later reported, "whether they were Rebells, or Loyalists, as they had the same Signals of white feathers, or paper in their hats." "To be Certain," he "Galloped up to them, at the Distance of 100 Yards and desired them to halt." When "some did," he related, "I then Asked them if they were for

147

King George," upon which "they immediately presented and fired Confusedly, hit my horse but missed me."[1]

Skene had been probing the loyalties and identities of New York provincials since at least July, but he remained uncertain what to make of them. He was aware that for the difficulties the British forces had faced in their push southward "some blame is laid on the Inhabitants being Spies and without doubt they are." Yet he had seen how Burgoyne's "Manifesto inviting the Inhabitants to return to their duty, and take the Oath of Allegiance…brings in Many" and was "well Satisfied his Humanity will Conquor more than the Sword."[2] Either inveterate Loyalists who had concealed their political principles under rebel rule were now coming forward, demonstrating the degree to which such political identities could be dissimulated, or one-time rebels were returning to the fold, whether out of genuine conviction or opportunism. As early as mid July, in fact, Skene had already been reporting that, "the Country come in fast to General Burgoynes Manifesto." Skene had himself been "honored…with his instructions as Commissioner" and had "his Orders to sett out Immedeately for Castleton to receive the different inhabitants Submission."[3] The oaths of allegiance recorded and the certificates issued to the submissive inhabitants by Skene and others would, it was hoped, help fix the provincials' political identities and make them legible upon demand.

The "feathers, or paper in their hats" were less explicit, less reliable, and more easily fabricated or assumed, but certificates as well as feathers could be falsified, forged, or stolen, and both allegiances and identities feigned. Yet identification was imperative and steps, however imperfect, had to be taken, at a gallop, if the war were to be won by anyone. Those who lived these

---

[1] Skene to Lord Dartmouth, 30 August 1777, APSED, Film 391, Reel 15, No. 1780, DLAR. "Skene, Philip," *ANB*.

[2] Skene to Lord Dartmouth, 30 August 1777, APSED, Film 391, Reel 15, No. 1780, DLAR.

[3] Skene to Lord Dartmouth, 15 July 1777, APSED, 1765-1782, Film 391, Reel 15, No. 1768, DLAR.

contests had to work out ways to identify themselves and others, if they were to survive the conflict and come out where they wished to be on the other side.

The need to distinguish Patriot from Loyalist was perhaps most basic to the Revolutionary crisis of identification. The principal means of making these distinctions was to impose oaths of abjuration and allegiance. The identities established through such loyalty testing were certified and mobilized in turn in the form of loyalty oath certificates and related instruments. These documents were often in turn pre-requisites for securing other instruments of identification, including commissions, passes, and passports. Loyalty oath certificates were thus instruments fundamental to the construction and practice of practical identities in the face of the Revolutionary crisis of identification. More so than any other Revolutionary instruments of identification, loyalty oath certificates marked fundamental personal political identities, distinguishing members of one nation or polity from another, "British" subjects from "American" citizens, and tying individual identification to the formation of the state and nation.

As the war progressed—as lines shifted, refugees fled to one side or the other, and territories changed hands—both sides used oaths of allegiance to solidify their authority and weed out enemies in the jurisdictions they claimed. As either side occupied or recovered territories, they often instituted new rounds of loyalty testing, administering new oaths, or the same oaths yet again. These iterative processes of distinction and displacement amounted to extended processes of identification, ranging from the precise identification of individuals to the coarse ascription of identities to entire communities based on broad characteristics. In some cases loyalty testing was calculated to compel the local inhabitants to declare, finally, a loyalty one way or another, thereby committing themselves to a cause and a political identity. Loyalty tests, in such instances, were means of crystallizing, establishing, and externalizing notionally pre-existing loyalties. In other instances, loyalty oaths were administered to reconstitute the individual's dutiful relationship to his chosen sovereign—what one

British commander referred to as "making Friends to Government."[4] Moreover, following the

initial divisions and identifications of the late Imperial Crisis and early war, both sides—in an effort

to win the war of opinion—were willing to show some clemency and welcome back into the fold

those less notorious apostates who might be willing to demonstrate a change of heart.

Previous discussions of loyalty testing in Revolutionary America have focused principally on

how the practice polarized the conflict, even as it consolidated American identity and enacted the

new states' claims to sovereignty.[5] Harold Melvin Hyman has gone farther than most, exploring the

enforcement and administration of loyalty tests by committees of safety and the Continental Army

and examining the persecution of those resistant to subscribing loyalty tests, thus showing how

loyalty testing played out in everyday life, on the level of the individual. This chapter builds on

Hyman's work, but goes farther by establishing that loyalty testing and certification were parts of a

larger history of Revolutionary identification. Only in this larger context can we fully understand the

importance of loyalty certificates themselves as instruments of identification to be deployed in

ongoing practice—as more than incidental byproducts or tokens of oaths of allegiance, hitherto the

dominant focus of studies of loyalty testing. Only in this larger context, moreover, can we

---

[4] James Grant to _____, 26 December 1776, Brunswick, NJ, Papers of James Grant of Ballindalloch, 1740-1819, Army Career Series (1740-1805), Film 687, Reel 28, Letterbook 2, DLAR.

[5] The historiography of loyalty testing in the American Revolution is sparse. The topic has been dealt with principally in studies of loyalism, citizenship, and conscientious objection. Harold Melvin Hyman, *To Try Men's Souls: Loyalty Tests in American History*, (Berkley, CA: University of California Press, 1959), is the only book-length study of loyalty testing to deal substantially with the American Revolution and very nearly the only study of any length to give extended, focused attention to Revolutionary loyalty testing in its own right. For discussions of Revolutionary loyalty testing in other historiographies, see Jerrilyn Greene Marston, *King and Congress: The Transfer of Political Legitimacy, 1774-1776*, (Princeton, NJ: Princeton UP, 1987); James H. Kettner, *The Development of American Citizenship, 1608-1870*, (Chapel Hill, NC: University of North Carolina Press, 1978), 175, 177, 179-180, 188, 197; Douglas Bradburn, *The Citizenship Revolution: Politics and the Creation of the American Union, 1774-1804*, (Charlottesville, VA: University of Virginia Press, 2009), 57-59; Rogers M. Smith, *Civic Ideals: Conflicting Visions of Citizenship in U.S. History*, (New Haven, CT: Yale UP, 1997), 91-96, 102; Claude Halstead Van Tyne, *The Loyalists in the American Revolution*, (Gloucester, MA: P. Smith, 1959), 130-145, 318-326; Maya Jasanoff, *Liberty's Exiles: American Loyalists in the Revolutionary World*, (New York: Alfred A. Knopf, 2011), 24, 28, 40-41, 45; and Robert F. Oaks, "Philadelphians in Exile: The Problem of Loyalty during the American Revolution," *Pennsylvania Magazine of History and Biography*, 96: 3 (Jul., 1972), 298-319, 321-325. See also Charles Evans, *Oaths of Allegiance in Colonial New England*, (Worcester, MA: American Antiquarian Society, 1922); Nellie Protsman Waldenmaier, *Some of the Earliest Oaths of Allegiance to the United States of America*, (Lancaster, PA: Lancaster Press, 1944).

appreciate that formal loyalty testing and certification were but one of many ways in which

individual loyalties were parsed and documented; that the parsing of loyalties was but one of many

ways in which individual "American" identities were called into question and redefined, in both their

social and their political dimensions; and that loyalty certificates were but one part of a larger

complex of documents of several genres, dependent on one another, through which individual

identities were constituted and practiced.

Oaths of allegiance were long-standing tools employed within the British and other

European empires to bind subjects, officials, and military officers to their sovereigns. They had

been used repeatedly to test loyalties in the colonies, particularly in moments of instability, such as

after imperial and colonial regime changes, on the ascent of a new monarch, and during civil

conflicts like Bacon's Rebellion, among many other occasions. They were routinely required,

throughout the colonial period, to qualify for suffrage, office, and naturalization.[6] Between

occasions of general loyalty testing and the requirement of oaths from those holding office or

performing other public functions, many colonists had occasion to take more than a few oaths of

allegiance in their lifetimes. In 1771, one colonist claimed that he had, in his "Little time in Life,

taken the oath of Alegence to His Majestie seven times."[7] Notably, loyalty testing during both the

colonial period and the Revolution generally applied only to free adult white males. Women,

children, servants, and slaves were not considered to posses the independent political will, capacity

---

[6] See Hyman, *To Try Men's Souls*, chs. 1-2; Evans, *Oaths of Allegiance*; Miles Ogborn, "The Power of Speech: Orality, Oaths and Evidence in the British Atlantic World, 1650-1800," *Transactions of the Institute of British Geographers*, New Series, Vol. 36, No. 1 (January 2011), 109-125; Kettner, *American Citizenship*, chs. 4-5.

[7] George Wilson to Arthur St. Clair, 14 August 1771, *The St. Clair Papers*, William Henry Smith ed., (Cincinnati, OH: R. Clarke, 1882), I: 257-259. Cf. Jasanoff on the fact that a militia officer and county judge would have taken "repeated oaths of allegiance" throughout his adult life. *Liberty's Exiles*, 34.

for consent, or, in the case of slaves, mere personhood necessary to meaningfully and legitimately choose an allegiance, let alone swear an oath to it.[8]

Building on this shared imperial history, both sides of the Revolution would turn to loyalty testing to consolidate support and prosecute their competing claims to sovereignty.[9] Well before war broke out, and before the rebels themselves would institute loyalty oaths per se, opposition authorities had begun to make inward political identities practical and legible. During the decade preceding the Revolutionary War, the colonial opposition had used boycott agreements and associations, for example, as a primary mode of resistance to objectionable acts of Parliament. The willingness to subscribe and abide by these agreements had become a de facto test of political allegiance, setting non-subscribers apart, in the view of the opposition, as enemies of American liberties. The Massachusetts Solemn League and Covenant became the next such agreement and de facto loyalty test when it was established by the General Assembly, in June of 1774, in response to the Coercive Acts.[10] This agreement was largely superseded, in turn, by the Continental Association of September 1774. Established by the Continental Congress, the Association would be circulated for subscription and enforced throughout the colonies by county and local committees of safety. Failure to sign the Association marked an individual as an "enemy of the country" and brought ostracism, if not physical abuse, by committees and crowds of vigilantes. The Association thus became what Hyman has termed "the colonists' first standard loyalty test."[11]

---

[8] Linda K. Kerber, *Women of the Republic: Intellect and Ideology in Revolutionary America*, (Chapel Hill, NC: University of North Carolina Press, 1980), 52, 121; Holly Brewer, *By Birth or Consent: Children, Law, and the Anglo-American Revolution in Authority*, (Chapel Hill, NC: University of North Carolina Press, 2005), 132-134, 148, 154, 157-160, 163, 166, 167, 172, 173.

[9] The division of Americans into Patriots and Loyalists was, as Jasanoff has recently reminded us, an active and coercive process of "threats, violence, the imposition of oaths, and ultimately war." *Liberty's Exiles*, 24.

[10] Hyman, *To Try Men's Souls*, 63. Cf. Richard D. Brown, *Revolutionary Politics in Massachusetts: The Boston Committee of Correspondence and the Towns, 1772-1774*, (Cambridge, MA: Harvard UP, 1970), 191-192, 200, 219.

[11] Hyman, *To Try Men's Souls*, 65; T.H. Breen, *American Insurgents, American Patriots: The Revolution of the People*, (New York: Hill & Wang, 2010), ch. 6; Don Higginbotham, "War and State Formation in Revolutionary America," *Empire and Nation:*

In these early stages of organized resistance, rebel authorities sometimes also employed ad hoc instruments of identification certifying loyalty and good citizenship, itself an emerging category of political identity by which the opposition, and later the rebels, began to define themselves against the subjects of the King and Parliament. These instruments appear to have functioned primarily to settle particular cases of contested identity and secure to those suspected of British sympathies an identity as good citizens. They bore only minimal resemblance to the mass tests and certifications of loyalty (to one side or another) represented by the Association and the formal loyalty testing that would characterize wartime governance. It was in this manner that the Committee of Correspondence of Worcester, Massachusetts, issued in September of 1774 a certificate testifying that [John?] and Daniel Goulding had so far satisfied them as to their previous questionable behavior that they "do now Esteem them as good members of Society and are determined…to do all in our Power that they be treated as Such…and do now Recomend them to be treated in ye like manner by all the good People in ye Province of the Massachusetts Bay."[12] The Committee thus attempted to restore and secure the impugned identity of the Gouldings as "good members of Society" by means of a hybrid instrument of identification that promised them the backing of what authority the Committee could command, while at the same time recognizing that, at least as yet, their powers were very indefinite. They could only recommend respect for their certificate from other residents or the other committees of Massachusetts. No hierarchy of authority over identity had as yet been established.

Once war broke out, British governors, other officials, and military commanders would increasingly take up loyalty testing as a tried and true practice of identification to reconsolidate

---

The American Revolution in the Atlantic World, Petter S. Onuf and Eliga H. Gould eds., (Baltimore, MD: Johns Hopkins UP, 2005), 59.

[12] Worcester, MA, Committee of Correspondence, Certificate in favor of [John?] and Daniel Goulding, 5 September 1774, U.S. Revolution Collection, Box 1, Folder 4, AAS.

support for royal government and prevent the further spread of rebellion. After the battles of

Lexington and Concord and the beginning of the siege of Boston, General Gage issued a

proclamation offering amnesty to Americans willing to swear renewed allegiance to the King.[13]

Soon thereafter, toward the end of May 1775, General Gage wrote from Boston to Governor Legge

in Halifax, Nova Scotia, to warn him that, "several of the Inhabitants of this Province, were

Emigrating to yours, and as they carry their Seditious principles with them, might become

troublesome to you." Legge had best, Gage advised, "be upon your guard, and have them closely

watched," for "Some you may depend will use every means to Poison the minds of the People they

settle amongst."[14] Legge took Gage's warnings to heart and instituted a close watch on new

immigrants arriving from New England. Along with his letter in response, Legge sent Gage a list of

thirty-two "persons Arrived here from New England," largely "Fisherman & Traders" (hailing from

Marblehead, Salem, Plymouth, Cape Ann, and Dartmouth), and divided into groups by their place of

origin and port of arrival—Halifax or Lunenburg. No doubt to help weed out the malcontents,

Legge had "Obliged [them] to take the State Oaths before they have been allowed to take out new

Registers for their Vessels or Certificate from myself." Moreover he had resolved that he would

"hereafter more particularly inquire into the inducements that have Obliged them to Quit their

Country, & into their principals as to their Allegiance & Dutiful Behaviour to the Government of

Great Britain."[15]

Later that year, after the King, in August, had declared the recalcitrant colonies in rebellion,

Gage himself reissued his earlier amnesty proclamation. Meanwhile, Lord Dunmore, the embattled

governor of Virginia, had instituted loyalty testing in an initially promising but ultimately failed

---

[13] Hyman, *To Try Men's Souls*, 96-97.

[14] Gage to Legge, 24 May 1775, Thomas Gage Papers, Volume 129, WLCL.

[15] Legge to Gage, 9 June 1775, Thomas Gage Papers, Volume 129, WLCL.

attempt to shore up support for royal government in the colony. Throughout the remainder of the

war, British officials and military commanders, in the name of the Crown and under its authority,

would repeatedly offer amnesty and protection to (nearly) any rebel adherent who would renounce

the rebellion, swear an oath of allegiance to the King, and bear themselves henceforward as true and

loyal subjects—sometimes by simply engaging no longer to aid or countenance the rebellion,

sometimes by engaging to take up arms in the King's cause.[16]

On the American side of the conflict, the outbreak of war in April of 1775 increased the

urgency of local efforts to establish individuals' political identities, employing tools such as the

Association as well as less formal scrutiny of individuals.[17] Soon, provincial authorities were lending

further support to these efforts. While some provincial authorities called on the Continental

Congress to establish a standard loyalty oath, the Congress, still focused on conciliation with Britain,

declined to involve itself.[18] The provinces, left to their own devices, avoided committing to formal

oaths of allegiance and concomitant claims to independent sovereignty. Between the outbreak of

war and the Declaration of Independence the following year, provincial authorities of the several

colonies, in cooperation with county and local committees, would continue informal loyalty

testing—examining suspected persons, pressuring inhabitants to sign the Continental Association or

one of a variety of provincial and local associations, and disarming, confining, or paroling those who

---

[16] Hyman, *To Try Men's Souls*, 97, 98-99, 108. The stipulation of military service as a condition of favor from the Crown
was made likewise in the case of those—African American slaves—who did not need, strictly speaking, to renounce
adherence to the rebellion, never having been allowed a free choice one way or the other, but who needed to earn or
furnish reciprocal service for the freedom "granted" and the protection afforded by the Crown (whose commanders
were largely interested in freeing or receiving slaves only in so far as they might be employed in turn to fill out the ranks
or provide auxiliary support for the Royal Army). See Jasanoff, *Liberty's Exiles*; Cassandra Pybus, *Epic Journeys of Freedom:
Runaway Slaves of the American Revolution and their Global Quest for Liberty*, (Boston: Beacon Press, 2006); Douglas R.
Egerton, *Death or Liberty: African Americans and Revolutionary America*, (New York: Oxford UP, 2009); Sylvia R. Frey, *Water
from the Rock: Black Resistance in a Revolutionary Age*, (Princeton, NJ: Princeton UP, 1991).

[17] Hyman writes that the news of Lexington and Concord led to an increase in "Tory-hunting" throughout the colonies.
To Try Men's Souls, 70. See also Jasanoff, *Liberty's Exiles*, 28; Mary Beth Norton, *The British-Americans: The Loyalist Exiles in
England, 1774-1789*, (Boston: Little, Brown, & Co., 1972), 24.

[18] Hyman, *To Try Men's Souls*, 70.

refused.[19] In early May of 1775, the Massachusetts Provincial Congress would recommend that, in

order to distinguish the "enemies to the rights of mankind, and the interest of America" known to

be in the colony "from those who have shewn a disposition to be friendly to their Country," local

committees should,

> inquire into the principles and conduct of such suspected persons; and...cause all such to be
> disarmed, who do not give them full and ample assurances, in which they can with safety
> confide, of their readiness to join their countrymen on all occasions in defence of the rights
> and liberties of America.

It was also recommended "likewise that they take effectual steps to put it out of the power of such

persons to obstruct, by any means whatever, the measures which shall be taken for the common

defence."[20]

In early August of the same year, in response to advice from General Washington, the

Massachusetts Provincial Congress appointed a committee charged to "strictly examine into the

characters and circumstances of all such persons" coming out of Boston as refugees and to take into

custody those who "shall appear to be enemies of this Country."[21] In the second week of August,

the committee of Newbern County, North Carolina, declared that, "those who have not subscribed

the Articles of Association, have sufficiently testified to the publick that they are enemies to the

liberties of America" and ordered that such persons be disarmed.[22] The following month, the North

Carolina Provincial Congress resolved that each town or county committee should appoint a

Committee of Secrecy, Intelligence and Observation empowered "to take up and examine all

---

[19] On the South Carolina Association, in particular, see Hyman, *To Try Men's Souls*, 72; J. William Harris, *The Hanging of Thomas Jeremiah: A Free Black Man's Encounter with Liberty*, (New Haven, CT: Yale UP, 2009), 86-87, 89-91, 122-125, 126-127, 137-138, 147. Norton writes of the provincial defense associations being used as means to "identify the disaffected." *British-Americans*, 26. Cf. Alexander Innes to the Earl of Dartmouth, 10-13 June 1775, Charleston, SC, APSED, Film 391, Reel 13, No. 1307, DLAR.

[20] *AAO*, Series 4, II: 793.

[21] Massachusetts Provincial Congress, 7 August 1775, *AAO*, Series 4, III: 313.

[22] Committee of Newbern County, North Carolina, 14 August 1775, *AAO*, Series 4, III: 100. Cf. order by the North Carolina Provincial Congress, 2 March 1776, that "suspected persons" be disarmed, *AAO*, Series 4, V: 65-67.

suspected persons, and, if necessary, send them to the Provincial Council or the Committees of Safety for their respective Districts."[23]

In mid January of 1776, the Maryland Convention provided for the disarming, paroling, emigration, or arrest of those who refused to sign the provincial association and ordered that all signed copies of the association, along with a list of non-associators, be forwarded to the Convention.[24] In March, the Provincial Congress of New Jersey ordered "all suspected persons removing into this Colony" to "return to the place they came from" unless they might properly be arrested as "delinquents," or "unless such persons produce certificates from the Committee of the City, Township or County from whence they came, that they have signed the General Association recommended by the Continental or their Provincial Congress, and have not, by any subsequent act, contravened the same; or that they are deemed to be well affected to the cause of American freedom."[25] In June the committees of Milford and Stratford, Connecticut resolved, "That it be the duty of the Authority, Selectmen, Committee of Inspection, Commissioned Officers, Constables, Grand Jurors, Tavern-Keepers, and Ferrymen" to "search and examine all transient travelling suspected persons; and if such persons cannot give satisfaction to said Inspectors that they are friendly and well-affected to the cause of American liberty" to take them into custody and bring them before the proper authorities for further examination.[26]

---

[23] North Carolina Provincial Congress, 9 September 1775, *AAO*, Series 4, III: 205-209.

[24] Maryland Convention, 16 January 1776, *AAO*, Series 4, IV: 755-757.

[25] New Jersey Provincial Congress, 2 March 1776, *AAO*, Series 4, IV: 1618-1619. Cf. *JCC*, 18 June 1776, V: 464: "That no man in these colonies, charged with being a tory, or unfriendly to the cause of American liberty, be injured in his person or property, or in any manner whatever disturbed, unless the proceeding against him be founded on an order of this Congress, or the Assembly, convention, council or committee of safety of the colony, or committee of inspection and observation, of the district wherein he resides; provided, that this resolution shall not prevent the apprehending any person found in the commission of some act destructive of American liberty, or justly suspected of a design to commit such act, and intending to escape, and bringing such person before proper authority for examination and trial."

[26] Committees of Milford and Stratford, CT, 10 June 1776, *AAO*, Series 4, VI: 798. In New York City, in May of 1776, suspected Loyalists were disarmed. In June, Patriot crowds assaulted Loyalists and drove many out of the city. Jasanoff, *Liberty's Exiles*, 30.

Under the pressures of war, however, it was the rebel military authorities who led the way in adopting formal loyalty tests and certificates. Well before the colonies had declared themselves to be independent states, which might require oaths of allegiance and establish treason laws, the Continental Army and other military units in the field deployed oaths of enlistment, office, and fidelity as means to exclude the uncommitted from active service and to govern their soldiers and officers. The higher stakes that depended on the loyalty of those in American military service once war was opened in the spring of 1775—combined with the fact that those who had taken up arms against royal forces had already declared themselves traitors—dictated some measure, however anomalous or risky, for verifying the loyalties of all military men.[27]

On May 8th of 1775, the Massachusetts Provincial Congress had adopted an oath to be taken by all soldiers and officers of the newly forming provincial army (excluding general officers, who took a different oath). The oath-takers swore to serve faithfully in the army and in defense of "the estates, lives and liberties" of Massachusetts and the other colonies against "ministerial tyranny" and all other enemies; to obey the army's regulations and the orders of superior officers; and to report any "traitorous conspiracies, attempts and designs" that came to their knowledge.[28] By late May some commissions in the Massachusetts Provincial Army bore certificates that the named officer "took and Subscribed the Oath appointed to be Taken" or had "appeared and repeated the Oath required by Congress to be taken by the officers of the Massachusetts army."[29]

The first article of the Continental Army's Articles of War required that all those in the Continental service give their signatures binding themselves to obey all of the succeeding articles

---

[27] Hyman, *To Try Men's Souls*, 73.

[28] *The Journals of Each Provincial Congress of Massachusetts in 1774 and 1775*, (Boston: Dutton & Wentworth, 1838), 201.

[29] Commission of James Crickett as Lieutenant Colonel, 19 May 1775, Certificate 20 May 1775; Commission of Zacheus Crocker as Lieutenant, 19 May 1775, Certificate 26 June 1775, Sol Feinstone Collection, Film 1, Reel 2, Nos. 888, 889, DLAR.

detailing the duties and disciplines of the soldier and the penalties for acts in aid of the enemy, detrimental to the cause of the army, or otherwise contrary to duty or discipline.[30] By at least the end of July 1775, an oath of enlistment was also established for soldiers in the Continental Army. This is evident in that on the 26th, Washington pardoned Levi Woods, a soldier convicted by court martial of being absent without leave, "threatening to leave the army," and "refusing to take the Oath."[31] On the 29th of July, the Continental Congress prescribed an oath of fidelity in office for the Paymaster, Commissary, and Quarter Master Generals and their deputies.[32] On September 20th, the Continental Congress established a new set of Articles of War that included an oath of fidelity and faithful service to be taken by all soldiers and non-commissioned officers.[33] The combination of signing the current Articles of War and swearing an oath of enlistment would continue to be the basic test of enlistees' loyalties and political identities. Thus, recruiting instructions that Washington issued in October of 1776 would stipulate that, "The Men inlisted...are to be Subject to the Rules & Articles for the Government of the Army published by Congress the 20th Sepr 1776 and are to sign those Articles," and that, "When any Person is enlisted you are as soon as convenient to take him to some person duly Authorised by the above Articles to take the Oath there Prescribed."[34] Some states, meanwhile, provided their own oaths of enlistment, even for units raised as part of the Continental Army. Thus the Rhode Island General Assembly, in late October of 1776, resolved on

---

[30] *JCC*, 30 June 1775, II: 111-123.

[31] Washington, General Orders, 26 July 1775, *PGWDE*, Revolutionary, I: 172-173.

[32] Waldenmaier, *Some of the Earliest Oaths*, 3.

[33] Waldenmaier, *Some of the Earliest Oaths*, 4.

[34] Washington to Colonel Edward Hand, 11 October 1776, *PGWDE*, Revolutionary, VI: 536-537. Cf. William Ripley, Enlistment Oath, 19 August 1777, Mss., Boston, Sol Feinstone Collection, Film 1, Reel 3, No. 1213, DLAR: "Boston. August. 19th. 1777— / I the Subscriber do hereby inlist myself into the Service of the United States of America to Continue that Service untill the 10: of January. 1778. & I do hereby engage to be under the Command, and faithfully to observe and obey all such Orders as I from Time to Time Shall receive from the Officers appointed to Command me, & to be under all Such Regulations as shall or may be provided for the Government of the Army of the aforesaid States / Willim Ripley[.]"

"the form of enlistment" of soldiers "in the battalions of the state of Rhode Island...in the service of the United States of America."[35]

Officers received certificates attesting to their oath, either inscribed on their commissions or issued as separate instruments. These certificates proved the legitimacy of their commissions and their authority to act in their appointed offices. Soldiers, upon enlisting, signed the Articles of War, swore the oath of enlistment, and signed enlistment papers. These papers became the official record of their obligation to serve. In contrast to their officers, soldiers do not appear to have been issued, as a matter of standard practice, certificates of the oath or signatures enacting their enlistment. As such they possessed comparatively little power over how they were identified in the context of war. Enlistment records, in the hands of the officers, served instead as instruments to govern and discipline soldiers by confirming the particular identities they documented.

In the civil sphere, some colonies began to certify provisional loyalties even before they had declared themselves independent. This largely took the form of changes to the oaths or the institution of new oaths required of officeholders, declaring loyalty and obedience to the provincial government, for the time being, and no longer to the King, until his and his ministers' abuses of power had been corrected. Thus in March of 1776, South Carolina established an oath for all provincial officers by which they swore to support the new interim constitution.[36] In early May of 1776, the General Assembly of Rhode Island passed an act replacing the King's name and authority in all official documents with that of "The Governor and Company of the English Colony of Rhode

---

[35] Rhode Island General Assembly, Form of an Oath of Enlistment, 28 October 1776, John Russell Bartlett ed., *Records of the State of Rhode Island and Providence Plantations,* (New York: AMS Press, 1968), VIII: 21-22. Cf. the similar oath prescribed for the recruiting of a new regiment, Rhode Island General Assembly, 21 November 1776, *An Act for raising a regiment, to serve for three months,* Bartlett ed., *Records of the State of Rhode Island,* VIII: 42-44; Rhode Island Interior Committee, Form of an Oath of Enlistment, 5 December 1776, Records of the States of the United States, Rhode Island, 1775-1818, Film 285, E4, Reel 1, Minutes of the Interior Committee, DLAR; and Rhode Island General Assembly, *An Act for raising, embodying, supplying and paying, two regiments of infantry, each consisting of seven hundred and fifty men; and a regiment or train of artillery, consisting of three hundred men, for the defence of the United States, in general, and of this state, in particular,* 10 December 1776, Bartlett ed., *Records of the State of Rhode Island,* IX: 61-64.

[36] Kettner, *American Citizenship,* 175.

Island and Providence Plantations," and suspending the practice of dating documents by the year of his majesty's reign (see Chapter 3). The act also provided new oaths of office for the full range of commissioned civil and military officers of the colony, each oath declaring that the juror would be "true and faithful" to the "colony" and obedient to the laws and authorities established by the General Assembly.[37] Connecticut adopted similar legislation the same month. In June, Rhode Island adopted a test oath to be tendered to those suspected of being enemies to American liberty.[38]

Unstandardized loyalty certificates, for a variety of purposes, continued to serve the day-to-day practice of Revolutionary identities in the period before the Declaration of Independence and the institution of formal American loyalty testing and certification. And, indeed, they survived in parallel with more formal or standardized documents thereafter. Such ad hoc instruments were issued at all levels and took as many forms as there were occasions and authorities. They were issued by governmental bodies, officials, or military officers to private citizens or to other officials or officers, as well as by private citizens to each other. In late June of 1776, for instance, Anthony Bleecker, Major in the First Regiment of the militia of the City of New York provided a certificate "that the bearer hereof Ebenezer Hazard Esqr: Post Master under Authority of the Honl the Continental Congress, Has always approved himself a Sincere and Steady friend to the Liberties of America & has leave of Absence for three days, and may be Allowed to Pass and repass at his pleasure."[39] Similarly, for his return journey from Philadelphia to his home in Maryland in July of 1776, the Reverend David Love, who would later leave Maryland as a Loyalist refugee, secured a

---

[37] Rhode Island General Assembly, 4 May 1776, *An Act repealing an act, entitled "An act for the more effectually securing to His Majesty, the allegiance of his subjects, in this his colony and dominion of Rhode Island and Providence Plantations;" and altering the forms of commissions, of all writs and processes in the cours, and of the oaths prescribed by law.* Bartlett ed., *Records of the Colony of Rhode Island,* VII: 522-526. The following October, the General Assembly would explicitly resolve that any town officials in the state who had not subscribed the required "test" were disqualified from further service in their offices and were to be replaced. Rhode Island General Assembly, 28 October 1776, Bartlett ed., *Records of the State of Rhode Island,* VIII: 22.

[38] Kettner, *American Citizenship,* 175, 175n2.

[39] Bleecker, Certificate and Pass for Ebenezer Hazard, 24 June 1776, H338, Ebenezer Hazard Papers, Item 9, APS.

letter from Colonel Henry Hill certifying the unexceptionable nature of Love's business and his harmlessness, "in order to save him the trouble of being interrupted by any who may be strangers to his unblemished conduct in regard to the affairs of these States."[40] At the end of October 1776, Benjamin Smith and Samuel Smith of the committee of Sandisfield, Berkshire County, Massachusetts, certified that Solomon Smith "is, a true friend to the States of America" and requested that he be allowed to travel unhindered.[41] Such instruments worked primarily to persuade rather than command, and therefore were akin to letters of introduction and recommendation.

While provincial and local authorities carried on informal loyalty testing and enforcement, General Washingotn became concerned that too many Loyalists still enjoyed too much liberty (and anonymity) and might pose a threat to both military operations and the cause in general. To address his concerns, Washington deployed detachments of the Continental Army on loyalty testing missions to areas of critical concern in late 1775 and early 1776. One expedition, under General Charles Lee, targeted Rhode Island, and another, at the same time, swept Long Island; a third would return to Long Island, this time under Lee. Each expedition imposed its own distinct loyalty oaths or paroles on suspected Loyalists, independent of the provincial civil authorities.[42] Lee in Rhode Island imposed oaths not to aid the King's troops with goods or intelligence and to obey the Continental Congress or provincial legislature if called to military service in defense of American liberties.[43] The first Long Island expedition imposed oaths to surrender all arms and paroles not to act against the measures of the Continental or Provincial Congress.[44] The second Long Island

---

[40] Henry Hill, Certificate issued to David Love, 9 July 1776, Philadelphia, Sol Feinstone Collection, Film 1, Reel 1, No. 541, DLAR.

[41] Benjamin Smith and Samuel Smith, Certificate and Pass for Solomon Smith, 31 October 1776, Sol Feinstone Collection, Film 1, Reel 3, No. 1275, DLAR.

[42] Hyman, *To Try Men's Souls*, 74-76.

[43] Oath of Allegiance, Rhode Island, 1775, APSED, Film 391, Reel 14, No. 1614, DLAR.

[44] Hyman, *To Try Men's Souls*, 75.

expedition, under Lee, imposed paroles not to convey intelligence to the enemy, to report

"treasonable Practices" that came to the juror's knowledge, to observe the laws and regulations of

the Continental Congress, and not to dissuade others from serving the American cause.[45]

Washington and Lee believed such tests should be imposed in every province.[46] But the civil

government of each province subjected to these expeditions protested, on the grounds that they

invaded civil authority and violated subjects' civil rights. The Continental Congress ultimately

adopted a resolution prohibiting further loyalty testing of the civilian population by the Continental

Army.[47]

Soon thereafter, the Declaration of Independence marked a turning point in the definition of

American allegiance and brought renewed civil loyalty testing throughout the new states.[48] The

Declaration itself was widely circulated as a loyalty test to be subscribed, superseding the Continental

Association before it.[49] Moreover, following the Declaration of Independence, the states

themselves, having now claimed sovereignty in their own right, abandoned their earlier reticence to

demand allegiance, matching the British in the imposition of formal oaths of abjuration and

allegiance. Beginning in the autumn of 1776, state governments once again established new oaths of

allegiance and oaths of office for civil and military leaders.[50] In September of 1776, for instance, the

New Jersey legislature passed an act directing that Justices of the Peace confront all those suspected

---

[45] Loyalty Oath, Long Island, 1776, BDSDS. 1776, AAS. In early March of 1776, Lord Stirling wrote from New York to the president of the New Jersey provincial congress that, "General Lee has thought it expedient that the enclosed test be offered to all suspected persons in this Province, and to remove all such as will not subscribe to it; and intends to have it immediately carried into execution." Stirling to Samuel Tucker, 5 March 1776, *AAO*, Series 4, V: 133.

[46] Hyman, *To Try Men's Souls*, 75-76.

[47] Hyman, *To Try Men's Souls*, 76-77.

[48] Jasanoff, *Liberty's Exiles*, 31. As Jasanoff points out, the American victory at Saratoga and the entry of France and Spain into the war deepened the division between Patriot and Loyalists and spurred new and more punitive test acts and acts providing for the arrest of Loyalists or the confiscation of their property (40).

[49] Hyman, *To Try Men's Souls*, 78.

[50] New Jersey established a new oath for state officials in September of 1776. Hyman, *To Try Men's Souls*, 81.

of disloyalty with an oath of allegiance, and that state officials and officers take oaths of office.[51] By

1778, every state had adopted an oath of allegiance to be subscribed by private citizens (not just

officeholders and officers).[52] Rhode Island, for instance, imposed an oath by which the juror swore

to "be True and faithful to the State of Rhode Island and Providence Plantations," to "demean

myself as a True and Faithful Subject thereof," and not to "convey Intelligence to or hold

correspondence with the Enemy or do any thing which shall have a Tendency to injure the said State

or either of the United States of America."[53] Like the Continental Association, these state oaths of

allegiance were imposed and enforced by committees of safety—with the assistance of the militia

and, sometimes, detachments of the Continental Army.[54]

Independence likewise renewed the need for certifying loyalties within the military

establishment, as well as among civilians. In the early autumn of 1776 General Gates wrote from

Ticonderoga to the President of the Continental Congress to recommend a new round of oaths for

officers and soldiers. "Your Excellency and the Congress will see clearly the Propriety," Gates

wrote, "of a Military Oath being administered to every Officer and soldier of the Army; especially

now, that the United States of America are wisely declared independent." He urged that, "we ought,

by every Method in our Power, to persuade our Friends as well as our Enemies, that we will support,

---

[51] *PWL*, I: 215n1: An Act for the Security of the Government of New Jersey, 19 September 1776, *Acts* (September 13, 1776-March 17, 1777), 2-3. Cf. Governor William Livingston's proclamation of 25 September 1776 empowering particular high officials of state to administer the oaths of office required by the above act of state civil and military officers. *PWL*, I: 152. See also Governor William Livingston's proclamation of 5 February 1777 "strictly charging and commanding" New Jersey justices of the peace who had been "remiss" in fulfilling their duty under this act to do so. *PWL*, I: 214-215. Cf. Livingston to John Witherspoon, 7 May 1777, on the institution of the Council of Safety in response to the failure of local magistrates to properly administer the "Treason Act." *PWL*, I: 322-324.

[52] Hyman, *To Try Men's Souls*, 85.

[53] Henry Northrup, Oath of Allegiance, Rhode Island Council of War, 31 December 1777, Records of the States of the United States, Rhode Island, 1775-1818, Film 285, E4, Reel 1, Minutes of the Council of War, DLAR. Thomas Cranston, Oath of Allegiance, Rhode Island Council of War, 7 January 1778, Records of the States of the United States, Rhode Island, 1775-1818, Film 285, E4, Reel 1, Minutes of the Council of War, DLAR. Cf. Rhode Island General Assembly, 9 February 1778, appointing a committee to draft a new "oath of fidelity and allegiance to this state." Bartlett ed., *Records of the State of Rhode Island*, VIII: 353.

[54] Hyman, *To Try Men's Souls*, 85-86.

and render permanent the noble Establishment of our Independence." "The Commission to each Officer," Gates advised, "should also correspond with the Oath, and be made subordinate to the Supreme Power of the Congress, under the new System." Any "Inconsistency…may turn to the Prejudice of those, whom the Fate of War may put into the Hands of the Enemy, and expose us to the just Censure of the Impartial."[55]

In October of 1776, the Continental Congress resolved that soldiers in the Continental Army must swear obedience to their officers and allegiance to the United States.[56] That same month they prescribed an oath of abjuration, allegiance, and faithful service for all Continental officials and officers.[57] In February of 1778, the Congress would adopt a new oath of office for Continental officials and military officers, now requiring the juror to acknowledge the independence of the United States; deny that the inhabitants thereof owed any allegiance to Great Britain; abjure personal allegiance to the King; swear to defend the United States against King George and his heirs; and swear to serve faithfully and to the best of his ability in his appointed office. The officers of the Continental Army took the new oath over the spring months of 1778, receiving certificates that they had done so.[58] These were issued sometimes using printed forms, sometimes in manuscript, the latter sometimes with significant variations in the oath's wording.[59] In March of 1778, for instance, Lafayette issued a manuscript certificate to Lieutenant William Stuart, on a slip of paper (roughly

---

[55] Gates to the President of Congress, 23 September 1776, Horatio Gates Papers, 1726-1828, Film 23, Reel 3 (Correspondence, July 1776 - October 1776), DLAR. Cf. Jacob Ford, Jr. to Governor William Livingston of New Jersey, proposing that the state's militia officers "Renew their Commissions and take an Oath of Test to the State," because, he believed, the loyalties of many were suspect and had not been properly tested as yet. *PWL*, I: 134-135.

[56] Hyman, *To Try Men's Souls*, 82.

[57] Waldenmaier, *Some of the Earliest Oaths*, 4.

[58] Hyman, *To Try Men's Souls*, 82-83; Waldenmaier, *Some of the Earliest Oaths*, 6-14. Cf. Josiah Harmar, Oath of Allegiance and Abjuration, 11 May 1778, Valley Forge, Josiah Harmar Papers, Volume 1, WLCL; Ebenezer Hazard, Oath of Allegiance, Abjuration, and Office, as Surveyor of the Post Offices and Post Roads, and Inspector of dead Letters to the General Post Office, 22 June 1778, Ebenezer Hazard Papers, Item 15, APS.

[59] Waldenmaier, *Some of the Earliest Oaths*, 7-9, 14. Cf. Washington, General Orders, 7 May 1778, announcing the oath and directing how it shall be administered, including the stipulation that, "The Generals administring the Oath are to take Duplicates of the same and to grant Certificates when it was made." *PGWDE*, Revolutionary, XV: 68-70.

two inches by six) certifying that Stuart "took, before me, the Oath of Allegiance to the United

States of America, [...] and Abjuration and Renunciation of Obedience or Allegiance to George the

Third, King of Great-Britain, according to the Resolutions of Congress of February the third,

1778."[60]

With each new round of loyalty testing among the civilian population, individuals were

required to report to a particular place, or were confronted by deputations moving door to door, and

required to take the oath in front of a designated official, either military or civil.[61] Often the

individual would be required to "subscribe" the oath—either signing his name or leaving his mark in

a register or on a copy of the oath. In the latter case, each subscriber might sign a separate copy, or

a group or queue of subscribers might sign a single copy. In some cases the authorities kept bound

volumes of sheets, each bearing several printed blanks of the prescribed oath, filled in succession

with name and date of appearance and subscribed with the signature or mark of the juror. On the

British side, several such volumes survive, for instance, recording oaths of allegiance to Britain made

in South Carolina in 1780 and 1781, including, usually, the date of the oath; the name of the juror;

sometimes the juror's occupation, trade, status (e.g. "Esqr."), or place of residence inserted with the

name in the form of the oath; the juror's signature; and the signature of the witnessing official.[62]

By imposing oaths of allegiance in this way and keeping the appropriate registers, the

authorities of either side were enabled to test the loyalties of the populace in a given area, at a given

---

[60] Lafayette, Certificate of Oath of Allegiance and Abjuration, Issued to William Stuart, 14 March 1778, Sol Feinstone Collection, Film 1, Reel 2, No. 723, DLAR. See Waldenmaier, *Some of the Earliest Oaths*, 15, for reference to another oath certificate issued by Lafayette.

[61] In the case of the Association, at least, mass swearing ceremonies had also sometimes been held. Hyman, *To Try Men's Souls*, 65.

[62] Great Britain. Colonial Office. South Carolina: Original Correspondence, Film 550b, Reel 14 (CO 5/527-535), CO 5/527-534, DLAR.

time, and sort out recusants. The resulting records, likewise, enabled the authorities to verify the

identity of an individual, at a later date, as a juror or non-juror—whether they still needed to take the

oath or already had; whether they should be treated as an enemy or a friend; with what privileges

and responsibilities they could be trusted; how much mobility they could be allowed if they

requested a pass. Such archives, however, could readily be consulted only by the immediate

authorities that held them and were, in any case, cumbersome to search.

To mobilize these records of oaths of allegiance, while securing individuals against repeated

harassment, and to allow multiple authorities to verify an individual's identity, officials on both sides

issued certificates attesting to each juror's oath.[63] Oaths and loyalty tests more generally were

increasingly receipted in various certificates as war got underway. Through these means the

identities defined in terms of ideology or allegiance became part of individuals' everyday practical

identities. Thus these certificates (and analogous documents) amalgamated with the proliferating

instruments of identification deployed in both civil and military spheres—not to mention persisting

regimes of slave and servant passes, freedom papers, cancelled indentures, and the like. Political

ideology had entered the realm of portable, legible identity for individual civilians.

The certificates in question often employed printed forms, with blanks completed by hand,

on small slips of paper—four by six inches, perhaps, at the largest. Surviving examples from

Pennsylvania feature ornamental borders surrounding a form certifying that the named individual,

whose occupation or residence was sometimes included, had "voluntarily taken and subscribed the

OATH of Allegiance and Fidelity as directed" in an act of the state Assembly. The certificate would

---

[63] The practice of requiring oaths of allegiance and of issuing certificates to the individual taking the oath continued in
some places for at least several years after the war. See John Gill, Certificate of Oath of Allegiance and Fidelity issued to
John Rhodes, Pennsylvania, 11 October 1785, Sol Feinstone Collection, Film 1, Reel 1, No. 381, DLAR. This certificate
is in the same form, both textually and materially, as the loyalty oath certificates issued during the war, especially in
Pennsylvania and was likely left over from batches of blanks printed during the war, though new printings may have
been made for post-war use. The text indicates that the oath taken was that mandated under the Act of General
Assembly passed 13 June 1777.

be dated and signed by the witnessing official, though often no seal was affixed. Instead, a printed placeholder—often "LS" inside a broken circle—was left unaltered. In some cases, the certificate was also numbered, to identify it as a unique instrument and to index it to an archive, as with "No. 818" issued by Plunk[e]t Fleeson to "Francis Allison Junr of Philadelphia Physician" on August 14[th], 1777, under the act of 13 June 1777.[64] New batches of very similar certificate forms were printed and employed under succeeding test acts.[65] In October of 1779, for instance, Fleeson issued a certificate to John Fryhoffer, using a form very similar to that for the certificate issued to Allison, but this time under the act of 5 December 1778.[66] Local variations abounded. In Barstable, Massachusetts, for instance, in April of 1778, Justice of the Peace Nathaniel Freeman issued a manuscript certificate, bearing his signature and his seal, declaring that, "On the 30th Day of March AD 1778. Personally appeard Revd. A. Williams & Voluntarily took ye Oath of Alligiance to this State before me the Subscriber."[67]

Loyalty oath certificates were to be kept, if not carried, by the individual to exhibit to inquiring authorities. The liabilities involved in not presenting such certificates discouraged the individuals from casting off the labels constituted by the documents, except when confronted by agents of the other side or when hoping to shift allegiance. A November 1776 act of the Rhode

---

[64] Fleeson, Certificate of oath of allegiance by Francis Allison, Jr., 14 August 1777, [Philadelphia?], Sol Feinstone Collection, Film 1, Reel 4, No. 2035, DLAR. See also the very similar certificate, under the act of 13 June 1777, issued after the war by John Gill, J.P., to John Rhodes, 11 October 1785, Sol Feinstone Collection, Film 1, Reel 1, No. 381., DLAR; and Henry Slagle, Certificate of Oath of Allegiance by Henry Sprinkle, 10 June 1778, York, Pennsylvania, under act of 13 June 1777, printed by Hall and Sellers, sm # Am 1778 Penn Gen Ass 15615.Q (Zinman), LCP.

[65] In October of 1783, shortly after the close of the war, Lieutenant Colonel Josiah Harmar was issued one such certificate after swearing and signing the oath of allegiance prescribed by the act of the Pennsylvania General Assembly passed December 5th, 1778. Certificate of oath of allegiance for Josiah Harmar, 6 October 1783, Philadelphia, Josiah Harmar Papers, Volume 1, WLCL. See also, in this same volume, Harmar's oath of abjuration of allegiance to George III, allegiance to the U.S., and oath of office as Lieutenant Colonel, 11 May 1778, Valley Forge, PA.

[66] Fleeson, Certificate of Oath of Allegiance by John Fryhoffer, 19 October 1779, sm # Am 1779 Penn Gen Ass 15621.Q (Zinman), LCP.

[67] Freeman, Certificate of Oath of Allegiance for Rev. A. Williams, 13 April 1778, Barnstable, MA, M-4190.1.2, MR: Single Items [uncatalogued], WLCL. Thank you to Curator of Manuscripts Barbara de Wolfe for brining this item to my attention.

Island General Assembly, for instance, suspended or reversed the execution of previous legal

judgments—and prohibited further such judgments—in favor of any person who had not,

"subscribed the test prescribed by an act of this state, or…taken the affirmation, or produced the

proper certificate by said act required."[68] The following March, the General Assembly resolved that,

since many of the state's inhabitants had refused to swear the prescribed oath "or produce a

certificate, agreeably to the requisitions of said act," and had "thereby manifested themselves

unfriendly to the liberties of this, and the other United States," therefore those inhabitants were not

to be "permitted in future to subscribe said test, or declaration, without permission first had from

this Assembly."[69] Once certified, political identity was not to be shed at convenience.

Where certificates were unavailable, individuals on both sides of the conflict looked to

instruments of their own devising, with varying degrees of success. Loyalist Alexander Pepperrell,

for instance, having finally secured from the Continental Congress "leave to quit America" in early

1777, after a year and a half as a prisoner in New Hampshire, was soon captured by the British ship

HMS *Grey-Hound* on his way to British-held New York City in his newly purchased ship, bearing a

cargo of lumber. Taken to New York, Pepperrell saw his ship and cargo sold off and himself

---

[68] *An Act in addition to an act, entitled "An act empowering the members of the upper and lower houses of Assembly, to tender to such of the inhabitants as are herein mentioned a declaration or test, for subscription,"* 21 November 1776, Bartlett ed., *Records of the State of Rhode Island*, VIII: 39. Cf. the 9 February 1778 resolution of the Rhode Island General Assembly providing that those who had not taken the prescribed test oath or affirmation be excluded from jury duty. Bartlett ed., *Records of the State of Rhode Island*, VIII: 352.

[69] Rhode Island General Assembly, 24 March 1777, Bartlett ed., *Records of the State of Rhode Island*, VIII: 187. Cf. Rhode Island General Assembly, 18 August 1777, granting permission to Clark Brown to subscribe the test and initiating a thirty day period during which anyone who has not previously subscribed may do so, after which special permission will once again be required. Bartlett ed., *Records of the State of Rhode Island*, VIII: 291; Rhode Island General Assembly, 29 December 1777, granting permission to Caleb Remington to take the test oath, Records of the States of the United States, Rhode Island, 1775-1818, Film 285, E4, Reel 1, Minutes of the Council of War, DLAR; Rhode Island General Assembly, 8 January 1778, granting permission to John C. Greene to take the test oath, Records of the States of the United States, Rhode Island, 1775-1818, Film 285, E4, Reel 1, Minutes of the Council of War, DLAR; Rhode Island General Assembly, 14 April 1778, permission to the freemen of Tiverton and Little Compton who have not subscribed the test act to do so, Records of the States of the United States, Rhode Island, 1775-1818, Film 285, E4, Reel 1, Minutes of the Council of War, DLAR; Rhode Island General Assembly, 6 May 1778, setting a final deadline of September 1st to subscribe the test act, except for those currently minors or serving in the army or at sea, Bartlett ed., *Records of the State of Rhode Island*, VIII: 405-406.

"deprived of every thing but my cloaths," all this "notwithstanding I produced letters from Colo. Campbell and others, showing my loyalty & attachment to Government, and that what I had done was by their advice and recommendation."[70]

Those who could not or would not identify themselves wholly with one side or another often found navigating the Revolutionary crisis of identification challenging, if not impossible. Conscientious objectors—including Quakers, Moravians, and others—were perhaps the most afflicted. In some places their refusal to fight, or sometimes even declare, for one side or the other cast them into the ranks of the enemy, or at least of suspected persons, and earned them treatment as prisoners of war.[71] In other places, provisions were made to accommodate such convictions— even providing instruments of identification to certify certain individuals' distinctive standing and exemption, on stipulated terms, from some of the duties of citizenship or subjecthood. New York, for instance, eventually accommodated its Quaker residents' unwillingness to swear oaths by allowing twelve non-Quakers to swear as proxies in place of each inoffensive Quaker.[72] But such provisions often did not fully resolve unease over liminal political identities. Thus, in April of 1777, there came before the Rhode Island Council of War the case of Isaac Walling of Gloucester, who had been drafted for militia duty and, when he refused to comply, had "some of his Stock…seized for Fines." Walling "shewed a Certificate, dated in Smithfield March 1. 1777. Signed by John Sayles Esq. Assistant, that he…had taken the Affirmation prescribed by a late Act of this State in Case of Tender Consciences" and requested "Relief." The certificate he had exhibited to the Council had

---

[70] A. Pepperrell to the Earl of Dartmouth, 15 May 1778, Craven Street, London, APSED, Film 391, Reel 16, No. 1862, DLAR. Pepperrell enclosed in his letter to Dartmouth two of the letters of recommendation he had vainly proffered to his British captors in New York "for your Lordships perusal," renewing these letters' functions as instruments of identification. For letters of recommendation secured by another Loyalist fleeing America, see Moses Kirkland to the Earl of Dartmouth, 20 September 1775, APSED, Film 391, Reel 14, No. 1526, DLAR.

[71] See Robert F. Oaks, "Philadelphians in Exile: The Problem of Loyalty during the American Revolution," *Pennsylvania Magazine of History and Biography*, Vol. 96, No. 3 (Jul., 1972), 298-319.

[72] Hyman, *To Try Men's Souls*, 91.

evidently been insufficient to satisfy the local officials who had drafted him for service. The Council, for its part, ordered that Walling's seized property not be sold until the General Assembly could give a judgment in the case, while specifying that the property remained liable to sale if the Assembly did not deign to grant Walling the relief he sought.[73]

That loyalty testing and certification functioned as an integrated system is suggested by a variety of state laws and enforcement measures. In May of 1777, for instance, the Virginia legislature passed an act declaring that "all free born male inhabitants of this state, above the age of sixteen years, except imported servants during the time of their service" were to swear and sign an oath prescribed by the act before the tenth of October. The oath could be taken before any local Justice of the Peace, who was to "give a certificate thereof"—dated, signed, and sealed— "to every such person" who swore and subscribed the oath. The Justice of the Peace was directed to "keep fair registers of the names of the persons so sworn or affirmed, and the time when," and to submit each year to the clerk of the county court "a true list of the names" of those sworn the preceding year, certified by his signature and seal. In the meantime, each county court was to "appoint some of their members to make a tour of the county, and tender the oath or affirmation" to those required to take it. They were to report "the names of such as refuse" to take the oath or affirmation to the county commander of the militia, who was to disarm the "recusants."

Besides parsing the loyalties of Virginia inhabitants in this manner, thereby documenting identities, the act instituted surveillance of strangers and suspicious persons. It directed "that all persons coming from any other of the United States into this state"—with the exception of prisoners of war, state or Continental officers and soldiers, and non-resident merchants and

---

[73] Rhode Island Council of War, Resolution re Isaac Walling 1 April 1777, Records of the States of the United States, Rhode Island, 1775-1818, Film 285, E4, Reel 1, Minutes of the Council of War, DLAR.

mariners belonging to "foreign powers in amity with the United States" and trading in the state's ports—were "to apply to one of the nearest justices after he enters this state," before whom they were to "take or subscribe an oath or affirmation, renouncing all allegiance to the king of Great Britain, and promising that he will not do any thing prejudicial to the independence of the United States of America, as declared by the General Congress." If they failed to comply, they were to be brought before a justice and tendered the oath. If they refused the oath, they were to be jailed until they did so or gave bond to leave the state.[74]

In New York, oaths of allegiance were drafted, imposed, and policed by a Committee for Detecting and Defeating Conspiracies, first established in September of 1776 and re-established, on a permanent basis, in mid 1778, as a Commission. In cooperation with local committees, the state militia, its own military company, and detachments of the Continental Army, the Commission scrutinized the New York populace, tendered the oath of allegiance, compiled lists of non-jurors, and punished those who refused to subscribe the required oaths or were otherwise judged to be disloyal. Subscription of the Commission's oath was ultimately made a prerequisite for suffrage, office, licensed professions, residence, and citizenship.[75] New Jersey's Council of Safety similarly oversaw oaths of allegiance and the disposition of those who refused to subscribe them.[76] Some, like Ezekiel Beech, who refused the oath, chose exile within the British lines in New York.[77] Some, like Richard Lewis, arrested for violating state pass laws, were released upon "taking the Oaths of

---

[74] *An act to oblige the free male inhabitants of this state above a certain age to give assurance of allegiance to the same, and for other purposes*, May 1777, Williamsburg, VA, *EAI*, Series 1, no. 15693 (filmed).

[75] On the activities of the Commission see Hyman, *To Try Men's Souls*, 88-90.

[76] The Council of Safety was instituted for this purpose after local justices of the peace had failed to satisfactorily carry out a charge to administer such oaths. See Livingston to John Witherspoon, 7 May 1777, *PWL*, I: 322-324.

[77] New Jersey Council of Safety, 20 January 1778, Records of the States of the United States, New Jersey, 1681-1786, Film 281, Reel 1, Minutes of the Council of Safety, DLAR.

Abjuration & Allegiance as by Law [prescribed]."[78] Others were simply taken into custody to have

the oaths tendered to them and were released once they had sworn and subscribed.[79]

The governments restored or established in British-occupied regions and cities like New

York, Philadelphia, and Charleston likewise often administered oaths of allegiance and issued

certificates to those who wished to declare and document their enduring or renewed loyalties to the

King, outside the provisions of particular amnesty proclamations. As early as May of 1777, the

Mayor of the City of New York, from which the rebel army had been driven the previous autumn,

was issuing loyalty oath certificates—including, apparently, to Loyalist refugees from New Jersey—

using printed forms, completed by hand and bearing his signature at bottom, that certified that the

named individual had "in my Presence, voluntarily taken an OATH, to bear Faith and true

Allegiance to HIS MAJESTY KING George the Third;—and to defend to the utmost of his Power,

his sacred Person, Crown and Government, against all Persons whatsoever."[80] In another instance,

though few of the corresponding certificates seem to have survived, the volumes recording oaths of

allegiance to Britain in South Carolina for 1780 and 1781 in some cases noted in the margin that a

"Certificate" was issued on a given date. While in some of the volumes occasional notations of this

sort were made in manuscript on an ad hoc basis, in others a printed blank for the date of the

certificate granted was included in the margin.[81] In some cases the process of granting certificates

<hr>

[78] New Jersey Council of Safety, 20 January 1778, Records of the States of the United States, New Jersey, 1681-1786, Film 281, Reel 1, Minutes of the Council of Safety, DLAR.

[79] New Jersey Council of Safety, 20 January 1778, Case of Andrew Mills, Records of the States of the United States, New Jersey, 1681-1786, Film 281, Reel 1, Minutes of the Council of Safety, DLAR. Cf. New Jersey Council of Safety, 21 January 1778, Cases of Frederick Cole and Abraham Man, required to post bond as well for appearance at a subsequent court, Records of the States of the United States, New Jersey, 1681-1786, Film 281, Reel 1, Minutes of the Council of Safety, DLAR; New Jersey Council of Safety, 26 January 1778, Cases of Enoch and Isaac Vreeland, Records of the States of the United States, New Jersey, 1681-1786, Film 281, Reel 1, Minutes of the Council of Safety, DLAR.

[80] See five such certificates issued to residents of Bergen County, 15 May 1777 (according to the date of four of the five certificates, the other lacking a date), Sir Henry Clinton Papers, Volume 21, Folder 9, WLCL.

[81] For examples of individual, ad hoc manuscript notations regarding the issuance of certificates, see Great Britain. Colonial Office. South Carolina: Original Correspondence, Film 550b, Reel 14 (CO 5/527-535), CO 5/533, ff. 46,

was iterative, one certificate based upon another. Thus the manuscript notation in the margin of the oath of allegiance form for John Ray, dated the 31st of May 1781, recorded that, "[Ray] Produced a Certificate of having taken the Oath—a Certificate Granted."[82]

The form of a loyalty oath certificate issued to John Pamor, Sr., in Charleston, South Carolina, in February of 1781 makes explicit the value attached to such certificates in themselves as evidence of loyalty on an ongoing basis. The certificate likewise illustrates the iterative constructions of identities through multiple instruments of identification. Pamor signed an oath of allegiance, made out in manuscript, to the British King. He was then issued a certificate, using a printed form, filled in by hand, under the name of Lieutenant Colonel Nisbet Balfour, Commandant of Charleston, and witnessed by militia Captain Thomas Walker, who had witnessed Pamor's subscription of the oath itself. The document stated that the recipient had presented to Balfour "a Memorial…setting forth that he was very desirous to have it in his power to show every mark of allegiance and affection to his Majesty's present government, to which he was most sincerely well affected; and humbly praying that he might have an opportunity to evince the sincerity of his professions." "The said Memorial," the form continued, "was referred to persons of loyalty and integrity, well acquainted with the characters and past conduct of the inhabitants," who had "reported in favour" of the recipient. The instrument certified that the bearer had subscribed a "declaration of his being a true and faithful subject" and concluded by declaring the recipient "restored to the free exercise of his trade or profession, and the full privileges enjoyed by the loyal

---

DLAR. For volumes with the printed form for noting the issuance of certificates, see Great Britain. Colonial Office. South Carolina: Original Correspondence, Film 550b, Reel 14 (CO 5/527-535), CO 5/530-531, DLAR. On the British imposition of oaths of allegiance, cf. Jasanoff, *Liberty's Exiles*, 45.

[82] Great Britain. Colonial Office. South Carolina: Original Correspondence, Film 550b, Reel 14 (CO 5/527-535), CO 5/533, ff. 46, DLAR.

inhabitants of Charles-Town."[83] This instrument was to constitute in practice an identity as a recognized and pardoned subject of the King with whom others bearing an analogous identity could legitimately deal commercially or professionally. The instrument constituted, in the eyes of the British authorities, the reborn social personhood of the bearer and his identity as a member of the community whose representatives recognized him as such.

As wider swathes of territory and population were subsumed in the theater of war, the mobile military governments on each side needed instruments by which to identify, in a durable fashion, particular categories of civilians. On both sides, though especially on the British one, moreover, there was often little distinction between the military and the government in active theaters of war. Loyalty testing administered by the military often blurred into new rounds of civil loyalty testing as a given region came under control of one side or another. Perhaps most importantly, in the midst of a civil war that required each side to build and sustain loyalty among the populace, it was crucial to secure civilians from harassment or abuse by soldiers and officials. Likewise, only by offering some mechanism through which they could expect security would each side be able to lure new constituents.

Both sides, to disparate degrees, turned to instruments of identification to accomplish these ends. Typical of such instruments was a minimal form of a safe-conduct, often, but not always, certifying an oath of allegiance and requiring the subordinates of the issuing authority not to harm or distress the bearer. British military authorities began issuing such protections in return for oaths of allegiance from the civilian population at least as early as the invasion of Long Island in August of 1776. During the long British occupation of New York, loyalty oath or protection certificates would

---

[83] Balfour and Walker, Certificate of Loyalty of John Pamor, Sr., 24 February 1781, Charleston, SC, Great Britain. Colonial Office. South Carolina: Original Correspondence, Film 550b, Reel 14 (CO 5/527-535), CO 5/532, folios 80 and 81, DLAR.

be made prerequisites for vital supplies, privileges from the military and civil authorities, protection

of property, and participation in the local wartime government. Throughout the war, in the several

theatres, such certificates would prove, at best, unreliable protection from distrustful or

unscrupulous Loyalist raiders and plundering soldiers, and at worst constituted markers of disloyalty

when Patriots regained control of a given region. Nevertheless, the British deployed and civilians

sought these protections with each new occupation and campaign.[84] American military and, to a

greater extent, civilian authorities issued their own such protections in turn.

A good example of this practice can be seen in the New Jersey campaigns of the winter of

1776-1777, "the times that try men's souls," in Tom Paine's famous words. A sizeable cluster—at

least thirty—of British loyalty oath or protection certificates has survived from the British Army's

occupation of New Jersey in the latter months of 1776. Having chased Washington's army across

New Jersey and beyond, to the far side of the Delaware River, securing the province for the crown,

British and Hessian officers, left in command of the occupying forces by General Cornwallis for the

winter of 1776-1777, quickly began to administer oaths of allegiance and issue corresponding

certificates to the inhabitants of New Jersey—identified in the certificates by name, residence, and

occupation—who came forward, under the terms of General Howe's proclamation of November

30th, 1776, to declare themselves loyal subjects all along or to claim amnesty.[85] In one typical

example, General James Grant issued a signed certificate on the 12th of December "that the Bearer

Benjamin Hart has taken the Oath agreeable to the Proclamation of the 30th. November 1776." The

---

[84] Hyman, *To Try Men's Souls*, 98-105. On plundering of Loyalists by British troops despite protection certificates, cf. Van Tyne, *Loyalists*, 247.

[85] See, e.g., James Grant, Certificates of Oath taken under the Proclamation of 30 November 1776, Issued to Benjamin Hart, Farmer of Trenton, to David Howell, Ferryman of Trenton, 12 December 1776, Sol Feinstone Collection, Film 1, Reel 1, Nos. 522, 565, DLAR. On British and American loyalty testing in New Jersey, 1776-1777, see also Hyman, *To Try Men's Souls*, 78-82.

document further identified Hart by his occupation and place of resident—a "Farmer of Trenton."[86]

This and other certificates issued in the same or similar form were instruments meant to be borne—

deployed by "the Bearer"—to certify the jurors' official loyalties and legal status and thereby secure

them immunity from any affiliate of the issuing authority whom they might encounter.

Other New Jersey loyalty certificates made explicit that the bearer was not to be harmed or

harassed. This was crucial in New Jersey, where complaints were common that both Loyalist and

rebel troops and partisans, but particularly Britain's Hessian mercenaries, plundered the inhabitants

(when they did not do worse) without distinguishing political allegiances.[87] Rather than certifying

that the prescribed oath of allegiance had been taken and leaving the corollary of safe conduct

implicit, these variants centered on the function of the instrument as a safe conduct, leaving the fact

of the prerequisite oath marginal to the document. The text of the safe conduct issued by Hessian

Colonel Rall to Joshua Howell in December of 1776 was typical, declaring, over Rall's signature,

that, "Tis his Excellency General Howes express orders that no person presume on any account to

molest or injure Joshua Howell in his person or property."[88] The safe conduct issued to Thomas

---

[86] Grant, Certificate of oath of allegiance for Benjamin Hart, 12 December 1776, Sol Feinstone Collection, Film 1, Reel 1, No. 522. See also Grant's certificate of the same date and in the same form issued to David Howell, a "Ferry Man of Trenton," Sol Feinstone Collection, Film 1, Reel 1, No. 565, DLAR. For similar examples, see Grant, Certificate of oath of allegiance for Archibald William Yard, 30 November 1776, Trenton, NJ; Grant, Certificate of oath of allegiance for Timothy Howell, 30 November 1776; Grant, Certificate of oath of allegiance for Samuel Hill, 12 December 1776, U.S. Revolution Collection, Box 2, Folder 5, AAS.

[87] Van Tyne, *Loyalists*, 248. See also Governor William Livingston's proclamation of 5 February 1777 against the practice of militia detachments seizing property from residents both suspected and beyond suspicion. *PWL*, I: 214-215.

[88] Rall, Safe Conduct for Joshua Howell, December 1776, Sol Feinstone Collection, Film 1, Reel 3, No. 1179, DLAR. See also, Safe Conduct for William Jones; Safe Conduct for John Stevens; Safe Conduct for Benjamin Aarenson, December 1776, Trenton, NJ; Safe Conduct for John Aarenson, December 1776, Trenton, NJ; Safe Conduct for [Timothy Howell?]; Safe Conduct for John Cubberly; Safe Conduct for James Cubberly; Safe Conduct for Marmaduke Watson; Safe Conduct for Samuel Hill; Safe Conduct for Daniel Hutchinson, 12 December 1776; Henry Knight, Safe Conduct for Elijah Lanning, 13 December 1776; Rall, Safe Conduct for William Harcourt, 14 December 1776; Henry Knight, Safe Conduct for Samuel Obdyhe, 15 December 1776; John Hinricks, Safe Conduct for Moses Clayton, 17 December 1776; Hinricks, Safe Conduct for John Cox, 17 December 1776; de Gotterhall, Safe Conduct for Thomas Cox, 18 December 1776. U.S. Revolution Collection, Box 2, Folder 5, AAS. John Montressor, Safe Conduct for Thomas Hutchinson, December 1776, Sol Feinstone Collection, Film 1, Reel 2, No. 953, DLAR; Rall, Safe Conduct for Jeremiah Anderson, December 1776, Sol Feinstone Collection, Film 1, Reel 3, No. 1178, DLAR. See also, [Knox?], Safe Conduct for John Hall, 12 December 1776, Howe Papers, WLCL.

Emley on the 16th of December by J[ames?] Gamble adopted a similar form, heading the instrument

with the label "Protection," and declaring that, "All Officers Soldiers or Followers of the Armey are

hereby Strictly Forbiden to Molist or injure Thomas Emley of Burlington County in the Province of

New Jersey Famely or property as they will Answer the Same at their peril."[89] If loyalty oath

certificates were one side of the coin, these safe conducts were the other. In some instances this was

very nearly literally the case, with a safe conduct on one side of the paper and a loyalty oath

certificate on the other, as in the instrument issued to Andrew M[erson?] on December 12th, 1776.[90]

These instruments took a variety of forms. The certificates issued of both types were

sometimes wholly in manuscript, sometimes printed forms filled in by hand.[91] They were sometimes

issued only in English, with or without the countersignature of a Hessian officer that might be

recognized by Hessian troops encountering the bearer.[92] Sometimes they were issued with the text

in English on one side or at the top and the same text in German on the back or at the bottom.[93]

---

[89] Gamble, Safe Conduct for Thomas Emley, 16 December 1776, Bordentown, NJ, U.S. Revolution Collection, Box 2, Folder 5, AAS. For another of these instruments employing the label "Protection," see, de Gotterhall, Safe Conduct for Thomas Cox, 18 December 1776, in the same folder. For a "Protection," using the same language, but this time using a printed form, filled in by hand, see Robert Mackenzie, Safe Conduct for Benjamin Smith, 24 December 1776, Princeton, NJ, Sol Feinstone Collection, Film 1, Reel 2, No. 863, DLAR. Cf. John Duychinck's account of how, having been an American militia officer, he crossed into British lines and accepted a British protection when British forces came to New Jersey and took control of the majority of his property. Duychinck to Greene, 26 September 1777, Papers of Elias Boudinot, 1773-1812, Library of Congress, Film 732, Reel 1, DLAR. On Duychinck's case, cf. Richard K. Showman ed., *Papers of General Nathanael Greene,* (Chapel Hill, NC: University of North Carolina Press, 1976-2005), II: 166-167.

[90] J. Tinker, Safe Conduct and Certificate of oath of allegiance, 12 December 1776, U.S. Revolution Collection, Box 2, Folder 5, AAS.

[91] For such an instrument issued using a printed form, filled in by hand, see Robert Mackenzie, [Safe Conduct?] for Samuel Rogers, 14 December 1776, U.S. Revolution Collection, Box 2, Folder 5, AAS. See also, Mackenzie, Safe Conduct for Benjamin Smith, 24 December 1776, Princeton, NJ, Sol Feinstone Collection, Film 1, Reel 2, No. 863, DLAR.

[92] For such instruments with countersignatures or certificates by Hessian officers, see Henry Knight, Safe Conduct for Elijah Lanning, 13 December 1776; Knight, Safe Conduct for Samuel Obdyhe, 15 December 1776, Bordentown, NJ. U.S. Revolution Collection, Box 2, Folder 5, AAS. John Montressor, Safe Conduct for Thomas Hutchinson, December 1776, Sol Feinstone Collection, Film 1, Reel 2, No. 953, DLAR. See also [Knox?], Safe Conduct for John Hall, 12 December 1776, Howe Papers, WLCL.

[93] See Safe Conduct for Marmaduke Watson, U.S. Revolution Collection, Box 2, Folder 5, AAS.

Some were issued entirely in German.[94] They were predominantly quite small—slips about two

inches by five. They were brief in their text and offered a minimum of identifying information—

typically name, residence, and occupation or trade—and either a single signature or a signature plus

countersignature to serve as authentication. They seem never to have merited seals. These

certificates were often issued on neatly cut slips prepared, most likely, in advance, or on printed

forms made to order. But they were on occasion scribbled out on scraps torn from larger sheets or

from ledgers, pay tables, muster rolls, or other forms and record books ready to hand (sometimes

with the lines marking off columns visible under the text of the certificate), whether as a way of

coping with shortages of paper and blank forms or else expressing an ad hoc approach.[95]

These certificates were, in essence, labels to aid the institutional memory of the British Army

and the imperial and colonial governments—small slips of paper effectively pinned to the locals like

a naturalist's specimen card to make visible who was who and to mark off which individuals had

been properly examined. The small size, fragility, lack of full standardization, sometimes casual or

sloppy form, and the fleeting circumstances under which they were issued suggest the ephemeral

nature of these certificates. They were meant to be temporary, interim instruments to meet

immediate contingencies and imperatives.

However ephemeral the instruments, they constituted a great deal of paperwork and

represented a considerable investment of time and effort. British General James Grant noted at

Brunswick, New Jersey, in December of 1776 that though the people "in this Rebell Province…are

at least as violent as the Inhabitants of the New England Government," yet, "many of them from

---

[94] See Robert Mackenzie, [Safe Conduct?] for Samuel Rogers, 14 December 1776, U.S. Revolution Collection, Box 2, Folder 5, AAS.

[95] For an example of a manuscript instrument of this sort written on what appears to be a slip cut from a ledger or muster roll, see Colonel Rall, Safe Conduct and Loyalty Oath Certificate, December 1776 / February 1777, Sol Feinstone Collection, Film 1, Reel 3, No. 1179, DLAR. See also, for another such example, [Knox?], Safe Conduct for John Hall, 12 December 1776, Howe Papers, WLCL.

fear & for protection—come in to sign the Declaration of the 30th: of November so I am constantly employ'd in making Friends to Government tho' I believe them to be very bad Subjects."[96] (Grant clearly entertained no illusions that the formal re-identification effected by these oaths bespoke changes in political conviction.) Ambrose Serle, likewise, back in New York City in late 1776 and early 1777—when Grant was issuing certificates in New Jersey—remarked in a January letter to Lord Dartmouth how, "my Time is exceedingly taken up in making out Pardons for Rebels, who are coming in for them by Hundreds."[97]

Soon, Washington and his army, after re-crossing the Delaware on Christmas 1776, pushed the British forces back across much of New Jersey. Despite previous conflicts with civil authorities over loyalty testing by the Continental Army, by the end of January 1777, to counteract the British amnesty and loyalty testing, Washington had proclaimed his own amnesty and instituted new rounds of American loyalty testing in the portions of New Jersey he controlled. Those who had taken the British oaths and accepted British protections, along with the populace more generally, were given thirty days to swear (or re-swear) allegiance to the United States and receive in turn protection for their persons and property.[98] Washington established no standard oath for this test, and the officers administering it were left to formulate texts to meet the circumstances.[99] How widely these oaths varied and how many forms the written instruments took is unclear. Some examples survive, however. On February 22, for instance, a few days before the amnesty period expired, Anthony Cook of Hunterdon County subscribed his name to a slip of paper bearing a manuscript oath by which he declared that, "I will bear full faith and true Allegiance to the United States of North

---

[96] Grant to _____, 26 December 1776, Brunswick, NJ, Papers of James Grant of Ballindalloch, 1740-1819, Army Career Series (1740-1805), Film 687, Reel 28, Letterbook 2, DLAR.

[97] Serle to Dartmouth, 1 January 1777, APSED, Film 391, Reel 15, No. 1727, DLAR.

[98] Hyman, *To Try Men's Souls*, 79-80. See also, *PWL*, I: 251n2.

[99] Hyman, *To Try Men's Souls*, 80-81.

America And Will to the Utmost of my power Maintain the Independence of the Same as declared by the Hond Continental Congress."[100]

Washington found, to his frustration, that many who had accepted British amnesty and protection certificates during the British occupation, even when they had done so under duress, now scrupled to recant their oaths of allegiance to the King. Washington explained in a letter to John Hancock that though,

> The People generally confess they were compelled to take protection and subscribe the declaration, yet it furnishes many with Arguments to refuse taking any active part; and further they alledge themselves bound to a neutrality at least. Many conscientious People who were well wishers to the Cause had they been bound to the States by an Oath, would have suffered any Punishment rather than have taken the Oath of Allegiance to the King, and are now lost to our Interest, for want of this necessary tie. Notwithstanding the Obligation of the Association, they do not conceive it to have the same effect of an Oath.

Washington judged that they had lost a significant advantage by allowing the British to be the first to tender oaths of allegiance in New Jersey, and he urged that the remaining states should adopt oaths before the British could usurp them. "I have often thought," he wrote, "the States have been too negligent in this particular and am more fully convinced of it from the Effect Genl Howe's excursion has produced in New Jersey." From these recent lessons and the experience of generations stretching back to "the first institution of civil Government," Washington urged "every State to fix upon some Oath or Affirmation of Allegiance to be tendered to all the Inhabitants without exception, and to out law those that refuse it."[101]

Meanwhile, the British army continued to shore up loyalties among the inhabitants of those portions of New Jersey it still controlled. Many of the certificates and safe conducts issued in

---

[100] Anthony Cook, Oath of Allegiance, 22 February 1777, U.S. Revolution Collection, Box 3, Folder 1, AAS. Thomas Stevens subscribed an oath in the same language on this same date. Thomas Stevens, Oath of Allegiance, 22 February 1777, U.S. Revolution Collection, Box 3, Folder 1, AAS.

[101] Washington to Hancock, 5 February 1777, *PGWDE*, Revolutionary, VIII: 249-253. Cf. Washington to William Livingston, 16 April 1777, regarding the case of Colonel Duychink and suspicions concerning the motives of those seeking to swear the American oath under Washington's amnesty, as well as the question of swearing the American oath after having sworn the British oath. *PWL*, I: 308-309.

November and December 1776 by British officers in New Jersey would now become compound instruments of identification, as certificates of later oaths were added to the safe conducts. A large majority of the documents issued by Grant and other British and Hessian officers during the winter of 1776-1777 bear notations on the reverse attesting to the named individual having subsequently sworn another oath (the notation bearing a date distinct from the original date of the instrument). Many of these notations on instruments dated originally in late 1776 indicate that the subsequent oaths were sworn near the end of the winter or early the following spring, especially February of 1777.[102] These notations made the original instruments into certificates of two distinct identities. They documented compliance with two different rounds of loyalty testing and, possibly, two different legal moments, embodying a portion of the bearer's personal history and perhaps imbuing the instrument's certification of professed loyalty with additional weight.

On the American side, Washington's loyalty testing in New Jersey had met renewed objections from civil authorities. For the remainder of the war, the Continental Army refrained from imposing distinct loyalty tests on the civilian population. Nor would the Continental Congress establish a civilian loyalty test, which it left to state and local civil authorities, though the Continental Army sometimes assisted in the implementation of state test acts.[103] The British Army faced no such opposition or constraints and would continue to administer loyalty tests to civilians in occupied territory for the remainder of the war.

Much the same practices as were employed in New Jersey were repeated by the British in subsequent campaigns. When British forces under Archibald Campbell gained the upper hand over the rebels in Georgia in late 1778 and early 1779, Campbell and his naval counterpart Admiral

---

[102] See, for some among the many examples, the certificates, referenced above and below, in U.S. Revolution Collection, Box 2, Folder 5, AAS.

[103] Hyman, *To Try Men's Souls*, 82, 95. Cf. Richard B. Morris, *The Forging of the Union, 1781-1789*, (New York: HarperCollins, 1988), 74-76. See also William Livingston to John Witherspoon, 7 May 1777, requesting a detachment of Continental soldiers to assist and protect the New Jersey Council of Safety. *PWL*, I: 322-324.

Parker issued a proclamation offering amnesty or, in the case of consistent Loyalists, protection in return for an oath of allegiance to the King and abjuration of allegiance to the Continental Congress. Campbell soon reported the great success of this measure to his superior in New York, Sir Henry Clinton, describing how, "the Inhabitants, from all parts of the Province flock, with their Arms to the Standard, and cordially embrace the benevolent Terms which have been offerd." Campbell set up patrols of Loyalist units and militia to secure the province from the enemy, and offered rewards for the capture of "every Committee and Assembly Man" and "every Lurking Villain who might be sent from Carolina to Molest the Inhabitants."[104] Those who complied with the terms of the amnesty were issued instruments certifying their oaths of allegiance and abjuration, promising protection, and authorizing them to reside and travel within prescribed limits—thus combining the multiple functions of a loyalty oath certificate, safe conduct, parole, and pass. These instruments used a printed form produced for the purpose. The top half of the form gave the text of the oath, with a blank where the name of the juror was to be inserted. The bottom half, addressed "To all Officers, Civil and Military," and dated at Savannah in 1779, in a month and on a day to be inserted in each case, declared the specific rights privileges that the bearer was to be granted.[105]

Ultimately, neither side could give much credit to loyalty oath certificates as proofs of actual loyalty, having seen so many Americans swear multiple successive and contradictory oaths, switching their allegiances back and forth, or wait until circumstances compelled or opportunity enticed them to declare any allegiance at all. Why then did these certificates matter? Because they were

---

[104] Campbell to Clinton, 16 January 1779, Savannah, GA, Sir Henry Clinton Papers, Volume 52, Folder 4, WLCL.

[105] Form of a Loyalty Oath Certificate, 1779, Savannah, GA, Sir Henry Clinton Papers, Volume 52, Folder 5, WLCL. Somewhat unusually, the blanks left in this form for variant pronouns suggests the possibility that women (presumably adult and unmarried) might be tendered the oath and issued this instrument, though it is possible these blanks were meant simply to accommodate the possibility of including more than one man on a single instrument, which was done in some similar instruments, in some cases, requiring plural pronouns.

foundational to the Revolutionary practice of identification in their particular moment,
distinguishing as well as possible one side from the other, friend from foe, "American" citizen from
British subject. They embodied practical political identities in the midst of a civil war, tying
individual identification to the formation of new states. They were useful, at same time, in securing
derivative, dependent, or compound instruments of identification. The following chapter explores
the use of one such class of instruments, passes and passports, as instruments vital to the practice
and governance of Revolutionary identities on the move.

Chapter 5

Passes

Within days of the battles of Lexington and Concord, the Massachusetts rebel forces

surrounding Boston had begun stopping post riders who attempted to reach the city. On April 22,

Peter Mumford, on his way through Roxbury, was stopped "by a Man unknown to me" then

"ordered before a Man who[se] Name I was told was Thomas." Mumford was told he could not be

allowed to take the mail to Boston, "and after detaining me some time, [Thomas] gave me a Letter,

and a pass through a Body of armed Men to Cambridge," where he was to deliver his letter to

General Ward. The General in turn demanded the mailbag, broke the lock, and removed and read

the letters directed to officers of the British Army and one to the Speaker of the Massachusetts

House of Representatives. Mumford was then given back the mail and received "a pass through a

Number of Armed Men to Charlestown," where he proceeded to the Post Office at Boston.[1] Less

than three weeks later, General Gage would write in frustration from Boston to a Lieutenant

Colonel Caldwell, that, "It is now next to Impossible to get any Intelligence to you, as the Posts are

stopped, and every person thro' the Country searched."[2] With the exception of General Ward, all of

the individuals who had detained Mumford remained anonymous, and if Mumford regarded their

---

[1] Depositions of Peter Mumford, [24?] April 1775 and 24 April 1775, Thomas Gage Papers, Volume 128, WLCL. The second of these two successive depositions (one probably a copy of the other) is followed by the certificate of JP Belcher Noyes that on the 24th Mumford swore to the truth of the deposition. Mumford's fellow post rider John Noble reported a very similar ordeal. Noble was stopped near Charlestown on his way to Boston from Portsmouth. He was taken to General Ward. His mailbag was taken, opened, and later returned, after which he was given "a Pass Thro' a number of Arm'd Men to Charlestown," from whence he made his way to the Boston Post Office and later the same day subscribed and swore to the truth of his account of these events before a Justice of the Peace. Deposition of John Noble before John Hill, Justice of the Peace, Suffolk County, MA, 24 April 1775, Thomas Gage Papers, Volume 128, WLCL.

[2] Gage to Caldwell, 10 May 1775, Thomas Gage Papers, Volume 128, WLCL. Gage pointed out to Caldwell that he might judge of the truth of this by "by the method I take to send you this," though what this, presumably covert, method was is not clear.

authority as suspect (in part precisely because of their anonymity), their de facto power meant that he had to comply with their directions. In contrast to his interrogators, his own identity and mobility were multiply subjected to examination.

The military lines around Boston were among the first of those that were to divide the American landscape over the succeeding eight years of war, marking friendly from enemy territory and delimiting zones of travel. Authorities at all levels, civil and military, increasingly sought to regulate the flow of information, goods, and people within and across such lines. Toward that end, they issued and regulated passes and passports, requiring travelers to negotiate overlapping pass regimes. Those Americans accustomed to thinking of themselves as free subjects of the King found themselves subjected to pass requirements reminiscent of those that had hitherto almost exclusively regulated the movement of bound labor. The Revolution thus brought a temporary but profound shift in the practice of American identities in relation to degrees of freedom.

Passes and passports, of many varieties, were the principal instruments of identification for those on the move during the Revolution. Each document implicitly identified the grantee as a person of a particular sort, meeting certain criteria, and worthy of being trusted with the right to travel. Some passes, moreover, explicitly attested to one or more facets of the bearer's identity. They were almost always issued to proven friends or known enemies (such as Loyalists going into exile or paroled prisoners of war). Many passes issued to friends, indeed, attested to their loyalty to the cause or even to the fact that they had sworn particular oaths of allegiance. Some passes issued to enemies attested to their honorable behavior or to their having sworn a parole. Thus passes and passports were instruments largely derivative of loyalty testing and the certificates it produced, as discussed in the previous chapter.

Passes operated within three overlapping realms. The first was the social or economic realm of bound labor—chattel slavery, indentured servitude, and seafaring labor—in which pass regimes were imposed to limit mobility. These established regimes, fundamental to colonial labor systems, continued in operation through the Revolution, albeit under new conditions. The second realm was that of civil regulation—pass regimes imposed by civilian governments on the general populace. Civil pass requirements had been less common in the colonial period, with the exception of restrictions on travel in certain frontier territories and requirements imposed to prevent the flight of debtors. But civil pass regimes proliferated with the advent of the Revolution and became fundamental to mobility during the conflict. The third realm was the military. This included both pass regimes imposed upon military personnel and those that military authorities imposed on civilians. These requirements regulated civilian travel in the proximity of and within military camps and garrisons, within sensitive theatres of war, and across lines separating friendly from enemy territory.

There was no centralized authority for any of this. Individual Americans could face pass requirements from more than one realm. And the authorities of the several realms often found themselves cooperating or conflicting with one another in the regulation of the same persons and populations. Passes and passports granted at the several levels of government varied greatly in form and sophistication, from the more elaborate passes, including physical descriptions and printed forms, mandated by the New Jersey pass law of 1777, to simple manuscript notes declaring that a given party was to be allowed to pass unhindered. Powers that claimed the authority to require and issue passes embraced both civil and military realms and ranged from the Continental Congress and the Continental Army down through provincial congresses and state committees of safety to militia officers, local committees, and bands of vigilantes. As a result, Americans who wished to travel, or even lead quiet lives in their own locality, had to repeatedly negotiate and certify their identities.

Travelling or residing within a politically distinct realm, either British or "American," was fraught enough. Crossing the lines to or from enemy territory was still more so.[3]

At the same time, the political distinctions embodied in passes were inflected by social status. The passes available to or required of the African American slave were very different from those available to or required of the refugee woman, the private soldier, or the gentleman prisoner of war; the passport issued to the middling artisan would likely not reflect the same solicitude as the passport issued to the genteel close acquaintance of the issuing official. Chapter 7 will examine the experiences of marginalized populations—particularly women and African Americans—as they attempted to navigate Revolutionary regimes of identification. This chapter examines passes as they applied to persons understood to be capable of bearing such instruments in their own right—largely free adult white males—yet who would have found the pass regimes to which they were subjected uncomfortably reminiscent of those used to regulate the unfree.

The lines established around Boston as the siege of the city set in were not, at least at first, assumed to mark off domains that corresponded with the loyalties of the populations they contained. The process of sorting people by loyalty was at first a self-sorting: royal officials and certain Loyalists had fled to Boston or abroad during the preceding years of crisis and many city residents retreated to the countryside during the British Army's occupation of Boston and the imposition of the Coercive Acts. From the beginning of open hostilities, more and more Americans sorted themselves, as they sought refuge under whichever army and government they supported. Others sought to reconstitute divided families. When the siege of Boston set in very suddenly following the unexpected battles of Lexington and Concord, many supporters of the resistance

---

[3] For the latter, see numerous examples in Records of the States of the United States, New Jersey, 1681-1786, Film 281, Reel 1, Minutes of the Council of Safety, DLAR.

found themselves trapped in the city under British marshal law. Many Loyalists, likewise, found themselves at large in a New England countryside dominated by opposition sentiment and the armed forces of the resistance. With certain caveats, it was clear to each side that they needed to shed dissenting populations by allowing them to pass to the enemy domain, though without carrying supplies or sensitive information.

In the days immediately following the British retreat to Boston from Lexington and Concord, the Boston town meeting had sent a committee to General Gage requesting that those Bostonians who wished might be allowed to leave the city. In the course of the subsequent negotiations, Gage agreed that, once "the Inhabitants in general" had surrendered their arms to the care of the Selectmen, "all such Inhabitants as are inclined may depart from the Town with their Family And their Effects…by land and Water…within the limits prescribed by the Port Act," for which purpose "he would desire the Admiral to lend his boats to facilitate the removal of the Effects of the Inhabitants, and allow carriages to pass and repass." Gage asked that in return "a letter might be wrote to Dr. Warren Charman of the Committe of the Provincial Congress that thos persons in the Country who may incline to remove into Boston with their Effects may have liberty so to do without Molestation." A letter to this effect was addressed to Dr. Warren by the Selectmen, who emphasized the unanimity of the town meeting in acceding to this arrangement.[4] Thus far reasonable and mutual accommodation was the order of the day.

Neither side, however, was eager to cooperate too fully with their enemies or to risk allowing them too many resources, and each had an interest in portraying the other as tyrants, imposing their will on a maltreated people. Thus the rebels—through the Continental Congress—were eager to publicize what they saw as Gage's duplicity and the imprisonment of desperate Americans in Boston

---

[4] Selectmen of Boston to Joseph Warren, [23?] April 1775, Thomas Gage Papers, Volume 128, WLCL. In requesting the surrender of the Bostonians' arms, Gage assured the committee that the arms would be "Marked with the names of the respective Owners…And that the Arms afforesaid at a Suitable time would be Returned to the Owners."

under arbitrary rule. In an appeal to the people of Ireland for support, during the early weeks of the

siege, the Congress described how "The neighbouring farmers" having "repelled the attack" on

Lexington and Concord, "all communication between the town and country was intercepted."

Trapped in Boston, "the citizens petitioned the General for permission to leave the town, and he

promised on surrendering their arms, to permit them to depart with their other effects." But "the

General violated his faith":

> Under various pretences, passports were delayed and denied; and many thousands of the
> inhabitants are at this day confined in the town in the utmost wretchedness and want——The
> lame, the blind and the sick, have indeed been turned out into the neighbouring fields; and
> some, eluding the vigilance of the sentries, have escaped from the town, by swiming to the
> adjacent shores.[5]

On the same day that the Continental Congress decried Gage's delay, Dr. James Warren

addressed a confidential letter to Gage, advising him that "great Complaints are made respecting the

Delays in removing the Inhabitants of Boston" and that he should feel himself assured "that this

People irritated as they have been, will not with any tolerable Degree of Patience suffer the

Agreement made between you and the Inhabitants of Boston to be violated." Warren acknowledged

himself "very sensible of the Formalities which Gentlemen in your Situation generally think

yourselves obliged to observe," but urged Gage to ignore "the mad Advice of Men who I know

have deceived you" and "consider whether you are to sacrifice the Interest of Grt Britain, and the

Peace of the colonies, to mere Forms."[6]

Gage, for his part, felt justified in withholding passports, at least until the rebel forces and

the Congress had made the stipulated arrangements for those who wished to take refuge in the city

to do so. His authority over identification and mobility in and out of the city was far from complete,

---

[5] *Journal of the proceedings of the Congress, held at Philadelphia, May 10, 1775,* (Philadelphia: William and Thomas Bradford, 1775), *EAI,* Series 1, no. 14569 (filmed), 213, 219.

[6] Warren to Gage, 10 May 1775, (emendations incorporated), Thomas Gage Papers, Volume 128, WLCL.

however, given the disordered circumstances and the multiple authorities governing the city and its harbor. Gage found that inhabitants had already been leaving the city, with official permission and passes, though he had not formally granted such leave and though arrangements had not been made for the admission of refugees from the countryside. With marked anxiety, Gage wrote to his counterpart in the Royal Navy, Admiral Graves,

> of Numbers of the Inhabitants getting out of Town, with Passes Signed by you, two of which I have seen. As it is of the greatest Consequence they should be kept in, till the whole have leave to retire, and that it is regulated for the friends of Government to come in without Molestation, I am to beg the favour of you to grant no more passes for the present, without a Cirtificate of their having my leave.[7]

Gage was not in a position to demand obedience from Graves. He had to seek cooperation and mutual coordination. Graves in turn, however, assured Gage that while he had granted "a few passes" to leave the city, he had issued them only "to some known friends to Government, And to an inconsiderable number of transient people; & fishing Vessels." Nevertheless, he was prompt to assure Gage that he would not "permit any more to leave the Town but such as produce to me Your Excellency's Certificate of leave."[8]

This new coordination, and effective centralization of the administration of identity and mobility across the British lines around Boston, was soon embodied in instruments such as that issued to a "Mr. Williams" on the 1st of May, in the following form:

> Head Qrs. Boston 1st. May 1775 / The Bearer, Mr. Williams, has the Commander in Chief's permission to pass to & repass from Noddle's Island to this place as often as he has occasion; he having given security to carry no people from hence, or bring any thing off the Island without leave from His Excelly or the Admiral— / Rt. Donkin Aide Camp / NB. his own Servants row him. / To all concerned / Approved / Saml Graves[9]

---

[7] [Thomas Gage] to Samuel Graves, 25 April 1775, Thomas Gage Papers, Volume 128, WLCL. The author of this note did not sign it, but from the context, contents, and handwriting, it seems clearly to have been sent by Gage.

[8] Graves to Gage, 25 April 1775, Thomas Gage Papers, Volume 128, WLCL.

[9] Smauel Graves, Pass for Henry Howell Williams, 1 May 1775, Noddles Island Papers, MHS.

Within a few days of Graves' assurances to Gage—the 28th by one British officer's recollection—"Passes were granted to such of the inhabitants, as chose to leave the town, with their Families; but were allowed to carry nothing out, except their bedding and houshold furniture."[10] Despite Gage's apparent uncertainty as to whether the rebels would reciprocate by permitting Loyalist refugees from the countryside to go to Boston, by the 30th the Massachusetts Committee of Safety drafted a letter agreeing to the arrangement. They had accordingly appointed "officers…for the giving permits for the above purpose one at the Sign of the Sun at Cha[r]lestown and another at the house of mr. John [Greaton?] at Roxbury."[11]

Once passes out of Boston began to issue with Gage's approval, sometime in May, they seem to have taken the form of slips of paper roughly the size of present-day checks, on which were printed a brief form, to be filled in and emended as necessary by the issuing officer. When Margaret Jepson received permission to leave Boston with her family, her pass was as follows (manuscript indicated by single quotation marks):

> 'To The Field officers in the Lines' / Boston, May [blank], 1775 / PERMIT '[Margaret] Jepson', together with his Family, consisting of 'Seven' Persons, and 'their' Effects, to pass 'Over the Lines—' between Sunrise and Sunset. / By Order of his Excellency the Governor. / No Arms nor Ammunition is allowed to pass. 'Nor Merchandize'

---

[10] Journal of an officer of the 47th Regiment of Foot, after 1783, mssHM 66: 13, HL. See also the description of the agreement regarding issuing these passes, the process by which they were issued, and the emigration from the city regulated by these passes in Extract of a Letter to a Gentleman in Philadelphia, 21 May 1775, *AAO*, Series 4, II: 666: "The arms being delivered, orders were issued by the General, that those who inclined to remove must give in their names to the Selectmen, to be by them returned to the Military Town Major, who was then to write a pass for the person or family applying, to go through the lines, or over the ferry; but all merchandise was forbid; after a while, all provisions were forbid; and now all merchandise, provisions, and medicine. Guards are appointed to examine all trunks, boxes, beds, and every thing else to be carried out; these have proceeded such extremities, as to take from the poor people a single loaf of bread, and half pound of chocolate; so that no one is allowed to carry out a mouthful of provisions; but all is submitted to quietly." See also Washington to Hancock, 4-5 August 1775, *PGWDE*, Revolutionary, I: 223-239, n29, n36: "General Gage has at length liberated the People of Boston, who land in Numbers at Chelsea every Day, the Terms on which the Passes are granted as to Money Effects & Provisions correspond with Mr Noyes's Letter."

[11] Massachusetts Committee of Safety to [Gage?], 30 April 1775, U.S. Revolution Collection, Box 1, Folder 6, AAS. This copy is a draft. Emendations have been followed to produce the clean text as quoted above.

On the back, under her name, were written the names of Margaret's mother, two aunts, a sister, a daughter, and an unspecified male relative, servant, or slave Benjamin.[12] The form made clear that only individuals, their families, and their personal effects could leave the city—they could take with them no supplies of war or, as the issuing officer clarified in an emendation, commercial goods, from which the rebel forces might profit. The bearers—and potential bearers—of these passes were thus identified as exclusively private, civilian, and domestic persons. Though implicit in the printed form, the issuing officer in this case specified that it was the field officers commanding in the lines who would accept or reject the passes as legitimate. The passes would be accepted only "between Sunrise and Sunset." Nighttime crossings of the lines would have been more difficult to regulate: the dark would have made it easier for travelers to conceal illicit goods and persons, disguise themselves, or use forged or altered passes.[13]

According to the records of the Town Major, Captain James Urquhard, between June 20th and September 26th of 1775, he issued 1,018 passes of the sort Margaret Jepson received, permitting inhabitants of Boston to leave the city and join the rebels in the countryside. Urquhard, on Gage's orders, had overseen two censuses of the inhabitants of Boston (not counting British troops and accompanying personnel), for June 24th and October 2nd of the same year. The first found 6,247 inhabitants, leaving 5,229 after the passes had been granted (indicating perhaps that Urquhard

---

[12] Permit to pass through British lines for Margaret Jepson and family, May 1775, Misc. Bd. 1775 May, MHS. The lack of a precise date and the absence of a signature from the issuing officer (though the pass is officially issued on the authority of Governor Gage) may indicate that this was a draft, but this is not certain.

[13] Sentries were, in fact, commonly ordered to permit no one to pass the lines at night. See, e.g., the account of an American sentry refusing to allow Lady Auckland to pass the lines at night to attend her wounded and imprisoned husband, detaining her instead in her boat all night. Journal of an officer of the 47th Regiment of Foot, after 1783, mssHM 66, HL.

counted the number of people authorized to leave by the passes issued, rather than the number of

passes issued), and the second found 5,389.[14]

Meanwhile, even as the Massachusetts and Continental armies mobilized for war, the

members of the Provincial Congress and their agents—along with many other civil officers—were

frantically meeting, travelling hither and yon, and generally working to keep the wheels of civil

government turning, while considering their relation to Great Britain and the forms that might be

taken by potential independent states. The civil identities of these officers and the demands of their

tasks had to be accommodated across a landscape dominated increasingly by military discipline.

Thus by the 7th of May 1775, orders had issued to the Massachusetts forces "That all officers of the

guard pay obedience to orders signed by the President of the Congress to the members of the same,

which are to be in the following form; viz.,

> To the guards of the Colony Army:—
> Pursuant to a resolve of the Provincial Congress, you are hereby ordered to permit ———,
> a member of this Congress, with his company, to pass and repass with his company at all
> times.[15]

In part—regardless of its particulars—this order represented a formal (re)assertion of the civil

authority over the military: the royal governor had typically been commander in chief of the colonial

militia, and now the President of the Provincial Congress was to be obeyed in the same capacity.

The members of congress, likewise, as high-ranking civil officers were to be allowed a freedom of

movement (if possessed of the appropriate pass) that was enjoyed by very few others. The pass

itself was to be authenticated by two principal marks: the proper form, introduced here to the

---

[14] The censuses broke down the inhabitants into whites above and below the age of 16, each group divided in turn into male and female; male "negros" above 16; "negro women and children"; and "Negros whose Masters are out." James Urquhart, Census of Boston, 9 October 1775, Thomas Gage Papers, Volume 136, WLCL.

[15] 7 May 1775, *The Orderly Book of Colonel William Henshaw*, (Boston: J. Wilson, 1877), 23. See also the resolves of the Provincial Congress adopting this form of a pass and the order to the provincial army to pay obedience to passes in this form. Massachusetts Provincial Congress, 6 May 1775, *AAO*, Series 4, II: 789. On the printing of these passes, see Rollo G. Silver, *Government Printing in Massachusetts, 1751-1801*, (Charlottesville, VA: Bibliographical Society of the University of Virginia, 1963), 176.

community of official knowledge, and the signature of the President of the Provincial Congress.[16]

The pass was to be borne by the member of Congress named therein. But under these

circumstances, the authorization—though not the identification, in any particular sense—extended

to encompass the member's "company" (presumably any person travelling with the member). In

this respect the member of Congress, as constructed by this pass, assumed a role homologous to

that of the head of household or master (of servants or slaves) to whom an authorization of mobility

was issued, as in the British passes issued to emigrants leaving Boston.[17]

Sentry lines continued to regulate travel around Boston and its neighboring towns for the

remainder of the siege. General pass requirements for soldiers and civilians prevailed, though

Washington and other authorities also issued specific injunctions or temporary restrictions. Thus on

July 7th, 1775, a few days after he took command, Washington included in his general orders that,

"The Guards on the Roads leading to Bunker's Hill, are ordered not to suffer any person to pass

them, unless an Officer is sent down from the Lines to order it, or they will be severely punished."[18]

On the 26th of the same month, Washington ordered "All Passes to be discontinued for the future,

and no person to be admitted into the Lines, unless introduced by an Officer, who can vouch for

him, or by Order of the Officer commanding in the Lines."[19] Individuals were from time to time

---

[16] It is perhaps implicit that the form of the pass would be printed, with particulars and the signature added by hand.

[17] It may likewise be useful to note the (transitive) connection with the use of the metaphor of "family" to refer to the suite of staff and aides de camp surrounding a high ranking military officer, including George Washington, who counted Alexander Hamilton, the Marquis de Lafayette, Tench Tighlman, and John Laurens, besides others, among his "family." See Washington to Anthony White, 25 August 1775, *PGWDE*, Revolutionary, I: 365; Washington to Charles Lee, 10 February 1776, *PGWDE*, Revolutionary, III: 282-284; Washington to Joseph Reed, 23 January 1776, *PGWDE*, Revolutionary, III: 172-175. The same metaphor was likewise employed by slaveholders—especially owners of large plantations in the southern colonies—to refer to all their dependents, including slaves (those related to them by blood and those not, alike), many of these planters self-consciously playing the role of the Biblical patriarch. See Rhys Isaac, *Landon Carter's Uneasy Kingdom: Revolution and Rebellion on a Virginia Plantation*, (New York: Oxford UP, 2004), 59, passim.

[18] Washington, General Orders, 7 July 1775, *PGWDE*, Revolutionary, I: 71-75.

[19] Washington, General Orders, 26 July 1775, *PGWDE*, Revolutionary, I: 172-173. On the 22nd of October, Washington forbade further boats to come over to Winnisimit from Boston. Joseph Reed to Loammi Baldwin, 22 October 1775, Loammi Baldwin Papers, 1768-1872, Box 1, Item 41, Houghton Library, Harvard University, Cambridge, MA.

granted passes to cross the lines or allowed to go forward with flags of truce to hold conferences with those inside the enemy's lines regarding personal business.[20] Before the end of the year, Washington would write to General Artemas Ward that, "The Applications for Liberty to go to the lines, are so frequent, that they cause much trouble." Ward was empowered therefore to "Grant passes to such as you may think proper," though Washington recommended "that the officer who will attend upon these occasions be a person of sense & one who will carefully attend to the conversation of those who meet on the Lines."[21]

Washington coordinated with the civil authorities to prevent mishap. Thus in early August of 1775, on advice from Washington, the Massachusetts General Court appointed a committee, "whose duty it shall be to give constant attendance at the place where the people coming out of Boston to Chelsea shall land, and strictly examine into the characters and circumstances of all such persons" (see Chapter 4). The committee was to remand to the General Court "any of the said persons" who "shall appear to be enemies of this Country."[22] Soon the question of permitting persons to pass out of Boston was complicated by the outbreak of smallpox in the city and the need to screen emigrants for the disease and block or isolate those suspected of bearing it.[23]

---

[20] See Horatio Gates to Artemas Ward, 27 November 1775, granting permission, on behalf of Washington, to two individuals to "accompany a Flagg to [the] Lines, to see if they can Obtain any satisfactory Answer to The Business they came about." Horatio Gates Papers, 1726-1828, Film 23, Reel 2 (Correspondence, Nov. 1769 - July 1776), DLAR. See also Joseph Ward to Horatio Gates, 6 December 1775, and Gates to Ward, 7 December 1775, Horatio Gates Papers, 1726-1828, Film 23, Reel 2 (Correspondence, Nov. 1769 - July 1776), DLAR.

[21] Washington to Ward, 17 December 1775, *PGWDE*, Revolutionary, II: 569.

[22] Massachusetts General Court, 7 August 1775, *AAO*, Series 4, III: 313.

[23] See Washington's query to his council of war regarding whether inhabitants of Boston who had received passes to leave the city should be allowed to come out given the current incidence of smallpox in the city. Council of War, 2 November 1775, Cambridge, MA, *PGWDE*, Revolutionary, II: 279-284. Se also Loammi Baldwin on the more general distress of emigrants from Boston and the possibility that blocking them from coming farther will cause them to perish of hunger and cold. Baldwin to Washington, 26 November 1775, Chelsea, MA, MS Am 1811, Loammi Baldwin Papers, 1768-1872, Box II, Item 154, Houghton Library, Harvard University, Cambridge, MA. On December 13th, Robert Harrison wrote to Baldwin on Washington's order, informing Baldwin "that notwithstanding his orders, some of the persons that came out last from Boston have been at this camp, one he has seen himself—he is exceedingly desirous to prevent a measure that may prove of fatal consequence to the Army & therefore Enjoins, that you will make it publickly known to these people and all others that may be sent out that they do not come here without special leave obtained

Regulating passage and distinguishing, in the process, between friend and foe, persisted as a major preoccupation of commanders on both sides until the British evacuated the city and the siege lifted. Near the end of October 1775, General Howe issued a proclamation that, "WHEREAS several of the Inhabitants of this Town have lately absconded to join, it is apprehended, His Majesty's Enemies assembled in open Rebellion," he did therefore "forbid any Person or Persons whatever, not belonging to the Navy, to pass from hence by Water or otherwise, from the Date hereof, without my Order of Permission given in Writing." Ships were likewise prohibited from receiving any person without a written pass from Howe himself or under the direct orders of the Admiral. Anyone leaving the city without a proper pass would be executed under martial law if caught, and "treated as Traitors," if they escaped, "by Seizure of their Goods and Effects."[24]

When the British had evacuated the city and the siege was over, in mid March of 1776, access to Boston was still regulated by passes. The day after the British left, a "Committee for taking care of the Boston poor" prepared to enter the city, bearing "a permitt from his Excellency Genl Washington to go in."[25] That same day, merchant William Green secured "a permit from Genl. Washington to Go into boston," where he hoped to have an early opportunity to buy up any goods he might resell.[26] Because of the persisting smallpox outbreak, officers and soldiers were initially prohibited from visiting the city unless they had a pass or were ordered there. Greater liberty would be given to visit the city once it was clear the infection had been eradicated. Inhabitants were free to

---

first of him & that If they do, they will be immediatly Imprisoned." Loammi Baldwin Papers, 1768-1872, Box 1, Item 29, Houghton Library, Harvard University, Cambridge, MA.

[24] Howe, Proclamation, 28 October 1775, Boston, MA, *EAI*, Series 1, no. 14085 (filmed).

[25] Committee for taking care of the Boston Poor, to Loammi Baldwin, 18 March 1776, MS Am 1811, Loammi Baldwin Papers, 1768-1872, Houghton Library, Harvard University, Cambridge, MA.

[26] William Green to ______, 18 March 1776, Cambridge, MA, Schoff Revolutionary War Collection, Box 1, WLCL.

return immediately, but they had to apply to the "proper persons...appointed at the Neck and at Charlestown-Ferry to grant them passes."[27]

Smallpox was not Washington's only concern. While the British evacuation ships still lingered off New England, he worried the British army might launch a surprise attack. He made sure to establish guard boats and lookouts accordingly. Yet "there is one evil I dread," he wrote to Josiah Quincy on the 24th of March, "& that is their Spies." "I could wish therefore," he explained,

> that the most attentive watch was kept to prevent any Intercourse between the Ships & Main—for this purpose, and to prevent suspected persons (for I have no doubt but that trusty Soldiers, Sergeants, and even Commissioned Officers in disguise will be sent out) from travelling about, I wish a dozn or more of Honest, sensible, and deligent Men were Imployed to haunt the Communication between Roxbury and the different landing Places nearest the Shipping, in order to question, cross question &ca all such Persons as are unknown, & cannot give an acct of themselves in a strait, & satisfactory line—

Washington proposed that Quincy hire such men accordingly, promising to pay whatever wages Quincy promised them. Washington was anxious to prevent the enemy gaining intelligence of his army's situation and, at the same time, to keep apprised of enemy movements.[28]

Even before the Boston crisis, passes had been tools of the colonial resistance. Crowds or bands of vigilantes sometimes used such instruments to impose identities on their targets and to give formal embodiment to the authority they had arrogated to themselves. In January of 1775, for instance, a crowd lead by Ethan Allen and Seth Warner in Sunderland, Vermont flogged a local justice of the peace who had presumed to continue in his duties under royal authority. Allen and Warner then issued the beaten Benjamin Hough a certificate stating that he had "this day received a

---

[27] Washington, Orders, 19 March 1776, *AAO*, Series 4, V: 421. Months after the siege of Boston had ended, it appears passes were still being used to regulate movement in the face of ongoing concerns about smallpox. Thus on August 13th, 1776, Boston selectmen issued to Ebenezer Simpson a certificate that he had been "so smoak'd and cleansed as that in our Opinion he may be permitted to pass into the Country without Danger of Communicating the Small-Pox to anyone." U.S. Revolution Collection, Box 2, Folder 4, AAS.

[28] Washington to Quincy, 24 March 1776, *PGWDE*, Revolutionary, III: 528-529.

full punishment for his crimes committed heretofore against this Country" and declaring that "our inhabitants are ordered to give him, the said Hough, a free and unmolested passport toward the City of New-York, or to the westward of our Grants, he behaving as becometh."[29]

The town and county committees that had, since the autumn of 1774, emerged as de facto Revolutionary governments had likewise turned to pass regimes to govern local inhabitants— especially those suspected of "disloyalty"—and to serve the cause by controlling the flow of people, goods, and information through their districts, sometimes in cooperation with provincial authorities. Since early 1775 the Boston committee of correspondence had coordinated with its counterparts in the rest of the province and region to prevent aid reaching the ministerial army in the city. In February they circulated a resolution that "no teams be suffered to load in, or after loading to pass through, any town in this province for Boston" if they carried goods that might be of use to the royal troops "except the teamster can produce from the committee of Correspondence for the town where he loaded, an instrument, certifying his name, place of abode, the particulars of his load, the person who sends, and to whom to be delivered in Boston."[30] In early May of 1775 the Massachusetts Provincial Congress advised local committees throughout the province to identify and disarm local enemies and "take effectual steps to put it out of the power of such persons to obstruct, by any means whatever, the measures which shall be taken for the common defence."[31] On May 22nd, the Worcester Committee of Correspondence accordingly "determined [that the] several persons herein Named be Agreable to Resolution of [...] Congress forthwith disarmed and

---

[29] Allen and Warner, Passport for Benjamin Hough, 30 January 1775, *AAO*, Series 4, II: 217. The text of the passport here is given in Hough's subsequent deposition in New York before Daniel Horsmanden on the 7th of March 1775.

[30] Boston Committee of Correspondence to the Woburn Committee of Correspondence, 25 February 1775, MS Am 1811, Loammi Baldwin Papers, 1768-1872, Box II, Item 187, Houghton Library, Harvard University, Cambridge, MA. In a similar manner, in October of 1775, the Committee of Providence Rhode Island established a system of certificates prevent shipments of provisions from reaching the enemy via Newport and to allay suspicions of the same. Committee of Providence, 6 October 1775, *AAO*, Series 4, III: 974-975.

[31] Massachusetts Provincial Congress, 8 May 1775, *AAO*, Series 4, II: 793.

that they do not depearte [this] town without a permitt in writeing from the Commitee of [Correspon]dance of the town of Worcester."[32] In July, the Massachusetts Provincial Congress confided ten prisoners taken on Long Island to specified towns in Worcester County, stipulating "That the Prisoners shall not be at liberty to pass over the line of the Town where they are respectively stationed, without a pass from the Selectmen of such Town, after they have arrived therein."[33] Such pass regulations became common practice.

More generally, indeed, pass regimes served as much to regulate enemies as to protect or empower friends. From early in the conflict, one major form passes took was the passport granted to Loyalists exiled or granted permission to emigrate. Like the justice of the peace driven from Vermont by Allen and his associates, other royal officials and Loyalists were given passes to enable their flight and ultimate exile, at least once they had made any proper restitution for their imputed crimes. As the conflict developed, the practice became more formalized, as local committees and provincial congresses or committees of safety began to issue numerous passports to "disaffected" would-be emigrants. In January of 1776, for instance, having previously imposed a state Association that all freemen were to sign as a pledge of their loyalty, the Maryland Convention resolved that "if any...non-Associator shall choose to quit this Province and go beyond the sea, then the Committee of Observation of the County to which he belongs, may, and is hereby empowered to grant him a

---

[32] Worcester Committee of Correspondence, 22 May 1775, U.S. Revolution Collection, Box 2, Folder 1, AAS. See also the Masscahusetts Committee of Safety, confiding Frenchman M. Viart to the Worcester Committee of Correspondence, to be confined to the town, 11 July 1775, U.S. Revolution Collection, Box 2, Folder 2, AAS. Other local committees dispatched identified enemies to the Provincial Congress or Committee of Safety to be dealt with, either by being placed under restrictions on their movement and behavior or by issuing them passes to take refuge with the British in Boston. See Committee of Northborough to Artemas Ward, 17 May 1775, *AAO*, Series 4, II: 632; Committee of Malden to the Massachusetts Committee of Safety, 25 May 1775, *AAO*, Series 4, II: 708.

[33] Massachusetts Provincial Congress, 13 July 1775, *AAO*, Series 4, II: 1515. For the Massachusetts Council stipulating the permissible mobility of another suspected person, a Worcester resident, see Massachusetts Council, 15 December 1775, Watertown, MA, U.S. Revolution Collection, Box 2, Folder 2, AAS. See also Horatio Gates to ______, 4 January 1776, Horatio Gates Papers, 1726-1828, Film 23, Reel 2 (Correspondence, Nov. 1769 - July 1776), DLAR, confiding prisoners to be confined or released at Worcester.

passport to leave this country in peace...carrying with him his property, or any part thereof."[34] Thus

those who chose not to identify themselves as rebels or "Americans" were offered passports

identifying them as enemy subjects and exiles.

The application for and receipt of a pass into the enemy lines often represented the choice

of one identity (and a corresponding instrument of identification) over another. Such a pass—at

least for adult males—was not uncommonly the alternative to taking an oath of allegiance to the

state, to the United States, or to the British Crown, and accepting the corresponding loyalty oath

certificate or safe conduct. A non-juror would often be required to leave the state and the United

States more generally on the one hand, or the province and the protection of the British armed

forces and Crown on the other.[35]

Pass requirements also continued to be imposed on particular Loyalists who remained in

Patriot territory, to restrict their mobility and prevent their acting against the Patriot cause. Thus in

July of 1776, the Committee of Northborough, Massachusetts, resolved that five "persons

unfriendly to the cause for which the United Independent States of North America are contending"

should be "confined to the limits of their respective farms" and "that they should not pass said

bounds on any occasion whatever, without leave in writing from the major part of said Committee,

unless it be to attend publick worship [or] funerals in their own town."[36] Shortly thereafter, a

convention of the committees of Hutchinson, Templeton, Athol, and Petersham, Massachusetts,

resolved to continue previously imposed restrictions on local "Tories" in Petersham under which it

---

[34] Maryland Convention, 16 January 1776, *AAO*, Series 4, IV: 755-757.

[35] Ezekiel Beech of New Jersey, for instance, having refused to comply with the demand of the New Jersey Council of Safety, in January 1778, that he "take the Oaths to Government," was granted "leave to go according to his request" into "the Enemy's Lines," provided that, "he depart this State for that Purpose in three days from the date hereof, by the way of Elizabeth Town to Staten Island," the commanding officer at Elizabethtown being "directed to send him over to the Island." New Jersey Council of Safety, 20 January 1778, Records of the States of the United States, New Jersey, 1681-1786, Film 281, Reel 1, Minutes of the Council of Safety, DLAR.

[36] Committee of Northborough, MA, 10 July 1776, *AAO*, Series 5, I: 179.

was stipulated "that they should not go out of the Town of Petersham without a pass, signed by the major part of the Committee of Correspondence of said Town."[37]

Travel passes were sometimes granted to Loyalists or prisoners of war, usually on parole, who were otherwise confined to a particular locale. Typically this was a privilege reserved to gentlemen, who, it was understood, could give their word of honor in a way that common soldiers or citizens could not. Thus on the 31st of May 1775, a committee appointed by the Connecticut House of Assembly issued to lieutenants John Feltham and Arthur Wadman of the British army, captured at Ticonderoga and since assigned to reside in Hartford, a pass "on their parole of honour, to visit their friends in the province of New Jersey and New York with a servant each," requesting "all men to whom these presents shall come" to allow them " to pass without molestation from this place into the said provinces of New Jersey and New York" and to treat them "with all that respect and honor which is due to gentlemen of their character."[38] In September of the following year, Governor William Livingston of New Jersey would grant to "Andrew Elliot Esqr., a Gentleman of the most amiable Character & unblemished Integrity and Honour, and thence universally respected by all his Acquaintance," a pass to travel and reside within New Jersey "without Molestation or Interruption by any Person whatsoever on Account of his political Sentiments (he refraining from saying or doing anything to the Prejudice of the States of America) or under Colour or Pretext of his having exercised any Office under His Britannic Majesty."[39] (Passes were also granted to lower ranking prisoners for more limited travel or to allow servants to rejoin the officers they served.[40])

---

[37] Convention of Committees of Safety, Petersham, MA, 12 July 1776, *AAO*, Series 5, I: 245-246.

[38] Committee of the Connecticut House of Assembly, Pass for Arthur Wadman and John Feltham, 31 May 1775, Hartford, CT, copy, Thomas Gage Papers, Volume 129, WLCL. See also William Livingston, Pass for Andrew Elliot, 25 September 1776, Sir Henry Clinton Papers, Volume 18, Folder 26, WLCL.

[39] William Livingston, Pass and Protection for Andrew Elliot, 25 September 1776, Princeton, NJ, Sir Henry Clinton Papers, Volume 18, Folder 26, WLCL.

[40] Cf. William Atlee, Pass for Sergeant Sutherland, prisoner of war carrying letters and accounts related to his regiment from Lancaster to Reading, PA, 21 August 1776, *AAO*, Series 5, I: 1094; James Read, Pass for Sergeant Sutherland,

In other cases authorities were more guarded, especially when the proposed travel involved passage into enemy territory. Thus in January of 1776, Washington denied a paroled prisoner's request to travel to Nova Scotia to join his family.[41] In February, the committee of New York City hesitated to grant an applicant a pass to visit the royal governor of the province, William Tryon, for fear that the applicant might give Tryon sensitive information.[42]

Some passes and passports were granted to deserters or defectors. These instruments served to certify this identity and protect the bearers within their former enemy's lines, allowing them some mobility, though often within fairly constrained limits and with a sense that only limited trust was being conferred. Military authorities commonly granted such passes to deserted enemy soldiers once they had been interviewed and any useful intelligence they could offer recorded. Typically the passes thus granted also translated the bearer's identity from soldier to civilian, as deserters from the enemy were not generally considered eligible or desirable as recruits into the American military service. Civilian authorities also granted such passes. Thus in July of 1775, the committee of the Massachusetts Provincial Congress appointed to examine the case of deserted British seaman Thomas Neat (or Neal) resolved "that he ought to be discharged and set at liberty" and recommended him "for a pass, to be signed by the Secretary, to go to New-York, there to apply for

---

returning to Lancaster from Reading, 22 August 1776, *AAO*, Series 5, I: 1094. For servants joining or rejoining imprisoned officers, see Committee of Reading to the Committee of Lancaster, 2 September 1776, *AAO*, Series 5, II: 120; Committee of York, PA, 4 September 1776, *AAO*, Series 5, II: 181; A. Gordon to the Committee of Lancaster, 5 September 1776, *AAO*, Series 5, II: 181; Committee of Lancaster, 11 September 1776, *AAO*, Series 5, II: 287; Committee of Lancaster, 26 September 1776, *AAO*, Series 5, II: 546; Committee of Lancaster, 12 October 1776, *AAO*, Series 5, II: 1008.

[41] Horatio Gates to John Knight, 24 January 1776, Horatio Gates Papers, 1726-1828, Film 23, Reel 2 (Correspondence, Nov. 1769 - July 1776), DLAR. On the same day, Washington denied a request by another prisoner to go into Boston to solicit his exchange since all appearances indicated that an exchange would not be allowed and that the prisoner would not be permitted to return. Gates to Henry Edwin Stanhope, 24 January 1776, Horatio Gates Papers, 1726-1828, Film 23, Reel 2 (Correspondence, Nov. 1769 - July 1776), DLAR.

[42] Henry Remsen to Joseph Hallett, 6 February 1776, *AAO*, Series 4, IV: 110-1111.

a further pass, as he proposes to go to Virginia."[43] In August of 1775, Horatio Gates, Adjutant General of the Continental Army, ordered that "Ric[h]ard Holland a Deserter from the fourth Regiment, or Royal Welch Fuzileers, is to be permitted to pass where he pleases" once he had been removed from Cambridge as far as Worcester.[44] In February of 1776, in a similar manner, the New York Provincial Congress granted a passport to Niles Christian stating that, "The bearer hereof...late Mate of the transport Ship Harriet, who has escaped from the said ship, and whose former stated place of residence was at Charlestown, Massachusetts-Bay, is hereby permitted to pass to Cambridge, in Massachusetts-Bay."[45]

Provincial authorities beyond Massachusetts had begun issuing passes and passports on an ad hoc basis by the early months of the war, in the summer of 1775. (Thus Robert Rogers that autumn gleaned documents from Pennsylvania, New York, and New Hampshire.) In June of 1775, the New York Provincial Congress issued to Brook Watson and "his suite" a passport to Quebec addressed "To all Officers in the service of the Colonies, Members of Committees, and others of the friends of AMERICAN liberty." The passport testified that "the said Brook Watson is a true friend to this Country and its rights" and asked that the addressee "give him every assistance, and shew him all the civilities in your power." The passport was to be engrossed and signed by the president and secretaries of the Congress.[46] The same month, the New York Congress received the application of Joseph Johnson, a Mohegan missionary on his way home to Connecticut from the Oneida country. He and his companions were "fearful of travelling without a passport or a letter of

---

[43] Massachusetts Provincial Congress, 1 July 1775, *AAO*, Series 4, II: 1468. See also the account of Neat's desertion, travel, and arrest as a suspicious person. Committee of Biddeford to the Massachusetts Provincial Congress, *AAO*, Series 4, II: 1127.

[44] Gates, Orders to James Mitchell Varnum, 8 August 1775, Horatio Gates Papers, 1726-1828, Film 23, Reel 2 (Correspondence, Nov. 1769 - July 1776), DLAR. These orders also directed Varnum to convey several prisoners to Worcester, from whence they were to be sent to Springfield to be confined.

[45] New York Provincial Congress, 29 February 1776, *AAO*, Series 4, V: 320.

[46] New York Provincial Congress, 20 June 1775, *AAO*, Series 4, II: 1307.

safe conduct, which may afford them peace and protection in their journey."[47] The Congress

granted Johnson a passport, declaring themselves "well convinced of the friendly disposition of the

said Joseph Johnson to the inhabitants of the American Colonies, and of his intentions and good

offices to preserve and maintain peace and harmony between them and the Indian Nations."[48] By

the end of November 1775, the Rhode Island Interior Committee was advising the governor on

who should receive passes.[49] By early 1776, the Committee of Albany, New York, had reportedly

declared it "necessary that every friend to liberty, travelling through their District, to have a passport

from some Committee of the place from whence he came."[50]

As the war advanced in new theatres, so did sentry lines and pass regimes. Regulations

varied depending on local circumstances. The capitulation of Montreal negotiated by American

General Richard Montgomery in November of 1775, for instance, provided "that trade, in

general...shall be carried on freely as heretofore, and passports shall be granted for that purpose,"

---

[47] Joseph Johnson, Petition, 21 June 1775, *AAO*, Series 4, II: 1047.

[48] New York Provincial Congress, Passport for Joseph Johnson, 22 June 1775, *AAO*, Series 4, II: 1311. On his return journey in August of 1775, Johnson would once again petition the Congress for a passport: "I also humbly beseech your Honours to grant me a passport for myself, that I may return home unmolested in these perilous times, and if there should be occasion, that I might pass and repass to and from the country of the Six Nations to New-England, or elsewhere, as business might call me at any time." *AAO*, Series 4, III: 436-438. The passport was granted. *AAO*, Series 4, III: 886.

[49] See, e.g., Rhode Island Interior Committee, 29? November 1775, 30 November 1775, 18 December 1775, Records of the States of the United States, Rhode Island, 1775-1818, Film 285, E4, Reel 1, Minutes of the Interior Committee, DLAR. See also, Rhode Island Interior Committee, 12 December 1775, forbidding anyone to go on board British ships without permission from the governor or deputy governor. Records of the States of the United States, Rhode Island, 1775-1818, Film 285, E4, Reel 1, Minutes of the Interior Committee, DLAR. In December of 1775, the Committee of Chesterfield County, Virginia, charged Edward Johnston with "having passed to Norfolk in violation of a passport granted for his safe conduct to Colonel Woodford's camp" and ultimately cited him for having "wilfully violated the proclamation of the Committee of Safety [of Virginia], and the promise he made under which he obtained the passport." Committee for Chesterfield County, VA, 6 December 1775, *AAO*, Series 4, IV: 200.

[50] Comfort Sands, a member of the New York Committee of Safety, who was "about to make a journey to and beyond Albany" in April of 1776, applied to the Committee for the necessary certificate and was issued one certifying that he was "a respectable and useful Member of the Provincial Congress of this Colony, and of this Committee of Safety; that he has steadily exerted himself as a sincere and active friend to the liberties of this country, and as such lie is hereby most cordially recommended to all friends to American liberty." New York Committee of Safety, Passport for Comfort Sands, 29 April 1776, *AAO*, Series 4, V: 1480-1481.

and that "passports shall also be granted to those who may want them for the different parts of this Province or elsewhere, on their lawful affairs."[51] The following January, General Wooster, now in command at Montreal, suspended the granting of passports for the Indian trade, so as to prevent intelligence and goods reaching the enemy through that channel.[52] By May the commissioners to Canada from the Continental Congress, empowered to grant passports for the Indian trade, reopened the trade and began issuing passports.[53] By the autumn of 1776, after the American withdrawal from Canada proper, the Americans at Ticonderoga, Crown Point, and other northern posts would begin policing travel through the borderlands. Besides regulating passes for soldiers and officers, they issued passes to civilian travellers, coordinated with civilian authorities to arrest those travelling without passes, and identified enemy agents based on the British passes they bore.[54]

The establishment of pass regimes around New York City had begun by early 1776, while the siege of Boston was still in progress. By mid February, General Charles Lee of the Continental Army had established sentinels in New York City and was coordinating the regulation of passes with civil authorities—at first primarily for visitors to the isolated royal governor on his ship off shore. Thus on February 12th, Lee gave orders that "the sentinels on the wharf" were "to suffer those who

---

[51] Capitulation of Montreal, 12 November 1775, *AAO*, Series 4, III: 1597.

[52] Wooster to a Committee of the Continental Congress, 5 July 1776, *AAO*, Series 5, I: 13.

[53] *The journals of the proceedings of Congress. Held at Philadelphia, from January to May, 1776,* (Philadelphia: R. Aitken, 1776), *EAI*, Series 1, no. 15145 (filmed), 117; Benjamin Franklin, Samuel Chases, and Charles Carroll to John Hancock, 1 May 1776, Montreal, *AAO*, Series 4, V: 1166.

[54] See Horatio Gates to the Cumberland County Committee of Safety, 1 August 1776, Horatio Gates Papers, 1726-1828, Film 23, Reel 3 (Correspondence, July 1776 - October 1776), DLAR; *PGWDE*, Revolutionary, V: 587n1; Thomas Hartley to Gates, 10 August 1776, 11 August 1776, Horatio Gates Papers, 1726-1828, Film 23, Reel 3 (Correspondence, July 1776 - October 1776), DLAR; Gates to Philip Schuyler, 20 August 1776, Horatio Gates Papers, 1726-1828, Film 23, Reel 3 (Correspondence, July 1776 - October 1776), DLAR; Gates to Egbert Benson, 22 August 1776, Horatio Gates Papers, 1726-1828, Film 23, Reel 3 (Correspondence, July 1776 - October 1776), DLAR; Quin John Freeman to ___, 14 September 1776, Horatio Gates Papers, 1726-1828, Film 23, Reel 3 (Correspondence, July 1776 - October 1776), DLAR; Benedict Arnold to Gates, 16 September 1776, Horatio Gates Papers, 1726-1828, Film 23, Reel 3 (Correspondence, July 1776 - October 1776), DLAR.

produce a pass from the Committee of Safety to go on board the Governour's ship."[55] On the 15th

of February, the New York Provincial Congress issued a pass authorizing the newly appointed

mayor of New York City and the city magistrates to board the governor's ship, so that the mayor

could be "qualified."[56] On the 21st, the Congress granted a pass to Zachariah Sickles to go to

Nutten Island to retrieve some of his property.[57]

In March of 1776, the New York Provincial Congress complained of "the interruptions

given to the persons having Passports from this Congress" occasioned by General Charles Lee's

determination to cut off communication with Governor Tryon. Once Tryon had explained his

seizure of a cargo of flour on its way to New York, Lee would permit provisions to be sent to

Tryon's ships, if the Congress thought it best, but declared no persons would be allowed to go to or

from the ships, "as he could not permit a personal communication to be any longer kept up."[58] The

Congress ultimately acceded to Lee's strictures. When an application was made to the Congress

soon thereafter to go on board one of the British ships to claim a seized boat, the Congress "refused

to give permission," noting that, "Major-General Lee has cut off all communication with said ship,

and through his conduct and orders the passports of this Congress are of no avail."[59] A few days

later, the Congress would attempt a compromise, granting a request for a passport to go on board

one of the British ships, but requiring the grantee to give his parole not to communicate intelligence

to the enemy.[60]

---

[55] Charles Lee, 12 February 1776, *AAO*, Series 4, IV: 1123.

[56] New York Provincial Congress, 15 February 1776, *AAO*, Series 4, V: 269.

[57] New York Provincial Congress, 21 February 1776, *AAO*, Series 4, V: 295.

[58] Report of a Committee of the New York Provincial Congress, 4 March 1776, *AAO*, Series 4, V: 532-533.

[59] New York Provincial Congress, 5 March 1776, *AAO*, Series 4, V: 337.

[60] New York Provincial Congress, 11 March 1776, *AAO*, Series 4, V: 367.

By mid April of 1776, its commanders satisfied that the British had left Boston for good but concerned that their next target might be New York, the main body of the Continental Army was established in New York City. Here, as at Boston, sentry lines were established, guards placed at the ferries, and pass requirements imposed. Continental officers were soon issuing passes to military personnel and civilians. Thus on the 18th of April, Adjutant General Horatio Gates, "at Head Quarters in New York," issued to Thomas Tomlin Pritchard an instrument addressed "To all Officers Civil & Military & All Others whom it may Concern" and directing that Pritchard be allowed "to Pass to New Windsor in the Province of New York, & to remain there; he behaving as Becometh."[61]

By July Washington was working to coordinate his pass system with civil authorities. Who had authority to issue passes, for what purposes, and to whom? In his general orders for July 9th, Washington directed that "Passes to go from the City are hereafter to be granted by John Berrien, Henry Wilmot and John Ray Junr a Committee of the City appointed for that purpose." These civil appointees were to issue passes to civilians. "Officers of the Guards at the Ferries and Wharves," Washington admonished, "to be careful in making this regulation known to the sentries, who are to see that the passes are signed by one of the above persons." At the same time, sentries were "to be careful no Soldier goes over the Ferry without a pass from a General Officer."[62] Less than a week later, Washington wrote to the Secret Committee of the New York Convention that "The Gentlemen appointed to give Passes to Persons leaving the City, I am informed decline acting." He warned the committee that, "Great Inconvenience will ensue to the Citizens, if this Business should

[61] Gates, Pass for Thomas Tomlin Pritchard, 18 April 1776, Horatio Gates Papers, 1726-1828, Film 23, Reel 2 (Correspondence, Nov. 1769 - July 1776), DLAR. See also Anthony L. Bleecker, Pass for Ebenezer Hazard, 24 June 1776, New York, H338, Ebenezer Hazard Papers, Item 9, APS.

[62] Washington, General Orders, 9 July 1776, *PGWDE*, Revolutionary, V: 245-247.

be committed to Officers of the Army, who from their Ignorance of the Inhabitants as well as other Reasons are wholly improper for the Management of it."[63]

The committee appointed to give passes may have changed their minds and agreed to act, because Washington, four days later, once again gave general orders that " John Berrian, Henry Wilmot and John Ray Jun: a Committee of the town are appointed to give passes to Citizens going over the ferries."[64] The distinction between military and civilian passes, and who had authority over what, remained unclear. On July 21st, Washington discharged from custody a Sergeant Ballard, held "for having presumed to give a pass to a person to cross the East river," he "appearing to have done it more thro' Ignorance than Design." Washington warned, however, that, "if any inferior officer shall hereafter take such a liberty; he will be severely punished."[65] Soon civilian demand for passes to leave the city was so great that the relevant committee had to be expanded. On the 12th of August, Washington announced in his general orders that, "The business of granting passes proving burthensome to Messrs Berrien, Ray & Wilmot; three others are added to them, viz.: William Goforth, John Campbell and Samuel Cowperthwaite, any passes signed by either of them are to be allowed."[66] Despite these measures, some military officers occasionally issued passes to civilians. Thus on August 30th, General George Clinton issued an instrument to "Permit the Bearer Ebenezer Hazard Esqr. Depy Post Master Genl to pass the Guards at all Times[.]"[67]

---

[63] Washington to the Secret Committee of the New York Convention, 13 July 1776, *PGWDE*, Revolutionary, V: 298-299.

[64] Washington, General Orders, 17 July 1776, *PGWDE*, Revolutionary, V: 352, 353: "officers and soldiers who want passes over the ferries are to apply to their own Brigadier General; And the General desires that they will give no passes to officers or soldiers of another brigade; The officers at the Ferry Guards to attend to this order particularly and make it known to the sentries."

[65] Washington, General Orders, 21 July 1776, *PGWDE*, Revolutionary, V: 411.

[66] Washington, General Orders, 12 August 1776, *PGWDE*, Revolutionary, V: 672.

[67] Clinton, Pass for Ebenezer Hazard, 30 August 1776, H338, Ebenezer Hazard Papers, Item 11, APS.

On the other side of the military-civilian divide, the New York Convention soon moved to curtail the passes they issued, while seeking to secure respect for those they did. Thus, early in August the Convention resolved, "That this Convention will not in future grant Passes…unless to Members and Officers of this Convention, or to such persons who may be by them employed during the time of their actual service." At the same time, the Convention ordered "That a Letter be wrote to General Washington, requesting him to issue general orders that every Member or Officer, or other person having a Pass from this Convention, may be permitted to pass without interruption."[68] Writing to Washington, Nathaniel Woodhull, President of the Convention, noted that members of the convention and those in its service, "having frequent Occasion to pass and repass where Guards are placed are often impeded," and suggested that Washington give orders to let them "pass without Interruption." "And lest Mistakes should arise with Respect to Members," Woodhull reassured Washington, "it is intended that each one shall have a Certificate thereof signed by the President."[69] Two days later, Washington ordered that, "Passes signed by the President of the Convention, of New York, are to be deemed authentic, and noticed as such by officers attending at the ferries."[70]

Meanwhile, Washington continued to tighten security around New York City. On the 7th of August, he ordered a subaltern officer and twenty men to be stationed at the Hoboken Ferry, "for examination of passengers."[71] Such measures were revised each time the army relocated. By mid September, having been pushed to the northern end of Manhattan by the British army, Washington

---

[68] New York Convention, 5 August 1776, *AAO*, Series 5, I: 1475-1476.

[69] Woodhull to Washington, 6 August 1776, *PGWDE*, Revolutionary, V: 589-591. Washington responded to Woodhull on the 8th, assuring him that "I shall pay proper attention to your Members & persons employed in their service and give It in Genl Orders that they be permitted to pass our Guards without Interruption." *PGWDE*, Revolutionary, V: 642.

[70] Washington, General Orders, 8 August 1776, *PGWDE*, Revolutionary, V: 618-619.

[71] Washington, General Orders, 7 August 1776, *PGWDE*, Revolutionary, V: 591-593.

on the 20th issued orders from Harlem Heights that, "Genl Green is to appoint some careful officer at Burdett's ferry to examine passengers, and see that none come over but such as have proper passes—Genl Mifflin is to do the same on this side, to prevent disaffected, or suspected persons, from passing."[72]

By the late autumn of 1776, New York City was firmly in British hands and Washington and his army were retreating across New Jersey toward the Delaware. Each new camp by each army brought new sentry lines and pass regimes affecting not just soldiers but local civilians. And with each major British occupation—of Philadelphia, Newport, Savannah, Charleston—pass regimes were enacted like those established around Boston and New York. Meanwhile, civilian governments throughout the states perpetuated their own pass regimes. New York City itself became a special case in both the military and civilian realms. After capturing the city in the autumn of 1776, the British occupied it for the remainder of the war. The lines separating American New Jersey from British New York City became some of the most important and stable of the war. Numerous refugees and others sought to cross this threshold, and military and civilian authorities on both sides spent a great deal of time and energy vetting applications for, issuing, and regulating passes to cross it.[73]

The British military and the Loyalist counterparts of the rebel committees of safety administered their own regimes of identification, with corresponding instruments. As they fortified cities against rebel attacks and planned imminent campaigns, they had to prevent rebel spies from infiltrating the city, control the outflow of intelligence and of supplies, prevent anyone from escaping the city to join the rebels, and regulate the influx of Loyalist and African American

---

[72] Washington, General Orders, 20 September 1776, *PGWDE*, Revolutionary, VI: 347-350.

[73] At least as early as December 1st, 1776, Washington, at New Brunswick, NJ, was conducting negotiations by letter with British General Howe for the exchange of prisoners in and out of New York City. See Washington to Howe, 1 December 1776, *PGWDE*, Revolutionary, VII: 247-248.

refugees. In British New York, a Superintendent General, Andrew Elliot, and the police magistrates under him, acted as the relevant authorities. Using forms printed for the purpose, under their name, Elliot and the magistrates issued passes authorizing movement into, out of, and within British New York, on Manhattan and Long Island.[74]

More comprehensive provincial and state pass regimes were soon layered on top of evolving local regimes and ad hoc procedures. By March of 1776, the Provincial Congress of New Jersey had adopted something of an in-between measure, in the form of "An Ordinance to prevent persons deserting places in danger of being attacked, and for restraining such as are dangerous to the common cause from taking refuge in this Colony." They directed those who had abandoned their duty as citizens or the support of their family in other colonies to return home. And they ordered,

> That all suspected persons removing into this Colony, shall immediately return to the place they came from; unless their behaviour in this Colony shall render their detention as delinquents proper; or unless such persons produce certificates from the Committee of the City, Township or County from whence they came, that they have signed the General Association recommended by the Continental or their Provincial Congress, and have not, by any subsequent act, contravened the same; or that they are deemed to be well affected to the cause of American freedom.[75]

In late autumn of the same year, Governor William Livingston would advise the state assembly that, "through the Credulity and Inattention of some of those who have hitherto been entrusted to grant Passes to Travellers, I have the greatest Reason to believe...many have been very improperly and imprudently granted." Livingston recommended that the state legislature newly empower trusted

---

[74] In contrast to the commissions, passes, and other instruments issued by the provincial and, later, state governments after the outbreak of the war, these passes, like nearly all other instruments issued by British military and Loyalist civilian authorities during the Revolution, defined time in terms of Royal sovereignty, giving the date of issuance in terms of the "Year of his Majesty's Reign"—tying the identity and mobility of the bearer and the authority of the issuing official to the sovereignty of the Crown. Andrew Elliot and Magistrates of Police, Pass issued to David Love, 21 July 1780, New York City, for repeated travel to and return from Long Island, Sol Feinstone Collection, Film 1, Reel 1, No. 312, DLAR. See also Andrew Elliot and Magistrates of Police, Passport issued to Mrs. Deborah Cornhoven, 27 July 1782, New York City, NY, Transcription of Copy, New Jersey. Revolutionary War. Numbered Manuscripts, 1770's-1890's, Film 678, Reel 5 (Mss. Nos. 1581-2210), No. 1582, DLAR.

[75] New Jersey Provincial Congress, 2 March 1776, *AAO*, Series 4, IV: 1618-1619.

persons to grant passes, and at the same time that it immediately "stop all Communication between this State and the Enemy's Quarters, that shall not be directed by proper Authority."[76]

By November of 1776, the New York Committee of Safety was already moving to revise their state's existing pass regime to address the "great Abuses...daily committed in the granting of Passes without sufficient Examination, to Persons inimical to the State" and to provide means to better "detect counterfeit Passes." Each county committee was to appoint "two judicious Men of known Attachment to its Interest" for each district "who shall grant the Passes…to such Persons only of whose Principles, they shall be fully satisfied." Passes were to use printed forms supplied by the state and be signed by one of the two secretaries of the state convention. The grantee was to fill in "his Name" in his own "Hand-writing," and the issuing official was to date and countersign. Each pass was to specify the grantee's "Place of Abode" and "the Place to which he may proceed." Residents had to carry passes when they moved about and any stranger was subject to arrest "unless he comes from some other State, and brings a Pass from the same."[77] The New York state and county committees of safety were joined by the Committee and, later, the Commission for Detecting and Defeating Conspiracies in the State of New York, charged with a variety of duties in regulating documented and undocumented persons.[78]

Back in New Jersey, in June of 1777, the General Assembly authorized the Governor and Council of Safety "to grant Passports or Permissions to pass through any Parts of this State; and also to authorize such and so many Persons in every County within the same, to grant such Passports and Permissions, and under such Regulations as they shall think necessary." They were to detain

---

[76] Livingston to the New Jersey Assembly, 21 November 1776, *PWL*, I: 183.

[77] New York Committee of Safety, 7 November 1776, Fishkill, NY, *EAI*, Series 1, no. 14928 (filmed).

[78] See *Minutes of the Committee and of the First Commission for Detecting and Defeating Conspiracies in the State of New York, December 11, 1776 – September 23, 1778, with Collateral Documents; to which is added Minutes of the Council of Appointment, State of New York, April 2, 1778 – May 3, 1779*, 2 vols., *Collections of the New York Historical Society for the Years 1924-1925*, (New York: 1925), I: 35, 36, 53, 60, 134, passim.

any suspect characters "travelling without such Passports or Permissions, until they shall satisfy" the authorized official in question of their being well-affected to the State, or of their travelling without any Designs injurious to it." "Every Person," moreover, "convicted of counterfeiting any such Passports or Permissions," was to "suffer six Months Imprisonment."[79]

Thus empowered, Governor Livingston, five days later, issued a proclamation designating by office those empowered to grant these passports and permissions, and specifying the form they were to take. The passports were to name and describe the bearer by approximate age, complexion, height, and eyes, and specify where he was authorized to travel, "behaving himself civily." The passport was to be dated, with the county and place of issuance noted, and was to be "subscribed" by the issuing officer "with his Name and Title of Office." The proclamation also stipulated that, "all Ferrymen and Innkeepers within this State" were "prohibited to convey over any Creek or River, or to entertain any Traveller (excepting the said Officers hereby authorized to grant such Passports or Permissions, and all Persons belonging to the Army of the United States)" who "shall refuse to produce such Passport or Permission upon being thereto requested, which every Ferryman and Innkeeper is hereby enjoined to do."[80]

Fitful attempts at coordination also proceeded. New Jersey authorities, through the Council of Safety, from 1777 onward worked with its counterparts in other states, the Continental Army, and the Continental Congress to police lines separating American New Jersey from British New York. In addition to the military passes needed to cross the military lines at the New Jersey coast, the New Jersey government forbade anyone to cross the lines in either direction without a proper civil passport. (By early 1777, New Jersey Authorities had found that simply requiring Loyalists to post

---

[79] 4 June 1777, *Acts of the General Assembly of the state of New-Jersey. At a session begun at Princeton on the 27th day of August 1776, and continued by adjournments*, (Burlington, NJ: Isaac Collins, Printer, 1777), *EAI*, Series 1, no. 15460 (filmed), 63. See also *PWL*, I: 183n2.

[80] William Livingston, Proclamation, 9 June 1777, Haddonfield, NJ, Sol Feinstone Collection, Film 1, Reel 2, No. 1007, DLAR.

bond that they would remain within the state and behave themselves had not prevented a number of such bonded persons from fleeing the state across British lines.[81]) The Council of Safety meted out a variety of punishments to those who violated passport requirements in crossing the lines. In January of 1778, the Council released Caleb Owins, charged with "having gone into the Enemy's Lines & returning without the License prescribed by Law," only once he agreed to enlist in the New Jersey Battalions.[82] The previous day, the Council had required Mrs. Hannah Ward, charged likewise with "going into the Enemy's Lines & returning into this State without the Permission for so doing required by Law," to give a £300 bond to appear at the next Court of General Quarter Sessions.[83] Harmin Bosin's case, adjudged about a week earlier, illustrated the threat seen behind such unauthorized crossings. Bosin was indicted for "going into the Enemy's Lines since the Treason Law & returning into this State as a Spy." He was given "five days to consider whether he will enlist in our Service, or be committed for his Trial."[84] Richard Lewis, who had not, it appears, crossed the lines in either direction, was examined that same day "for travelling thro' the Country without a Passport," and was required to take "the Oaths of Abjuration & Allegiance as by Law subscribed" before being released.[85]

---

[81] See William Livingston to the New Jersey Assembly, 19 February 1777, *PWL*, I: 243-244.

[82] New Jersey Council of Safety, 29 January 1778, Records of the States of the United States, New Jersey, 1777-1778, Film 281, E4, Reel 1, Minutes of the Council of Safety, DLAR. See also, in the minutes for 19 January 1778, the judgment against Joseph Morse, Jr., "it appearing that he had been into the Enemy Lines & returned into this State, without the Permission by Law required—Agreed that he be committed for Tryal to Morris Town Gaol."

[83] New Jersey Council of Safety, 28 January 1778, Records of the States of the United States, New Jersey, 1777-1778, Film 281, E4, Reel 1, Minutes of the Council of Safety, DLAR. Hannah Higgens, indicted a little less than two weeks earlier, 16 January 1778, "for coming from the Enemy's Lines into this State, without the Licence required by Law," was likewise required to give bond for appearance at the next Quarter Sessions.

[84] New Jersey Council of Safety, 20 January 1778, Records of the States of the United States, New Jersey, 1681-1786, Film 281, Reel 1, Minutes of the Council of Safety, DLAR.

[85] New Jersey Council of Safety, 20 January 1778, Records of the States of the United States, New Jersey, 1681-1786, Film 281, Reel 1, Minutes of the Council of Safety, DLAR.

In Pennsylvania, in June of 1777, the Provincial Congress moved, much as New Jersey and New York had, to exclude dangerous strangers. The Congress recommended that all committees throughout the province "pay the strictest attention to the examination of all strangers or persons travelling through the City or Counties, and permit no persons travelling through the City or Counties to remain therein, unless they produce a pass or certificate from the City, County, or District Committee from whence they last came." The Congress further recommended that the committees "furnish proper passes to all friends to American liberty, upon their application therefor."[86] Meanwhile, from 1776 onward, the Council of Safety, and later the Supreme Executive Council, adjudged numerous applications for passes to cross into enemy lines—most commonly at Philadelphia or at New York—to travel to the western frontier, or to travel through the state. During the British occupation of Philadelphia, from September 1777 to June 1778, the provincial government coordinated with Washington and other Continental Army commanders to regulate passage of persons and goods in and out of the city.[87]

In Rhode Island, similarly, during the British occupation of Newport (1777-1778), the state Council of War received numerous applications to travel or relocate to the British-held island, or to come from the island into American-held territory. The minutes of the Council contain dozens of resolutions permitting such travel, often from a specific embarkation point, in a specified vessel, or with limited personal property and goods.[88] Some of the granted passes survive. On the 29th of November 1777, for instance, the Council of War issued a pass, in the name of the State, dated at Providence and signed by the Council's clerk, certifying that, "The following Persons are permitted

---

[86] Pennsylvania Provincial Congress, 25 June 1776, *AAO*, Series 4, VI: 964-965.

[87] *Records of Pennsylvania's Revolutionary governments, 1775-1790: (Record Group 27) in the Pennsylvania State Archives*, Harry E. Whipjey et al eds., Microfilm, Reel 30: Applications for Passes, 1776-1788.

[88] See, Records of the States of the United States, Rhode Island, 1775-1818, Film 285, E4, Reel 1, Minutes of the Council of War, DLAR.

to go upon Rhode Island in the Cartel Vessel now going. (viz) / Mr. Richard Backhouse, late Purser of the British Ship Syren. / Mr. Thomas Greene— / Mr. Townsend Goddard.— / Mrs. Bathsheba Fairchild."[89]

It was probably impossible for Americans who took to the road during the Revolution to keep track of the multiple pass regimes. Securing all of the instruments for travel was likewise difficult. And it was far from certain that these would be sufficient to certify a traveller's identity in the eyes of all those he or she might encounter. Travellers, accordingly, often sought to supplement or substitute for prescribed passes a variety of additional instruments of identification. In this way they interwove the practices and instruments of private or social identification with those of the official pass regimes.

In some instances travellers supplied themselves with documents or objects that were not in themselves instruments of identification, but which could betoken their political loyalties or social connections. When the American Colonel Israel Shreve sent his son John home to his mother after the boy had visited him in camp, he gave him a letter of instructions for his journey and fatherly admonitions to behave well at home and be dutiful to his mother. In a postscript, Shreve directed his son to "Keep this Letter," as "it will Do for a pass," should anyone think John was a deserter from the army, a runaway servant, or a proper candidate for recruitment or conscription. It would also advertise that he was the son of a Patriot in active service, and so likely not a Loyalist or an enemy agent.[90]

---

[89] Records of the States of the United States, Rhode Island, 1775-1818, Film 285, E4, Reel 1, Minutes of the Council of War, DLAR.

[90] Israel Shreve to John Shreve, 12 June 1776, Sorel, NJ, Transcription, Letters found in the case of John Shreve—Invalid #3890, New Jersey. Revolutionary War. Numbered Manuscripts, 1770's-1890's, Film 678, Reel 6 (Mss. Nos. 2211-2403), No. 2314, DLAR.

Given the numerous authorities involved in issuing and regulating passes, individuals often had to coordinate with a tangle of authorities. In February of 1776, for instance, Alexander Ross applied to the Maryland delegates to the Continental Congress for "a passport to Lord Dunmore," who he claimed owed him money. The delegates ultimately recommended him to the Maryland Council of Safety for a passport, fearing that the Congress would not be able to address his request for quite some time and judging that "a license from your honourable Board will be, at least, as effectual."[91] The Council of Safety in turn gave Ross "a permit to pass" to the Virginia Committee of Safety, writing to the latter that "as his business is to be settled in your Colony, we leave the propriety of granting him a further passport to your determination."[92] The Virginia Committee of Safety in turn gave him a letter to the Committee of Hampton, who ultimately "declined giving him any passport."[93]

Individuals' abilities to mobilize social resources heavily influenced their control over their identities and therefore their access to mobility. Thus on January 9th of 1776, Washington issued an instrument to John Austin and Joseph Collidge directing whoever might read it to allow the two men "to pass from hence to Canada on their private business, being recommended to me as friends to the United Colonies."[94] In June of that year, John Leaver of Tryon County, NY, applied to the Provincial Congress of New York for a passport to Pennsylvania. Because "the Members of said County" testified that he was "a friend to the American cause," Leaver was granted a certificate that,

---

[91] Maryland Delegates in the Continental Congress to the Maryland Council of Safety, 25 February 1776, *AAO*, Series 4, IV: 1491-1492.

[92] Maryland Council of Safety to the Virginia Committee of Safety, 7 March 1776, *AAO*, Series 4, V: 95.

[93] Maryland Council of Safety to the Maryland Delegates to the Continental Congress, 17 April 1776, *AAO*, Series 4, V: 960-961.

[94] Washington, Pass for John Austin and Joseph Collidge, 9 January 1776, Sol Feinstone Collection, Film 1, Reel 3, No. 1623, DLAR. The pass was signed by Washington and countersigned by secretary Stephen Moylan. Notations on the pass from August 1776 indicate that the two men acted at least once as couriers between General Wooster at Montreal and General Montgomery at Quebec.

"This Congress having received satisfactory information that the bearer, Mr. John Leaver, is a friend to the cause of America, therefore he is permitted to pass unmolested."[95]

The closer to the army and the more involved with its affairs they became, the more civilians were likely to find themselves entangled in military identification regimes. This was especially the case when they ventured into army posts. Civilian contractors, such as wagoners or sutlers, and "official" camp followers, were typically registered and licensed, and often issued long-term passes. Instruments were also issued to such persons on an ad hoc basis. In early October of 1776, General Gates issued a pass, addressed to "All whom it may Concern," explaining that, "Captain Casdorp—with his Company of Carpenters, consisting of thirty four Men, lately in the Service of the United States of America, having discharged their Duty with Dilligence; Ability & Faithfulness," were, "hereby permitted to pass from hence to Philadelphia." Gates requested "All Committees of Safety, Officers at the Different posts upon the Communication and others…to Aid and Assist them on their March."[96]

Since such persons were civilians acting for the military, the certification of their identities was often hybrid in character. Thus in March of 1776, the New York Committee of Safety issued an instrument in manuscript on a largish sheet of letter paper, addressed "To Every Committee and to Every friend to Liberty in the United Colonies," certifying that, "[t]he Bearer hereof Mr Daniel Hinslee of the City of New York, Butcher" had "Contracted with Mr Abraham Livingston (the Contractor for Supplying the Continental Troops in this City with rations accorded by Congress with a Quantity of fresh beef[)]." Because "the said Daniel Hinslee" was accordingly "under a Necessity of going into the different parts of this Colony as well as into the Colony of Connecticut

---

[95] New York Provincial Congress, 26 June 1776, *AAO*, Series 4, VI: 1431-1433.

[96] Gates, Pass for Captain Casdorp et al., 3 October 1776, Ticonderoga, NY, Horatio Gates Papers, 1726-1828, Film 23, Reel 3 (Correspondence, July 1776 - October 1776), DLAR.

to purchase and procure Cattle to fulfill his said Contract," the Committee "therefore recommended that he be suffered to pass and repass with such Cattle as he may be able to procure unmolested."[97] Similar passports were issued to several other contractors or sub-contractors employed by Livingston in gathering cattle.[98]

Unaffiliated civilians in or near a camp itself were more worrisome. They might promote disorder, drain army provisions, bring disease, encourage desertion, or any number of other evils—or they might prove to be enemy spies. Commanders continually struggled not only to keep soldiers within bounds but also to keep the civilian population from bringing confusion to the army. Early in the autumn of 1776, General Gates of the Northern Army declared that, "Whereas, either led by Curiosity, or from some sinister design, many Persons intermix with this Army, Continue therewith as long as they find Convenient, and again depart, without having any Certificate from the Committee of Safety of the place where they belong, or a pass from Head Quarters here," therefore,

> The General Orders that any Person, not properly belonging to this Army, who shall be found to have been within the Limits of this Encampment above the Space of One Hour, without having given in his Name and Business either at Head Quarters, or to a Field Officer of some of The Regiments, and Obtained a proper Certificate thereof, shall be confined, Tried by a General Court Martial, and Punished as the Nature of the Offence shall Appeal to Deserve:—The General Expects Al Officers will be Careful in discovering such Delinquents.[99]

Washington and other commanders likewise issued passes (similar to those issued to soldiers) to civilians with legitimate reasons for contact with the American forces. In September of 1777, at the

---

[97] New York Committee of Safety, Pass for Daniel Hinslee, 30 March 1776, New York, NY, Sol Feinstone Collection, Film 1, Reel 4, No. 1996, DLAR.

[98] See New York Committee of Safety, Pass for Ryer Schermerhorn, 28 March 1776, *AAO*, Series 4, V: 1411; New York Committee of Safety, Pass for Henry Hegeman, 30 March 1776, *AAO*, Series 4, V: 1418.

[99] Gates, Orders, 28 September 1776, Orderly Book: Northern Army, 10 July 1776 – 3 June 1777, Horatio Gates Papers, 1726-1828, Film 23, Reel 18 (Orderly Books, August 1758 - February 1783; Returns, January 1756 - November 1778), DLAR.

"Camp near Potssgrove," Washington signed a pass declaring that one James A. Esqr., "the bearer of this, has liberty to pass to and from the Continental Army."[100]

Establishing and governing individual political identities was fundamental to the prosecution of war and the contest for sovereignty in Revolutionary America. But the identities in question were as often fluid and mobile as fixed and settled. Passes both enabled and restricted the mobility of individual identities, mobilizing but also channeling Revolutionary "Americans" between and across lines defined by political divisions and military imperatives. The pass regimes established amid the Revolutionary crisis of identification, indeed, brought greater regulation of mobility to wider swathes of American society than ever before, giving many who had hitherto enjoyed relative freedom of movement a taste of the type of regimes used to govern unfree labor. Pass regimes were established, and the challenges of mobile identification faced, by both civilian and military authorities, in a revolution defined by a complex intermixture of civil and military conflict and transformation. Policing the boundaries of the military communities created by the conflict—as well as establishing and governing the identities of their constituent individuals—was no less essential to the practice of revolution and civil war than was governing the identities and mobility of the civilian populations, communities, and polities. The following chapter explores how identities were contested, defined, and transformed along the uncertain frontier between the civil and the military Revolution. As such, it marks a shift from the focus in the preceding four chapters on individual genres of identification papers back to more integrated histories and a focus on particular contexts or realms of identification in the final three chapters. With this shift in focus, these

---

[100] Washington, Pass for James A., 25 September 1777, Camp near Potssgrove, Sol Feinstone Collection, Film 1, Reel 5, No. 2127, DLAR.

concluding chapters illuminate the interstices and occluded histories of the Revolutionary crisis of

identification as explored to this point.

Chapter 6

Military

Because the Revolution was a composite political and military conflict, defining identities within that context was a dual process of identification. And yet even as military and civilian domains overlapped, there was a frontier between them that imperfectly divided the civilian from the military population, civil from military law. Along this frontier, many Revolutionary identities were defined and the margins of the Revolutionary conflict were delimited. To cross from one identity to another meant to be recreated—in part from the elements of one's civilian identity and in part from scratch. Military recruitment was thus a continual process of double identification: first establishing the relevant facets of the candidate's civilian identity to judge his (or her) eligibility, and then fashioning military identities for those enlisted. This dual process of identification revealed the dynamics of exclusion and coercion that shaped Revolutionary identification more generally and constructed the United States.

Like political citizenship, to which it was closely related, military service described one form of participation in the Revolution and thus of membership in the polity. In this era of exclusively male political personhood, especially, military service was understood to properly entail, if not full citizenship, at least free subjecthood. The bounds of military service, accordingly, had to be defined in harmony with acceptable structures of dependence and autonomy, as well as period understandings of who could legitimately be considered an autonomous agent. At the same time, the Revolutionary military conflict was a necessarily practical affair. Those who served had to meet minimum requirements of physical and mental capacity, both as individuals and as members of groups defined by certain cultural stereotypes. Acceptable military recruits or conscripts were thus

defined by a complex of characteristics, including race, gender, age, physical capacity, and loyalty.

Military service nevertheless offered opportunities for self-advancement for slaves, servants,

children, other dependents, and the free but poor. There were many, as such, who had incentives to

dissimulate the criteria for military service. Recruiting officers and muster masters, in turn, had

quotas to fill and a war to fight, and so had incentives not to scrutinize candidates too closely. At

the same time, however, these officers faced penalties for fraud or negligence. Commanders

likewise had every reason to make sure their ranks were filled with capable, reliable, and acceptable

soldiers, as well as strong temptations to blame failures in battle on unsatisfactory rank-and-file.

Identification on the frontiers of military service in the Revolution was, thus, a continual, multi-sided

contest to define and redefine individual identities.

Revolutionary military service incorporated a greater proportion of the populace than had

typically served either in peacetime militias or in previous wars. But even in the early stages, at the

local and provincial level, recruiting was explicitly structured by age ranges and implicitly by gender

and race.[1] When, in July of 1775, the Continental Congress added its voice to the chorus of calls for

mobilization it resolved, "That it be recommended to the inhabitants of all the united English

---

[1] See Committee of Worcester County, MA, 29 August 1774, *AAO*, Series IV, I: 795-797; Extract of a Letter from
Worcester, 27 September 1774, *AAO*, Series IV, I: 806; Don Higginbotham, *The War of American Independence: Military
Attitudes, Policies, and Practice, 1763-1789*, (Boston: Northeastern UP, 1983), 10, 61; Convention of Maryland, 8 December
1774, *AAO*, Series IV, I: 1031-1033; New Castle County, DE, 21 December 1774, *AAO*, Series IV, I: 1022; Fairfax
County, VA, 17 January 1775, *AAO*, Series IV, I: 1145; Association of the Inhabitants of Fairfax County, 17 January
1775, *AAO*, Series IV, I: 1145. In Great Britain, minimum ages for holding officers' commissions had been legislated,
though very loosely enforced, since the late seventeenth and early eighteenth centuries. Age minimums for service in the
general infantry had risen from fifteen in the thirteenth century to eighteen by the middle of the eighteenth century.
Holly Brewer, *By Birth or Consent: Children, Law, and the Anglo-American Revolution in Authority*, (Chapel Hill, NC: University
of North Carolina Press, 2005), 137. By the time of the Revolution in the colonies, the minimum age for militia service
and the age of militia obligation had settled generally at sixteen years old (having dropped from eighteen in Virginia as of
1775, and rising to eighteen in Pennsylvania in 1776). The Massachusetts militia law of 1776 would require all men from
sixteen to fifty years old to enroll in the militia. John W. Shy, *A People Numerous and Armed: Reflections on the Military
Struggle for American Independence*, Rev. ed., (Ann Arbor, MI: University of Michigan Press, 1990), 32. Pennsylvania added
to a minimum age a requirement of parental consent for enrolling children below twenty-one years of age in the militia.
Brewer, *By Birth or Consent*, 138.

Colonies in North America, that all able bodied effective men, between sixteen and fifty years of age in each colony, immediately form themselves into regular companies of Militia."[2]

When the newly formed Continental Army began recruiting in the summer of 1775, identification of potential recruits was guided by a complex of stipulations designed to exclude objectionable persons from the ranks. In a letter to Congress shortly after taking up his command of the Continental Army at Cambridge, Massachusetts, Washington had noted the large "Number of Boys, Deserters, & Negroes which have been listed in the Troops of this Province," and remarked that "the Dismission of those unfit for Duty on Account of their Age & Character would occasion a considerable Reduction" of the troops in arms.[3] The new recruiting instructions for the Continental Army issued, even as Washington wrote his letter, by newly appointed Adjutant General Horatio Gates specified that recruiting officers were "not to Enlist any Deserter from the Ministerial Army, nor any Stroller, Negro or Vagabond, or Person suspected of being an Enemy to the Liberty of America, nor any under Eighteen Years of Age." Nor were the recruiting officers to enlist "any Person who is not an American-born, unless such Person has a Wife and Family, and is a settled Resident in this Country."[4] These instructions excluded those whose credibility or commitment to the cause could not be verified or assumed. And they excluded all African Americans, slave or free, from service. The instructions also suggest a perceived need to steer clear of those who lacked the sort of social identity by which their characters could be judged (and enforced) to begin with, but also by which they could be located were they to go missing as deserters. Those who came as ostensible deserters from the enemy or as strangers to the locality in which they enlisted, moreover, were suspect as potential if not actual spies or traitors.

---

[2] *JCC*, 18 July 1775, II: 187-190.

[3] Washington to the President of Congress, 10-11 July 1775, *PGWDE*, Revolutionary, I: 85-97.

[4] 10 July 1775, Cambridge, MA, Broadside, (Watertown, MA: Printed by Benjamin Edes, 1775), *EAI*, Series 1, no. 14243 (filmed).

When General Washington issued new recruiting orders the following October, he delimited

the pool of acceptable recruits by combining a precise upper age limit with the common but less

well-defined exclusion of children and the elderly. He added a variety of other exclusion criteria.

The first article of the instructions stipulated that,

> You are not to inlist any but Freemen able of Body & under the age of 50 carefully avoiding
> all persons Labouring under any Lameness or other Defect of Body prejudicial to the
> Service. If any such persons or any Boys or decripit persons are brought into the Service the
> Officer inlisting them will be chargeable with the Expence they may be to the publick.

A draft of the same instructions had originally specified the minimum age of recruits as seventeen,

but this lower age threshold was omitted in the final instructions, perhaps to allow the recruiting

officer greater discretion in judging which potential recruits were mere "boys" and which were

sufficiently mature.[5] (These new instructions, likewise, allowed free African Americans to enlist.)

Persistent or obviously fraudulent enlistment of legally excluded or otherwise unfit recruits could

bring punishments up to and including dishonorable discharge from the service, or worse.[6]

---

[5] Washington to Edward Hand, 11 October 1776, *PGWDE*, Revolutionary, VI: 536-537. His circular recruiting
instructions of January 1777 would set the minimum age for recruits at seventeen and the maximum age at fifty.
PGWDE, Revolutionary, VIII: 44-45. Washington would resort instead to the broader, informal exclusion of the upper
and lower extremes of the age spectrum when he was driven to reiterate the stipulation in his general orders of
November 1776. "No Boys," he ordered, "(under the idea of Waiters, or otherwise) or old Men, to be inlisted—if they
are, they will be returned on the hands of the officer, without any allowance for any expence he may be at." General
Orders, 10 November 1776, *PGWDE*, Revolutionary, VII: 129-130.

[6] In August of 1782, for example, Ezra Badlam would be discharged from the army for, "Neglect of duty and
unofficerlike conduct in ministering and forwarding to the Army as Recruits for the Massachusetts Line several persons
precluded by the Laws of the State and others unfit to perform the duty of soldiers in the field." These included British
deserters, foreigners, "boys undersized," "a negroe lame in the ancle," and "an idiot." *PGWDE*, Revolutionary, XII:
683n1. Despite such efforts to exclude those unqualified—by age, sex, incapacity, unfreedom, or other status—from the
service, complaints that the army was diluted or burdened with those unsuitable for service would continue throughout
the war. Explaining and attempting to excuse the controversial evacuation of Fort Ticonderoga in 1777, General Arthur
St. Clair would insist that only a portion of the garrison had been fit for duty, "many of those mere boys." St. Clair to
Bowdoin, 9 July 1777, and St. Clair to Washington, 11 July 1777, *St. Clair Papers*, William Henry Smith ed., (Cincinnati,
OH: R. Clarke, 1882), I: 425-426, 429-433. Later the same summer, General Schuyler would complain to Congress that
of the Continental troops under his command, fully a third of them consisted "of Boys, Negroes & aged Men not fit for
the field or any other service." Samuel Adams to Roger Sherman, 11 August 1777, *LDC*, VII: 452-453. Reporting the
same account from Schuyler, see also Adams to James Warren, 12 August 1777, and Adams to William Heath, 13
August 1777, *LDC*, VII: 461, 473-474. Heath would write in return regarding the Massachusetts forces, "As to the
ability of body of the men I can not fully determine. The greater part that I saw appeared able, but it is more than
probable that there were some men advanc'd in life, and some lads and a number of negroes (the latter were generally
able bodied, but for my own part I must confess I am never pleased to see them mixed with white men)." Washington,
in turn, seems to have had to contend with at least one general under his command who was more willing to enlist boys

In the midst of the succeeding winter, in January of 1776, the Continental Congress would adopt instructions for the recruiting service in which they would resolve, "That the recruiting officers ought to be careful to inlist none but healthy, sound and able bodied men, and not under sixteen years of age."[7] A year later, Washington issued circular recruiting instructions directing officers to "enlist none but freemen above the age of Seventeen & under that of Fifty of Sufficient Stature & Ability of body to discharge all the Offices of a private Soldier," such recruits "to be free from Lameness or other bodily Infirmity, that may render them Incapable to support the fatigues of a Camp." They were not to enlist any British deserters, "nor any person of disaffected or Suspicious Characters with respect to the American Cause."[8] Later in the war, in February of 1780, the Continental Board of War would recommend a uniform system of recruiting, across the states, in which an officer dispatched to the recruiting rendezvous in each state would "examine the fitness, or unfitness of the drafts and recruits for service," rejecting any that were improper. "To prevent all disputes respecting the proper age of the drafts and recruits," it was "farther resolved that no person shall be received as such, who shall be under the age of eighteen, or above that of fifty," with the exception of healthy boys of at least fifteen, who might be enlisted as musicians or officers' servants.[9]

The process of American military recruitment during the Revolutionary War thus shows the practice of identification on the ground, as a means of policing one of the key boundaries of active

---

under sixteen years old, as long as they were "of Good Growth & firm Constitutions." See Higginbotham, *War of American Independence*, 415n5. In May of 1778, General Alexander McDougall would despair of the recruiting and conscription effort in which he was engaged. "I have but Little Hopes of the Batalions being filled," he wrote to Washington, "All the mean and wicked arts are practised, which the craft of man can invent, to screen men from the draughts, or to render them ineffectual, by engaging Deserters & prisoners; old men and boy for Substitu[t]es." McDougall to Washington, 6 May 1778, *PGWDE*, Revolutionary, XV: 64-65.

[7] *JCC*, 17 January 1776, IV: 63-64.

[8] Washington, Circular Recruiting Instructions, 12-27 January 1777, Morristown, NJ, *PGWDE*, Revolutionary, VIII: 44-45.

[9] *JCC*, 8 February 1780, XVI: 248-251.

citizenship, in part by demanding documentation for those who wished to cross the border, one way or the other. Those who wanted to enlist, to be exempted from conscription on the grounds of age, disability, or other status, or to be discharged from service (as they thought better of their commitment or if personal and family crises arose) had to furnish proof of their age, unfreedom, or exemption for other cause, or otherwise convince the relevant officer that they were excluded by established criteria.[10] Parents who petitioned for the discharge of children who had enlisted without their consent had to prove that those children were under a certain age. Masters who demanded the discharge of their ostensible servants and slaves had to prove their authority over or ownership of the individual in question. Few explicit and detailed accounts of how officers verified or others proved their ages, freedom, or other identity in these cases survive. But some sense of the several ways these processes played out can be gleaned from clues found in muster rolls, recruiting returns, and officers' diaries and correspondence.

In many cases when officers recorded excluding particular soldiers from service on the grounds of age they did not specify how they determined the individual was "above age" or "under

---

[10] Mintz has suggested that, "in a society without reliable birth records, a boy could simply lie about his age or find and adult who would testify that he was sixteen or older." Steven Mintz, *Huck's Raft: A History of American Childhood*, (Cambridge, MA: Harvard UP, 2004), 62. This was undoubtedly true to a certain extent, and, as both Mintz and Higginbotham note, recruiting officers under pressure to meet quotas would have had an incentive to accept such claims without too much scrutiny (though, as we have seen, Washington and others attempted to impose penalties to discourage such practices). Higginbotham, *War of American Independence*, 391. For a take similar to Mintz's on the motives of recruiting officers and their willingness to look the other way regarding age, see Brewer, *By Birth or Consent*, 129-130. But it is not clear how common this was; how simple it was for underage boys to find adults willing to lie, even perjure themselves on their behalf; or how readily recruiting officers and muster officers accepted undocumented assertions of age, whether true or fraudulent. At the same time, while recognizing the important role that decentralization, inconsistency, and unreliability of birth records played in structuring identification by age during this period, we also need to recognize the historically contingent nature of standards of reliability and evidence, in recordkeeping and otherwise. On the historical contingency of standards of evidence and record keeping, see Barbara J. Shapiro, *A Culture of Fact: England, 1550-1720*, (Ithaca, NY: Cornell UP, 2000); Shapiro, *"Beyond a reasonable doubt" and "probable cause": Historical Perspectives on the Anglo-American Law of Evidence*, (Berkley, CA: University of California Press, 1991); Mary Poovey, *A History of the Modern Fact: Problems of Knowledge in the Sciences of Wealth and Society*, (Chicago: University of Chicago Press, 1998). And we need to consider what degree of imprecision and unreliability recruiters and others were willing to accept, while still, in some instances, requiring proof of age. The idiosyncrasies of individual recruiters and the variable circumstances of different recruiting drives likely also had substantial influence on the degree of scrutiny and standard of proof regarding the ages of potential recruits.

age," or how a particular candidate "Prov'd himself Over Age."[11] Other soldiers, already serving in the ranks, were dismissed or excused from duty as "Unfit for service through age."[12] In other instances, an officer might provide a little more detail, noting, for instance, that a particular candidate had been judged "under age by Certi[ficate]," but without specifying whether the document in question was a certificate of birth (probably a certified copy from a church register), a certificate of baptism, a formal attestation from an acquaintance, or something else.[13] In some cases, as Holly Brewer has suggested, recruiters may have been as concerned with the fact of a recruit's signature on an enlistment paper as with whether the recruit was eligible to sign or make his mark— the form may have been as important as the intent or capacity of the individual.[14]

Because the surviving records tend to lack detail and to offer absolute categorizations, they can obscure the ambiguities of the processes involved in arriving at an identification. Occasionally, hints of the importance of individual officers' ad hoc judgments emerge, as in a note indicating that a particular candidate was "I belive over age."[15] Proof of a potential enlistee's identity may have frequently rested on the willingness of the candidate himself to swear to being free, of a particular age, not previously enlisted in another unit, and so on, and risk the penalties provided for in case of

---

[11] See *PAA*, Series V, VII: 145, 915, 242 (Michael Huber).

[12] "Muster and Pay Rolls of the War of the Revolution, 1775-1783," *CNYHS*, XLVIII (1915), 359.

[13] *PAA*, Series V, VII: 149 (John Huber). In other circumstances and in later eras, individuals needing to prove facts about themselves of similar intangibility and illegibility to that of age—such as citizenship, place of birth, lineage, length of residence, or "good moral character"—to claim freedom, a passport, diplomatic protection, suffrage, naturalization, inheritance, eligibility for office, or release from impressment into the British Navy, would often rely on a combination of their own sworn depositions, certificates and attestations from family, friends, colleagues, patrons, and acquaintances, and certified copies or extracts from town or church records of birth, baptism, marriage, or the like. See the numerous examples in "Passport Applications, 1795-1905," NARA M1372; "Naturalization Petitions for the Eastern District of Pennsylvania, 1795-1930," NARA M1522; "Proofs of Citizenship Used to Apply for Seamen's Certificates for the Port of Philadelphia, Pennsylvania, 1792-1861," NARA M1880; "Miscellaneous Lists and Papers Regarding Impressed Seamen, 1796-1814," NARA M1839. See also Rebecca J. Scott and Jean M. Hébrard, *Freedom Papers: An Atlantic Odyssey in the Age of Emancipation*, (Cambridge, MA: Harvard UP, 2012).

[14] Brewer, *By Birth or Consent*, 129-130.

[15] *PAA*, Series V, VII: 208 (Jacob Coss).

perjury. Though enlistment papers were primarily intended to prove voluntary enlistment for a particular period and on particular terms, many also included a description of the subscriber (as a means to prevent bounty hopping, desertion, and the like), varying in detail, but usually including, at the very least, the enlistee's age. Signed enlistment papers for the Pennsylvania militia in 1777, for instance, typically began with the formula used in the case of "I George Alexander aged Twenty Three years," or "I, William Alley, aged Twenty one years."[16] Enlistees in the First New York Regiment in the midst of the war put their signature or mark on muster rolls describing their person, including physical features and their age.[17]

Not uncommonly, the uncertainty regarding the particulars of a soldier's identity came through in omissions and approximations. In many cases, the age column for a particular soldier would simply be left blank.[18] In others, the lack of knowledge was made explicit, the column for "age" being completed with "Unknown."[19] When the soldier could provide some point of reference for the length of his life, or when the recording officer felt confident enough to judge by appearances, an approximate age was sometimes given, as in the "Abt. 30 yrs." recorded for Abraham Gambell.[20] An enlistee's place of birth or origin tended to decrease in specificity the

---

[16] *PAA*, Series V, VII: 658-659, passim.

[17] "Muster and Pay Rolls of the War of the Revolution, 1775-1783," *CNYHS*, XLVIII (1915), 391, passim. When it came to self-identification by age—independent of the context of military recruiting—Fischer's research has identified regionally specific tendencies among Americans to distort, exaggerate, round, or falsify their ages ("age heaping") depending on the particular culture of age (resulting in general tendency to give older ages in Virginia, for instance, or a bias towards youth among younger adults and towards old age among older adults to different degrees in both New England and the backcountry). David Hackett Fischer, *Albion's Seed: Four British Folkways in America*, (New York: Oxford UP, 1989), 103, 323, 694, 696. These tendencies evident in regional cultures likely had an influence on how individuals from each region identified themselves by age in the process of recruiting, and the heuristics with which recruiters and others evaluated these self-identifications.

[18] See *AMDMR*, 629 (Simon Perry; John Buckannan).

[19] See *AMDMR*, 630 (Henry Clarage).

[20] *AMDMR*, 630. Approximate or estimated ages may have been used more commonly than is evident from the explicit language of the lists and registers themselves, and regional cultures of age heaping may have influenced different recruiters, from and recruiting in different locales, to approximate or round ages differently. But without indication in the register or independent evidence concerning the registering of particular soldiers, it is impossible to determine

further this place fell from the site of enlistment. Those from the immediate region were often identified by town or county—sometimes farm or plantation—while those from other states or from overseas were most commonly identified only by state, country, or geographical region.

Because military enlistment offered servants, slaves, children, and other dependents opportunities for liberation, while masters and parents strove to maintain control of their dependents, recruiting officers and commanders had frequently to contend with disputes regarding the freedom of potential enlistees or their legal capacity to consent to enlistment. The legal structures of subordination that prevailed in colonial society, defining mastership, authority, and dependence, remained largely in place through the Revolution. The Continental and state governments, as well as the British military governments, largely worked with masters and parents, and established regulations, to preserve the authority of these parties. The recognized rights and authorities on the part of masters and parents—and the general social structuring by mastery and dependence—posed a challenge to military recruitment and the regulation of identity and mobility during the Revolution more broadly. Not only had potential citizen-soldiers to be identified in their own right, but the nature and degree of their dependence on others had to be determined in order to establish their right to consent or travel.

The tension between state needs and private authority was repeatedly made salient in attempts to prevent recruiting officers' efforts to fill their quotas and complete their units from violating the rights of parents and masters. Thus, a resolution of the Continental Congress, in early 1776, ordered, "That no apprentice whatsoever be inlisted within the colonies of New Jersey,

---

whether a number entered in an age column was meant as a precise or approximate age. In fact, just as recruiters may have had an incentive in many cases to admit underage recruits and overlook, or even abet, falsification of recruits' ages, they may also have had an incentive not to document or record their decision-making and judgment process in regard to recruits' ages—regardless of the level of integrity they aspired to, or the degree of good faith with which they approached the question of age verification—since such records would only provide evidence of the uncertainty, lack of evidence, and individual judgment that likely went into many such decisions and would open up their practices to scrutiny.

Pensylvania, the counties on Delaware and Maryland, as a soldier in the army or navy of the United Colonies, without the consent of his master or mistress first obtained in writing." As a corrective to prior violations of this principle, it was directed, "that all apprentices now inlisted as soldiers in said army or navy, without such consent, be immediately discharged from the service, on the application of his master or mistress, upon payment of all just and reasonable charges of their inlistment."[21] Maryland, in its recruiting act of March 1778, banned the enrollment of "any servant whatever, until emancipated and set at liberty."[22] In a similar manner, the October 1780 Maryland act allowing for the enlistment of "any able bodied slave, between sixteen and forty years of age, who voluntarily enters into the service" required that any such enlistment take place "in the presence and with the consent, and agreement of his master."[23]

Parents and masters who found that their male dependents had enlisted or been drafted without their consent could (and did) apply to have them discharged. In September of 1775, Continental Adjutant General Horatio Gates wrote to General Artemas Ward, explaining that the bearer of his letter was a resident of New Hampshire who "says he has a Negroe Slave Named William Mingo who was a Runaway, & has enlisted in one of the Regiments at Roxbury, and in a Company at present Commanded by Lieut Everet Parker." Though the claimant did not know the colonel of the regiment or the captain of the company, he said he "has seen the Slave, & thinks he can produce him to you." Gates directed that "if he has good Ground for his pretension, the General desires the Negroe may be deliver'd to Him, & beggs you will examine & Judge the Matter."[24] What "Ground for his pretension" the claimant might present, what counterproofs the

---

[21] *JCC*, 30 January 1776, IV: 103-104.

[22] *AMDMR*, 316.

[23] *AMDMR*, 367.

[24] Gates to Ward, 29 September 1775, Horatio Gates Papers, 1726-1828, Film 23, Reel 2 (Correspondence, Nov. 1769 - July 1776), DLAR.

ostensible runaway might offer, and more generally on what basis Ward might "Judge the Matter"
remained unspecified. This left a great deal of discretion in the hands of the adjudging officer.
Similarly, in March of 1777, the Rhode Island Council of War resolved that, "Mr. Ichabod Cole of
Warren having represented that a certain Negro Man Slave, called Caesar, belonging to his Father
Benjamin Cole of Warren, is detained on Board the Continental Ship Warren John Hopkins Esq
Commander," therefore it was "recommended to the Hon. Commodore Hopkins forthwith to
discharge the said Negro if the above Facts shall appear to be well founded."[25] Whether Caesar was
"detained" onboard against his will, or had fled there and chose to remain as a free seaman, with the
captain's backing, is not clear. Nor, again, was it specified how the commander was to judge the
case. In at least one instance, a putative slave owner simply had the recruiting officer jailed when he
enlisted the "Negro Man" the slaveholder claimed as his slave.[26] On the other end of the social
spectrum, when Bryan Fairfax of Virginia returned home from the north in the autumn of 1777, he
"found they had put [my Son Tommy] on the Militia Roll and draughted him tho' under the Age
required." But Fairfax immediately applied for his discharge and "had him excused."[27]

The highly uneven balance of power was evident as well in the treatment of the poor and
socially marginal who began to be forcibly conscripted into a military overwhelmingly defined by its
politically free male actors. A few years into the war, recruiting having become more difficult, some
states resorted to conscription laws and less exacting requirements for enlistment. Among the first

---

[25] Rhode Island Council of War, 11 March 1777, Records of the States of the United States, Rhode Island, 1775-1818,
Film 285, E4, Reel 1, Minutes of the Council of War, DLAR.

[26] See Rhode Island Council of War, 19 March 1778, Records of the States of the United States, Rhode Island, 1775-
1818, Film 285, E4, Reel 1, Minutes of the Council of War, DLAR.

[27] Fairfax to Washington, 21 September 1777, *PGWDE*, Revolutionary, XI: 280-282. Despite provisions to the contrary,
and despite the remedies established my law and the protests of masters and parents, however, recruiters appear to have
continued to knowingly recruit underage boys (or neglected to inquire to closely regarding their age); apprentices
sometimes successfully fled their masters and entered the service without being recovered; and those seeking substitutes
to serve in the ranks in their places often targeted boys, apprentices, and servants. Mintz, *Huck's Raft*, 62-63; Brewer, *By
Birth or Consent*, 129-130.

targets of such measures were transients and the unemployed or destitute, classed as "vagrants,"

who had long been treated, in British and American law, as probable threats to the peace and safety

of the community, as burdens on the public resources, and a rightfully subject to the coercive

supervision of the state through such measures as workhouses, conscription into the army, or

impressment into the navy.[28] Coercive poor laws had often swept children of all ages into the

poorhouse or the workhouse along with their families, and might then bind them out as apprentices

and servants, as was done in Boston. But conscription measures aimed at vagrants typically marked

off a minimum age at which they might be drafted into military service and, implicitly, treated as

adults, even as vagrants often suffered a set of age limits and provisions different from those applied

to the "settled" or self-supporting population. A Maryland act of March 1778, for instance, ordered

the conscription of "every idle person above eighteen years of age, who is able bodied and hath no

fixed habitation, nor family, nor any visible method of getting an honest livelihood, and who may be

adjudged by the lieutenant of the county, or any field officer, to come properly under the above

description of a vagrant."[29] This act gave field officers the discretion to judge whether potential

---

[28] See John Pound, *Poverty and Vagrancy in Tudor England*, 2nd ed., (New York: Longman, 1986); A.L. Beier, *Masterless Men: The Vagrancy Problem in England, 1560-1640*, (New York: Methuen, 1985); Felicity Heal, *Hospitality in Early Modern England*, (New York: Oxford UP, 1990); Christopher Tomlins, *Freedom Bound: Law, Labor, and Civic Identity in Colonizing English America, 1580-1865*, (New York: Cambridge UP, 2010); Josiah H. Benton, *Warning out in New England*, (Boston: W.B. Clarke Company, 1911); Ruth Wallis Herndon, *Unwelcome Americans: Living on the Margin in Early New England*, (Philadelphia: University of Pennsylvania Press, 2001); J.R. Hutchinson, *The Press-Gang Afloat and Ashore*, (New York: E.P. Dutton, 1914); Denver Brunsman, *The Evil Necessity: British Naval Impressment in the Eighteenth-Century Atlantic World*, (Charlottesville, VA: University of Virginia Press, 2013); John K. Alexander, *Render them Submissive: Responses to Poverty in Philadelphia, 1760-1800*, (Amherst, MA: University of Massachusetts Press, 1980); Michael B. Katz, *In the Shadow of the Poorhouse: A Social History of Welfare in America*, (New York: Basic Books, 1986); Simon P. Newman, *Embodied History: The Lives of the Poor in Early Philadelphia*, (Philadelphia: University of Pennsylvania Press, 2003).

[29] *AMDMR*, 316. The act gave the governor and council authority "to discharge any person adjudged a vagrant, if in their judgement such person does not answer the above description." The British Parliament, similarly passed new "press acts" in 1778 and 1779, which ordered, as Higginbotham notes, "that all able-bodied persons guilty of disorderly conduct who did not follow lawful trade or employment were to be inducted into the King's service." Higginbotham, *War of American Independence*, 124. The Maryland general conscription act of October 1780 would call for recruits as young as sixteen years old, though capping the upper age limit at forty-five. *AMDMR*, 366-367. Virginia, in 1778, had instituted a draft of single men from the militia, without children, who were eighteen years old or older. *PGWDE*, Revolutionary, XIII: 513n3. The British forces, facing similar recruiting problems as the Revolutionary War continued, would likewise open the ranks to men from sixteen to fifty years old. Higginbotham, *War of American Independence*, 123-

conscripts met the description of a vagrant and, in doing so, whether they were "above eighteen years of age."[30] Provisions of this sort endowed government agents with sweeping power over the identities, and thence the fates, of individuals who could not mobilize sufficient social resources to effectively contest an agent's determination regarding their status and broader identity.

If forced conscription of the poor constituted one way in which unfreedom shaped the citizen's army, objectification of the individual soldier's body represented another. Military service entailed submission of one's physical person to both the control and the scrutiny of formal superiors. This began with the recruiting officer's evaluation of the suitability of an individual's social and physical selves for military service. Was the individual free to enlist, or was he a dependent? Was he of age and capable of consent? Was he of an age to be mentally and physically capable of military service? Was he of sound body and mind, capable of performing his duty as a soldier? Was he in fact a "he"? Any of these questions could lead to an interrogation of the individual and his family or acquaintances, and to a physical examination, possibly in very invasive ways. This could range from measuring a potential soldier's height or weight, considering his clothing, speech, or manners, testing his physical or mental capacity, looking at his skin for brands, scars, or tattoos that might indicate enslavement or a criminal history, searching for disqualifying injuries, signs of illness, or lameness, or even examining private body parts to confirm male status.

Washington's recruiting instructions of January 1777, for instance, specified that when new recruits were mustered there was "a Surgeon to be present" to help identify those who should "not

---

124. In May of 1781, Maryland would lower the age threshold for the conscription of adjudged vagrants from eighteen to sixteen years old. *AMDMR*, 374.

[30] *AMDMR*, 316. A similar act three years later, in May of 1781, would once again authorize such discretion, though only on the part of the county lieutenant, while lowering the age threshold of conscriptable vagrants to sixteen years old.

pass Muster for defects pointed out in these Instructions."[31] The Rhode Island recruiting instructions for its Continental battalions in February of 1777 similarly specified that when new recruits were mustered there was "a Surgeon to be present" to aid in determining whether the recruits were subject to disqualifying "Defects" or met the stipulated requirements, being "Freemen, above the Age of Seventeen, and under that of Fifty, of sufficient Stature and Ability of Body to discharge all the Offices of a Private Soldier" and "free from Lameness, or other bodily Infirmity, that may render them incapable to support the Fatigues of a Camp." As was typical, the expenses incurred for every soldier who did not pass muster were to be paid by the recruiting officer who had enlisted him despite "defects," whether knowingly, to fill his quota, or from insufficient diligence.[32]

In a telling instance, when officers under William Barton, on command at Newark, suspected that a newly recruited soldier might in fact be female, they began with a disguised test of the recruit's social identity, before moving on to the conclusive physical examination. By the evening of the day following the recruit's enlistment, Barton had been "Inform'd" by his officers "of Several Circumstances which gave me reason to believe that it was A she." Already suspicious, and Barton dining out that evening, the officers at dinner had called in the new recruit and "desired [him] to hand the Tankard to the Table[,] he did so and Made A Courtesy [curtsey] at the Delivery, which was suppos'd to be Accidental." On his return, Barton was told of the incident and other causes of suspicion and became "Determind to know the Certainty" then and there. The recruit was called in once more and told by Barton, drawing on the established enlistment protocol, that "I had suspicion of his being lame" and would have him examined for soundness. Barton "Desired Capt. Flavin to Afficiate as Doctor in searching." The Captain began his examination "and soon [made]

---

[31] Washington, Circular Recruiting Instructions, 12-27 January 1777, Morristown, NJ, *PGWDE*, Revolutionary, VIII: 44-45.

[32] Rhode Island Council of War, 24 February 1777, Records of the States of the United States, Rhode Island, 1775-1818, Film 285, E4, Reel 1, Minutes of the Council of War, DLAR.

the Discovery by Pulling out the Teats of A P[l]ump Young Girl, which [caused] Great divertion."

Quite literally exposed, the "Young Girl" explained that she had left home and enlisted as a soldier because her father would not allow her to marry the young man she wished to wed. Apparently unsympathetic, and still greatly amused, Barton the next morning "orderd the Drums to beat her Threw the Town with the whores march...which was Curious seeing her dress'd in mens Clothes and [the] whores march Beating."[33]

In this case, a young dependent, legally subservient to her father's governance and representation, had crafted an identity in order to enlist. Underage, she could not have done so even if she were male, but the subterfuge offered a chance of escape, and possibly proximity to her (unidentified) intended, along with potential future self-determination. Moreover, the military's depersonalizing and by definition male uniforms could disguise (albeit ineffectively in this instance) her previous identity. It was ultimately this dependent's ingrained, gendered habits and gesture of deference that betrayed her. The exposure of this identity, as signified by her physical body, was instantly transformed from an official and quasi-medical examination into an overtly sexualized moment in which the socially superior male authority figures—triply authoritative by virtue of social rank, military rank, and sex—mocked the exposed inferior, reasserting the identity as a dependent child and female that she had tried to escape. The re-imposed female identify was further stigmatized with accusations of sexual impropriety. Escorted out of town, in the incongruous costume that symbolized her transgression, with drummers beating the traditional "Whore's March," the young woman was put in her place as a disgraced social inferior, as well as a dishonored, discharged soldier, drummed out of the service.

---

[33] William Barton to _______, 17 November 1778, Elizabethtown, NJ, Sol Feinstone Collection, Film 1, Reel 1, No. 81, DLAR. Cf. Robert Fridlington, "A 'Diversion' in Newark: A Letter from the New Jersey Continental Line, 1778," *New Jersey History*, Vol. 105, Nos. 1-2 (Spring/Summer 1987), 75-78.

Entering military service involved a recreation of individuals' identities, translating civilians into soldiers, re-classifying them as subject to military command and martial law. A militarized identity consisted principally of two elements drawn from a man's pre-enlistment identity and from the liminal period surrounding his initial recruitment: the soldier's social location (his town of origin or residence, his occupation, who enlisted him) and his physical characteristics. These elements would be combined with the soldier's command or military location. As the experience of war brought mounting problems of administration and discipline, both American and British military authorities increasingly sought means to verify the identities of the soldiers under their command.

The organization of the military by hierarchy and into units, where officers and comrades developed and reinforced personal knowledge of each other, provided one basic foundation of military identities. Such familiarity served in a military context much as local communities did in a civilian context. This semi-official, institutionalized personal knowledge was supplemented by written records and instruments of identification. These took the form, on the one hand, of enlistment papers, muster rolls, and other returns of the members of each unit—records that would more and more over the course of the conflict make use of physical descriptions to identify individual soldiers. The written records of military identities on the other hand, when mobilized, took the form of a variety of passes and certificates (including, under a broader definition, the commissions discussed in Chapter 3.) Together these records and instruments constituted an archive of individual militarized identities.

The reorganization of the hodgepodge American troops gathered around Boston in the summer of 1775 into coordinated and effective forces required, in the first instance, identifying what forces in fact were available. This same fund of knowledge would, in the longer perspective, serve the governance of the army, when regulating pay, provisions, reinforcements, furloughs, and the like. This process began prior to the institution of the Continental Army, with the muster rolls of provincial units and the local knowledge of particular soldiers and officers. But to a greater extent than other Revolutionary regimes of identification, the Continental Army centralized its efforts. Through this process, large numbers of men and boys were drawn further—or newly—into identities as soldiers but also as Americans.

As the Massachusetts provincial forces organized for open war and laid siege to Boston in the days following Lexington and Concord, orders were issued—accompanied by a model blank form to be employed—requiring each regimental commander "now in camp, or that may hereafter arrive" to "take an exact list of the officers and soldiers by name, and make daily returns to the Adjutant-General of the number of officers and soldiers under his command."[34] This was not merely an inventory, but also a process that transformed a body of unofficial volunteers, many of whom were not formally under military command, into an army of enlisted soldiers, who could be governed as such. Shortly after the inventory was prescribed, it was likewise ordered

> That as many men as are not enlisted, and incline to remain in the army, enlist immediately, in order that it may be ascertained what number it may still be necessary to be raised in each town to complete the complement of troops for this Province, and to forward to each town their remaining quota.[35]

This process was neither rapid nor entirely successful, and several days later further orders were issued requiring company commanders to make "exact return of the number of men in each company now in camp, and how many of the abovesaid men in each company are enlisted for the campaign, and how many of the enlisted are gone home."[36]

The inventory was necessary for basic administrative purposes, including provisioning. To speed their completion, it would soon be ordered that after the 11th of May the Commissary General was to "supply no regiment, with their allowance of provisions till the Adjutant, or some other

---

[34] *The Orderly Book of Colonel William Henshaw*, (Boston: J. Wilson, 1877), 21 April 1775, 15.

[35] *Orderly Book of Colonel William Henshaw*, 27 April 1775, 18-19.

[36] *Orderly Book of Colonel William Henshaw*, 30 April 1775, 20.

suitable person belonging thereto, has presented him with the number and names of the persons belonging thereto, signed by the commanding officer of each company belonging thereto. Such orderly sergeant to take a list of his own company."[37] Over the course of the summer months, the new Continental Army authorities would build on these initial registrations, while seeking to further cement and crystallize these militarized identities by requiring not only officers but common soldiers as well to make oaths of enlistment and fidelity (see Chapter 4).

It was soon evident that further clarification was needed. Having submitted themselves as soldiers, once their identities had been militarized, neither enlistees nor their recruiting officers could exercise the same control over the enlistees' identities—the enlistees could not shed their military identities as easily as they had taken them on; nor could they exercise even so much self-determination within the constraints of these identities as to choose their own command locations. Thus, on the 6th of May, recruiting officers were instructed, "That no person who may have received enlisting orders, and in consequence thereof, has enlisted men, presume to dismiss any person who is enlisted, upon any consideration, whatever, nor presume to re-enlist any person that is already enlisted, without special orders from the General."[38] The troubling freedom with which soldiers attempted to reposition themselves—while recruiting officers and commanders competed with each other for the valuable resources constituted by the soldiers—was not quelled, however.

Within a few days of taking command of the Continental Army in Cambridge, General Washington would remark in his general orders that "A Complaint of the most extraordinary kind" had reached his ears. It was reported "that Soldiers inlisted in one Regiment, have been seduced to reinlist into others, by Agents employed for that purpose under the specious promises of money, or leave of absence from the army." This was "a procedure so subversive of all order, discipline, and

---

[37] *Orderly Book of Colonel William Henshaw*, 9 May 1775, 24.

[38] *Orderly Book of Colonel William Henshaw*, 6 May 1775, 22.

of the very Existance of the army" that it "cannot be forgiven." As such, "the strictest Orders are

therefore given against such practices," which would be severely punished.[39] Seven months later

Washington would express "no small degree of astonishment" upon seeing in the returns that

soldiers were being discharged without authorization. He warned, accordingly, "that if any Colonel,

or Commanding Officer of a Regiment, presume in future to discharge a man without proper

Authority, for so doing, he will be put in Arrest and tried for disobedience of orders." It seemed

evident to him that "To have Men inlisted one day, and discharged as it were the next, without any

Action, or apparent cause, to disqualify men for service, must have a bad appearance in the Returns

sent to Congress, especially when the list of Deserters, comes to be added to it."[40]

Regulation required ever more elaborate documentation of individual soldiers. Within three

months of the initial orders for returns of names and numbers, the commander of the

Massachusetts forces would order a more precise register of the identities of the soldiers of the

provincial army. This census would define more clearly each soldier's social and physical person, for

future purposes of governance and discipline. On the 14th of June general orders were issued

directing "That each colonel of a regiment take and keep a list of his men, their names, when

enlisted, place of residence, age, stature, and complexion, and order the roll to be called every

morning and evening."[41] A nearly identical command, of the same date, was noted as a general

order in the orderly book of the Connecticut company under William Coit, suggesting collaboration

in this project by the armies of several provinces, rather than of Massachusetts alone.[42] Early the

---

[39] General Orders, 7 July 1775, *PGWDE*, Revolutionary, I: 73.

[40] General Orders, 12 February 1776, *PGWDE*, Revolutionary, III: 299-300: "To remedy these evils, as far as possible, it is directed, in cases where discharges are really necessary, that the Commanding Officer of the regiment do produce the man, (solliciting the discharge) to the Brigadier Genl of his brigade, who is to examine accurately into the matter, and not to give a discharge for Sickness of a temporary duration."

[41] *Orderly Book of Colonel William Henshaw*, 14 June 1775, 33.

[42] "Orderly Book kept for William Coit's Company," *Orderly Book and Journals Kept by Connecticut Men while Taking Part in the American Revolution, 1775-1778*, (Hartford, CT: Connecticut Historical Society, 1899), 20.

following month private Samuel Bixby, a member of the Massachusetts militia hailing from Sutton, recorded in his journal that there had been

> orders from the congress that the capt. of the Several companges Shall take the length of Every Soldier & the town where in they belong and where they was born & where they are Servants or Sons & how old and when inlisted and who under and when they had got it to return it to the co[lonel].[43]

It is not clear whether Bixby had simply been late in hearing of the orders of the 14th of June; whether the orders in question were regimental rather than general; or whether they had been restated more recently. Bixby's attribution of the orders to the Provincial Congress seems to have been a misunderstanding (though, strictly speaking, general orders issued to the militia might be said to come from Congress). Regardless, the substance of the orders was the same, directing that the soldiers were to be described physically and located socially. Significantly, it appears that only the "men" (certainly privates, and likely non-commissioned officers) were to be subjected to such physical description. Officers were not to suffer such indignity, which could impugn their honor by suggesting they might desert, and implied that, like men of lower status, they could be so anonymous that a written description would be necessary.

Although the project of describing all soldiers was never systematically undertaken, even within the Massachusetts provincial army, descriptive registration would form an important part of military identification during the Revolution. It would become increasingly prevalent as the war progressed, particularly as part of recruiting. It had, in fact, long been a common practice in the British armed forces to record physical descriptions and other identifying information for common soldiers and seamen. Even when enlistment papers from, for example, the French and Indian War

---

[43] Samuel Bixby, Diary, 3 July 1775, I, Mss. Octavo Volumes, AAS. Caroline Cox, *A Proper Sense of Honor: Service and Sacrifice in George Washington's Army*, (Chapel Hill, NC: University of North Carolina Press, 2004), read's "take the length of Every Soldier" in a metaphorical sense, translating it as an order to "get their histories (2)." But it is clear from the full text of Bixby's entry and from the general orders of 14 June recorded by Henshaw that to "take the length" in this case referred literally to taking the height or "stature" of the soldiers.

did not include physical descriptions, they often included a recruit's age.[44] (Such records and descriptions were less commonly compiled for militia units.) Washington himself, as a provincial officer in the 1750s, had compiled descriptive muster rolls of his men, including their names, date and place of enlistment, age, height, occupation, "Country," and "Description" (complexion, hair color, marks, habits of speech, and other characteristics).[45]

By June of 1775, New Hampshire units were listing men by name, occupation, place and county of residence, and age.[46] As early as February 1776, recruits for Maryland artillery companies were registered by name, place of birth, height, occupation, and age.[47] A return of enlisted men in the 1st New Jersey Regiment for June 1776 lists the men by name, date of enlistment, person who enlisted them, "Place of abode," age, "Person" (meaning height in feet and inches), and complexion.[48] At least as early as the autumn of 1776, orders given to officers sent on recruiting missions for the Continental Army directed that they were to take detailed, physical descriptions of the soldiers they enlisted, including their age, size, complexion, hair and eye color, and "natural or accidental mark[s]."[49] By August of 1776, some enlistment returns for Maryland units destined for the Continental service featured descriptions including stature, place of birth, hair color, and age.[50]

---

[44] See the New Hampshire enlistment papers from 1758 transcribed or abstracted in Isaac W. Hammond ed., *Rolls and Documents relating to Soldiers in the Revolutionary War*, (Manchester, NH: John B. Clarke, Public Printer, 1889).

[45] See Washington, Roll of Company, 1 August 1756, *PGWDE*, Colonial, III: 306.

[46] See "A list of Cap Hzekiah Hutchins Compy," 9 June 1775, "A list of Cap Winborn Adams Company," 2 June 1775, no. 1-117, and "A list of Cap Winthrop Rowe's Compy," 3 June 1775, no. 1-119, Hammond ed., *Rolls and Documents*.

[47] *AMDMR*, 563

[48] William Winds, Descriptive Muster Roll, 1st New Jersey Regiment, 13 June 1776, Ticonderoga, New Jersey. Revolutionary War. Numbered Manuscripts, 1770's-1890's, Film 678, Reel 6 (Mss. Nos. 2211-2403), No. 2243, DLAR.

[49] *Instructions to the officers appointed to recruit in New-York, for the service of the United States of America*, (Fishkill, NY: Printed by Samuel Loudon, [November?] 1776), *EAI*, Series 1, no. 15184 (filmed).

[50] *AMDMR*, 54.

Muster rolls and "Description & Size" rolls for the Virginia line by 1777, and again in 1780, recorded age, stature, occupation, place of residence, and other information.

When ordering a new round of recruiting and conscription from militia units in February of 1778, the Continental Congress would direct that each state submit "complete lists of the men drafted, with a description of their persons, their age, stature, the places of their abode, and the regiment and company from which they shall have been drafted."[51] In New Hampshire, muster rolls including physical descriptions were compiled, in some cases, by March of 1778. Along with name, rank, residence, date of enlistment, and advance received, the roll of Captain Davenport Phelps' company included a column simply headed "Description." The descriptions consistently included age and height, sometimes "Dark" or "Light complected," occasionally eye or hair color, pockmarks, or a "Thick" build. Significantly, only men from the rank of Sergeant down were so described. The Captain and the two Lieutenants were listed by name and rank, but the remaining columns were left blank.[52]

The practice of descriptive registration spread. By at least the middle years of the war, enlistment rosters and muster rolls for New York regiments would include "age."[53] By January of 1780, some officers in Massachusetts regiments had begun keeping descriptive lists of the soldiers under their command.[54] When, in June of 1780, Massachusetts began a new round of recruiting to reinforce the Continental Army, those enlisting the new soldiers were directed to give details, including their names, stature, complexion, trade, town of residence, and their age.[55] Descriptive

---

[51] *JCC*, 26 February 1778, X: 199-203.

[52] March 1778, Hammond ed., *Rolls and Documents*, 119-120.

[53] See "Muster and Pay Rolls of the War of the Revolution, 1775-1783," *CNYHS*, XLVIII (1915), 594-596, 600-618, 393.

[54] "Muster and Pay Rolls of the War of the Revolution, 1775-1783," *CNYHS*, XLVII (1914), 262

[55] Massachusetts General Court, 5 June 1780. See a descriptive list of five Massachusetts recruits (Harwood, English, Reynolds, Coleman, and Seabels), U.S. Revolution Collection, Box 1, Folder 2, AAS. This list itself—probably a draft or

muster rolls of much the same type, including the age of the soldiers, were in use in New Hampshire

units by the end of the war.[56] Even when such details were omitted from rolls and rosters in the

later years of the war, age often remained as a key identifying characteristic. Thus, rolls of substitute

recruits from Prince George's County, Maryland, from 1780, include only their names, country of

birth, and age, while a list of recruits from the same county in July of 1781 would add to these only

the recruits' agreed period of service and remarks on their current assignments.[57]

If records of soldiers served a variety of goals, their most fundamental purpose was to "call

the roll," by which means individuals absent without leave could be detected. That procedure—in

combination with the system of passes, sentries, and guards—required soldiers to remain within a

certain distance of camp. As well, by consulting descriptions of rank-and-file soldiers, officers and

government officials were better able to advertise and recapture deserters, identify bounty-hoppers

and other offenders, recognize spies, and enforce passes and other restriction on mobility. In

August of 1777, commanders in the Continental Army complained that Colonel John White "and

other officers of the Georgia Battalion" had been "inlisting some men out of the Continental Army

who were already inlisted in other regiments." Thus, it was directed that,

> All officers from whose corps it is suspected any men have deserted, & inlisted into Col.
> White's battalion, are instantly to make out lists of their names, with proper descriptions of
> their persons & dress—and deliver them to their brigadier, or officer commanding their
> brigade, who will immediately send a suitable officer of the brigade to Philadelphia; to
> examine Col. White's battalion, agreeable to his request; who will deliver up their deserters, if
> any shall be found in his corps—these officers will at the same time, apply to the officers

---

set of notes for making up the formal list—is undated, but entries corresponding to the recruits listed in *Massachusetts Soldiers and Sailors of the Revolutionary War*, (Boston: Wright & Potter, 1896-1908), (Jacob Harwood of New Salem; Joseph English of Salem; Enos Reynolds; Solomon Coleman of Ipswich; and Darius Seables) all indicate that they were included on a "descriptive list of men raised to reinforce the Continental Army for the term of 6 months, agreeable to resolve of June 5, 1780, returned as received of Justin Ely, Commissioner,...at Springfield, July 11, 1780. For a descriptive list of this type from the same recruiting cycle, see "Muster and Pay Rolls of the War of the Revolution, 1775-1783," *CNYHS*, XLVII (1914): 301-303. See also Orderly Book, 6th Massachusetts Regiment, 1782, U.S. Revolution Collection, Folio Vol. 3, AAS, which includes descriptive muster lists.

[56] "Muster and Pay Rolls of the War of the Revolution, 1775-1783," *CNYHS*, XLVII (1914): 322.

[57] *AMDMR*, 338, 381.

commanding the gallies, and other vessels of war, at Philadelphia, and below the city, for leave to search their vessels, for deserters; and they are desired to permit such searches accordingly.[58]

By these means, the information constituting the military identities of suspected deserters was to be transferred up the chain of command, aggregated, and then dispatched. The order likewise illustrates how categories of deserters were easily blurred, as it implied that some thought to have deserted to White may have instead taken to the sea service. And, most importantly, it brings out the way that soldiers, by crossing the boundaries of "local," official knowledge, supplemented by the looser knowledge of the civilian community of their location, could evade, at least for a time, the constraints of military identities—until that knowledge was mobilized to enable their apprehension.

More generally, when absences were noted and it was concluded that the soldiers had deserted—usually fleeing military service entirely—descriptions were furnished to those charged with tracking them down. By February of 1776, General Washington would attempt to give greater system and regularity to this process. He ordered that, "In case of desertion, the Commanding Officer of the regiment or Corps, is immediately to report the Deserter, or Deserters, to his Brigadier General, giving an exact description of the man—the town he comes from &c." The commanding officer was likewise expected "to cause proper Steps to be taken for apprehending [such deserters]." It was further stipulated that "A Reward of Five Dollars, will be paid to any person, or persons, who shall apprehend and bring a Deserter into the Camp, upon obtaining a Certificate from the Brigadier of the service performed."[59]

Such descriptions were accordingly often inserted in newspaper advertisements, offering rewards for the capture and return of the deserter. Many took roughly the form of the following item, dated 12 June 1775 at Waterbury, Connecticut, and published in the *Connecticut Currant*:

---

[58] General Orders, 13 August 1777, *PGWDE* Revolutionary, X: 596.

[59] General Orders, 12 February 1776, *PGWDE*, Revolutionary, III: 299-300.

Deserted from the subscribers company in Col. Wooster's Regiment, one James Parker, a transient Irishman, about 36 years of age, middling stature, his face pitted with gun-powder, short black hair, had on a light colour'd coat, and is a taylor by trade. Whoever shall take up said deserter, and return him to the subscriber, shall be reasonably rewarded, by
THOMAS PORTER.[60]

A few days later, a similar advertisement appeared in the *Norwich Packet* offering twenty dollars for the return of deserter Thomas Clark, "belonging to the 7th Company of the 6th Regiment" of the Connecticut forces. Clark was described as "about 30 Years of Age, of middling Stature, light Complexion, pitted with Small-Pox, and has many Pimples on his Face." It was noted that Clark, when he deserted, was wearing "a light coloured Fustain Coat, a Callicoe Waistcoat, a Pair of Drab Breeches and white Stocking," and that he had stolen two silver watches.[61] As the war went forward, the newspapers were increasingly riddled with such advertisements.[62]

Officers, in contrast to the closely described common soldiers, were typically identified only by name, rank, unit, state, date of commission, residence, or status (e.g. "esquire," "gentleman"). Physical description—except in a very different sense, in character sketches or heroic narratives— would have insultingly lumped genteel officers with common or "vulgar" persons associated with physical labor and the physical body. Such descriptions of officers would likewise, according to the logic of the elite culture of honor, have been superfluous.[63] When assessing the current state of military forces in preparation for reorganization or new rounds of recruiting, state and Continental

---

[60] *Connecticut Courant*, 19 June 1775, 4, *AHN*

[61] *Norwich Packet*, 15-19 June 1775, 3; and 19-26 June 1775, 3. *AHN*.

[62] See *Connecticut Courant*, 26 June 1775, 3; and 3 July 1775, 4; *Pennsylvania Packet*, 10 July 1775, 1; *New England Chronicle, or Essex Gazette*, 21-27 July 1775, 3; *Providence Gazette*, 29 July 1775, 4; *Massachusetts Spy*, 9 August 1775, 3; *Connecticut Gazette*, 11 August 1775, 3; *Massachusetts Spy*, 16 August 1775, 4; *New England Chronicle, or Essex Gazette*, 17-24 August 1775, 4; and 31 August 1775, 4. See also numerous additional advertisements headed "Deserted," 1775-1783, *AHN*.

[63] On the cultures of gentility and honor, both in direct relation to the Revolutionary military and more generally, see Cox, *A Proper Sense of Honor*; Charles Royster, *A Revolutionary People at War: The Continental Army and the American Character, 1775-1783*, (Chapel Hill, NC: University of North Carolina Press, 1979); Richard L. Bushman, *The Refinement of America: Persons, Houses, Cities*, (New York: Knopf, 1992); Sarah Knott, *Sensibility and the American Revolution*, (Chapel Hill, NC: University of North Carolina Press, 2009); Joanne B. Freeman, *Affairs of Honor: National Politics in the New Republic*, (New Haven, CT: Yale UP, 2001).

authorities might seek both reports of the number of men in each unit and detailed registers of the rank-and-file, but only a minimal matrix of identity for the commanding officers. When Massachusetts set out to reorganize its militia in the autumn of 1779, for instance, the Council issued orders for returns from the county Brigadiers "of the Name, Rank & place of Abode of every Officer...as also what Vacant officers there are in each Brigade."[64] Though officers' physical characteristics were not registered as those of common soldiers increasingly were, descriptions of such characteristics, based on the personal knowledge of subordinates, fellow officers, or private connections could be mobilized, when need be, either to advertise an officer who had become a fugitive or to locate and identify one who was missing or captured.[65]

Military identities were mobilized in the forms of passes and certificates. While military and civilian requirements for identification (and their concomitant instruments) overlapped, each subset was structured and operated in distinctive ways, representing distinct realms of authority. Identification of soldiers and officers formed not only the means of governing the countryside and prosecuting the war but also part of a complex system of internal military governance and identification—comprising uniforms, passwords, commissions, enlistment records, muster rolls,

---

[64] John Hancock to Oliver Prescott, 13 September 1779, Sol Feinstone Collection, Film 1, Reel 1, No. 512, DLAR.

[65] See, for instance, the description of a missing French officer, who had volunteered in the American service, furnished by Franklin in September of 1783, on behalf of the officer's friends and family, as an aid to initiating inquiries as to his whereabouts and welfare. *LDC*, XXI: 246n2. In the course of the war, occasional attempts would also be made to adapt such descriptive registers to the governance of prisoners of war, as a means to prepare for the recovery of any who might escape and become fugitives. Following the surrender of British forces under Burgoyne at Saratoga in October of 1777, the Continental Congress would order General Heath, in charge of the prisoners, "to cause to be taken down the name and rank of every commissioned officer, and the name, former place of abode, occupation, size, age, and description of every non-commissioned officer and private soldier, and all other persons comprehended in the convention." *JCC*, 8 November 1777, IX: 881-882. Heath would soon report that General Burgoyne had refused to comply with the Congress's orders beyond giving a list of the prisoner's names, "asserting that no president can be produced in Military History of more being given," Heath to Washington, 26 November 1777, *PGWDE*, Revolutionary, XII: 411-412. In response Congress would insist that the order was "a measure naturally resulting from the articles of Convention, which the conquering party has a right to avail itself of for its own security, and that this measure would have been strictly justifiable had no just suspicion of the want of good faith in the party surrendering, presented itself," *JCC*, 27 December 1777, IX: 1058-1064.

patrols, and many other components. Passes issued to soldiers came in numerous types: for

furloughs, couriers, duty on detachment, escorting prisoners, going to the hospital when sick, and

obtaining supplies, among many other purposes.[66] Military passes were most commonly issued to

individual soldiers and officers, but, like civilian passes and passports, were sometimes issued to

groups—sometimes an entire company, consisting of dozens of men.[67]

Establishing a system of passes was intrinsic to the earliest war effort. Article XV of the

Massachusetts articles of war, established in April 1775, dictated that "All non-commissioned-

Officers and Soldiers, who shall be found one Mile from the Camp, without Leave in writing from

their commanding Officer" should be tried and punished by regimental court martial.[68] The Articles

of War passed by the Continental Congress for the Continental Army at the end of June of the same

year included this same regulation—in nearly identical language—as Article XVI.[69] This basic

stipulation would be reiterated by commanders in their orders as month succeeded month.[70] And

variations on orders requiring written passes to cross the lines, be absent from camp, or take a leave,

formed a persistent theme running through commanders' orders for the duration of the war, from

beginning to end. Such pass requirements, as imposed on the rank and file, were intended not

simply to prevent disorder, but to combat desertion. Soldiers found outside the lines without proper

authorization were suspected of attempted or actual desertion. Regulations frequently specified that

---

[66] In March of 1783, with the war effectively over, General Horatio Gates "recommended to the troops to make regimental Gardens, for the purpose of raising Greens Vregitables for their own Use" and directed that, "in order to collect a sufficient quantity of seeds, Commanding Officers of regiments, will give passes to as many trusty soldiers as they judge necessary to go into the country and be absent not exceeding ten days." Gates, General Orders, 24 March 1783, Orderly Book: Newburgh & New Windsor, 1 February 1783 – 8 April 1783, Horatio Gates Papers, 1726-1828, Film 23, Reel 18 (Orderly Books, August 1758 - February 1783; Returns, January 1756 - November 1778), DLAR.

[67] See Gates, Pass for Captain Casdorp et al., 3 October 1776, Ticonderoga, NY, Horatio Gates Papers, 1726-1828, Film 23, Reel 3 (Correspondence, July 1776 - October 1776), DLAR.

[68] *Rules and Regulations for the Massachusetts Army,* (Salem, MA: Printed by Samuel and Ebenezer Hall, 1775), *EAI*, Series 1, no. 14244 (filmed), 9.

[69] *JCC,* II: 115.

[70] See Bixby, Diary, 12 October 1775, I, Mss. Octavo Volumes, AAS.

the "Leave" or pass must be in writing. Writing made the authorization both mobile and somewhat more independent of the person thus authorized. The pass could—if standard forms were used, signatures were known, and proper seals and other marks of authentication employed—make this identification independently and repeatedly verifiable. The fact that large numbers of soldiers were substantially illiterate—or at least unable to write more than their names, if that[71]—made an instrument of identification still more independent of the individual soldier, who might well be incapable of reading it, let alone altering it credibly or forging a new one.

Passes varied greatly in form, sophistication, and specificity. Those issued by military officers authorizing passage of sentries, pickets, and guards were commonly simple statements of identification and authentication. They were often little more than handwritten notes on small slips of paper— some no bigger than a modern band-aid— or else very brief printed blank forms filled in with sparse details. Often, such passes were in effect written orders, directing the reader, for example, to "Permit [blank] to pass the Guards from Head Quarters" or "to & from the Camp [at X]."[72] A pass might request or order the reader to "Permit the Bearer hereof," who would then be named, "to pass" the guards or sentries, or from a particular point of origin, to a specified destination, concluding with "By his Excellency's Command" or "By the General's Order," the signature of the secretary or aide de camp, and the location and date of issuance.[73] Lacking seals, a physical description of the bearer, or the bearer's signature, among other possible devices, such passes relied on the expectation that the signature or handwriting of the issuing officer—and the

---

[71] On literacy among Continental soldiers, see Cox, *Proper Sense of Honor*, 4, 8, 33, 53, 69, 127, 249.

[72] See J[onathan?] Ward, Pass for Lieutenant [Ezra Moore?] Beaman, 9 June [...?],U.S. Revolution Collection, Box 1, Folder 1, and J[onathan?] Ward, Pass for Lieutenant Ezra Beman, 28 July 1775, U.S. Revolution Collection, Box 2, Folder 2, AAS.

[73] See George Johnston, Pass for Samuel Bonnel from Head Quarters at Morristown to New Brunswick, 29 March 1777, Sol Feinstone Collection, Film 1, Reel 2, No. 680, DLAR.

general rubric of the pass—would be recognized by the soldiers and officers in the district, or, in less ideal cases, could at least be verified by sending to the point of issuance for confirmation.

Passes, as compared to signs (passwords) and countersigns, were more individuated modes of identification. They did not, in all cases, substitute for the baseline knowledge of the daily password and countersign. But they provided—or were prescribed as—more secure forms of individual identification than could be transmitted orally. The validity of passes still depended ultimately on a chain of authority inhering in a successive hierarchy of officers. Thus, from time to time, it became necessary, either to combat the use of fraudulent passes or to cut off channels of travel and communication convenient for smuggling or espionage, to issue orders declaring all passes, or all passes of a certain description, invalid for certain purposes.[74] By temporarily suspending a pass regime, some of its key advantages—greater portability and ease of decentralization—were sacrificed precisely for the "flaws" of the purely oral system, which narrowed the field of discretionary authority to a few persons, with concentrated control over how their permissions were distributed. Before the end of July of 1775, Washington ordered "All Passes to be discontinued for the future." From then on, at least for the time being, "no person [was] to be admitted into the Lines, unless introduced by an Officer, who can vouch for him, or by Order of the Officer commanding in the Lines."[75] For the time being, the personal and (possibly) oral authority of trusted officers was restored to primacy.[76]

---

[74] On the 6 of May 1775, for instance, orders were issued "That the commanding officer of the guard at Charlestown permit no person to go into Charlestown with any provision whatever, with or without a pass." Two weeks later it was ordered "That the sentry placed at the bridge permit no person to pass on to Lechmore's Point, without an express order from head-quarters, till further orders." *Orderly Book of Colonel William Henshaw*, 6 May 1775, 22; 20 May 1775, 27. In a similar manner, general orders on July 7th, 1775, directed "The Guards on the Roads leading to Bunker's Hill…not to suffer any person to pass them, unless an Officer is sent down from the Lines to order it, or they will be severely punished." General Orders, 7 July 1775, *PGWDE*, Revolutionary, I: 71-75.

[75] Washington, General Orders, 26 July 1775, *PGWDE*, Revolutionary Series, I: 172-173.

[76] Near the end of November a private in the Massachusetts line recorded orders issued by General Ward ("Genl. Words ordors") that reinforced the distinction between those who were required to carry written identification and proofs of authorization to travel and those who were authorized to issue but were not required to carry them. The general ordered

Military commanders spent considerable time and energy administering pass regimes, showing how the measures were essential yet flawed. In late July of 1776, General Nathanael Greene wrote to Washington that, "I am so confind, writing passes &ca that it is impossible for me to attend to the duties of the day, which in many instances prejudices the service." "I must beg leave to Recommend to your Excellencys consideration," Greene continued, "the appointing an officer to write & sign the necessary pases...if it was put in General Orders that pases signd by him should be deemd Authentick as if sign'd by me, it would leave me at liberty to pursue the more important employments of my Station."[77] The following day, Washington issued orders that, "General Greene being particularly engaged at present, passes signed by Lieut: Blodget, are to be allowed sufficient to enable persons to cross the ferries."[78]

The use of printed forms for military passes was one solution, and made the instruments themselves more legible to others. At least as significantly, printed forms provided greater security against fraud. The standardization of text, format, and physical form made departures from any of these more noticeable and emendations more detectable; the exclusive means needed to print forms (relative to handwritten forgery) and the greater cost and difficulty of obtaining them likewise increased the barriers to fraud. The effectiveness of printed forms depended on insisting that only documents produced upon them would be accepted, and on ensuring that an adequate supply of the sanctioned forms was available to those authorized to issue them.

Regulations of this sort were established and forms printed for a wide variety of instruments of identification, though universal standardization was never achieved. When, in the summer of

---

"that the commanding offercer of the main gard Purmit no Person to send letters into Boston who has any c[onference?] with the Enemy or go Beyond our Sentries with out a written order from the Genl. Exsept Genl. officers & adicamps By Whom varbil ordors are to Be obayed as if written." Bixby, Diary, 29 November 1775, I, Mss. Octavo Volumes, AAS.

[77] Greene to Washington, 25 July 1776, *PGWDE*, Revolutionary, V: 459-461.

[78] Washington, General Orders, 26 July 1776, *PGWDE*, Revolutionary, V: 470-471.

1777, Washington reiterated requirements that officers obtain furlough passes from their brigadiers before they could leave camp, he stipulated that, "The Adjutant General will furnish each Brigadier applying, with printed furloughs for the purpose, which alone are to be made use of."[79] Likewise, when Gates issued orders for the regulation of furloughs for both officers and men in December of 1782, he announced that, "Printed furloughs (the blanks for which are to be furnished by the Quarter Master) will be given by the commanding Officers of Brigades to the non-commiss'd Officers and privates in their commands" who were granted leave under these orders.[80]

Some passes included physical descriptions of the bearer, again to prevent misappropriation and to add to their persuasive authenticity. The descriptions sometimes quoted the enlistment, muster, or hospital records of the soldier's unit, which were increasingly likely to include physical, social, and biographical characteristics. When, for instance, private Jabez Alexander received a medical discharge from the Continental Army at Ticonderoga in October of 1776, the document included a certificate from a surgeon that Alexander "is Rendered unfit for further Service this campaign by Reason of his having the fever & ague"; a certificate from the Lieutenant Colonel of Alexander's regiment that he was "convinced that the Complaint of Jabez Alexander is not factitious" and recommending his discharge; a signed acknowledgment by Alexander that he had received the full pay due him; and, finally a certificate of discharge from General Gates. The certificate from the Lieutenant Colonel of Alexander's regiment, at the heart of the portfolio, described Alexander as a "Soldier in Capt. Gates Company of the Regiment under my Command

---

[79] Washington, General Orders, 7 June 1777, Middlebrook, NJ, *PGWDE*, Revolutionary, IX: 630-632.

[80] Gates, General Orders, 11 December 1782, Orderly Book: Newburgh & New Windsor, 31 October 1782 – 31 January 1783, Horatio Gates Papers, 1726-1828, Film 23, Reel 18 (Orderly Books, August 1758 - February 1783; Returns, January 1756 - November 1778), DLAR. The following month, Gates issued orders concerning the issuing and registration of discharges and furloughs for injured and disabled soldiers using printed forms with blanks left for the particulars. Orders, 1 January 1783, Orderly Book: Newburgh & New Windsor, 31 October 1782 – 31 January 1783, Horatio Gates Papers, 1726-1828, Film 23, Reel 18 (Orderly Books, August 1758 - February 1783; Returns, January 1756 - November 1778), DLAR.

Aged 21. Years 1 Month 19 Days 5 foot 8 Inches Brown hair Dark Eyes Dark Complexion

belonging to the town of Halborough."[81]

The integrity of the pass system required specifying from time to time which officers were

empowered to grant which types of passes. These stipulations reflected both the divisions of

command and authority and the degree to which applicants for passes could only be properly known

by officers under whom they served. In early July of 1776, for instance, with the Continental Army

ensconced in New York City, Washington revised pass regulations to meet the new circumstances,

ordering the officers of the guards at the ferries and wharves "to be careful no Soldier goes over the

Ferry without a pass from a General officer."[82] Shortly thereafter, Washington clarified that,

"officers and soldiers who want passes over the ferries are to apply to their own Brigadier General,"

and that the Brigadiers were to "give no passes to officers or soldiers of another brigade."[83] One

brigadier could not properly judge whether an applicant might be spared from another brigadier's

command. Nor could he confidently judge the characters of such applicants, lacking the

institutional or community knowledge available to him regarding individuals under his own

command. Four days later, Washington ordered that "Passes to officers and soldiers" were only to

be issued by "a Major General; the Brigadier General of the Brigade to which the person belongs;

the Adjutant General, or General's Secretary, or Aide-de-Camps."[84] The following day he was

forced to specify that, "Passes from Col. Knox, for the officers and soldiers of the Artillery only, to

be sufficient to pass the ferries."[85] On August 31st, in response to a query from General William

---

[81] Medical Discharge of Jabez Alexander, 11 October 1776, Ticonderoga, NY, Horatio Gates Papers, 1726-1828, Film 23, Reel 3 (Correspondence, July 1776 - October 1776), DLAR.

[82] Washington, General Orders, 9 July 1776, *PGWDE*, Revolutionary, V: 245-247.

[83] Washington, General Orders, 17 July 1776, *PGWDE*, Revolutionary, V: 352-353.

[84] Washington, General Orders, 21 July 1776, *PGWDE*, Revolutionary, V: 411.

[85] Washington, General Orders, 22 July 1776, *PGWDE*, Revolutionary, V: 419. In a similar manner, early in August, Washington ordered that "Passes signed by the Quarter Master-General, or his Assistant Mr Hughes for persons in that

Heath, Washington clarified that "As to passes signed by Colos. of Regiments they are not to be permitted; none but those under the hand of a Brigadier general or one of superior rank, are to have any reguard paid to them unless you hear something farther from me on that subject."[86]

Beyond the use of passes to govern lines and camps in general, both soldiers and officers were sometimes issued passes to facilitate a particular mission, identifying them as authorized travellers and distinguishing them from deserters and spies. In early May of 1776, in New York City, for instance, Captain Isaac Bolster, by order of Colonel Learned issued to Sergeant James Scott, along with Moses Hood and Benjamin Powers, an instrument directing the reader to allow the three "to pass & Repass to take up all Deserters from the Continentall Army, wherever they shall find them," and requesting "the assistance of the Selectmen & Committees of Each Town to assist the above Named Persons in securing said Deserters if found."[87] In December of 1776, in a document issued at Ticonderoga, Colonel Anthony Wayne requested "All Officers Civil and Military…to forward Major Frazer the bearer hereof to Congress with all Possible Despatch."[88] Courier passes, likewise, were commonly issued to soldiers, officers, or post or express riders to facilitate their passage. Often these consisted of little more than brief signed notes from the dispatching officer— frequently written on the cover of the dispatch being carried—directing that the bearer was to be allowed to pass, in some cases to "pass express"—with the least possible delay.[89]

---

department to cross the Ferries to be admitted as sufficient." Washington, General Orders, 4 August 1776, *PGWDE*, Revolutionary, V: 556-557.

[86] Washington to Heath, 31 August 1776, *PGWDE*, Revolutionary, VI: 183. For Heath's query, see Heath to Washington, 31 August 1776, *PGWDE*, Revolutionary, VI: 182.

[87] Coloneal Learned and Isaac Bolster, Pass for James Scott et al., 2 May 1776, U.S. Revolution Collection, Box 2, Folder 3, AAS.

[88] Wayne, Pass for Major Frazer, 4 December 1776, Sol Feinstone Collection, Film 1, Reel 3, No. 1657, DLAR.

[89] See John Clark Jr. to Washington, 27 October 1777, *PGWDE*, Revolutionary, XII: 27-29n; Washington to James Potter, 5 November 1777, *PGWDE*, Revolutionary, XII: 137n; James Mitchell Varnum to Washington, 8 November

When soldiers fell ill, they were often issued a pass or "ticket" to go to a specified military hospital.[90] These passes implicitly or explicitly certified that the soldier was in fact ill, in the judgment of the issuing officer. Commanders were aware that these passes were, in their own way, open to abuse. Thus, General Gates, in early July of 1776 instructed the commander at Fort George to be "very Careful Sir! to prevent any Desertion of those who are sent to the Genl. Hospital; some Villains, may perhaps feign themselves sick, merely with design of gaining an Opportunity of Deserting."[91] In other cases soldiers and officers were given extended leaves to recover their health at home or elsewhere, and were issued special furlough passes accordingly.[92] General furlough passes were required for both soldiers and officers taking leaves of absence for other reasons.

In so far as military pass regimes were meant to distinguish soldiers on authorized leave or missions from mere deserters, military commanders had also to look to civilian authorities to help enforce these regimes of identification. The fundamental question of this type of identification was whether the person in question was (or should be) a soldier or a civilian. Any person who might plausibly be taken for an able-bodied adult male therefore lived and travelled with a continually unstable identity and through a climate of persistent suspicion. The burden of proof was largely upon individuals to prove who they were. Civilian authorities were often enlisted, or acted on their

---

1777, *PGWDE*, Revolutionary, XII: 176-177n; William Livingston to Washington, 9 November 1777, *PGWDE*, Revolutionary, XII: 180-181n; Varnum to Washington, 9 November 1777, *PGWDE*, Revolutionary, XII: 185-187n; Varnum to Washington, 10 November 1777, *PGWDE*, Revolutionary, XII: 205n; Varnum to Washington, 12 November 1777, *PGWDE*, Revolutionary, XII: 218-219n. See also courier passes on additional correspondence from Varnum to Washington, November 1777, *PGWDE*.

[90] See Washington, General Orders, 7 August 1776, *PGWDE*, Revolutionary, V: 591-592, for reference to "the usual Ticket" issued to sick soldiers being sent to hospital.

[91] Gates to Peter Gansevoort, 7 July 1776, Horatio Gates Papers, 1726-1828, Film 23, Reel 2 (Correspondence, Nov. 1769 - July 1776), DLAR.

[92] See John Lauring, Furlough for Colonel Seth Reed, 19 August 1776, Albany, NY, Copy, Horatio Gates Papers, 1726-1828, Film 23, Reel 3 (Correspondence, July 1776 - October 1776), DLAR; Loammi Baldwin to Mary Baldwin, 12 October 1776, 23 October 1776, MS Am 1811, Loammi Baldwin Papers, 1768-1872, Box 1, Item 112, 113, Houghton Library, Harvard University, Cambridge, MA

own, to regulate the mobility and scrutinize the identity of soldiers or suspected soldiers. Local and county committees of observation and safety, in particular, played important roles in this regard by building on their surveillance of strangers and suspicious persons more generally. This role was reflected in the passes issued by military commanders that ordered and requested "all Officers Civil & Military" or all civilian "committees" to allow the bearers to pass.[93] Committees could play particularly important roles in locating deserters, who would attempt to pass as civilians or as discharged soldiers, and often tried to return to their home communities. Thus, in August of 1776, General Gates wrote from Ticonderoga requesting the assistance of local committees in discouraging "the Scandalous desertion that has prevail'd in this army," by, "seizing & sending under a proper Guard, all Stra[g]lers, & persons who are not supplied with a written pass under my hand or the hand of some Publick Officer Authoris'd by me."[94]

State and local laws and regulations reinforced the role of civil authorities in policing the margins of military governance and identification. In early August of 1776, the New Jersey Convention prohibited any "person or persons belonging to, or coming from, the Army in the State of New-Jersey…to go over any of the Ferries in or travel through said State without a pass, signed either by General Mercer, Colonel Griffin [Samuel Griffen], or Colonel [Clement] Biddle."[95] In Pennsylvania, a state act of February 1777 required constables to arrest and bring before a Justice of the Peace "any person, who shall be suspected to be a Deserter," and provided for rewards for anyone apprehending a deserter. It provided penalties for harboring or failing to report a known

---

[93] See, as discussed above, Gates, Pass for Captain Casdorp et al., 3 October 1776, Ticonderoga, NY, Horatio Gates Papers, 1726-1828, Film 23, Reel 3 (Correspondence, July 1776 - October 1776), DLAR. See also Gates, Pass for Thomas Tomlin Pritchard to New Windsor, NY, 18 April 1776, Horatio Gates Papers, 1726-1828, Film 23, Reel 2 (Correspondence, Nov. 1769 - July 1776), DLAR.

[94] Gates to the Committee of Safety of Cumberland County, [VT?], 1 August 1776, Ticonderoga, Horatio Gates Papers, 1726-1828, Film 23, Reel 3 (Correspondence, July 1776 - October 1776), DLAR.

[95] *PGWDE*, Revolutionary, V: 685n3.

deserter, as well as for buying and selling uniforms or equipment belonging to the United States, or for "caus[ing] the colour of such cloaths to be changed." A suspected deserter brought before a Justice of the Peace and examined might be identified as such "by his confession, or the testimony of one or more witness or witnesses, upon oath or affirmation," or if, "by the knowledge of such Justice of the Peace, it shall appear that such suspected person is an inlisted Soldier, and ou[ght] to be with the troop or company to which he belongs." The act also provided that,

> [I]f any able-bodied man shall travel, or come into any part of this State, without a pass from some Justice of the County, or some other Justice of the Peace, from whence he may have come; or, if a Soldier, from his Commanding Officer; every such person so travelling, or coming into the State as aforesaid, shall be deemed and taken to be a Deserter, and within the meaning of this Act, except the contrary be made appear.[96]

Apart from discouraging desertion and providing for more consistent apprehension of deserters, this act, and its latter provision in particular, more generally reinforced the multiple overlapping regimes, civil and military, that required passes for travel and secure mobilization of identity within Revolutionary America.

The frontier between the civilian and military spheres was a key site in the identification of individual Americans during the Revolution. On the military side, regimes of identification and governance established and regulated militarized identities—homologous with but largely distinct from other contemporary identity structures of dependence and subordination—for those admitted to or forced into military service. The frontier, on the other side, excluded many marginalized groups and individuals, whether or not they wished to fight, from military service and the qualified forms of citizenship and self-determination that it implied. These people were also, to a large degree, nominally excluded from the Revolution, as from political participation and self-

---

[96] Pennsylvania General Assembly, *An act, to discourage desertion, and to punish all such persons as shall harbour or conceal deserters,* 20 February 1777, *EAI*, Series 1, no. 15501 (filmed).

determination more generally. As part and parcel of this ascribed apoliticality, they were largely excluded from or subordinated by the evolving regimes and instruments of identification. They were at the same time subjected to a variety of regimes, instruments, and assumptions designed to subordinate and constrain them. The following chapter examines how marginalized groups—particularly women and African Americans—were subordinated rather than liberated by regimes of identification but nonetheless navigated Revolutionary identification to fashion and enact their own identities and to claim some measure of self-determination.

Chapter 7

Margins

Even as the adult white men of Revolutionary America struggled over their identities as

citizens or subjects, it was members of marginalized populations—notably women, children,

indentured servants, and African Americans (both slave and free)—who lived most precariously on

the line between freedom and unfreedom and whose power over their own identities was most

uncertain. The conflict's disruptions offered them new opportunities to reshape their identities or

claim new degrees of self-determination. But any such efforts entailed contest with other, usually

much more powerful, parties who held stakes in how they were identified. These contested

identifications, and the experiences of these marginalized groups amid the Revolutionary crisis of

identification, were centered on cultures of hierarchy that structured instruments and practices of

identification more generally.

The instruments of identification through which these marginalized groups contested and

practiced identities were in some cases the same sorts of passes, passports, letters, and certificates

employed in the identification of enfranchised persons. But they included as well genres that were

distinctive to and defined by these persons' marginal or dependent status, as ascribed to them by

personal or social "masters." These documents included, among many others, slave and servant

passes; advertisements and posters describing fugitive slaves and servants; freedom papers;

specialized letters or certificates tailored to the nominal apoliticality of women, children, and

servants; and registers of ostensible slaves "carried off" by the British. These instruments could be

deployed or required by others to constrain the dependent persons they identified. But the

individuals themselves also found ways to manipulate these instruments to their own advantage, as they attempted to seize greater power over how they were identified. In their efforts to define or deploy chosen identities, these persons struggled simultaneously with exclusion from the instruments available to enfranchised groups and with the regimes of identification designed to subordinate them.

These instruments and the contests of identification they enacted were framed by basic assumptions delimiting marginalized populations. Marginalized persons were almost universally ascribed identities as dependents—typically of adult white males, whether heads of households or "masters." For many, dependence was assumed unless they could prove otherwise. Presumption ran against African Americans, young or lower class boys and men, children more generally, and women, when any of these attempted to travel or act at law in their own right. They could be taken up as runaway slaves, servants, seamen, children, or wives, or denied any capacity to self-determination or consent (such as enlisting in the military or choosing exile with the enemy). As a function of their ascribed subordination they were nominally excluded from participation in the political or military struggles of the Revolution—or were defined as racial or cultural outsiders—but were everywhere and in profound ways entangled with the conflict. Their histories reveal the hierarchical and exclusive assumptions behind the Revolutionary regimes of identification explored thus far while at the same time demonstrating that the most coercive and contested Revolutionary identification took place on the margins.

When marginalized groups struggled against regimes of identification used to stymie their self-determination, they continued the struggles embedded in pre-Revolutionary hierarchical and coercive social orders. Those systems of bound labor had been designed to bind the servant's or slave's identity and physical person closely to his or her master. Most indentures (including articles of apprenticeship) explicitly restricted the mobility of the servants or apprentices—who were required to obtain their master's leave, often in writing, to "absent" themselves from his vicinity. In the case of slaves, restrictions on mobility and pass requirements were imposed by custom or statute, rather than individual contract. The authority of masters over servants in these and other respects was, in law, analogous to the authority of parents (especially fathers) over children and husbands over wives, of heads of household over dependents. This authority included the right to restrict their mobility and to speak for them or pass approval regarding any agreements or obligations they might enter into, including indentures, apprenticeships, contracts of other sorts, maritime service, or military enlistment.[1] The analogous legal authority of masters over slaves was carried to a still further extreme by the denial of legal personhood, by which the slave became legally an extension of the master, like his other property.[2]

Established structural limits on their social resources constrained marginal persons' ability to control their own identities even in basic ways. The ability of individuals to know and to prove their own ages, or to provide persuasive or legally determinant proof of many other facets of their identities—including places of birth and residence, freedom (or lack thereof), character, credit, respectability, social rank, name, or race—depended heavily on individual circumstances. The problematic availability of birth and other age records, for instance, was an obstacle for individuals across the social spectrum, but the potential for incomplete records tended to be greater the lower

---

[1] On bound labor and the authority of masters see Daniel Vickers, *Young Men and the Sea: Yankee Seafarers in the Age of Sail*, (New Haven, CT: Yale UP, 2005), ch. 7; Richard B. Morris, *Government and Labor in Early America*, (New York: Columbia UP, 1946); Christopher L. Tomlins, *Freedom Bound: Law, Labor, and Civic Identity in Colonizing English America, 1580-1865*, (New York: Cambridge UP, 2010); Holly Brewer, *By Birth or Consent: Children, Law, and the Anglo-American Revolution in Authority*, (Chapel Hill, NC: University of North Carolina Press, 2005).

[2] See Walter Johnson, *Soul by Soul: Life inside the Antebellum Slave Market*, (Cambridge, MA: Harvard UP, 1999); Orlando Patterson, *Slavery and Social Death: A Comparative Study*, (Cambridge, MA: Harvard UP, 1982); David Brion Davis, *The Problem of Slavery in Western Culture*, (Ithaca, NY: Cornell UP, 1966); Eugene D. Genovese, *Roll, Jordan, Roll: The World the Slaves Made*, (New York: Vintage Books, 1976); Thomas D. Morris, *Southern Slavery and the Law*, (Chapel Hill, NC: University of North Carolina Press, 1996).

the individual fell within the social hierarchy.[3] In part this likely reflected lower degrees of family

literacy and education (which translated into fewer written family records, including birth and

baptism registers in the family Bible), less stability (which would mean greater chance of disruption

or loss of family records, as well as less visibility in the records of institutions like churches or town

government), and social roles that may have occasioned fewer instances requiring age verification,

such as voting, holding office, or inheriting property.

The disparity in documentary foundations for age (and for identity more generally) was

particularly pronounced for slaves. Some slaveholders kept meticulous records of slave births,

purchases, age at purchase, and other matters, either for purposes of valuation, or as part of the

paternalist construction of slaves as part of the patriarchal "family" and "household."[4] But, in

general, the dearth of records that corresponded to slaves' comparatively lower status was

exacerbated in their case by their legal lack of personhood. This encouraged inattention to

recording of their identities—except where it served the masters' interests—and, in some cases,

deliberate obfuscation of their identities as part of the larger tactic of social control through

enforced ignorance.[5] On the other hand slave owners had incentives to record and so be able to

deploy identifying descriptions as a means to recover fugitive slaves.

---

[3] For brief treatments of the patchy, limited, and decentralized nature of identification records and civil registration in the American states at this time, see Pamela Sankar, "State Power and Record-keeping: The History of Individualized Surveillance in the United States, 1790-1935," PhD diss., (University of Pennsylvania, 1992), 20-24; Robert Gutman, "Birth and Death Registration in Massachusetts. I. The Colonial Background, 1639-1800," *The Milbank Memorial Fund Quarterly*, Vol. 36, No. 1 (Jan., 1958), 58-74. On similar issues in the French Atlantic and Louisiana in the late eighteenth and early nineteenth centuries, see Rebecca J. Scott and Jean M. Hébrard, *Freedom Papers: An Atlantic Odyssey in the Age of Emancipation*, (Cambridge, MA: Harvard UP, 2012).

[4] See Rhys Isaac, *Landon Carter's Uneasy Kingdom: Revolution and Rebellion on a Virginia Plantation*, (New York: Oxford UP, 2004); Drew Gilpin Faust, *James Henry Hammond and the Old South: A Design for Mastery*, (Baton Rouge, LA: Louisiana State UP, 1982); Erskine Clarke, *Dwelling Place: A Plantation Epic*, (New Haven, CT: Yale UP, 2005).

[5] See, especially, though focused primarily on a later period, Janet Duitsman Cornelius, *"When I can read my title clear": Literacy, Slavery, and Religion in the Antebellum South*, (Columbia, SC: University of South Carolina Press, 1991).

The uncertainty regarding basic facets of servants' and slaves' identities, including age, was evident when, having fled their bondage, they were described in fugitive advertisements. Thus, when, in January of 1775, John Stevenson of New Haven, Connecticut, advertised the flight of "two indented Servant Men," he described one as "about 19 years old" and the other as "about 23 years old."[6] When, that same day, Philip Clampher of Philadelphia described his runaway "Irish servant LAD," he guessed his age as "about 19 or 20 years of age."[7] The following day, Samuel Philips advertised in a New York City paper that "two indented Mulatto boys" had deserted his service, one "about 20 years of age" and the other "about 18 years of age."[8] When, later that month, Thomas Burton of Philadelphia advertised "a mulatto boy" as a runaway, he described him as "about 17 or 18 years of age."[9] Fugitive advertisements more generally often described servants or slaves as "aged about" a certain number of years. Some did not even give an approximate age, identifying the fugitive only as a "boy," "lad," or "man."[10]

Servants and slaves had frequently fled their bondage during the colonial period. But the Revolution brought them new opportunities to do so. With many masters more frequently absent because of the war, dependents found more occasions for escape and self-determination. Disruptions of social labor regulation and local oversight brought further opportunity, as did the

---

[6] *Connecticut Journal*, 11 January 1775, 3, *AHN*.

[7] *Pennsylvania Gazette*, 11 January 1775, 3, *AHN*.

[8] *New York Journal*, 12 January 1775, 4, *AHN*.

[9] *New York Gazette*, 16 January 1775, 4, *AHN*.

[10] In many cases, it may have been judged unnecessary to identify, for example, a fugitive slave by age. However, were a record of the fugitive's precise age readily available, it is unclear why the author of the description would not give the precise age (unless this lack of precision expressed disdain regarding the details of a slave's identity). Though born well after the Revolution, Frederick Douglass would begin his later *Narrative of the Life of Frederick Douglass*, (Boston: 1845), with the telling comment that, "I have no accurate knowledge of my age, never having seen any authentic record containing it. By far the larger part of the slaves know as little of their ages as horses know of theirs, and it is the wish of most masters within my knowledge to keep their slaves thus ignorant. I do not remember to have ever met a slave who could tell his birthday. They seldom came nearer to it than planting-time, harvest-time, cherry-time, spring-time, or fall-time. A want of information concerning my own was a source of unhappiness to me even during childhood. The white children could tell their ages. I could not tell why I ought to be deprived of the same privilege."

warring armies themselves, in which fugitives might find a haven as soldiers, servants, or camp followers. Thousands of slaves in fact fled during the course of the war, many to the shelter of the British army and the freedom it offered or was believed to offer.[11]

Whether or not they fled (or rebelled as an enslaved population), African Americans, and slaves in particular, were commonly presumed to sympathize with the enemy. As such, it was feared, they might act as a fifth column, perhaps in concert with white Loyalists. In October of 1775, Richard Henry Lee blamed the failure to stop Lord Dunmore raiding Norfolk, Virginia and stealing the local printing press on the fact that, "It happened when the good men of that place were all away, and none but Tories & Negroes remained behind."[12] In July of the following year, the Committee of Correspondence of Newark, New Jersey wrote to General Washington seeking further protection by the military, expressing anxiety that "Our Country [is] destitute of Inhabitants" and "Our Wives & Children unprotected either from the Enemy without or the Tories & Negroes in the midst of us."[13]

In response to such anxieties, slaveholding communities, especially in the southern states, increased citizen and militia patrols to prevent gatherings of slaves; to identify possible fugitives on the road; and to seize small watercraft that might be used for escape to British ships. In some cases slaves were relocated from coastal or otherwise threatened regions to keep them out of enemy hands and to limit their opportunities for flight. Vigilance was increased and both slaves and African

---

[11] On the wartime flight of slaves and their fate thereafter, see Sylvia R. Frey, *Water from the Rock: Black Resistance in a Revolutionary Age*, (Princeton, NJ: Princeton UP, 1991); Cassandra Pybus, *Epic Journeys of Freedom: Runaway Slaves of the American Revolution and their Global Quest for Liberty*, (Boston: Beacon Press, 2006); Douglas R. Egerton, *Death or Liberty: African Americans and Revolutionary America*, (New York: Oxford UP, 2009), ch. 2-3; Benjamin Quarles, *The Negro in the American Revolution*, (Chapel Hill, NC: University of North Carolina Press, 1961); Gerald W. Mullin, *Flight and Rebellion: Slave Resistance in Eighteenth-Century Virginia*, (New York: Oxford UP, 1972) ch. 4.

[12] Lee to Washington, 22-23 October 1775, *PGWDE*, Revolutionary, II: 217-218.

[13] Newark Committee of Correspondence to Washington, 4 July 1776, *PGWDE*, Revolutionary, V: 207-208.

Americans more generally were more closely watched.[14] In some places additional pass requirements and restrictions on mobility were imposed. Thus in May of 1775, the committee of Newburgh, New York, resolved that slave owners in the district were not "on any account whatever" to "suffer his or their Negro or Negroes to be absent from his dwelling house or farm, after sun-down, or send them out in the day time off their farm without a pass." Slaves caught abroad contrary to these regulations were to be punished with up to thirty-five lashes.[15]

When slaves or servants did flee, masters employed much the same measures to recover them as before the Revolution. Many published advertisements in newspapers, announcing the fugitive's flight, describing his or her person, clothes, manners, and other characteristics, and often offering a reward, while warning others not to harbor or employ the runaway.[16] Masters supplemented these advertisements with broadsides posted in public gathering places.[17] Many, no doubt, hoped that the enforcement of pass requirements would lead to the recapture of fugitives.

Subordinated persons, however, often manipulated regimes and instruments of identification for their own ends. It was not uncommon, for instance, for slaves fleeing their masters to take with them—in addition to clothes and select other goods—an old, stolen, or forged pass. Such a pass might allow the fugitive to get some distance from his or her master before being suspected by those

---

[14] See Frey, *Water from the Rock*, 57-61, 85; Frey, Sylvia R., "Between Slavery and Freedom: Virginia Blacks in the American Revolution," *Journal of Southern History*, Vol. 49 (1983), 383, 385-386; Egerton, *Death or Liberty*, 50, 61, 69, 73.

[15] Committee of Newburgh, NY, 15 May 1775, *AAO*, Series 4, II: 606-607.

[16] On fugitive advertisements, see David Waldstreicher, "Reading the Runaways: Self-Fashioning, Print Culture, and Confidence in the Eighteenth-Century Mid-Atlantic," *William and Mary Quarterly*, Series 3, Vol. 56, No. 2 (Apr., 1999), 243-272; Gwenda Morgan and Peter Rushton, "Visible Bodies: Power, Subordination and Identity in the Eighteenth-Century Atlantic World," *Journal of Social History*, Vol. 39, No. 1 (Autumn, 2005), 39-64; Jonathan Prude, "To Look upon the 'Lower Sort': Runaway Ads and the Appearance of Unfree Laborers in America, 1750-1800," *Journal of American History*, Vol. 78, No. 1 (Jun., 1991), 124-159.

[17] Thus, at the end of February, 1774, shortly after the Boston Tea Party and just before the Intolerable Acts were to descend on Boston and Massachusetts, Richard Derby of Salem had printed a broadside advertising the flight from his service of "a NEGRO MAN, named Obed, about 25 Years of Age," describing in addition his features, place of birth, and probable clothing, and offering three dollars reward. 28 February 1774, Salem, MA, BDSDS. 1774, Broadsides Collection, AAS.

met on the road, or it might be modified to dissimulate the fugitive's identity and suit the needs of a longer journey. When Ebenezer Sayer, for instance, advertised the flight of his slave Pomp in December of 1774, he made special note that, "Said Negro before his Elopement, procur'd a counterfeit Pass, changing his own Name and his Master's." "All Persons," Sayer wrote, "are cautioned against being deceived by such Artifice."[18] (How Sayer knew of the false pass was unexplained.) George Reynolds of Shepherdstown, NJ, in September of 1782, likewise noted of his runaway slave Will that he had "a forged pass" and that "no regard is to be paid thereto."[19]

Some masters heard second or third-hand that their runaway servant or slave had acquired such an instrument. A slaveholder advertising in the *Connecticut Gazette* in February of 1776 wrote of the fugitive slave Harry that, "he (as I hear) has a counterfeit Pass."[20] John Hall of Cecil County, Maryland, advertising the flight of husband and wife Toney and Rachel in April of 1779 included that, "It is thought they have a pass with them."[21] Other masters, familiar enough with what was apparently a common practice, simply remarked the possibility that the fugitive had acquired a pass of one sort or another. John Barnes of Poughkeepsie, New York, in February of 1775, advertised the flight of his slave Caesar, noting that he "probably has a counterfeit pass with him."[22] A Virginia master, the following June, wrote of his runaway slave, "I don't doubt but he has procured a forged Pass."[23] Christian Wirtz noted of fugitive Dan in December of 1779 that he would "if possible procure a pass."[24] Gunning Bedford, advertising the flight of his slave "SAM, alias SAMUEL

---

[18] 20 January 1775, *New Hampshire Gazette*, (Portsmouth, NH), 4, *AHN*.

[19] 18 September 1782, *New Jersey Gazette*, (Trenton, NJ), 3, *AHN*.

[20] 23 February 1776, *Connecticut Gazette*, (New London, CT), 4, *AHN*.

[21] 10 July 1779, *Pennsylvania Packet*, (Philadelphia, PA), 1, *AHN*.

[22] 27 February 1775, *New York Gazette*, (New York, NY), 4, *AHN*.

[23] 24 June 1775, *Virginia Gazette*, (Williamsburg, VA), 4, *AHN*.

[24] 5 January 1780, *New Jersey Gazette*, (Trenton, NJ), 1, *AHN*.

THOMSON" in May of 1783, suggested that, "he may possibly have a forged pass."[25] It was common enough for fugitives to acquire such passes that some advertisements explicitly remarked when a fugitive lacked one. Thus in December of 1777, John Jones of Mount Holly, New Jersey, advertising the flight of his slave Quash, wrote that, "As he has a large bundle with him, and without a pass, it is thought he will be easily detected."[26]

The ease with which fugitives might secure passes to aid their escape depended to some degree on their varying social resources—especially their access to literacy, their own or another's. Some masters, at least, were very conscious of this dynamic and noted the relevant circumstances in their advertisements. When Rovin fled his master at East Chester, New York in March of 1775, the latter included in his advertisement the fact that, "it is imagined he has got a pass, being very intimate with a Negro fellow, who can write."[27] John Jones of Southward, Pennsylvania, advertising the flight of his slave Newry in April of 1776, noted that he had " been creditably informed the said Negro has obtained a pass from a certain THOMAS ADAIR, and says he is his property." Adair, he explained was a mariner lately arrived from Scotland.[28] (Newry's connection to Adair and the latter's motives remained unexplained.) In February of 1777, a master advertising the escape of a slave named Bill, wrote that, "It is supposed he is gone towards New-York, or Long-Island, in Company with some other Negroes and white Persons, who it is probable may forge a Pass for him."[29]

Marginalized groups could also draw on some instruments meant, if not exactly to empower them, to certify desirable identities. Manumitted slaves, or those who wished to claim identities as

---

[25] 17 May 1783, *Pennsylvania Packet*, (Philadelphia, PA), 4, *AHN*.

[26] 10 December 1777, *New Jersey Gazette*, (Burlington, NJ), 3, *AHN*.

[27] 9 March 1775, *New York Journal*, (New York, NY), 2, *AHN*.

[28] 20 April 1776, *Pennsylvania Ledger*, (Philadelphia, PA), 1, *AHN*.

[29] 5 February 1777, *Connecticut Journal*, (New Haven, CT), 4, *AHN*.

such, could proffer manumission papers as proof of their freedom if it came into question.[30] Thus

Pompey, a former slave of Quaker Cornell Stevenson of Burlington County, New Jersey, could

present the certificate of manumission signed by Stevenson and witnessed by two others on the 5th

of August 1776. The certificate described Pompey simply as "my Negro Slave—named Pompey—

Aged about fifty five—Years." The certificate was issued using a printed form of a manumission

certificate, suggesting the more general use of these instruments. A manuscript note at bottom

indicated that the certificate had been "Recorded in a Book kept by the Monthly Meeting of Friends

in Burln. By Saml. Allenson Clk." This registration might have provided some further record of the

manumission and some further support for Pompey's claim to freedom were his certificate to be

lost, stolen, seized, or destroyed.[31] In another case, a mother and daughter taken up in Stono, South

Carolina, and advertised as fugitive slaves in June of 1783, bore what was apparently presumed to be

a forged certificate of emancipation from their former master, dated four years earlier.[32]

Some fugitive slaves managed to steal or forge freedom papers and certificates. Thus in July

of 1776, advertising both the flight of a slave named Charles and the theft of goods Charles had

taken from his house, John Barnesley of Bristol, Pennsylvania, noted that, "The Mulatto had a pass

as a free Negro signed by Samuel Rhoads in Philadelphia."[33] John Tolly Worthington of Baltimore,

in April of 1782, wrote of his fugitive slave Saucy that he would "endeavour to get a pass and travel

---

[30] Of course, the custom of issuing such documents, and the common legal requirements that free African Americans carry either manumission papers or certificates of free birth, laid the burden of proof of his or her freedom upon the claimant to freedom. Thus these instruments, in themselves empowering and aids to African Americans' self-determination and self-identification, at the same time formed part of a larger documentary, legal, and social apparatus designed to maintain power and control over African Americans—especially the enslaved, but likewise the free—by the white colonials now turned rebels.

[31] Cornell Stevenson, Certificate of Manumission of Pompey, 5 August 1776, Springfield, NJ, Sol Feinstone Collection, Film 1, Reel 3, No. 1326, DLAR.

[32] 7 June 1783, *South Carolina Gazette,* (Charleston, SC), 1, *AHN.*

[33] 3 August 1776, *Pennsylvania Ledger,* (Philadelphia, PA), 3, *AHN.*

as a freeman."[34] In June of 1782, William Buchanan of Baltimore remarked concerning his fugitive

slave Fortune that, "it is suspected he procured a Pass which had been granted to a free Negro,

named JOHN."[35] In January of the following year, Daniel J. Adams of Wilmington, Delaware,

advertising the flight of his slave Charles, noted that a recently recaptured fugitive who had been in

company with Charles "informs [Charles] had obtained a pass from a free Negroe in this town, by

the name of Poll, under which name and pass he now passes."[36] That same month, Elizabeth

Cochran advertised the flight of her "likely Negro wench named Suck," noting that the fugitive had

"a pretended pass or certificate from Mr. Hailey, of her being free."[37] Hugh Cunningham of

Lancaster, Pennsylvania, writing in March of 1783, believed it "probable" that his runaway slave Sam

had "got a pass from some associates, and may pass for a freeman."[38] James Buchanan of Sussex

County, Delaware, advertising the flight of his slave Ben Lately in July of 1783, noted that, "He

probably will pass for a freeman, and is supposed to have a pass."[39]

Struggles over the identification of marginalized persons wove through the Revolution more

broadly as well, beyond the intense contests between master and fugitive. Both sides of the conflict,

most basically, parsed populations they sought to govern based, to one degree or another, on basic

assumptions and fundamental heuristics of identification that determined which persons could be

considered political actors or subject to the demands and rigors of war. Conflict over self- and

social identification may have been most fraught whenever the borderline between freedom and

---

[34] 18 April 1782, *Pennsylvania Packet*, (Philadelphia, PA), 4, *AHN*.

[35] 8 June 1782, *Independence Gazetteer*, (Philadelphia, PA), 3, *AHN*.

[36] 18 January 1783, *Pennsylvania Packet*, (Philadelphia, PA), 3, *AHN*.

[37] 3 February 1783, *Independent Gazetteer*, (Philadelphia, PA), 3, *AHN*.

[38] 9 April 1783, *Freeman's Journal*, (Philadelphia, PA), 2, *AHN*.

[39] 30 July 1783, *Freeman's Journal*, (Philadelphia, PA), 1, *AHN*.

subordination intersected with that between civilian and military statuses. Age, race, gender, and

freedom were used to identify those who could and could not enter military service, and those who

could or could not determine their own political identities. At the same time, these identifying

characteristics were used to identify which persons should be considered potential threats, in part

depending precisely on whether they might serve in the enemy's army or could be held politically

responsible.[40] Children below a certain age, for instance, were generally not required to swear the

oaths of allegiance that proliferated during the Revolution.[41]

One basic corollary of these assumptions was that certain portions of the population—

women, children, and the elderly—were considered to fall outside the bounds of legitimate warfare

and political responsibility. To violate these assumed exemptions was to act "without distinction of

age or sex" and to merit the opprobrium of "gentlemen," Christians, or "mankind." The conflict

was defined by free adult white males to be a conflict by and among—though not exclusively for—

free adult white males. In the heat of civil war, however, dependents were often seen, for practical

purposes, as very real, and potentially threatening, political and military actors.[42] It was recognized

---

[40] Thus, for instance, as Virginia prepared for war and possible invasion in the summer of 1776, the convention ordered
the evacuation from much of Princess Anne and Norfolk counties of Loyalist or suspected white inhabitants and slaves
of military age. See *PGWDE*, Revolutionary, IV: 259n1. What qualified as "military age" for slaves may or may not have
been congruent with the range of age allowed or prescribed for free white recruits. The October 1780 Maryland act
allowing for the enlistment of slaves limited the provision to those "between sixteen and forty years of age": *AMDMR*,
367.

[41] Children below the prescribed age thresholds were generally considered both incapable (or unauthorized) to make
their own political decisions and unlikely, through sheer lack of mental and physical capacity, to pose a military or
political threat (making the binding of their wills with an oath unnecessary). Brewer, *By Birth or Consent*, 134; Harold M.
Hyman, *To Try Men's Souls: Loyalty Tests in American History*, (Berkley, CA: University of California Press, 1959), chs. 3-4;
Nellie Protsman Waldenmaier, *Some of the Earliest Oaths of Allegiance to the United States of America*, (Lancaster, PA:
Lancaster Press, 1944); James H. Kettner, *The Development of American Citizenship, 1608-1870*, (Chapel Hill, NC: University
of North Carolina Press, 1978), 198. See also, *PGWDE*, Revolutionary, XVIII: 442n9.

[42] The question of their political identities would remain in contention long after the war, as legislatures and the courts
attempted to work out to what degree dependent women and children were to be identified with their husbands and
fathers or held liable for the political decisions of their male heads of household. Linda K. Kerber, "The Paradox of
Women's Citizenship in the Early Republic: The Case of Martin vs. Massachusetts, 1805," *American Historical Review*, Vol.
97, No. 2 (Apr., 1992), 349-378; Linda K. Kerber, *Women of the Republic: Intellect and Ideology in Revolutionary America*,
(Chapel Hill, NC: University of North Carolina Press, 1980), ch. 4-5; Kettner, *American Citizenship*, ch. 7.

that the assumption that these persons were uninvolved or harmless could let them act as spies,

saboteurs, smugglers, and the like.

Women and children in particular cut highly ambiguous figures. As the battle of New York

City approached in August of 1776, American General Alexander McDougall anxiously reported to

Washington concerning a woman calling herself Mary Debeau. When examined by McDougal,

Debeau related how she, along with seven men, eight or nine women, and ten children had travelled

by boat from Manhattan to Staten Island, where the British lay encamped, yet "no person

Questioned her or her Companions there, about her or their business, or on any other subject." In

like manner, when she returned, recently, from Staten Island to Manhattan along with ten or eleven

men and women, "the boat was not examined in crossing the Bay, nor any of the passengers

Questioned when they landed." Debeau claimed she could give no account of the British army

forces on the island, and she was cagey regarding the identities and business of her companions,

suggesting that they went "to Secure a place of retreat" or "to take their Famil[i]es out of Town."

McDougall explained to Washington in exasperation that, "She answers So evasively, that I am at [a]

loss to determine her true Character." To be safe he had "had her Searched by matrons for Papers;

but found none." McDougall noted that "From her appearance and deportment; I am inclined to

conclude, she is a follower of the Enemy's army." He closed by suggesting that the local committee,

"composed of Persons from every Quarter of the Town," could probably best identify her,

investigate the matter, and "discover her fellow passengers; if her Story be true."[43] If her story was

---

[43] McDougall to Washington, 19 August 1776, *PGWDE*, Revolutionary, VI: 77-78. See also General Heath's reluctance
to allow "Lady Johnson" to pass into New York City because she "is said to be a Lady of great art & Intrigue." Her
previous application had, Heath understood, been refused by the New York state Convention "on Account of Sr John's
Influence among the Indians." Heath to Washington, 9 January 1777, *PGWDE*, Revolutionary, VIII: 26-28.

true, it revealed the laxity of sentries and patrols on both sides, at least concerning parties largely

composed of women and children.[44]

The tendency to treat women, the young, and the elderly as less threatening, and thus less

subject to wartime governance and military security was so common that during the winter

encampment at Valley Forge, General Washington, intent on stopping illicit trade with the enemy,

was compelled to issue explicit orders directing that sentries were to, "seize all the provision and the

horses & Carriages drove by women & Boys, many of whom are employed as they think indulgence

will be allowed on Account of Sex and Age."[45] Two days later, Washington used his General Orders

to squelch a rumor that special indulgence had been given to a woman to carry a large quantity of

butter into Philadelphia.[46] The previous autumn he had ordered that women coming out of

Philadelphia only be allowed to pass if they understood they would not be allowed to return.[47] In

other instances, Washington expressed himself willing to allow women and children to go into

---

[44] The rebels knew very well, in fact, how useful women could be as couriers, spies, and informants—they drew on women in these capacities for important intelligence in a number of instances. Elias Boudinot, for instance, in December of 1777, as the Continental forces waited outside British-occupied Philadelphia, received, unsolicited, from "a little poor looking insignificant Old Woman," presenting herself under pretense of requesting a pass into the country to buy flour, a paper concealed in a "needlebook" that conveyed intelligence of General Howe's impending movements and possible attack. *PGWDE*, Revolutionary, XII: 538n1. The day before, information from two women in the neighborhood of Frankford, Pennsylvania, helped to identify a possible double agent in the Continental intelligence service. *PGWDE*, Revolutionary, XII: 514-515n.

[45] Washington to John Jameson, 1 February 1778, *PGWDE*, Revolutionary, XIII: 437-438. In other instances, guards and pickets seem to have been all too ready to suspect, stop, or harass women as possible smugglers, etc. See the complaints conveyed by Major John Clark, Jr. to Washington, 18 December 1777, *PGWDE*, Revolutionary, XII: 628-630. The British appear to have faced a problem similar to that encountered by Washington, in the willingness of some officers and men to permit women to pass without the proper authorizations. Thus John Le Roome, secretary to General Pattison, Commandant of New York City under the British, in July of 1780 wrote to Captain Thomas Ward to inform him that a "Miss Romine, having contrary to the Regulations of this Garrison, come into this City (to visit her Father, who is a Prisoner, and at present confined in the Sugar House) not having a Pass from the Commandant so to do, & on being asked how she came in produced a Pass from you, in Consequence of which I am directed by Major General Pattison to inform you, that in future you are not to permit any Person (Prisoners making their Escape from the Rebels & Rebel Deserters excepted) thro' your Post who cannot produce the Commandants pass to come in."

[46] Washington, General Orders, 3 February 1778, *PGWDE*, Revolutionary, XIII: 442-443.

[47] Washington, General Orders, 21 November 1777, *PGWDE*, Revolutionary, XII: 337-338.

British-held Philadelphia provided that they remain there, thus obviating the possibility of further illicit trade under their cover.[48]

Even those women travelling for evidently innocuous if not charitable purposes posed potential threats. Thus in April of 1778, from headquarters at Valley Forge, Washington wrote to Pennsylvania governor Thomas Wharton, then at Lancaster, that four "Ladies connected with the Quakers confined at Winchester in Virginia" had "waited upon me this day for permission to pass to York Town to endeavour to obtain the release of their Friends." Their passage even so far as Valley Forge might have been refused with some prudence. But "As they were admitted by the Officer at the advanced picket to come within the Camp, I thought it safer to suffer them to proceed, than to oblige them to return immediately to the City [Philadelphia]." "You will judge of the propriety of permitting them to proceed further than Lancaster," Washington wrote Wharton, "but from appearances, I imagine their request may be safely granted. As they seem much distressed, humanity pleads strongly in their behalf."[49] In a similar manner, the following month, Washington himself received a letter from the Governor of Maryland informing him that Maryland's government "had many Applications from People of this State for Leave to go into Phila." and "some of them want to return again." "We have not given Leave to any Body to go in," he assured Washington, "without permission from the Officer commanding the Continental Troops at some post on the way," and they had not "recommended any except" three women: "Mrs Stewart Mrs CaLDCleugh and Mrs McCall."[50] A year later, Colonel Israel Shreve wrote to Washington from Elizabethtown, New Jersey that there were "about twenty persons men Women and Children, Now Waiting at this post to go in the Enemys Lines, with passes from the Different States." "This business with the Situation

---

[48] See Washington to William Smallwood, 23 May 1778, *PGWDE*, Revolutionary, XV: 206-207. See also the request to which this was a response, Smallwood to Washington, 19-20 May 1778, *PGWDE*, Revolutionary, XV: 169-170n2.

[49] Washington to Wharton, 6 April 1778, Insert in *Exiles in Virginia...* (Philadelphia, 1848), M-4153, after page 63, WLCL.

[50] Thomas Johnson to Washington, 22 May 1778, *PGWDE*, Revolutionary, XV: 189.

of the post, I find," Shreve explained, "Calls for the Greatest Attention, As Our Enemys Wish to take Every Little Advantage they possably Can."[51]

African Americans were generally seen as best left out of the conflict. While consistently cast as potential labor, African Americans were only more reluctantly cast as potential rank and file soldiers. Though the British would recruit slaves and other African Americans to fight on their side, and though the American military would increasingly (but never fully) open its ranks to African Americans over the course of the war, both sides demonstrated some ambivalence over the practice of arming slaves or former slaves. They were often derided as poor excuses for soldiers, even while seen as a dire threat. Above all, they were not seen as parties to the conflict—potential citizens fighting for their own liberties.[52] The Americans, meanwhile, were outraged by British appeals to slaves, use of black soldiers en masse, and implicit incitements to slave rebellion—describing such measures as barbaric, one more example of how Britain had forfeited any legitimate claim to sovereignty over America. The more African Americans were kept out of the conflict however, the more remained within communities that, because of the war, lacked the adult white men who had ordinarily enforced subordination.

The supposition that slaves might not simply rebel but also act in concert with the enemy was one facet of the larger ambiguity in the perception of African Americans' political identities. African Americans, even if free, were excluded from any political franchise and laid under special legal restrictions. Slaves were politically and legally non-persons, supposedly without independent agency, unless they committed an offense for which they needed to be held responsible and

---

[51] Shreve to Washington, 26 May 1779, *PGWDE*, Revolutionary, XX: 637-638.

[52] See Lorenzo J. Green, "Some Observations on the Black Regiment of Rhode Island in the American Revolution," *Journal of Negro History*, Vol. 37 (1952), 142-172; Ira Berlin, "The Revolution in Black Life," *The American Revolution: Explorations in the History of American Radicalism*, Alfred F. Young ed., (Dekalb, IL: Northern Illinois UP, 1976), 353-355; Frey, "Between Slavery and Freedom," 387-394, 397-398; Frey, *Water from the Rock*, 77-80, passim; Egerton, *Death or Liberty*, 74-79; John Wood Sweet, *Bodies Politic: Negotiating Race in the American North, 1730-1830*, (Baltimore, MD: Johns Hopkins UP, 2003), ch. 5.

punished. In practice, however, individual slaves were certainly recognized to have individual personalities and, perhaps, convictions. It was not uncommon for them to be seen as "Tories." American patrols that took up Loyalist partisans, fugitives, and suspects took up slaves and free African Americans as well.[53] How they should be identified and treated, whether alike to or distinct from the white Tories remained ambiguous.

It was most common for marginalized persons to be identified passively, very nearly as objects, a striking contrast with the self-determined identities essential to the voluntaristic politics of revolution. Since women and children were exempted from the rigors of war, they were not uncommonly thought to be best removed from the theatre of war. Thus, in December of 1776, anticipating the imminent descent of British forces on their state, the Interior Committee of Rhode Island resolved that "whereas many of the Inhabitants" in the threatened towns were "Women & Children" who "must (if they Remain there) in Case of an Attack suffer extremely," and who "can be in no wise serviceable in defence," they should be removed to the interior of the state. The men, meanwhile, were not to leave but instead exhorted to meet the enemy with "Fortitude and Resolution."[54]

Likewise, African Americans were only sometimes treated as persons with political significance but were commonly treated as resources. When Town Major Urquhard, in the autumn of 1775, took the census in Boston at Gage's direction, the African American population was measured by an additional category of which no equivalent was applied to the white population:

---

[53] See, New York Committee for Detecting and Defeating Conspiracies, 31 December 1776, 2 January 1777, 5 March 1777, *Minutes of the Committee and of the First Commission for Detecting and Defeating Conspiracies in the State of New York, December 11, 1776 – September 23, 1778, with Collateral Documents; to which is added Minutes of the Council of Appointment, State of New York, April 2, 1778 – May 3, 1779*, 2 vols., *Collections of the New York Historical Society for the Years 1924-1925*, (New York: 1925), I: 57, 70, 178.

[54] Rhode Island Interior Committee, 6 December 1776, Records of the States of the United States, Rhode Island, 1775-1818, Film 285, E4, Reel 1, Minutes of the Interior Committee, DLAR.

"Negros whose Masters are out." Not only did the exceptionality of this category reflect the assumption that only "Negros" could be categorized in this manner, but the category also conflated the African Americans' race with slavery by implying that "Negros" as such—as opposed to black slaves—might have "Masters." By means of the same conflation, it likewise implied that the "negros" listed in the previous categories were necessarily and uniformly slaves. At the same time, these other categories divided them by age and, among adults, gender. This indicates that the men at least might have been considered possible sources of labor and, possibly, military service, along with the whites, though whether as individual persons in themselves or as slaves and property of their "Masters" is less easily read out of the census. The tally of passes issued by the Town Major and the calculation of the residual population were not divided by race (or by age or gender), suggesting that African Americans might in theory have been granted passes, under certain circumstances, though this census does not make clear whether any in fact received such passes.[55]

Whenever mentioned in correspondence or written records, African Americans who came to the attention of the (generally) white male authors were almost universally described by their "race"—as "blacks," "Negroes," or "Africans"—often without further individuation. Unless explicitly preceded by the designation "free," these terms were implicitly synonymous with "slave" and certainly synonymous with "subordinate" or "of low social standing." At the same time, much as women were regularly identified in terms of the men to whom they were attached as dependents, enslaved African Americans were almost always identified by their owners. Thus General Nathanael Greene identified an escaped slave who brought intelligence regarding British forces in July of 1776 as " A Negro belonging to one Strikeer at Gravesend."[56] General Hugh Mercer, later that month, referred to "two Negros" who brought him intelligence from Staten Island, one of whom was

---

[55] James Urquhard, Census of Boston, 9 October 1775, Thomas Gage Papers, Volume 136, WLCL.

[56] Greene to Washington, 21 July 1776, *PGWDE*, Revolutionary, V: 414

further identified in the record of his examination as "a Negro Slave belonging to Peter Peleyon of Richmond County on Staten Island."[57]

Seen primarily as labor resources, African Americans were identified primarily in terms of their bodies, beginning with their "race" and continuing with other characteristics. Age, physical capacity, and other traits of course also described the contributions that white soldiers and laborers could make to the military and political struggle. But such characteristics quite literally put prices on African Americans, as the property of others. Much as upper and lower age thresholds marked off the ranks of functional citizenship for military service, office-holding, and the like, the valuation of slaves marked off, though generally at younger lower boundaries and older upper boundaries than in the case of active citizenship, those who were judged too young or too old to provide appreciable labor value in excess of their maintenance costs.[58] Thus, Jonathan Trumbull, in his critique of the apportionment provisions of Article IX of the Articles of Confederation, argued that, "Negroes when young or Old are like Drones in a Hive," and proposed counting them for apportionment purposes only "from a certain Age, when they become usefull, to that Age, when they are unserviceable."[59] In March of 1779, a committee of the Continental Congress recommended that South Carolina raise battalions of "able bodied Negroes," whose masters were to receive a bounty and "A Certificate of the said inlistment Containing the age, and description of the Negro, and the price agreed on between the owner and the said Colonel, or other commanding officer."[60] The report specified that Congress should provide compensation for the enlistment of "each active able

---

[57] Mercer to Washington, 31 July 1776, *PGWDE*, Revolutionary, V: 528.

[58] Out of a very large historiography, see Eugene D. Genovese, *The Political Economy of Slavery: Studies in the Economy and Society of the Slave South*, 2nd ed., (Wesleyan University Press, 1989); Johnson, *Soul by Soul*.

[59] Trumbull to Henry Laurens, 1 December 1777, *PGWDE*, Revolutionary, XII: 502-503n3.

[60] 25 March 1779, *LDC*, XII: 242-244.

bodied Negro Man…of Standard Size and not exceeding…thirty five years of age."[61] When, in 1780,

Virginia needed to meet its quota of reinforcements for the Continental Army, the state offered as

an enlistment bounty "*a healthy sound negro*, between the ages of ten and thirty years, or *sixty pounds in

gold or silver*, at the option of the soldier, in lieu thereof."[62] With the coming of the peace, and the

British evacuation of New York, American authorities anxious that the British might abscond with

many valuable African Americans who had sought refuge behind their lines, but whom American

slaveholders considered their fugitive property, would push the British commanders to compile a

descriptive register of "of all Negroes who were sent off, specifying the Name, Age & Occupation

of the person, & the Name & place of the residen of his former Master," so that "Compensation"

could "be made by the Crown of G. Britain to the owners."[63]

Navigating the Revolutionary crisis of identification was a distinctive challenge for those

who, like free white women separated from their husbands or fathers, needed to act on their own

and negotiate with Revolutionary authorities, but who, by definition, were not supposed to have a

separate, formal civic identity. Those who became refugees may have faced this challenge most

directly. Margaret Roberts and Mary Knap, for instance, early on found themselves on the wrong

side of the lines when the ship on which they had been passengers was captured and taken to

Gloucester in the autumn of 1775. Perez Morton, secretary of the Massachusetts Provincial

Congress, reported to General Washington that "They say they have Husbands belonging to the 59th

Regt of Genl Gage's Army—And are desirous of seeing them." He had been directed, accordingly,

---

[61] 25 March 1779, *LDC*, XII: 246-248

[62] Act of October 1780, Chapter 3, in William Thomas Roberts Saffell ed., *Records of the Revolutionary War*, 3rd ed., (Baltimore, MD: C.C. Saffell, 1894), 496.

[63] Maryland Delegates to William Paca, 13 May 1783, *LDC*, XX: 249-250. For registers themselves, see New York: Inspection Roll of Negroes, 1783, *MPCC*, NARA, M332.

"to recommend to your Exy to permit them and 2 Children, to pass your Lines, in order to their proceeding into Boston."[64] Roberts' and Knap's self-identification had been accepted, likely because they were thought to pose little threat to the American cause and, perhaps, because their separation from their husbands had been beyond their control. They were identified only by their sex, their names, and their self-reported circumstances—the document carried no additional information to ensure that it was borne and used by the proper persons. Morton's letter indicated that Roberts and Knap would be "accompanying" the letter—it is not clear whether they were to bear the letter themselves, as a sort of letter of recommendation, or whether it was simply to be conveyed by others for them. The children—whether theirs or not—were not identified individually, even by sex, so little threat did they seem to pose.

Similar applications were made on behalf of children seeking to rejoin their parents. Early in July of 1775, for instance, Washington received an application from Daniel Murray on behalf of his two younger teenage brothers and a younger sister whom their father Col. John Murray—a mandamus councilor who had fled to Boston in the summer of 1774—wished to join him in the city. Unfamiliar with the circumstances of the case, Washington referred it to the Massachusetts Committee of Safety, who referred it in turn to the Provincial Congress, who ultimately rejected the application on the grounds of a standing policy prohibiting any entry into Boston. By the time Boston was evacuated the following spring, however, the three children had rejoined their father in the city and left with him for Halifax.[65] In November of 1780, the role of age in distinguishing those who were potential threats from those who were not was made explicit when the relative of a Loyalist couple, now in New York, petitioned for the couple's three children, the oldest of whom "does not exceed nine years of age," to cross the American lines and join their parents. "Their

---

[64] Morton to Washington, 4 Oct 1775, *PGWDE*, Revolutionary Series, II: 93-94.

[65] Daniel Murray to Washington, 6 July 1775, and notes, *PGWDE*, I: 69-70.

Innocence and youth," the petitioner wrote, "will cover them from public resentment and their incapacity to injure the State influence your Excellency to grant them permission."[66]

In so far as any of these efforts focused on the reconstitution of families and households, the concomitant identifications explicitly identified women and children by their dependence on a male head of household. Thus in December of 1775, the Interior Committee of Rhode Island voted to allow "Mrs. Sarah Robinson (Wife of Mr. Thomas Robinson)" and two male escorts "to go on board the Ship Ross and with the Wife of Joseph Greene and solicit the Liberty of the Two Sons of the said Mrs. Greene."[67] Through the course of the year 1777, during the British occupation of Newport, the Rhode Island Council of War spent a great deal of time issuing rulings and passes to regulate the movement of persons, largely wives and children of specified men, back and forth from the island to the mainland, as refugees attempted to find safer ground and rejoin families.[68] Similarly, after the fall of 1776, the New Jersey Council of safety regulated the passage of women and children across the lines in and out of British-held New York City. These migrants were defined largely as wives or children of specified men on the other side of the lines. Thus in January of 1778, the Council resolved that, "the following Persons have Permission to go to their Husbands in the Enemy's Lines (viz) Lydia Gormon Wife of John Gormon with her four Children and Sarah Copinger Wife of William Copinger & her three Children."[69] Six days later they granted "Deborah Ogden Wife of John Ogden" permission "to go to her husband, together with her Child & wearing

---

[66] John Henry to Thomas Sim Lee, 13 November 1780, *LDC*, XVI: 328.

[67] Rhode Island Interior Committee, 18 December 1775, Records of the States of the United States, Rhode Island, 1775-1818, Film 285, E4, Reel 1, Minutes of the Interior Committee, DLAR.

[68] See Records of the States of the United States, Rhode Island, 1775-1818, Film 285, E4, Reel 1, Minutes of the Council of War, DLAR: 20, 22 January; 17, 20, 22 March; 2, 4, 11 April; 15 May; 3, 11, 12, 13 June; 17 July; 1, 9, 12, 29 August; 1, 4, 5, 8, 29 September; 1 October; 14, 18, 27, 29 November; 8 December. For an example of the passes issued, see Rhode Island Council of War, Pass for Richard Backhouse et al., 29 November 1777, Records of the States of the United States, Rhode Island, 1775-1818, Film 285, E4, Reel 1, Minutes of the Council of War, DLAR.

[69] New Jersey Council of Safety, 14 January 1778, Records of the States of the United States, New Jersey, 1681-1786, Film 281, Reel 1, Minutes of the Council of Safety, DLAR.

Apparel."[70] Some women, however, were granted permission to cross over to the enemy in their own right. Thus, near the end of that January, the Council gave "Jane Foster" permission "to remove into the Enemy's lines."[71] Other women or children sought to visit or bring aid to husbands, parents, or other family members held prisoner.[72]

There was a basic disjunction between the perception of women as dependents and the assumptions behind the regimes that were adapted to identify them during the war but which were designed for the identification of autonomous (male) actors. This disjunction was brought to the fore when the customs of prisoner exchange—more particularly of officers—were adapted for women wishing to cross the lines, or whom their husbands or fathers wished to cross the lines. In these cases, the fact that households were being reconstituted—with women rejoining their male heads of household—served to bridge the two halves of the disjunction. Thus in November of 1776, the Continental Board of War wrote Washington concerning General Howe's request that a Mrs. Watts and a Mrs. Barrow, the latter the wife of the Paymaster, be permitted to cross the lines from the rebel side, into New York City, "to go to their Husbands." A Mr. Lewis, a member of Congress, had sought Congressional aid "to obtain the Release of his Lady whom the Enemy would not permit to come out." The Board suggested to Washington "the Propriety of obtaining Mrs Lewis & Mrs Robinson her Daughter with her Children in exchange for Mrs Watts & Mrs Barrow."

---

[70] New Jersey Council of Safety, 20 January 1778, Records of the States of the United States, New Jersey, 1681-1786, Film 281, Reel 1, Minutes of the Council of Safety, DLAR.

[71] New Jersey Council of Safety, 29 January 1778, Records of the States of the United States, New Jersey, 1681-1786, Film 281, Reel 1, Minutes of the Council of Safety, DLAR.

[72] See Washington to James Potter, 10 November 1777, *PGWDE*, Revolutionary, XII: 203, 203n2; Washington to Governor Wharton, 5 April 1778, requesting a passport, on behalf of Mrs. Mary Pemberton, for wagons to carry supplies out of Philadelphia to her husband and others confined as prisoners of the state, Insert in *Exiles in Virginia...* (Philadelphia, 1848), M-4153, after page 63, WLCL; Washington to Wharton, 6 April 1778, regarding four Quaker women wishing to travel to the Congress at York, PA, to petition for the release of the Friends held prisoner in Winchester, VA, Insert in *Exiles in Virginia...* (Philadelphia, 1848), M-4153, after page 63, WLCL. See also Mrs. Wilson to Major André, 12 March 1780, requesting permission to visit "Mr. Wilson" on board a prison ship, Sir Henry Clinton Papers, Volume 88, Folder 35, WLCL.

They asked that, "if you have not already permitted those Ladies to go into York or given Genl Howe a promise to that effect, that you will make the Release of our Ladies, if we may be allowed the expression, a necessary requisite." If Watts and Barrow were already gone to the British, Washington was requested to ask for Lewis and Robinson in return. "We do not imagine that you will be refused," the Board wrote, "but should you, we must recur to the unhappy Expedient of with-holding in future every simular Indulgence to those Ladies in our Power, who may desire to visit their Connections in the Army." They professed themselves "very sorry that our Enemies have compelled us to resolve upon any Thing which looks like severity, or indeed to lay any Restraint upon the fair Sex." (Washington was also to insist that Lewis and Robinson be allowed the same privileges in regards to baggage as Watts and Barrow.) In a closing thought, the Board suggested that "Perhaps if the Ladies cannot be exchanged upon the above Terms Mrs Lewis may be exchanged for Mrs Kempe."[73]

The Board's proposals engaged the customs of an exchange of officers, the genteel male equivalents of these "Ladies" in the standard practice of war. Among the genteel, persons were to be identified and exchanged as individuals, with particular exchange values depending on their rank, in the case of officers, or their social standing. Only rank-and-file were exchanged as batches of enumerated but wholly anonymous units. The insistence on equal privileges and treatment on both sides accorded with customs of prisoner exchange and treatment more generally, while the suggestion of alternate equivalencies for exchange (i.e. Lewis for Kempe) mirrored similar negotiations in the exchange of officers.[74] The entire episode was framed, in a larger sense, by the social structures of rank or class, in that these women were identified in terms of, and their mobility

---

[73] Board of War to Washington, 8 November 1776, *PGWDE*, Revolutionary, VII: 114-115.

[74] See Washington to Howe, 1 December 1776, *PGWDE*, Revolutionary, VII: 247-248, in which Washington acknowledges, announces, and proposes exchanges of particular officers "whose names are specified in the inclosed List," as well as the passage back and forth of those for whom equivalents had not yet been received, including " Capt. Hesketh of the 7th Regt his Lady, 3 Children and two Servant Maids" who "were permitted to go in a few days ago."

enabled by, their connections to influential men. Those who lacked social standing and connections were likely to be identified and regulated at the sentry line and the local camp, rather than dealt with through Congressional negotiations with the British commander in chief.

At the same time, the Board's discomfort applying these forms to women (perhaps especially genteel women) was evident. They asked to be "allowed the expression" the "Release of our Ladies," and they insisted they neither wished to be "severe" nor liked to "lay any Restraint upon the fair Sex." They further cast the entire episode in terms of the desire of men on both sides that these women—possessively "our Ladies" on the American side, "Mrs" in all cases—should cross the lines to "go to their Husbands." (In this period, "Mrs." by itself could be simply an honorific, indicating an adult woman of a certain age or possessed of property and did not necessarily indicate present or past marital status.) Casting the episode in terms of what the women wanted, in what was a realm of military operations and regulations, would have portrayed them as autonomous agents capable of self-determination and, perhaps, political decisions. Washington was ultimately able to stop Mrs. Barrow and Mrs. Kempe (Mrs. Watts had already been promised "that she should go") and recommended that they "write to their Husbands & connections to obtain Genl How's assurances" that Lewis and Robinson, with children and baggage, would be released and allowed to cross to the American side of the lines.[75] Here again it was these women's ability to mobilize their connections to influential men that was to enable their mobility and which defined their identities.

The practice of "exchanging" women and other dependents continued through the war. Thus, in December of 1777, American general James Clinton issued to Morris Hazard a hybrid instrument certifying his status as the bearer of a flag of truce for the purpose of making specified exchanges. Morris was to request of the British commander in chief "leave to bring his Children & Effects off Long Island where they are now detained, in exchange, for Mrs. Cathrine Cranner her

---

[75] Washington to the Board of War, 15 November 1776, *PGWDE*, Revolutionary, VII: 160-161.

Daughter Mary Cranner and a Negro girl Easter, together with their Effects, which are all permited to go to New York with this Flag." The same document authorized Zebulon Schofield, his wife and daughter, and Elizabeth Schenk to pass to New York (Clinton perhaps expecting future British reciprocity), "And those Persons Named in the Margin...to Navigate the Vessel, and return again with all convenient Speed unmolested."[76]

In other instances, passage of women (generally of high rank) through the lines to rejoin husbands was granted as a favor. These instances could make clear the degree to which women were treated as persons set apart from the political and military conflict. In December of 1777, for instance, when Joseph Galloway wrote to Washington to request permission for his wife and "her Household Furniture and Effects" to join him in Philadelphia from her current residence at their country estate, Galloway declared that, "Coud I imagine that a Contest of such Magnitude and Importance as the present between Great Britain and America is to be decided by, or in any Degree depended on a Matter of so trivial comparative Consequence as that of obliging me in the Gratification of my Desire I shoud immediately perceive the Impropriety, and not give you the Trouble of this Request."[77] Washington informed Galloway that it was not in his power to grant permission for his property to pass the lines, "Commissioners being appointed by the legislative Authority of this State to take cognizance of and to dispose of the personal property of those who have willingly gone over to the Enemy." But he professed he had "not the least objections to Mrs Galloways going to Philada" and would "be ready to furnish passports for that purpose whenever they are applied for."[78] Washington made the same answer, the same day, to John Potts, who

---

[76] Clinton, To all concerned, 5 December 1777, Sir Henry Clinton Papers, Volume 28, Folder 3, WLCL.

[77] Galloway to Washington, 18 December 1777, *PGWDE*, Revolutionary, XII: 630.

[78] Washington to Galloway, 20 December 1777, *PGWDE*, Revolutionary, XII: 649.

requested permission for his wife, children, and household furniture to pass into Philadelphia.[79] Property was subject to the conflict, and it might in any case prove useful to the enemy. But the enemy's wives did not come within the question.

Especially as the war wore on, some male authorities were less ready to dismiss women as unthreatening or apolitical, and more apt to apply stricter regulations to women's identities and mobility. Such regulations were often equivalent to those placed on men but were sometimes still self-consciously differentiated by sex. Thus, in April of 1777, Elisabeth Brewer was captured, along with several men, coming in and out of New Brunswick, New Jersey, by forces under Israel Putnam. The men were either held as prisoners or dismissed on parole. Brewer, after giving some information concerning other unauthorized travellers, expressed "an Inclination of entering the Hospital as a Nurse, in which employment she has been before employ'd at this place [Princeton]." Putnam explained to Governor William Livingston that, as "the Surgeon" gave her "a good Character," Putnam had "thot proper to detain her here for that purpose."[80] Brewer was, perhaps, shown more leniency as a woman, as well as on account of her good reputation and her useful skills. And she was assigned a position culturally gendered female—one to which the men were not and would not have been assigned—as the means of keeping her out of further trouble. Later that year, in the autumn of 1777, the General Assembly of New Jersey, in a distinct section of an act for regulating mobility, forbade "any Woman being a Subject of, or owing Allegiance to this Government" from attempting to go to or come from the enemy without proper "License, Permission or passport," on pain of fine or imprisonment for the first offense and death for the second.[81]

---

[79] Washington to Potts, 20 December 1777, *PGWDE*, Revolutionary, XII: 655

[80] Putnam to Livingston, 25 April 1777, Sol Feinstone Collection, Film 1, Reel 3, No. 1175, DLAR.

[81] *Acts of the General Assembly of the state of New-Jersey. At a session begun at Princeton on the 27th day of August 1776, and continued by adjournments till the 11th of October 1777*, (Burlington, NJ: Isaac Collins, 1777), *EAI*, Series 1, no. 15461 (filmed), 87.

During the lengthy occupation of Newport by the British, the Rhode Island Council of War would attempt to regulate the flow of persons—largely women and children—back and forth from the island to the mainland. In January of 1777, they ordered the apprehension of two men who had "come from Newport to North-Kingtown with a Number of Women and Children," apparently without prior authorization.[82] When it was discovered that these two men had brought over the group of women and children at the behest of an Overseer of the Poor in Newport, the Council issued an announcement clarifying that no "general Permit" had been given "for the Inhabitants of the Island of the aforesaid to Remove therefrom but only particular Individuals." As such, "for the future, not any Women or Children shall be suffered to be put ashore or Land in any part of this State whatever, without previous to their being sent...a List of the Names and Additions of the Women, & the Number and Age of the Children...be transmitted to this Council, who will thereupon inspect the Same" and determine and order whether the listed persons were to be allowed to land, and at what specified points.[83] At the same time, socially detached women could be seen as threats—potential spies for instance, or likely public charges. Thus in September of 1777, the Council of War ordered the Sheriff of Providence County to "take Mrs. Graves a transient Woman & remove her to the House of Mr Daniel Mowrey in the Town of Smithfield and if he refuses to keep her to place her to some other suitable place in the County their to remain until further orders."[84] In April of 1778, the Council ordered the arrest of Alice Davis and a search of the house

---

[82] Rhode Island Council of War, 20 January 1777, Records of the States of the United States, Rhode Island, 1775-1818, Film 285, E4, Reel 1, Minutes of the Council of War, DLAR.

[83] Rhode Island Council of War, 22 January 1777, Records of the States of the United States, Rhode Island, 1775-1818, Film 285, E4, Reel 1, Minutes of the Council of War, DLAR.

[84] Rhode Island Council of War, 26 September 1777, Records of the States of the United States, Rhode Island, 1775-1818, Film 285, E4, Reel 1, Minutes of the Council of War, DLAR.

where she lived, on suspicion that she was facilitating illicit correspondence with paroled enemy

prisoners of war, who were seen carrying letters to and from her house.[85]

Framed by broad ascriptions of dependence, marginal populations were generally excluded

from or subordinated in the core regimes of Revolutionary identification. Yet the burden of proof

lay on all individuals who might be perceived as of lower or subordinate rank to demonstrate that

they were either dependents travelling or acting with the written consent of their master, father, or

husband or were not in fact dependents at all. To prove the latter they might proffer cancelled

indentures, a certificate of discharge from a ship, manumission papers or certificate of free birth,

among other possible instruments.[86]

To the extent that women, children, and African Americans were excluded (or exempted)

from military service, they had no access to the concomitant instruments of identification. Letters

of introduction and recommendation, and the facets of identity they embodied, were likewise largely

class, gender, and race exclusive. Refugees or dependent migrants who were passed from one adult

white male authority to another were sometimes given or mentioned in instruments equivalent to

letters of introduction or recommendation, even if they were not the primary bearers, as in the case

of Knap and Roberts. Further exceptions appeared on occasions when members of political and

socially marginal groups were recruited as labor or support for the cause outside the discipline of

military structures. Thus on August 9th of 1775, an advertisement appeared in Philadelphia

addressed "To the Spinners in this City, the Suburbs, and County," declaring that "Your services are

now wanted to promote the American Manufactory, at the corner of Market and Ninth-streets,

---

[85] Rhode Island Council of War, 3 April 1778, Records of the States of the United States, Rhode Island, 1775-1818, Film 285, E4, Reel 1, Minutes of the Council of War, DLAR.

[86] Or, perhaps, a feme sole license as a woman authorized by legislative act to act independently in law or commerce. On feme sole bills see Kerber, *Women of the Republic*, 148-151.

where cotton, wool, flax, &c., are delivered out." "Strangers" who applied, however, were "desired to bring a few lines, by way of recommendation, from some respectable person in their neighbourhood"—perhaps to verify their skill in spinning, most likely to reassure that they were not opportunists who would make off with the raw materials. The stipulation reflected a recognition not only of the mobility of the laboring classes, including women, but also of the increased mobility spurred by the Revolution, especially in the case of refugees.[87]

The language, structure, and administration of many instruments of identification assumed that male heads of household or masters would oversee and represent the dependents who in fact carried the documents themselves. When Margaret Jepson received permission to leave Boston with her family, in May of 1775, the pass was made out to her in manuscript (see above), yet the printed section of the document specified travel with "his Family."[88] The juxtaposition of her name and the male possessive pronoun made clear the expectation that the bearers of these passes would be men. In particular, they were likely to be male householders with dependents and property. The pass identified persons not as individuals but within social units. Only a certain subset of the population—householders or heads of families—were to be identified and authorized in this manner. On the rebel side of the lines, when a committee of Charlestown, at the end of May, issued a pass confiding a refugee woman and her family to the care of the selectmen of Watertown, they wrote that, "we... Send to you Mrs Susannah Holman & her family Consisting of three persons."[89] Though Holman is presented, implicitly, as the head of household, the "three persons" of "her

---

[87] On mobility among the laboring classes and poor, see Waldstreicher, "Reading the Runaways"; Ruth Wallis Herndon, *Unwelcome Americans: Living on the Margin in Early New England*, (Philadelphia: University of Pennsylvania Press, 2001); Douglas Lamar Jones, *Village and Seaport: Migration and Society in Eighteenth-Century Massachusetts*, (Hanover, NH: University Press of New England, 1981).

[88] Permit to pass through British lines for Margaret Jepson and family, May 1775, Misc. Bd. 1775 May, MHS. The lack of a precise date and the absence of a signature from the issuing officer (though the pass is officially issued on the authority of Governor Gage) may indicate that this was a draft, but this is not certain.

[89] Committee of Charlestown to the Selectmen of Watertown, MA, 31 May 1775, U.S. Revolution Collection, Box 2, Folder 1, AAS.

family" are identified only by their dependence on Holman—the instrument does not even clarify whether these "persons" were Holman's children, other relatives, servants, or slaves. "Mrs" Holman herself may have been implicitly a dependent of an unspecified, absent husband. In much the same way, a committee of the Provincial Congress, two weeks later, confided to the care of the selectmen of Worcester " Mr[s] Tho' Bell with Twelve...family."[90]

Other passes issued throughout the war to civilian refugees would commonly adopt this same collective, household-structured approach to identification and authorization, though sometimes giving greater individual definition to the subordinated members of the household, as in Jepson's pass. Thus when, in early 1778, the Reverend Daniel Batwell chose exile in Europe rather than swear allegiance to Pennsylvania, the pass issued him for his journey to the lines at Philadelphia (where he was to seek another pass, from Washington, authorizing his crossing of the lines) gave permission for him to pass into Philadelphia "with his Family and such Baggage &c. as may be of absolute use to him and of no Service to the Enemy." At the end of the pass, it was specified that, "Mr Battwell's family consists of Mrs Bethea Batwell his Wife three of his Children George Elizabeth & Anne & Mrs Elizabeth Sherwin, the mother of Mrs Batwell also Elizabeth Hubbard. Servant maid of Mr Batwell's." The pass given to the wagoners who would carry the Batwell household to Philadelphia authorized them to transport simply "The Revd Mr D. Battwell & his Family, with his Effects."[91] Similarly, in November of 1779, the Supreme Executive Council of the Commonwealth of Pennsylvania issued a formal letter of recommendation, addressed "To all concerned," to Mrs. Mary Cassan, who wished to "go into the City of New York not to return again, recommending "the said Mary Cassan to the Officer commanding the troops next to the enemy that

---

[90] Committee of the Provincial Congress at Charlestown to the Selectmen or Committee of Correspondence of Worcester, MA, 16 June 1775, U.S. Revolution Collection, Box 2, Folder 1, AAS. Though the text of the document may alternatively read "Mr Tho' Bell," the receipt on the reverse for "My goods Safe to Worster" was signed by Hannah Bell, presumably the de facto head of the large household conveyed to Worcester and likely "Mrs. Thomas Bell."

[91] See *PGWDE*, Revolutionary, XIII: 613-15n1.

she be permitted to pass into the said City of New York at his discretion, with four small Children, and the necessary bedding and apparel."[92] The following February, in Charleston, South Carolina, General Benjamin Lincoln issued a pass declaring that "Mrs. Massey and her family are permitted to pass to Mr. Chisholm's plantation on John's Island under ye. sanction of a Flag."[93] In July of that year, Mathew Paterson, Justice of the Peace of Dutchess County, New York, allowed Lieutenant David Smith and three drivers to transport by wagon "to the Enemys out Post... the Familys of Abigal Smith 3 Children Eunis Brown 2 Children Deborah mc.Neil 4 Children Fabby Jackson 3 Children and marey Brundredg 3 Children whos Husbands are all now with the Enemy."[94]

As in several of the above cases, some instruments only identified the women bearing them as dependents in the most minimal way. Thus a pass or letter issued in June of 1780 by Governor William Livingston of New Jersey, addressed to the officer commanding U.S. troops as Elizabethtown, declared that "Mrs. Hona: French the Bearer has my Permission to go to New York upon her Engagement not to return into this state during the War."[95] With the exception of the prefix "Mrs.," which may or may not have indicated her marital status, French appears in this pass as the bearer and a traveller in her own right, proceeding alone towards an exile she has chosen for herself (if only from limited options). Likewise in July of 1782, Andrew Elliot, commandant of New

---

[92] Supreme Executive Council of Pennsylvania, Recommendation of Mary Cassan, 23 November 1779, Sol Feinstone Collection, Film 1, Reel 6, No. 2408, DLAR.

[93] Lincoln, Pass for Mrs. Massey, 25 February 1780, Sir Henry Clinton Papers, Volume 86, Folder 46, WLCL.

[94] Paterson, Pass for David Smith et al., 5 July 1780, Sir Henry Clinton Papers, Volume 96, Folder 59, WLCL. The women were to be allowed "to Take their bedding wearing apparel and a Sufficincy of Provision for their Support tile they arrive at Said out Post where they are to Resied." A further pass, 6 July 1780, by Colonel Elisha Sheldon, commanding on the lines, authorized Smith and the specified families and effects "to pass & repass the Guards as a Flagg."

[95] Livingston, Pass for Hon[oria] French, 5 June 1780, Sol Feinstone Collection, Film 1, Reel 3, No. 1423, DLAR.

York City, issued a pass to "Mrs Deborah Cornhoven to pass to Staten Island on her way out of the lines to New Jersey."[96]

When included in household passes, servants appeared as, often unnamed, dependents, much like children. In other instances they travelled independently—or at least in the absence of their master. But their passes often took the form of permissions from their masters and usually identified the bearer in those unequal terms (i.e. to whom the bearer was bound and subject). On both sides of the conflict, gentlemen prisoners were not uncommonly permitted to send for and travel with personal servants or slaves.[97] Such indulgence of parolees or prisoners entailed the issuance of instruments of identification and mobility, or addenda and modifications to instruments issued to the parolee or prisoner, to permit the servants or slaves to enter, travel in, or reside within the parolee's prescribed bounds. These servants at the same time represented labor power available to the enemy and potential additions to their rank-and-file, were the parolee allowed to return or venture to the enemy's lines. In some cases, these concerns were met by requiring the parolee to assume responsibility for the good behavior of his servant or slave—effectively offering a parole by proxy. In other instances, the captors sought ways to balance the potential loss of labor power or rank-and-file, and the potential accession of such to the enemy, by demanding equivalents—treating the servants or slaves as essentially fungible units of resource. This may also have served to balance out intelligence conveyed to the enemy by the servants sent in. Thus, in June of 1779, a Mr. Collins,

---

[96] Elliot, Pass for Deborah Cornhoven, 22 July 1782, Copy, New Jersey. Revolutionary War. Numbered Manuscripts, 1770's-1890's, Film 678, Reel 5 (Mss. Nos. 1581-2210), No. 1582, DLAR.

[97] See the complaint of the British prisoners held at Yorktown, PA, to the President of Congress that the local committee had, "taken from us our Servants," whom they had previously been allowed to keep, a deprivation that featured prominently among the outrages, insults, and "Violation of every law of Humanity" they had suffered at the hands of the committee. Edward Thompson et al. to John Hancock, Yorktown, PA, 12 July 1776, Papers of Elias Boudinot, 1773-1812, Library of Congress, Film 732, Reel 1, DLAR. For servants joining or rejoining imprisoned officers, see Committee of Reading to the Committee of Lancaster, 2 September 1776, *AAO*, Series 5, II: 120; Committee of York, PA, 4 September 1776, *AAO*, Series 5, II: 181; A. Gordon to the Committee of Lancaster, 5 September 1776, *AAO*, Series 5, II: 181; Committee of Lancaster, 11 September 1776, *AAO*, Series 5, II: 287; Committee of Lancaster, 26 September 1776, *AAO*, Series 5, II: 546; Committee of Lancaster, 12 October 1776, *AAO*, Series 5, II: 1008.

prisoner to the Americans in Boston, paroled and sent to British-held New York, was permitted to take with him "a negro[e] Servent to whome he was much attached," upon providing security "that a Black Should be sent out in his room or that [Mr. Collins] would Send his [servant] Back."[98]

As they navigated Revolutionary regimes of identification and, often, laid claim to identities of their own determination, marginalized and subordinated persons tested the structures of American society and the boundaries of the American Revolution. They cast into question what it meant to be an "American" and how "Americans" were to be identified. Other "Americans" tested the boundaries of the Revolution and Revolutionary identification in a very different sense, as they sought to secure their identities as "Americans" and U.S. citizens beyond the boundaries of the nascent republics. The following chapter explores how American identities and citizenship were negotiated and documented abroad in the course of the Revolution, as these categories and their practice were still in formation.

---

[98] Johonnat Gabriel to Joshua Loring, 8 December 1780, Sol Feinstone Collection, Film 1, Reel 2, No. 682, DLAR. Gabriel had provided the security that Mr. Collins, "an acquantence of mine of some years Stan[ding]," would comply with the stipulation that, "A Negro of his one of the four that ware in NYork Was Sent out or that the servt was returned," but neither had been done and Gabriel wrote to Loring in New York to request that Mr. Collins be compelled to comply, both to vindicate his personal honor and to preserve "that Publick faith Wich has bean Established by the [Commisary?/Comerisal?] oficers of both [armyes?] That no Onterruption may take place from Violation."

Chapter 8

Abroad

By October of 1779, Robert Montgomery was becoming distraught. After receiving no answer to four previous letters, he wrote once more to Benjamin Franklin, United States minister plenipotentiary at the court of France. "With the utmost distress," he wrote, "I find my Self Abandond by the Onley Gentleman in Europe from Whome I would Either Ask or Expect Protection as I Cannot Suppose that a Gentleman of Mr Franklins Knowledg in the world tho in the Most Exalted Station Could think it beneath him to Write a Merchant of the first Credit and Reputation."[1] More than two years before, Montgomery, a merchant from Philadelphia, had established his trading house in Alicante, Spain. After a year in his new home and having "Acquired Business and Consequence," he had written to Franklin in April of 1778. He offered his services to the Revolutionary cause, for which he professed great zeal, and requested that Franklin send him "a Certificate of what I am." He feared that should Spain and Britain go to war the Spanish governor would not accept his "Bear word" on this matter and would treat him as a British subject, banishing or imprisoning him, or seizing his goods.[2] Montgomery was one of many "Americans" abroad anxious to secure their identities as citizens of the new republic. But his appeal to Franklin made clear the two difficulties of such identification: lack of clarity about what U. S. citizenship actually was, and continuing reliance on the private documentation that tended to assist the better-off, whatever the revolutionary pretensions of the new nation.

---

[1] Montgomery to Franklin, [1-12] October 1779, *PBFDE.*

[2] Montgomery to Franklin, 5 April 1778, *PBFDE.*

In August of 1778 Montgomery had called on Franklin, John Adams, and Arthur Lee at Franklin's residence in Passy. He had sworn an oath of allegiance to the United States and had left with a certificate attesting to this fact and a passport signed by the three American ministers. But when Spain had indeed declared war on Britain the following summer, Montgomery's documents had proven unavailing. He had been arrested and his property seized, though, he wrote, "I know myself Guilty of No fault; but the Exect Semillarity between us and the English (Except in Sentiment)," and "Notwithstanding I have Every time that the foraigne Merchants Established here ware Called by the Governour to Declare of what Nation they ware, always declared and Subscribed Myself a Subject of the Thirteen United States of North America."[3]

Montgomery was released following his initial arrest, on the intervention of the Spanish minister of war. But he was subsequently sent to the interior of the country as a British subject after he insulted a Spanish official, who had then declared that, "I [Montgomery] have Never been in America, and that the passport and Certificate I Produced Signed by your Eccely. Mr Lee and Mr Adams, are no more than Counterfits and ware never Given by you."[4] Montgomery judged that a simple letter from Franklin authenticating his papers would confirm his identity, and he was beginning to feel wronged by the apparent lack of attention to his pleas. He had considered the documents "the Credentials that my Situation demands and Justice Entitles me to," and now he insisted to Franklin that "As well as any other Subject I find I am Entitled to all the Protection the Government I belong to Can Give Me," reminding him that, "in Europe [I] have None to Ask it

---

[3] Montgomery to Franklin, 26 June 1779, *PBFDE*. In a subsequent letter to Franklin (6 July 1779), Montgomery said he "had always Subscribed my Self a Subject of those States in the Anual List taken of foraign Merchants Established here." For merchants' enclaves in Spain, and local resentment of their failure to integrate or to acknowledge allegiance to Spain (which may have affected the treatment Montgomery encountered), see, Tamar Herzog, *Defining Nations: Immigrants and Citizens in Early Modern Spain and Spanish America*, (New Haven, CT: Yale UP, 2003), chapters 2 and 4 (esp. 82-91).

[4] Montgomery to Franklin, 12 August 1779, *PBFDE*.

from but your Excellency which I hope will Not Onley Pardon My Inportunitys but also afford me all the Releif in your Power."[5]

When he finally answered Montgomery, Franklin explained that, on first receiving the merchant's complaints, he had interceded with the Spanish ambassador in Paris, receiving assurances that, "there was no doubt but you would receive [relief] from the Court, as soon as it should be known that you were an American." And Franklin had subsequently received Montgomery's confirmation that he had been released. "But when," Franklin went on, "in a subsequent Letter you informed me that those Vexations were renewed, I began to apprehend there might be something in your Case or Conduct that I did not understand." He expressed himself "still at a Loss to conceive how the Certificate given you by me & Mr. Adams jointly can receive greater Force by my acknowledging it," and noted that, "with all the good Will Spain has manifested in many Instances for the Americans in general, I am surprized that you in particular should meet with so much Unkindness, unless you had given some Offence or some Cause for Suspicion." "For these Reasons," he explained, "I postponed answering some of your Letters, 'till I should be better acquainted with your Character, and with the Circumstances." He had now determined to intercede once more with the Spanish ambassador, and to "request that agreable to the Certificate you have received from the Commissioners here you may be considered and treated as an American, unless the Court has some good Reasons to consider you in another Light."[6]

How had Montgomery first proven to Franklin and his colleagues who he was? How had he demonstrated his claim to American citizenship and secured their certificate and passport? In his first letter to Franklin, in April of 1778, he suggested Franklin might remember him from some brief previous encounter. They both hailed from Pennsylvania and shared mutual acquaintances. "But

---

[5] Montgomery to Franklin, [1-12] October 1779, *PBFDE.*

[6] Franklin to Montgomery, 28 October 1779, *PBFDE.*

least you Should not Recollect or know me," he wrote, "I Must beg l[e]ave to Refer you to Mr.

Thomas Morris or to any of the Captains of Ships Belonging to Philadelphia of which I was one

many years and Inclose for your Inspection a Certificate from the Customhouse at Hampton in

Virgenia the Only Paper I have Left of the kind which may satisfy you as to that Perticular."[7] Had

they been at home in Pennsylvania, Montgomery might have appealed to testimonials from his

friends and business associates and to the general community's knowledge of his reputation. If he

had been baptized or married or had served time as a servant there he might have used church

records or cancelled indentures to confirm his nativity, his ties to the community, or his length of

residence. Montgomery insisted it would be useless to suggest he send to Pennsylvania for such

further proofs, as it would be "so long before I Could Get the Necessary Credentials from home I

Might Be Ruined in the Interim."[8] He had to make do with the proofs he had to hand and those he

could muster abroad. Not only his fortune but his honor was "Concerned in my being mintained in

our rights and Previliges at this Juncture." But, "as I have always Suported th highest Reputation

here as a Merchant and allso been honoured with an Intimacy with the Governour, Lieutenant

General Dn George Dunant with General Mace, and the first Spanish Familys in this City," he

declared, "I do not fear giving a very good account should either of the Minesters Require a General

Information of My Conduct Since my Establishment in this place."[9]

Backed by Franklin's second intercession, Montgomery ultimately proved his identity and

cleared his name with the Spanish authorities beyond all "*farther* Apprehension of being Molested in

future." He had, he wrote Franklin, "far Exceeded the Proofs Required on my Part by the Minister

[of War]," and the troublesome Governor of Alicante now appeared "Perfectly Satisfyed With the

---

[7] Montgomery to Franklin, 5 April 1778, *PBFDE*.

[8] Montgomery to Franklin, 5 April 1778, *PBFDE*.

[9] Montgomery to Franklin, 24 August 1779, *PBFDE*.

Justfycations I have Made." He had secured testimonials "by a Number of the first Merchents here

by all the Publick Brockers and by the Late English Vice Consul (who is a spaniard)," that,

> I have Always Declared myself and been Considerd an American Since My first Coming
> here, that being Apply'd to by the English Consul on business of his office Whilst here I
> Repeatedly Refused to know him for Any thing I Also Prove by the Governours Secretary
> and Others in that office that on My first Establishment I Enrol'd my Self on the List of
> Foraign Merchants An American and have Also Proved that My House Since my first
> Establishment has been Vulgarly Called the American House. And Not anything has ever
> been offerd in Contra to Any of thos Circumstances.

"As to My Credit as a Merchant and a Man of Probity," he wrote Franklin, "I beg l[e]ave to Refer

you" to the testimony of the several prominent merchant houses and bankers with which he dealt.

"In Philadelphia," he added, "there Are [few] Men in Trade that do not Know Me." His

acquaintance among Philadelphia merchants, in fact, included Joseph Wharton, who had been at

Passy when Montgomery had called the year before. Montgomery hoped these many aggregated

proofs would "Eradicate Every Suspition that Might have Arrose with you in My Particular."[10]

As it happened, Franklin and his colleagues were in a more awkward situation than

Montgomery seemed to appreciate. The American commissioners had been dispatched as

diplomats—to secure loans, war supplies, commercial treaties, eventually alliances, and, most

fundamentally, recognition of the sovereignty of the United States by the European powers.[11] But

they were soon beset by applications from the many Americans and would-be Americans abroad

who, like Montgomery, looked to them for aid, including, most fundamentally, means to secure their

identities as American citizens and the protections that might come with that status. In these

---

[10] Montgomery to Franklin, 20 November 1779, *PBFDE*. Montgomery would be troublesome again, near the end of the
war, when he undertook to arrange a treaty with Morocco, effectively arrogating to himself the character of a U. S.
diplomat. See Franklin to William Carmichael, 15 December 1783, *PBFDE*.

[11] See the collected instructions to the original commissioners. The Continental Congress, Instructions to Franklin, Silas
Deane, and Arthur Lee as Commissioners to France, [24 September-22 October 1776], *PBFDE*. See also Samuel Flagg
Bemis, *The Diplomacy of the American Revolution*, (New York: D. Appleton-Century, 1935), chs. 3-4; Jonathan Dull, *A
Diplomatic History of the American Revolution*, (New Haven, CT: Yale UP, 1985), chs. 6 and 9. On the importance of
recognition from European states to the establishment of the sovereignty of the United States, see David Armitage, *The
Declaration of Independence: A Global History*, (Cambridge, MA: Harvard UP, 2007), 85-87.

endeavors, supplicants faced the heightened suspicion of wartime, shifting and uncertain categories

of identity, and the lack of many or all of the resources on which they might have drawn to

substantiate their identities back home or in time of peace. These personal struggles, in turn,

intersected with the imperatives of governance, diplomacy, and war, drawing Franklin and other U.S.

representatives abroad into the larger Revolutionary crisis of identification. Neither dimension of

this crisis was much anticipated at the time or has thus far received much attention in the

historiography of the Revolution abroad.[12]

Montgomery was one of what the three commissioners in France described to the

Continental Congress in September of 1778, as a "multitude of Americans who are scattered about

---

[12] The historiography on the Revolution abroad (as distinguished from the contemporary or subsequent perception or influence of the Revolution) has been defined as almost exclusively, diplomatic, military, or biographical. For leading examples, see, Bemis, *Diplomacy of the American Revolution*; Richard Warner Van Alstyne, *Empire and Independence: The International History of the American Revolution*, (New York: Wiley, 1965); Dull, *Diplomatic History of the American Revolution*; Ronal Hoffman and Peter J. Albert eds., *Diplomacy and Revolution: The Franco-American Alliance of 1778*, (Charlottesville, VA: University Press of Virginia, 1981); Carl Van Doren, *Secret History of the American Revolution*, (New York: Viking, 1941), ch. 3. These (reasonable) preoccupations have obscured the important problems of governance, citizenship, state building, and identification faced by American agents and civilians overseas. The one significant exception is Catherine M. Prelinger, "Benjamin Franklin and the American Prisoners of War in England during the American Revolution," *The William and Mary Quarterly*, Third Series, Vol. 32, No. 2 (Apr., 1975), 261-294. Studies of identity during the Revolution may situate the formation of "American" identity within the British Empire and an Atlantic world, but rarely address the Americans abroad who were not diplomats and their deputies. Studies of Loyalists in exile are something of an exception. See Mary Beth Norton, *The British-Americans: The Loyalist Exiles in England, 1774-1789*, (Boston: Little, Brown, & Co., 1972); Wallace Brown, *The Good Americans: The Loyalists in the American Revolution*, (New York: Morrow, 1969); Claude Halstead Van Tyne, *The Loyalists in the American Revolution*, (Gloucester, MA: P. Smith, 1959); Lewis Einstein, *Divided Loyalties: Americans in England during the War of Independence*, (Boston: Houghton Mifflin Co., 1933); Maya Jasanoff, *Liberty's Exiles: American Loyalists in the Revolutionary World*, (New York: Alfred A. Knopf, 2011). See also studies dealing with African-American refugees and emigrants from Revolutionary America, especially Cassandra Pybus, *Epic Journeys of Freedom: Runaway Slaves of the American Revolution and their Global Quest for Liberty*, (Boston: Beacon Press, 2006); and Jasanoff, *Liberty's Exiles*. These historiographies, however, besides leaving out the Patriot side of the story abroad, tend to focus on the aftermath of the Revolution or on those who fled America. The experience and activities of Americans abroad needs to be understood as a sphere of action integral to the Revolution and rife with challenges of identification. Studies of individual experience abroad during the Revolution, when not focused on Loyalists, tend to focus on genteel individual or families, especially those on the grand tour, or on a particular subset of Americans abroad, such as medical students or artists, rather than on the larger phenomenon of American expatriates and Americans abroad. See Charles Warren, "A Young American's Adventures in England and France during the Revolutionary War," *Proceedings of the Massachusetts Historical Society*, Series 3, Vol. 65 (Oct., 1932 – May, 1936), 234-267; Whitfield J. Bell, Jr., "Philadelphia Medical Students in Europe, 1750-1800," *Pennsylvania Magazine of History and Biography*, Vol. 67, No. 1 (Jan., 1943), 1-29; Maurie D. McInnis, "Cultural Politics, Colonial Crisis, and Ancient Metaphor in John Singleton Copley's 'Mr. and Mrs. Ralph Izard'," *Winterthur Portfolio*, Vol. 34, No. 2/3 (Summer-Autumn, 1999), 85-108. See Einstein, *Divided Loyalties*, as a partial exception, considering multiple groups of Americans, of various loyalties, in Britain.

the various parts of Europe."[13] With the advent of the Revolution, many potential U.S. citizens were in Europe, on the high seas, and scattered around the world. In 1776, there were an estimated two to three thousand Americans in Britain alone—most there on business, for education, or travelling for recreation, along with a small number of Loyalist refugees (who had begun arriving in conspicuous numbers in 1774). Many more—Patriot, Loyalist, and undecided—ventured abroad during the Revolution, including to Britain.[14]

Much to the shock of prominent Loyalist refugees and zealous proponents of the counterrevolutionary war in America, most of the Patriots in Britain were allowed to remain, unmolested, though some were monitored or arrested as possible spies.[15] Whether under individual or collective pressure, for recreational or more serious purposes, many of these Patriots abroad eventually left Britain for the continent, some to return, some not. Many visited Franklin or other U.S. agents abroad, either simply to pay a call or to seek aid. Numerous others, who had been prisoners in Britain—civil or military—and escaped or were exchanged, sought out U.S. agents for

---

[13] Franklin, John Adams, and Arthur Lee to the President of Congress, 17 September 1778, Passy, Wharton, II: 722-725. See also the version of this same letter and the accompanying notes, Commissioners to the President of Congress, 17 Sept 1778, *PJADE*, VII: 42-46. In addition to those who sought oath of allegiance certificates and passports, as noted below, others sought payments as self-identified creditors of Congress; emergency funds as merchants in distress; relief and exchanges as prisoners of war; funds as escaped or exchange prisoners or as stranded seamen; and intervention with foreign governments. On such applications, see the above letter of 17 September 1778, as well as Franklin to John Jay, 20 August 1781, Wharton, IV: 643-647; and on the prisoners of war and seamen in particular, see Prelinger, "Benjamin Franklin and the American Prisoners of War." These were apart from the many applications from Europeans for aid in emigrating to America, letters of recommendation to Congress, passports for them or sea letters for their vessels, and commissions in the American military, among other favors. These applications are, in fact, more frequently addressed in the historiography than the applications of Americans or self-described Americans. For a concentrated treatment of one category of such applicants, see Prelinger, "Less Lucky than Lafayette: A Note on the French Applicants to Benjamin Franklin for Commissioners in the American Army, 1776-1785," *Proceedings of the Fourth Annual Meeting of the Western Society for French History*, 11-13 November 1976, Reno Nevada, (Santa Barbara, CA: Western Society for French History, 1977), 263-270.

[14] By the end of the war, there would be between five and six thousand Loyalist refugees alone in Britain. Brown, *The Good Americans*, 148. Many Americans sympathetic to the Revolution who were in Britain on the advent of war remained there, leading much the same lives they had before, though now their correspondence with home was less sure and their prospects for returning to America in the near future impossible to judge. Warren, "Adventures"; Bell, "Philadelphia Medical Students"; Prelinger, "Benjamin Franklin and the American Prisoners of War"; Brown, *Good Americans*, 148, 154-155; Van Doren, *Secret History*, ch. 3.

[15] The hanging of Major André in America later soured the welcome of rebel Patriots in Britain more generally. Warren, "Adventures," 243-244.

aid, passports, and advice.[16] Large numbers of others already on the continent included merchants, like Montgomery, resident in European ports. Others were apprentices to merchant houses, students abroad for medical education, and young artists seeking instruction or patrons. Young men and families took the Grand Tour. Still others had resettled in Europe—some in Britain, as the political commercial, and cultural center of the same empire, and some on the Continent, as expatriates. Some were war refugees or had been brought to Europe on captured ships and stranded or imprisoned.

This "multitude" comprised both friend and foe, not readily distinguishable one from the other. Some of the Loyalist refugees, indeed, travelled to or through France and the continent, adding to the U.S. agents' suspicions of "Americans" who came to call, and adding to the difficulties faced by "Americans" attempting to trade on their identities as such.[17] More generally, U.S. agents and American individuals in Europe had to contend with the realities of war, including espionage and infiltration. The British ministry sent agents to the continent and gathered information from a variety of less specialized sources. The U.S. agents abroad reciprocated. Desperate individuals, opportunists, and confidence tricksters attempted to take advantage of U.S. protection and resources. The monitory cases of treachery by Dr. Church and Benedict Arnold, among others, no doubt loomed large in the anxieties of those working abroad to further the Revolutionary cause. U.S. agents necessarily operated, and individuals lived and traveled, in a climate of suspicion, where deception and aliases were familiar tools and elements of their experience.[18]

---

[16] Prelinger, "Benjamin Franklin and the American Prisoners of War".

[17] See Norton, *Good Americans*, 92.

[18] In fact, most of the British spies were Americans: Wentworth, Bancroft, Vardill. See Van Doren, *Secret History*, ch. 3; Bemis, *Diplomacy of the American Revolution*; John A. Nagy, *Invisible Ink: Spycraft of the American Revolution*, (Yardley, PA: Westholme, 2010); Richard W. Van Alstyne, "Great Britain, the War for Independence, and the 'Gathering Storm' in Europe, 1775-1778," *Huntington Library Quarterly*, Vol. 27, No. 4 (Aug., 1964), 311-346; Dull, *Diplomatic History*; Brown, *Good Americans*, 154-155.

When faced with supplicants offering little if any corroborating evidence for the identities they claimed, U.S. agents abroad faced a dilemma: Deny aid to possible citizens in need? Or risk abuses of their confidence by granting aid or certification of citizenship without sufficient proof? Problematic cases began to present themselves very soon after the commissioners were situated in Paris.[19] In early February 1777, Franklin, Silas Deane, and Arthur Lee included in a letter to the Committee of Secret Correspondence an account of a man named Nicholas Davis. He had come to them "pretending to have served as an officer in India, to be originally from Boston, and desirous of returning to act in defense of his country." Davis had claimed, however, that some of his property had been seized by American privateers while en route to him from Jamaica, and he could no longer pay his passage home. On the strength of this report, they had advanced him thirty louis d'or, but later found that before he sailed from Havre he had drawn on them for "near 40 more." Because, they wrote, "in order to obtain that credit, he was guilty of several falsities, we now doubt his ever having been an officer at all." Sending along Davis's "note and draft" and informing the Committee that he had been entrusted with two "blanked" for Mr. Morris and that he had said his father was a clergyman in Jamaica, they asked the Committee to "take proper care of him."[20]

If, in the case of Davis, the commissioners were in fact overly trusting, and not simply deceived by false proofs, in subsequent cases they were more circumspect, whether as a consequence of lessons learned or because subsequent stories were less convincing. When a man claiming to be from the Carolinas and requesting a passport presented himself, they were less ready to credit his self-identification. Ralph Izard of South Carolina, the intended U.S. envoy to Tuscany, then in Paris, received the visitor in late March of 1778 and examined Franklin's wary letter of

---

[19] Dean had been there first, but in a more secret capacity, and even Franklin and Lee were not officially recognized yet.

[20] Franklin, Deane, and Lee to the Committee of Secret Correspondence, 6 February 1777, Wharton, II: 264-265. It is intriguing that the commissioners, having discovered the behavior of Davis, were suspicious of his having been an officer but not of his having been from Boston or an American at all.

introduction. Franklin informed Izard that, "The bearer says he is a native of Charleston, South Carolina" and had requested a "pass" to go to Italy. "I do not well understand the account he gives of himself," wrote Franklin, "He seems to be lost, and to want advice. I beg leave to refer him to you, who will soon be able to discover whether his account is true."[21] Izard in turn explained to Franklin that the man claimed to have been abroad so long that he had no acquaintance in his native South Carolina. The man said he was on his way from London to Livorno, where he was to take up a position as clerk to a merchant, and had come to Paris on his way, "to see the world" and, apparently, to request a "passport." As wary as Franklin, Izard wrote that, "As this account did not appear very satisfactory, I desired him to excuse my troubling you with any recommendation until he put it in my power to do it with propriety."[22] Neither Izard's account nor his own observations had reassured Franklin, who could form "no good opinion" of the traveler and decided to deny him the "pass."[23]

Franklin and Izard seem to have had very little to go on beyond the man's own account of himself, which was in the end unconvincing. The one means readily available to them by which to verify his identity was to consult someone from the society from which he professed to hail—in this case South Carolina, making Izard himself, by coincidence, an apposite choice. Such a person could be expected to know, directly or indirectly, the individual in question, or to judge the accuracy of the individual's knowledge of the society in question. In this case the man's ostensible long absence from South Carolina precluded this testimonial approach.

If their self-identifications would not satisfy, and they could not offer persuasive testimony by others on the scene, Americans abroad might present documents or artifacts that might indirectly

---

[21] Franklin to Izard, 27 March 1778, Wharton, II: 520.

[22] Izard to Franklin, 29 March 1778, Wharton, II: 522-523.

[23] Franklin to Izard, 30 March 1778, Wharton, II: 528.

serve to substantiate their identity claims. What types of documents did applicants offer?[24] U.S. authorities (both home and abroad) relied to a significant degree on the traditional modes of identification already examined in this study. Officers in the army or navy and some civil officials could proffer their commissions, for example.[25] Present or former private soldiers or sailors could sometimes, though much less consistently, show enlistment papers or certificates of discharge. Those coming from America during the war would in many cases have been issued certificates when they took oaths of allegiance and might carry these with them. Some would have passports from a state government or the Continental Congress. But not all had these documents to begin with, nor did the papers always survive the passage or remain in the intended hands. These documents would not have been, in any case, available to those already abroad, who now often sought them from Franklin and his fellow U.S. agents.

There were, thus, few standard or official instruments of identification that Americans might deploy abroad, even as the United States attempted to identify itself as a nation among nations. Many Americans abroad therefore bore private, social, or unofficial instruments. Members of certain religious societies—especially the Friends, or Quakers—sometimes carried certificates of recommendation or transfer from their congregation.[26] Members of the major professions might carry credentials or licenses, as well as testimonials from patients, clients, congregants, or fellow practitioners. Merchants, and others, could show the powers of attorney or letters of credit with

---

[24] Even in America there was no central register of residents or citizens. This was particularly troubling for those who had been caught unprepared by the Revolution and who sought equivalent documentation from the commissioners. See Pamela Sankar, "State Power and Record-keeping: The History of Individualized Surveillance in the United States, 1790-1935," PhD diss., (University of Pennsylvania, 1992), 20-24; Robert Gutman, "Birth and Death Registration in Massachusetts. I. The Colonial Background, 1639-1800," *The Milbank Memorial Fund Quarterly*, Vol. 36, No. 1 (Jan., 1958), 58-74. The commissioners also lacked access to the local knowledge available to their functional counterparts at home.

[25] Diplomatic agents, couriers, and some others could likewise present, in addition to their commissions, their instructions or letters of credence.

[26] These served as testimony to their character and piety, and as means to secure them welcome in other congregations of the same confession abroad. Bell, "Philadelphia Medical Students," 6-7.

which they had been entrusted. Students abroad for education sometimes brought certificates of previous degrees taken or apprenticeships completed.[27] Former apprentices and journeymen in commerce and trades often carried with them recommendations from their previous masters or employers when they went abroad.[28] When they could not offer any such relatively direct instruments of identification, individuals could often present indirectly substantiating documentation, like Montgomery's customs certificate or correspondence with known figures. Most pervasively, and often most importantly, travellers of the middling ranks and up commonly carried letters of introduction and recommendation, from the professional and official to the purely private. These could serve much the same purposes as more formal instruments and were such common accouterments of the respectable or genteel traveler (as opposed to the seaman, servant, slave, or laborer travelling at another's behest or with no social pretensions) that they were more or less expected and often crucial to the cases of applicants and travelers attempting to substantiate their identities in the eyes of U.S. officials abroad.

Despite justifiable fears of fraud and espionage—and the frustrating difficulty of distinguishing genuine U.S. citizens—the commissioners assured Congress in the autumn of 1778 that among the "multitude" of Americans in Europe "there are…some, we hope many, who are excellent citizens." In fact, they wrote, "Applications have been frequently made to us by Americans who have been some time abroad to administer the oath of allegiance to the United States, and to give them certificates that they have taken such oaths." They had "yielded to their importunity" in the cases of only three applicants—including Montgomery—and had warned even these that "such certificates are in strictness legally void, because there is no act of Congress that expressly gives us

---

[27] Bell, "Philadelphia Medical Students," 5

[28] Former indentured servants, likewise, could sometimes show their cancelled indentures.

power to administer oaths."[29] They expressed some anxiety about having to proceed on their own authority and discretion, writing that while "we hope we shall not have the disapprobation of Congress for what in this way has been done…we wish for explicit powers and instructions upon this head."[30] Many applicants, aside from certificates of citizenship or of their oaths of allegiance, sought passports and other authorizations or protections as American citizens to travel in Europe, venture to Britain, or return to the states with their family or property. But the commissioners, as in the case of oaths of allegiance and much else, had no instructions to meet these applications and would receive very few from Congress despite their urgent solicitations.[31] They would take it upon themselves to satisfy as many legitimate claims as they could, struggling to establish the legitimacy of the new states in the eyes of these potential citizens—furnishing some basis and reciprocity for their continuing loyalty—and the sovereignty of these same states before European powers.[32] Thus, to certify the official identities they helped construct, the commissioners and other American agents abroad developed their own versions of the instruments of identification—including loyalty oath

---

[29] Franklin, John Adams, and Arthur Lee to the President of Congress, 17 September 1778, Passy, Wharton, II: 722-725. "In three instances we have yielded to their importunity; in the case of Mr. Moore, of New Jersey, who has large property in the East Indies which he designs to transfer immediately to America; in the case of Mr. Woodford, of Virginia, a brother of General Woodford, who has been some time in Italy and means to return to America with his property; and yesterday, in the case of Mr. Montgomery, of Philadelphia, who is settled at Alicant, in Spain, but wishes to send vessels and cargoes of his own property to America." Similarly without explicit authorization, the commissioners had "also given two or three commissions by means of the blanks with which Congress intrusted us…and in these cases we have ventured to administer the oaths of allegiance." Franklin, John Adams, and Arthur Lee to the President of Congress, 17 September 1778, Passy, Wharton, II: 722-725. The commissions were given to "one to Mr. Livingston and one to Mr. Amiel, to be lieutenants in the navy." They had likewise administered "the oath of secrecy" to a secretary in their employ and speculated that they should administer oaths of both secrecy and allegiance to similar functionaries.

[30] Franklin, John Adams, and Arthur Lee to the President of Congress, 17 September 1778, Passy, Wharton, II: 722-725.

[31] Franklin, Adams, and Lee to the President of Congress, 17 September 1778, Passy, Wharton, II: 722-725. On requests for travel authorizations, see also Franklin, Adams, and Lee to Vergennes, 28 August 1778, Wharton, II: 698; James Smith to the Commissioners at Paris, 15 November 1778, *PCC*, NARA, M247, r128, i102, v4, p177-178; Lee to Franklin, 3 April 1779, ibid., v3, p10; Lee to All Captains and Commanders, 3 May 1779, ibid., p23-24; Richard Speakman to Franklin, 12 July 1779, *PBFDE*.

[32] On lack of instructions see Franklin, Adams, and Lee to the President of Congress, 17 September 1778, Passy, Wharton, II: 722-725; Franklin to John Jay, 20 August 1781, Wharton, IV: 643-647; Prelinger, "Benjamin Franklin and the American Prisoners of War," 262n1.

certificates and passports—that were increasingly employed by the new American states and long-employed by the European powers.

Foundational among these instruments were those that certified oaths of allegiance to the United States.[33] These oaths and the administration thereof by U.S. representatives—perhaps especially abroad, in the face of the European powers—were important marks and practices of the sovereignty the new states sought. The substance of Revolutionary oaths of allegiance affirmed the sovereignty of the new states (severally), and, often, denied the authority of Britain or any other power over them.[34] The oath commonly administered abroad was a truncated version of that required of those holding offices civil and military in the Continental service. The oath comprised an acknowledgment that the United States—each named individually—were "free, independent and sovereign states" that owed no allegiance to George III, an abjuration of any personal allegiance to the king, and a promise to "support, maintain and defend the said states" against George and his successors.[35] (The promise of faithful service in office was omitted.) Thus the oaths sworn and the certificates documenting them served primarily to construct the sovereignty of the several states, while indirectly establishing the allegiance of the juror.

---

[33] At home and abroad, oaths of allegiance, abjuration, and office constituted the nascent United States in much the same way as they had the British empire. See, esp., Miles Ogborn, "The Power of Speech: Orality, Oaths and Evidence in the British Atlantic World, 1650-1800," *Transactions of the Institute of British Geographers*, New Series, Vol. 36, No. 1 (Jan., 2011), 109-125; Harold Melvin Hyman, *To Try Men's Souls: Loyalty Tests in American History*, (Berkley, CA: University of California Press, 1959), chs. 1-2.

[34] The act of requiring, or even administering, such oaths in an official capacity was itself a claim to sovereignty. And both the substance of the oaths and the act of swearing bound the persons swearing the oaths to the new states and their cause, while thereby, at the same time, building their constituent citizenry.

[35] For the original oath from which this was adapted, see Hyman, *To Try Men's Souls*, esp. 211; Nellie Protsman Waldenmaier, *Some of the Earliest Oaths of Allegiance to the United States of America*, (Lancaster, PA: Lancaster Press, 1944). For examples of the oath as administered by the commissioners, see Joy Castle, 22 June 1778, *PCC*, NARA M247, r128, i102, v4, p20. From Solomon Townsend: Oath, 27 June 1778; from Thomas Hutchins, 6 March 1780, *PBFDE*. Castle and Townsend are not acknowledged by the commissioners as among the three persons to whom they claimed they had agreed to administer the oath by the time they wrote to Congress, 17 September 1778 (see above).

The loyalty oath certificates issued abroad may have been employed as proofs of American citizenship, but it was not always clear whether the oaths confirmed or created this identity.[36] The documents typically certified only that an individual had taken the oath, though in at least one early case the certificate added that the oath-taker was "thereby acknowledging himself a Subject of the said States."[37] In other cases, Franklin seems to have offered the oaths to naturalize Europeans as American citizens.[38] Amid the "multitude" of "Americans" or potential Americans roaming and continually flowing into and out of Europe were a number of individuals who acknowledged themselves not to be Americans, but who wanted to become so. Thus, the commissioners reported to Congress that,

> Several persons from England have applied to us to go to America. They profess to be friends to liberty, to republics, to America; they wish to take their lot with her, to take the oath of allegiance to the States, and to go over with their property. We hope to have instructions upon this head and a mode pointed out for us to proceed in.[39]

While the commissioners lacked instructions, the basic mode of naturalization proposed (seemingly outlined by the applicants themselves) was quite similar to what had been requested by persons who considered themselves Americans and who wished to have their citizenship affirmed. It was a mode that, in a few cases, the commissioners had adopted: an oath of allegiance and a certificate of the same; and a passport to America, including a grant of permission to transport property, and protection from American and allied ships of war and privateers. These were sometimes supplemented with letters of introduction and recommendation.

---

[36] A certificate was cited as proof of citizenship in Franklin to Montgomery, 28 October 1779, *PBFDE*.

[37] To Solomon Townsend, 27 June 1778, *PBFDE*. On the relationship between oral, script, and print legal cultures, see Ogborn, "The Power of Speech," 110.

[38] For this possibility, see John Paradise to Franklin, 2 October 1780, *PBFDE*; Franklin to Jay, 20 August 1781, Wharton, IV: 644.

[39] Franklin, Adams, and Lee to the President of Congress, 17 September 1778, Wharton, II: 722-725.

The difficulty of distinguishing the two groups by the mode employed to certify their citizenship suggests the difficulty of distinguishing the two groups at all. Each individual had to choose American citizenship. As such, one was not clearly an American citizen until one performed whatever appropriate form of fealty or service demonstrated one's choice; the process of affirming citizenship and having it affirmed was nearly homologous to the process of naturalization, in which an individual chose citizenship, declared allegiance, renounced allegiance to any previous sovereign (in this case George III) and was accepted as a citizen by the appropriate governmental body, acting on behalf of the community of citizens.[40]

The principal distinction between the two groups of applicants to the commissioners—those who considered themselves Americans and those who wanted to be—might in fact have been precisely their self-identification as one or the other. As the case of the Loyalists makes clear, of course, birth or a history of residence in what were now the states, and a history of family, social, and public connections there, did not necessarily translate into citizenship in the new polity. Such a personal history might be necessary to be considered a candidate for affirmation of a self-declared pre-existing citizenship, but it was not sufficient. At the same time, all of the "Americans" of the new polity came from, broadly speaking, the general pool of British subjects, and so it was not entirely clear that others from that same pool could not also be "Americans" in the new sense.[41]

---

[40] On the "volitional" nature of American Revolutionary citizenship, see James H. Kettner, *The Development of American Citizenship, 1608-1870*, (Chapel Hill, NC: University of North Carolina Press, 1978).

[41] The ambiguities were brought out when, in late 1778, the Congress sought Dr. Richard Price's allegiance and aid in administering their war effort. In December of that year the commissioners wrote to Price that, "it is the desire of Congress to consider him as a citizen of the United States, and to receive his assistance in regulating their finances." They invited him and his family to emigrate at Congressional expense and assured him of the efforts they would make to ensure an "agreeable" passage, reception, and settlement in America. Franklin, Lee, and Adams to Richard Price, 7 December 1778 (transmitting the Congressional resolution of 6 October 1778), Wharton, II: 853. Notably, the Congress did not invite Price to submit an oath of allegiance or to expatriate himself, and did not offer to naturalize him—though this may have been implied—but instead offered to "consider him as a Citizen of the United States," as though his American citizenship was a matter of course because of his sympathies for and work in support of their cause. Price, in declining the offer, cast the matter in different terms, pleading his lack of qualifications, his age, and his attachment to Britain. Price to Franklin, 18 January 1779, Wharton, II: 474.

Though the commissioners were conscious that they had no explicit powers to administer oaths of allegiance even to established Americans, they reconciled themselves to the necessity in limited early cases and would eventually conclude that they were implicitly "vested with consular powers, and…therefore capable of administering an oath."[42] When they administered an oath of allegiance to anyone who professed or was known not to be a U.S. citizen already, they were, in essence, providing naturalization on their own authority.[43] The ambiguities and the possible impropriety of their practices in this regard came out when John Jay, the U.S. diplomatic envoy to Spain, was requested to administer the oath of allegiance himself. The punctilious Jay would not only argue that the oath could only be offered to those who were already Americans (in some still undefined sense), but would object to the oath more generally as a means to establish United States citizenship, on the grounds that this identity was itself illusory.[44]

The case concerned Mr. John Vaughan, the son of Franklin's English friend and publisher. Vaughan was living in France and Spain during the Revolution to study commerce and the local languages to prepare for a commercial career based in America, where he and his parents intended he should establish himself. He accordingly sought to take the oath of allegiance before departing for the United States in the summer of 1781, and Franklin designated a proper person in Bordeaux to administer it. Vaughan planned to travel via Spain after leaving Bordeaux, however, and decided to delay taking the oath until he had reached that country. Upon arrival he sought out Jay and requested that he administer the oath, on the strength of a letter of recommendation from Franklin

---

[42] Franklin to Jay, 20 August 1781, Wharton, IV: 644.

[43] But they made a point of informing even acknowledged Americans affirming their citizenship that "such certificates are in strictness legally void, because there is no act of Congress that expressly gives us power to administer oaths." Franklin, John Adams, and Arthur Lee to the President of Congress, 17 September 1778, Passy, Wharton, II: 722-725.

[44] Jay to Franklin, 31 May 1781, Wharton, IV: 462-463.

to William Carmichael, Jay's secretary. Jay was uncertain, however, of his authority to administer the oath and whether it would be proper or advisable in this case. He wrote to Franklin:

> [Vaughan] desired me on his arrival at Madrid to administer to him an oath of allegiance to the *United States* in order to justify his calling himself an American, and to facilitate his pursuing his objects in this country and his passing from hence to America. I have no doubt but that his character and intentions are fair. He seems to be a sensible young gentleman, and I would with pleasure do him service; but as I knew he was not an American I could not represent him as such, nor could I comply with his request as to administering the oath, having no powers for that purpose either expressed or implied in my commission or instructions.[45]

Vaughan apparently already considered himself an American, or at least wished to begin identifying himself as such, but had not formally established his allegiance to the United States and so could not "justify his calling himself an American." By taking the oath, Vaughan seems to have thought, he would be effectively naturalized. Jay, on the contrary, seems to have considered that the oath could only confirm the allegiance of those who were already Americans.

Jay considered that Vaughan, to be recognized as an American, would need to be naturalized. But he objected, on two principal grounds, to the proposal that Vaughan might achieve this by swearing the oath of allegiance to the United States. First, Jay argued, while "I believe it to be the inclination as well as the interest of America to augment her number of citizens; but still her consent to admit a foreigner must be as necessary as his consent to be admitted." Secondly, he objected to the idea that anyone could be admitted as a citizen of the United States. He explained to Franklin that,

> it appears to me that an oath of allegiance to the *United States* can with propriety be only administered to servants of Congress, for though a person may by birth or admission become a citizen of one of the States, I can not conceive how one can either be born or be made a citizen of them *all*.[46]

---

[45] Jay to Franklin, 31 May 1781, Wharton, IV: 462-463.

[46] Jay to Franklin, 31 May 1781, Wharton, IV: 462-463.

Jay's interpretation suggests that the idea of national citizenship was still inchoate, given that the states were both newly formed and primarily concerned to maintain their own autonomy, having confederated only for the purposes of prosecuting the war, regulating their collective foreign affairs, and resolving disputes among themselves.[47] The oath of allegiance to the United States (as opposed to the many state oaths) was, in Jay's view, an oath for the faithful performance of public service in the common endeavor but did not correspond to a body politic of which the oath-taking party was thereby constituted a member. Though the notion and practice of a national citizenship, in addition to citizenship in the particular states, was in fact gaining prevalence among members of the Congress and the Continental Army—if not more generally—it was still a contested and largely undefined concept.[48] Nonetheless, lacking explicit authority even to administer oaths as agents of Congress, Franklin and his colleagues certainly could not have administered the oaths of individual states on their behalf. Jay assured Franklin regretfully, in conclusion, that "I wish these difficulties did not oppose my complying with the request of Mr. Vaughan, whom I am the more desirous of serving, as he appears to posses your regard."[49]

Franklin assured Jay that no pretense was being made, clarifying that "Mr. Vaughan is not indeed an American, but desires to become one." Franklin's response made clear that he did not

---

[47] On the nature of the confederation, see David C. Hendrickson, *Peace Pact: The Lost World of the American Founding*, (Lawrence, KS: University Press of Kansas, 2003); Jerrilyn Greene Marston, *King and Congress: The Transfer of Political Legitimacy, 1774-1776*, (Princeton, NJ: Princeton UP, 1987); Peter S. Onuf, *The Origins of the Federal Republic: Jurisdictional Controversies in the United States, 1775-1787*, (Philadelphia: University of Pennsylvania Press, 1983); Merrill Jensen, *The Articles of Confederation: An Interpretation of the Social-Constitutional History of the American Revolution, 1774-1781*, (Madison, WI: University of Wisconsin Press, 1966).

[48] See Richard B. Morris, *The Forging of the Union, 1781-1789*, (New York: Harper & Row, 1987), 74-76. Though persuasive in his argument for the de facto practice of a U.S. citizenship, beginning at least as early as 1777, Morris's argument relies largely on tacit acceptance of these practices by Congress, the British, and others. His claim that this matter was "settled" by acceptance of national and state citizenries by both American and British parties to the Peace of 1783 is less tenable. Leading scholarship on the history of American citizenship in the Revolutionary and early national periods demonstrates continuing contests and ambiguity. See, esp., Kettner, *American Citizenship*, chs. 7-9; Douglas Bradburn, *The Citizenship Revolution: Politics and the Creation of the American Union, 1774-1804*, (Charlottesville, VA: University of Virginia Press, 2009), ch. 1.

[49] Jay to Franklin, 31 May 1781, Wharton, IV: 462-463. See Franklin to Richard and Sarah Bache, 19 January 1782, Wharton, V: 119, for his account of Vaughan's activities and intentions during the Revolution.

consider that Vaughan's taking the oath of allegiance, even if witnessed by an American agent abroad, would constitute a naturalization. But at the same time he reminded Jay that, "the constitutions of most, if not all, of the States show a disposition to receive strangers by making the residence of one or two years entitle them to all the privileges of denizens without a formal naturalization." It appears that Franklin considered the oath as a means to facilitate Vaughan's acceptance in America (and perhaps to compel Vaughan to commit, once and for all, to the American cause), rather than as a sufficient mechanism for the creation of Vaughan as an American. It is not even clear that he intended "American" in this case to be synonymous with American citizen. He seems to have been suggesting that Vaughan was seeking not formal citizenship but the rights of a denizen, or even more minimally, assurance that he would not be treated as an enemy upon arrival in the United States.

Franklin and Jay could, it seems, agree that the new states should attract additional population and good citizens from abroad. If Franklin could persuade Jay that what was at issue was not formal naturalization, in which they as agents of the new confederation government actually enacted Vaughan's naturalization, but that they instead were simply facilitating Vaughan's practical membership in a particular state and community in America, they could perhaps find a way around Jay's scruples. "My brother ministers here I believe," Franklin wrote, "considered themselves as vested with consular powers, and to be therefore capable of administering an oath, and I have continued the practice, conceiving them to be better lawyers than myself."[50] The Congress, in fact, would never contest Franklin's authority in administering such oaths or issuing U. S. passports, even though they never gave him formal instructions in this regard.[51]

---

[50] Franklin to Jay, 20 August 1781, Wharton, IV: 644.

[51] Morris, *Forging of the Union*, 74-76.

Franklin did admit to Jay that, "I did not consider the matter in the lights you state it; I think your objections reasonable, and I wish the Congress would give some instructions about it." But Franklin suggested that even without powers to administer oaths, they might still, with propriety, witness the oaths of those wishing to take them. "On reflection," he wrote,

> there seems to me some difference between requiring an oath and being witness to the taking of an oath. He that requires another to take an oath ought to be vested with authority for so doing. But when a man is pleased to take an oath voluntarily may not any other person testify its being done in his presence. This I apprehend is the case of those which have been taken before us.[52]

In this way, Franklin seems to have been proposing, the ministers would be acting not as agents of the governments and people they represented, but as individuals of good character, fortuitously abroad and available to witness the oaths of those, on their own initiative, wishing to declare their choice of allegiance to the new polities and the principles for which they stood.

Of course, self-identified or would-be Americans abroad, who wished to travel to Britain, were not necessarily eager to put themselves on record as rebels—especially if they were in fact Loyalists trying to pass safely through the dominions of the rebels or their allies (or if they planned to wait out the contest before declaring themselves for the winner). U.S. agents abroad, as such, while grappling with uncertainties and dissensions among themselves, had also to contend with challenges to their authority in these matters from the very persons they sought to identify. In November of 1778, for instance, Dr. James Smith addressed a letter to Franklin, Adams, and Lee, explaining as patiently as he could how their insistence on his taking an oath of allegiance might kill him. Smith had, for several weeks, been seeking their aid as intercessors with the French government—first to secure duty-free passage of his goods through France and then, when these goods had been detained by customs at Calais, to secure their release. As it became apparent that the affair would drag on, he had written the commissioners to explain that his affairs in England

---

[52] Franklin to Jay, 20 August 1781, Wharton, IV: 644.

required his immediate attention and that he wished to have a pass thither for himself and his family. He had received in response what he termed a "very extraordinary Letter" in which the commissioners informed him that, "Your Request of a Passport, to go to England We do not think We can consistently grant, unless you previously Subscribe the Declaration and take the oath of Allegiance to the united States of America."[53] Having been an active partisan of the Revolution and having made himself obnoxious to the British ministry, he was astounded that the American agents should impose such a condition when, he wrote, they "must be sensible how fatal that Measure might prove to my Liberty & even life should it transpire in England before I could finish my private Business."[54]

"When I wrote that I was willing to give the most solemn assurances of my affection & duty to my Country," Smith marveled, "could it be supposed that I meant to expose myself to the wispers of secret enemies & the Rage of a merciless disapointed & consequently invetera[te] Administration[?]" "It must have accured" to the commissioners, "from a Momen[t's] reflection that I could only mean such assurances as were binding upon a man of honour and yet would not subject me to the Laws of England." He had, in any case, meant his application to be little more than a courtesy. "When I requested a passport," he explained, "I intended to pay you the usual Compliment payed to the public Ministers of my Country."[55] It pained him now to have to remind them, "that the power wherewith you are invested was never given to distress or indanger the Lives & Liberties of your Country men." Was this "the Reward of public Virtue? And shall the official Guardians of our Lives furnish the very means of our destruction without any possible be[ne]fit to our Country[?]" In any case, he informed them, "I have attentively perused all the public Acts of

---

[53] Franklin et al. to Smith, 17 November 1778, *PBFDE*; Smith to Franklin et al., November 1778, *PCC*, NARA M247, r128, i102, v4, p171-173.

[54] Smith to Franklin et al., November 1778, *PCC*, NARA M247, r128, i102, v4, p171-173

[55] Smith to Franklin et al., November 1778, *PCC*, NARA M247, r128, i102, v4, p171-173.

Congress & I do not find that they insist upon imposing the Oath of Allegiance upon any person going to England."[56] As it happened, he had the commissioners there. The authority they attempted to exercise in this and other like cases was largely of their own construction.

Rather than seek instruments of personal identification, many applicants instead sought documents, including passports, that would enable them to bring to America extensive personal effects, money, or trade goods. These passports, they hoped or assumed, by identifying the cargo as American and, more specifically, their property, would provide protection, at least from American and allied cruisers. It was in such cases that the commissioners' duties to serve and protect intersected most clearly with an implied obligation to govern Americans abroad.

In the course of the war Congress grew increasingly convinced that many Americans they had permitted to go abroad to retrieve property, along with many of the foreigners who said they were coming to settle in the states, were using their American passports to cover an illicit trade in British goods. Franklin, at least, attempted to further Congressional efforts to stop this practice, by requiring oaths, bonds, or testimonials before he would issue passports.[57] But he evidently became concerned that even those who were recommended were sometimes abusing the instruments he provided. In March of 1780, Thomas Digges, who was the source of a number of such recommendations, wrote to Franklin on behalf of Captain Jonathan Snelling, "a native of Boston…for many years past…employd in the Streights Trade to & from London," who was "well recommended to Me as an honest Am[erica]n" now "meaning to push out to his Home thro France" and desiring Franklin's advice (and implicitly his aid). Under the circumstances, Digges felt

---

[56] Smith to Franklin et al., November 1778, *PCC*, NARA M247, r128, i102, v4, p171-173.

[57] See the passport issued to Cyprian Sterry and John Smith, 24 September 1779, to return to America with their property, their application supported by "good Testimony" and Sterry having taking the oath of allegiance to the U.S. *PBFDE.*

compelled to insist on the good grounds he felt he had for making his previous recommendations. "As far as I have recommended the granting some late favors from You," Digges wrote, "I have not the least doubt the transactions are bona fide intended for the purposes mentiond—ie getting home property." He did not "mean by saying this, that some of the partys did not carry more than they had property to purchase," but "In the two instances wch." he "lately recommend" the "various persons" concerned were "every one natives & Citizens of A[merica]" and "were people whom I had proofs were honest."[58] Digges thus professed to have made a good faith effort to properly identify those he recommended and implied he could only be held so far responsible for any deceptions.

At the same time, Franklin, his colleagues, and other committed Patriots abroad feared Loyalists might disguise themselves as friends of the United States, acting either personally or as tools of the British ministry to undermine the Patriot cause.[59] Among other measures, Franklin imposed requirements (similar to those for transporting significant property to America) on those applicants who, like Smith, proposed to go to Britain—this in an effort to prevent the transmission of sensitive information to the enemy. Loyalists who had "converted" to the Patriot cause were perhaps the most suspect.[60] The case of James Cheston of Maryland, detained while travelling to England via France, illustrates both these suspicions and the complexities that these imperatives of identification involved.

---

[58] Digges to Franklin, 17 March 1780, *PBFDE*

[59] In reports that reached Arthur Lee, it was rumored that the Carlisle peace commission was to be accompanied by a number of secret Loyalists. Van Doren, *Secret History*, 78. Van Doren notes that, in reality, only two "informal agents," Berkenhout and Temple, "followed" the commission.

[60] Similar suspicions prevailed among the Loyalist exiles in American cities held by the British, and abroad in England or the West Indies, concerning those who had joined the Loyalist ranks after supporting or serving the rebel governments or armed forces, or after initial neutrality or indecision. See Van Tyne, *Loyalists*, 263. The British authorities, likewise, sometimes suspected Loyalist exiles, including Samuel Curwen, of being spies for the rebels. Van Tyne, *Loyalists*, 257n1.

By the autumn of 1780, Franklin's authority to restrict or authorize the travel of U.S. citizens to Britain (and perhaps elsewhere) was accepted by many Americans, largely merchants, resident in France. That autumn, several such persons in L'Orient arranged through Commodore John Paul Jones for the detention of Cheston and three other recently arrived Americans of suspect loyalty who proposed to go to England but lacked passports from home and had not taken oaths of allegiance to their states or to the United States. Cheston explained in his memorial to Franklin (20 October 1776) that the suspicious parties did not think it "proper in the Present Situation of Affairs, that Any Person Shou'd go to that Kingdom [Britain] without Your previous Approbation."[61]

"It has been Sugghested here," Cheston concluded, "that your Memorialist, left Maryland in a clandestine Secret Manner, Than which nothing can be More Injurious or Unjust." To prove it so, He takes the liberty of troubling Your Excellency with an advertisement, he inserted in the Baltimore Gazette last May And a certificate of Capt. Forbes's with whom he came here." Cheston had arrived from Maryland at L'Orient more than a month before and now waited there for Franklin's permission to go on to England. He explained that though he had spent much of his youth in England, he was a native of Maryland and had resided there for the previous decade as the representative of a British trading firm in which he was a partner. He wanted to go to England to liquidate his holdings in that firm and return to Maryland, where he claimed to have "a Wife and three Children and considerable property." Cheston freely admitted that he had disagreed with the movement for independence, but insisted that he had not actively opposed it. He had since concluded that the United States would indeed achieve a secure independence and that he would be happiest living in his native state. And so "he had Determined, Notwithstanding his former prejudice to become a good Subject of the Government under which he intended to reside, in every

---

[61] James Cheston to Franklin, 20 October 1780, *PBFDE.*

Sense of the word." He had not taken the oath of allegiance to Maryland because, like Smith, he had concluded that such an oath would put him in danger from the British during his voyage.

Cheston had been packed and prepared, ready to embark for Ostende on a Flemish ship, when the commandant of L'Orient summoned him, saying that "information had been lodged against him as a suspicious person" and that he would be required to give his parole not to leave that port "untill further orders." These particulars were later related by Jonathan Nesbitt, a Philadelphia merchant then in L'Orient, in a letter to Franklin. Nesbitt did not know who had lodged the information against Cheston, though he supposed them to be "warm friends to America" who were concerned that Cheston might convey intelligence to the British if allowed, as Cheston desired, to reach England via Ostende. Nesbitt assured Franklin that this could hardly be a valid concern, as Cheston had been warmly recommended to him in a letter Cheston bore from a Mr. Stephen Stewart, a "Gentleman" of Maryland and a strong supporter of the Revolutionary cause, with whose "Character" Nesbitt supposed Franklin might be acquainted. It was alleged that Cheston had left Maryland "in a Clandestine Manner," but Cheston had provided a certificate to the contrary from Captain Forbes of the ship on which Cheston had arrived. Forbes was of "an extraordinary good Character," Nesbitt judged, "not Capable of setting his hand to a falsehood."[62]

Letters of the same date to Franklin from John Paul Jones and the American merchant Samuel Wharton, both then at L'Orient, revealed that the "warm friends of America" were Wharton himself, a Captain Hall of Philadelphia, and Robert and Matthew Mease of Virginia.[63] These "American citizens," as Wharton labeled them, had informed Jones of the arrival of Cheston and three other men, also "Suspected Persons," and had persuaded him to advise the French commandant to prevent them travelling on to England until Franklin could be consulted. Wharton

---

[62] Nesbitt to Franklin, 20 October 1780, *PBFDE*.

[63] Jones to Franklin, 20 October 1780, *PBFDE*.

conceded that Cheston "appears a Gentleman of good Address and Understanding" and insisted that he had "not been moved to [this action] by any illiberal Motive, as I had not the least personal Knowledge of Mr. Cheston and his Companions."[64]

Whatever his personal merits and recommendations, Cheston, according to Wharton, admitted "to have acted uniformly against the Principles of the Revolution,— not to have taken the usual Oath to the State, and to have departed from Maryland, without permission of the Government." Cheston's three companions, likewise, gave no evidence that they had been granted "Liberty…To Pass from France to England."[65] As Jones explained to Franklin, "Mr. Cheston and his three Companions being Under no Tie on their Arrival in England, would naturally give information not only of what they know here, but of what they have Seen in America."[66] Wharton suggested more generally that in light of such risks,

> perhaps, during the War, It might be impolitic to suffer the Enemies of America to come to the ports of this Kingdom without permission, and from thence to pass to England, Where They would be closely interrogated, as well with Respect to the Situation of Affairs in the States, as of all Vessels, and Armaments, in the Harbours of our Ally.

The four gentlemen had demurred at Wharton's suggestion that they go to Passy to make their case to Franklin, determining instead to wait at L'Orient in expectation of his approval.[67] As Cheston dispatched his memorial to Franklin, Jones, in his own letter, informed the latter that, all of "These Men Say they are now willing to take the Oath of fidelity to the United States."[68] And while Smith had contested and Jay would later question his and the other agents' authority to require oaths, by this time Franklin felt confident in requiring oaths and, in fact, delegated to Jones "all the Power that

---

[64] Wharton to Franklin, 20 October 1780, *PBFDE*.

[65] Wharton to Franklin, 20 October 1780, *PBFDE*.

[66] Jones to Franklin, 20 October 1780, *PBFDE*.

[67] Wharton to Franklin, 20 October 1780, *PBFDE*.

[68] Wharton to Franklin, Jones to Franklin, Cheston to Franklin, and Thomas Smith to Franklin, all 20 October 1780, *PBFDE*.

in me lies of administring those Oaths in my Stead." He explained to Jones that "Those who do not chuse to take the oath, can have no Claim to [a] Passport from me; they must be considered as British Subjects, and in the Disposition of the Government."[69]

Franklin sent to Jones "Copies of the Oath taken by the Subjects of the United States, with Passes for such of the Gentlemen arrived from Maryland as chuse voluntarily to take the oath before you." "The Passes you give may be so worded," Franklin allowed, "as to prevent the Gentlemen preceeding sooner than you judge proper, if you have any Suspicion that dangerous Information may be obtained from them."[70] Franklin also wrote Nesbitt that, "I am sorry that anything happened in the Di[t]ention of your Friend, that is disagreable to you or to him." And he conveyed "Directions to Commodore Jones to receive his [Cheston's] Oath to the States & deliver him a Passport." However inclined to be of service to Nesbitt or his friend, Franklin noted that,

> as there are other Persons in Company, & I find there are Apprehensions that Intelligence early given in England either thro' Inadvertence or otherwise, may be prejudicial to the Interests of Persons concerned in the Ships going to America, and to the Publick I have left a little in M. Jones's Discretion as to the time of the Passports, commencing.

At the same time Franklin expressed his curiosity "to know, if he is any Relation of a M. Daniel Cheston whom I knew about 40. Years ago, & who then lived I think on Chester River," and requested Nesbitt would present Cheston his compliments and his apologies for not writing Cheston himself, due to an ongoing attack of gout.[71] Franklin hoped, possibly, to make some better sense of the episode in future. He may likewise have wished to perpetuate or renew the connections he had formed with Daniel Cheston via a person who may have been connected to him by family.

---

[69] Franklin to Jones, 1 November 1780, *PBFDE*.

[70] Franklin to Jones, 1 November 1780, *PBFDE*. Franklin wrote to Wharton on the same date: "I thank you for the Information relating to the Passengers arrived from Maryland. I have impower'd Comme. Jones to receive their oaths to the State, & then to give them Passports." Franklin to Wharton, 1 November 1780, *PBFDE*.

[71] Franklin to Nesbitt, 1 November 1780, *PBFDE*.

The vagaries of dealing in instruments of identification over long distances soon intervened to shape the process of Cheston's identification. Ten days after Franklin wrote to Jones authorizing him to administer oaths to Cheston and his companions, and dispatching copies of the form of oath and passport to be employed, Jones wrote to Franklin's grandson and secretary, William Temple Franklin, acknowledging receipt of previous letters and expressing solicitude for Franklin's recovery from his illness. He noted at the same time, however, that, "There is mention made in his Letters to Mr. Wharton and Mr. Nesbitt of Passports being sent to me with powers to Administer the oath to Mr. Cheston and others here." "But though I have made dilligent inquiry," Jones explained, "no Paper nor Power on that subject has yet come to my Hands." Jones reported that "Mr Cheston speaks of going to Nantes" but that he would "tell Mr. Nesbitt again my opinion that he [Cheston] ought not to stir without taking the Oath to the United States."[72] As it happened, Nesbitt had written Franklin the day before Jones, hoping "that Mr: Cheston (who will have the honor to deliver you this Letter) will find you perfectly recover'd." "No doubt," Nesbitt suggested, "it was a continuation of your illness that prevented your giving orders to Commodore Jones to receive Mr: Chestons oath to the States and deliver him a Pasport." In the meantime, Cheston, "being determind to go to England by the way of Ostend," had "taken the Resolution of waiting on your Excellency." Nesbitt confirmed him to be "Son to your old acquaintance Mr: Danl. Cheston who lived on Chester River."[73] On the nineteenth of November, at Passy, Cheston swore and subscribed the oath acknowledging the independence of the United States from Britain and its King, abjuring his own allegiance to King George, and swearing to defend the United States against George and his

---

[72] Jones to William Temple Franklin, 11 November 1780, *PBFDE*.

[73] Nesbitt to Franklin, 10 November 1780, *PBFDE*.

minions. Franklin certified the fact of the oath over his signature and title as Minister

Plenipotentiary from the United States of America to the Court of France.[74]

The Smith and Cheston cases brought out the ambiguous character of U.S. sovereignty and

of the authority of U.S. agents abroad, even among their constituents and supporters, let alone

skeptics and Loyalists. But they also exemplified the radically different applications for passports

that individuals made as U.S. citizens, or simply as Americans either friendly or neutral toward the

cause.[75] Applicants, some eager to take oaths, others not, sought travel authorizations, some to

travel in Europe or further afield; some, like Smith, to go to Britain; and some, as Smith ultimately

intended, to return to America. Americans abroad who were headed to sea (or across the channel)

needed protection from the ships of the U.S. and its allies. Those headed to the states often needed

(or believed they needed) a U.S. passport to gain entry to the states in the midst of war and

revolution (as well as, possibly, a British passport to cross through British lines).[76] Those travelling

through France or Spain needed to distinguish themselves from enemy Britons and sometimes

hoped to garner favors (like exemptions from customs duties) from the republic's French and

Spanish allies. Whatever their itineraries, American passports could ease their passage, especially in

countries or with officials sympathetic to the North American rebellion.

The uncertain definitions of U.S. citizenship, and its ambiguous relationship to being

"American" by birth or established residence, made the protections of a passport especially

attractive. Even those who felt their claim to American citizenship and friendship to the Revolution

---

[74] Cheston, Oath of Allegiance, 19 November 1780, *PBFDE*.

[75] U.S. agents also received applications for passports from foreigners seeking protection from the ships and agents of the U.S. and its allies. See note 97, below.

[76] See, for instance, Arthur Lee's letter to Franklin, 3 April 1779, concerning the application by a man named Hunter "for a pass-port to gain him admission into the State of Virginia or any other of the United States." Transcripts of Letters from Arthur Lee, William Lee, Ralph Izard, and the Joint Commissioners of the United States to France, 1776-80, *PCC*, NARA M247, r128, i102, v3, p10.

to be well established were often worried that their identities would not be recognized. Thus when

Dr. Upton Scott prepared to return to America after seeing to an inheritance in Ireland, he applied

to Franklin, through a letter from Thomas Digges, for a passport. Digges explained that Scott was

"an old & respected Citizen of Annapolis, where He practisd Phisick with reputation for many years,

and left that Country about four years ago with the approbation & good wishes of the Province."

Having settled his affairs in Ireland, he intended to return with the next British fleet to New York

and after "getting past the lines of New York" would make his way "back to His Country, Family &

Home." Though availing himself of Digges's intercession, Scott said he "formerly had the honour

to be known" to Franklin and now asked "the favour of You…to procure Him if possible some

written Instrument, which may save His Baggage & Effects from seizure should the vessel on which

He Embarks fall into the hands of an American Cruizer." Scott feared that "in which case, tho the

Doctor is a good friend to His Country, He may loose his Baggage, from the People who takes him

not knowing any thing about Him or His worth."[77] Scott was acutely conscious of how the

geographical and social limits of personal identities could be tested by travelling outside one's state

or county, let alone overseas. Likewise, whether he or his compatriots believed in a generalized U.S.

citizenry or community of "American" Patriots, transcending state boundaries, he knew he could

not rely on being recognized as an American when his captors had little ground on which to

establish his identity.

It complicated matters that passports at this period were not issued exclusively to citizens or

subjects of the issuing power. A traveler might carry several, from several powers, as well as letters

of recommendation and other instruments, public and private. (The commissioners, in addition to

applications for U.S. passports, received many requests that they intercede with France, Spain, or

---

[77] Digges to Franklin, 30 May 1780, *PBFDE*.

even Britain to secure an individual—and not always an American—a foreign passport.[78])

Americans and U.S. agents likewise had to accommodate local circumstances and the expectations

or demands of European governments. Thus in June of 1779, John Paradise and William Jones

wrote to Franklin that, "Being informed that the King's passport was absolutely necessary for them

to go out of France, they sent to Versailles for that purpose." The response they received led them

to ask Franklin "to insert in his passport what they [the French] seem to want namely, that Mr.

Paradise is an American gentleman born in Greece (if où ils sont nès must be taken literally,) and

that Mr. Jones is an Englishman with one valet de chambre."[79] The two men had found they must

bear both American and French passports, and that even this was not sufficient—they must have

their American passport modified to meet French requirements. In particular, the French seem to

have expected that the American instrument would identify the bearer more precisely in terms of

nativity and nation, as well as particularizing any auxiliary members of their suite. In all these

respects and many more, Americans and U.S. agents abroad had to work out among themselves and

the other powers involved the relationship between allegiance and mobility, U.S. citizenship and a

U.S. passport, American instruments of identification and those issued by other governments. As

with loyalty oath certificates, U.S. agents abroad—still acting almost entirely on their own

judgment—had to develop and administer the form, both textual and material, of several variants of

a U.S. passport.

From the spring of 1778 onward, Franklin and his fellow commissioners adopted two forms

of passports. One was an increasingly standardized letter to the commanders of American armed

---

[78] Applications were even made to Franklin on behalf of English subjects friendly to America but with no pretensions to being U.S. citizens who desired a French, Spanish, or other passport. See Digges to Franklin, 17 March 1780, *PBFDE*. U.S. representatives interceded more generally to secure the interests of US citizens, as when requesting that France fulfill a treaty promise to intercede on U.S. behalf with Barbary pirates; requesting arrangements for Americans to pass home without taxes on their property; and requesting passports for English cartel ships involved in prisoner exchanges. On these matters, see Franklin, Lee, and Adams to Vergennes, 28 Aug 1778, Wharton, II: 698.

[79] Paradise and Jones to Franklin, 1 June 1779, *PBFDE*.

vessels.[80] The other copied the form of French government passports and, in French, addressed all

who might read it.[81] Unlike the loyalty oath certificates, which Franklin and his colleagues issued in

manuscript, on an ad hoc basis, the passports they issued (which had began as manuscript

instruments) soon used printed forms produced in the private print shop Franklin established at his

residence in Passy. While the Passy press also and more famously printed Franklin's "bagatelles," it

proved most publicly valuable for high volume production of official documents—items relating to

Franklin's diplomatic mission or consular functions.[82] These documents included passports, sea

letters, bonds, promissory notes, orders on the American ministers' banker in Europe, Mr.

Ferdinand Grand, and a series of Congressional regulations relating to American privateering. The

first of the official documents printed at Passy seems to have been a series of blanks for the general

passport, on the French model, produced in the late summer or early autumn of 1779. On the 2nd of

August, Franklin issued Thomas Burdy a passport, for travel to England via Ostend, nearly identical

to a manuscript passport he had issued John Adams the preceding March, but this time using a

printed form.[83]

---

[80] See the American Commissioners, passport for William Moore, 23 June 1778, *PBFDE*; Franklin to "All Captains and Commanders of Vessels of War," 11 March 1779, *PBF*, XXIX: 95; passport for Cyprian Sterry and John Smith, *PBF*, XXX: 393; passport for Benjamin Carpenter, 14 March 1780, *PBFDE*.

[81] *PBF*, XXVI: 440-441n, XXIX: 79n. See passport for Thomas Burdy and accompanying editorial notes, *PBF*, XXX: 181-182.

[82] See Luther Samuel Livingston, *Franklin and his Press at Passy*, (New York: Grolier Club, 1914); Ellen R. Cohn, "The Printer at Passy," *Benjamin Franklin: In Search of a Better World*, Page Talbott ed., (New Haven, CT: Yale UP, 2005).

[83] Franklin, passport for Thomas Burdy, *PBF*, XXX: 181-182 and notes. For a passport of this same type, using a printed form, but from a different printing run, with small differences in the text (e.g., "empreinte" rather than "cachet"), see Franklin, passport for William Rawle and ___ Walker, 8 May 1782, *PBFDE*. Though it had not been clearly tied to a particular time or purpose, there is among Franklin's papers at the APS a manuscript blank form of a French royal passport, for one month, issuing on behalf of the King by Vergennes. The document is docketed on back as "Form of a Pass," and may possibly represent part of Franklin's efforts to gather information and models for the form of a U.S. passport. Papers of Benjamin Franklin, Miscellaneous Papers, LXXIV: 103, B:F85, APS. For an example of a French royal passport in this form, issued to an American, see passport for Josiah Harmar, 10 April 1784, Josiah Harmar Papers, Volume 45 (Commission and Passport Book—Flat File), WLCL.

These passport blanks represented the first of at least six different issues of passports, all
nearly identical in wording, though marked by significant typographical differences.[84] Besides saving
him time and labor, printed passports also eventually allowed Franklin, drawing on his expertise as a
printer in general, and especially as a printer of colonial currency, to better secure the passports he
issued from forgery or modification, taking the relative security and uniqueness of manuscript
documents in his own handwriting and translating it into print. In 1781, Franklin had a French type
founder cut a large custom script type. (The same founder may have produced an earlier custom
type for Franklin in the spring of 1780.[85]) The 1781 script, used to print subsequent runs of
passports, was probably designed by Franklin himself to stymie counterfeiters.[86] In contrast to the
situation back in America, the American mission seems to have faced no significant shortage of
paper, ink, or printing type. Franklin ordered large quantities of paper, including (ironically) custom
paper from England. And he was "constantly buying type," from both French and English
founders, during most of his stay in France, beginning with a 1777 order from the Fourniers.[87]

The process of evaluating applicants for passports was much the same as the process of
evaluating candidates to take the oath of allegiance. Often the eligibility and willingness to take the
oath were sufficient grounds to be granted a passport, assuming circumstances and policy permitted.
In many cases, and especially when the passport involved sensitive routes or destinations (e.g. to or
from Britain) or the transport of large quantities of goods, letters of introduction and
recommendation helped to establish that the applicant could be safely trusted with such a privilege.
In some cases, as with the ostensible Carolinian, local knowledge of a particular state's community

---

[84] *PBF*, XXX: 181-82.

[85] *PBF*, XXX: 89, 117.

[86] *PBF*, XXX: 89, 109.

[87] Livingston, *Press at Passy*, 111.

might be relevant. For that reason, perhaps, Franklin directed a man seeking a passport to Virginia to apply to Lee, the resident Virginian. From Lee's account of the man's application there is no indication that the man claimed a particular connection with Virginia, but only sought "a pass-port to gain him admission into the State of Virginia or any other of the United States."[88] While Lee had no authority to issue passports for admission to Virginia, he was likely to exercise greater influence with that state's government and society than would Franklin or Adams. Lee's handwriting, seal, language, and references were also bound to be more familiar and convincing to Virginia authorities, and thus less likely to be taken for forgeries.

In at least one other instance, Lee joined his personal identity as a Virginian (and his personal history of residence in London) with his public character as a commissioner of Congress in order to identify and protect a compatriot. On the 3rd of May 1779, in Paris, he issued a passport addressed "To all Captains & Commanders of Ships of War, armed Vessels & Privateers of or belonging to the United States of America," certifying "that the Bearer of this Mrs Ann Norton, widow of the late John Norton Esqr Virginia Merchant of London, is a native of the State of Virginia to which She is returning with her Family & effect[s]," and requesting that she "pass without molestation, in obedience to the Resolution of Congress for that purpose" and receive "every assistance & protection which her situation may require, & which the zealous attachment She has always shewn to the cause of her Country deserves." Lee signed the passport as "Arthur Lee Commissr. of Congress."[89] This passport echoed the pervasive uncertainty concerning the grounds and nature of citizenship in the new states, let alone the United States, by insisting both on the bearer's birth in one of what were now the United States and on her personal demonstrations of

---

[88] Lee to Franklin, 3 April 1779, copy, Transcripts of Letters from Arthur Lee, William Lee, Ralph Izard, and the Joint Commissioners of the United States to France, 1776-80, *PCC*, NARA M247, r128, i102, v3, p10.

[89] Arthur Lee, passport for Ann Norton, 3 May 1779, Transcripts of Letters from Arthur Lee, William Lee, Ralph Izard, and the Joint Commissioners of the United States to France, 1776-80, *PCC*, NARA M247, r128, i102, v3, p23-24.

loyalty to the Revolution or "the cause of her Country"—whether Virginia or America was left ambiguous.

The issue was complicated, in this case, by the fact that the bearer was a woman travelling more or less in her own right. While free women could be and act as Patriots, their political identities were much less clear than those of men. Women had certainly been recognized as subjects under the British Empire, and they were recognized as potential citizens of the several United States by most of the (male) Revolutionary leaders, but generally only in the sense that they were subject to and protected by the laws of the state, not in any active political sense. As long as the male head of household to whom underage and married women were bound was an established citizen, they could be identified as members of the citizenry, broadly understood, by virtue of these bonds. Unmarried women and widows were more difficult to identify. They could, with certain qualifications, own and administer property and generally act with considerable legal and economic autonomy. With rare exceptions, however, they could not vote or hold office. And they were still often identified and their connection to the state and community validated by defunct bonds to male subjects or citizens. Thus, in her instrument, after her name (itself prefaced with "Mrs"), Norton was identified first by the fact that she was the "widow of the late John Norton Esqr Virginia Merchant of London," and only then by her own place of birth, and still later by her political commitments.

In some instances, the American agents issued hybrid instruments of identification. An early example of the passport addressed to commanders of vessels, issued to "Willm More of the State of N Jersey in N. America," combined in one document a loyalty oath certificate and a passport. Moore had applied to the three commissioners on June 20th of 1778, explaining that he had been born in New Jersey, and had recently been in the East Indies, where both he and his brother held property. He now planned to transfer his property to the United States and desired a passport back to the Indies and then to the United States with a laden ship.[90] Three days later the commissioners

issued Moore a passport addressed "To all Commanders of Armed Vessels &ca. in the Service of or

belongn. to the United States." The instrument declared that "These may certify" that Moore had

"this day taken the oath & subscribed the declaration of Allegiance to the United States of America"

and that he had accordingly "received from us a Passport to go thro this kingdom in his way to the

E. Indies, from whence his intentions are, as he says, to return with his property to the United States

of America." The commissioners went beyond these certifications to affirm that "we believe his

Declarations aforesaid to be true & sincere"—offering their judgment and enlisting their credibility

on Moore's behalf.[91] This may have constituted a kind of bridge between the oath of allegiance

(which they could only claim to witness) and the passport (which they issued as a form of

recommendation). Similarly, in the 1779 passport he issued to Cyprian Sterry and John Smith, Jr., to

return to America, Franklin declared that the particulars of their identities, backgrounds, and

intentions had been "represented to me" and appeared "by good Testimony."[92]

The passport issued to Moore concluded by requesting "all Commanders of vessels of war,

belongn. to the United States of America or any of them & of Privateers & Letters of Marque &

Reprisal, belongn. to any Individuals of any of the sd. United States, to permit him to pass to the

said States with his marchandise & effects, unmolested."[93] Moore's passport and subsequent

---

[90] Moore to the American Commissioners at Paris, 20 June 1778, *PBFDE*. Moore was one of the three individuals to whom the commissioners had agreed to administer an oath of allegiance when they raised the issue with Congress, 17 September 1778, Wharton, II: 722-725.

[91] American Commissioners at Paris, passport for William Moore, 23 June 1778, Transcripts of Letters from Arthur Lee, William Lee, Ralph Izard, and the Joint Commissioners of the United States to France, 1776-80, *PCC*, NARA M247, r128, i102, v4, p20-21.

[92] Franklin, passport for Cyprian Sterry and John Smith, Jr., 24 September 1779, *PBFDE*. A note on the back of the draft of this passport states that, "On the 25th of Sept Mr Sterry took the Oath of Allegiance to the U.S."

[93] American Commissioners at Paris, passport for William Moore, 23 June 1778, Transcripts of Letters from Arthur Lee, William Lee, Ralph Izard, and the Joint Commissioners of the United States to France, 1776-80, *PCC*, NARA M247, r128, i102, v4, p20-21. It may be telling that though they certify Moore's oath of allegiance to the U.S., they identify him

examples of this increasingly standardized letter to commanders of vessels were consistently

couched in terms of request and recommendation rather than command.[94] The same was true of

the general passport, modeled on the French, even though French royal passports commanded the

King's subordinate officers to recognize and further the protection he had chosen to grant the

bearer ("...We wish and command you very expressly...").[95] In the case of the passport addressed to

commanders of vessels, the language of request was appropriate because it was addressed not only

to those in service to the Continental Congress but to military officers, privateer captains, and

commanders of vessels belonging to the individual states—over none of whom did the

commissioners have clear authority, though they could and did appeal to Congressional resolutions

in favor of particular classes of travellers to bolster their recommendations.[96] In other instances the

passport appealed primarily to the humanitarianism of the captains, as when Franklin issued

passports recommending ships supplying religious missions, or bearing charitable relief, or when he

issued passports to the ships of Captain Cook's expedition in the name of the advancement of

knowledge.[97]

In the case of the generalized passport, only a request and a pledge of reciprocity were

appropriate, since it was addressed by representatives of one confederation of sovereign states to the

officials of other sovereigns (and indeed issued within the territory of one such) whom they could

---

by state and by continent ("N. America") but not by U.S. citizenship or the U.S. as a country, state, or nation itself.
They likewise identify New Jersey as a state on a particular continent, but not as a member or constituent of the U.S.

[94] For a later example, see Franklin, passport for Cyprian Sterry and John Smith, Jr., 24 September 1779, *PBFDE*. The
docket note indicates that "nearly the same" passport was issued to W. Johnston & Walter Belt.

[95] See Form of a French Passport, Papers of Benjamin Franklin, Miscellaneous Papers, LXXIV: 103, B:F85, APS.

[96] See Franklin, passport for Cyprian Sterry and John Smith, Jr., 24 September 1779, *PBFDE*; Arthur Lee, passport for
Ann Norton, 3 May 1779, Transcripts of Letters from Arthur Lee, William Lee, Ralph Izard, and the Joint
Commissioners of the United States to France, 1776-80, *PCC*, NARA M247, r128, i102, v3, p23-24.

[97] Franklin, passport for Moravian supply ship, 22 June 1778, Wharton, II: 627-628; Franklin, passport for Captain
Cook, 10 March 1779, Wharton, III: 75-76; Franklin, passport for ship bearing Irish relief to West Indies, 7 February
1781, *PBFDE*.

not, by definition, command. This latter form may have served as much to construct the United States as credible sovereigns as to identify the bearer: it made an implicit claim to sovereignty in being issued by a minister of the United States in a document addressed to the European sovereigns from which the United States sought recognition; and it adopted much of the form and language used by one of those sovereigns.

The general passport, modeled on the French, is represented by an early example in manuscript (the printed form would come several months later): Franklin's passport for John Adams, John Quincy Adams, and a servant to travel from Passy to Nantes, as they prepared to embark for home. The passport was written in French—it would, of course, most likely be read and evaluated by French officials, and French was likewise the principal international language or lingua franca among the European powers. It was issued under Franklin's name and title ("Nous Benjamin Franklin Ministre Plenipotentiaire des treize Etats Unis de l'Amerique septentrionale"). In the body of the passport Franklin "requests all those concerned" ("Prions touts ceux qui sont a prier") to "allow to pass securely and freely the honorable John Adams subject of the said States going to Nantes with his son and a Servant without offering or allowing to be offered them any Hindrance, but on the contrary to give them all Aid and Assistance, as we would in similar Cases all those recommended to us." The passport was valid for three months; it was dated at Franklin's house in Passy, 7 March 1779; and it was signed by Franklin, countersigned by one of Franklin's secretaries, and sealed with Franklin's personal coat of arms.[98]

Notably, the passport identified Adams as a "subject" of the "thirteen United States of north America." It thus employed a category of political membership (subject instead of citizen) more familiar and acceptable to the officials of European monarchies. But at the same time it posited a category of membership and collective identity transcending the individual states, though the states

---

[98] Franklin, passport for John Adams et al., 7 March 1779, *PBFDE*.

were themselves identified as a plural collective of polities united by common geography. Even in the case of someone like Adams (a former and future ambassador, a leading member of the Continental Congress) so tightly associated with the confederation as a whole, Franklin could only deal in highly ambiguous terms in attempting to articulate the relationship of the individual to the confederation and to one or more of the individual states, as well as the nature of the confederation itself—its terms disputed and still without a fully ratified charter. Even in passports addressed primarily not to European officials but to commanders of American ships, Franklin and others not uncommonly dealt in the same ambiguous articulations of U.S. political membership. Thus in his passport for Sterry and Smith to return to the United States with their property, he identified them as "Natives of America & Subjects of the United States."[99]

The ways in which applicants for passports identified themselves suggested further ambiguities. When, in July of 1779, Richard Speakman wrote from Ghent to request a passport from Franklin, he identified himself as "a Native of America" who was "now waiting at this place— with my Wife & Children for an Opportunity to Return" to his native country. He was, however, "at a loss how to find the most Eligible way" and "as an American Subject" hoped Franklin would advise him "& also to send a passport for travelling to the place your Excellency advises us to go to" embark for America. In closing, he signed himself "Richd Speakman[,] son of Tho Speakman formerly of Boston[,] Carpenter." His lineage and occupation (or that of his father?) particularized his identity, situated him socially, and may have been meant to establish some connection with Franklin personally, or else substantiate his claim to be an American by referencing persons and circumstances with which Franklin might be familiar. In explaining his connection to Franklin as a representative of the United States, Speakman identified himself first and foremost by his identity as a "Native of America," a social identity of an essentially apolitical cast, especially in the context of a

---

[99] Franklin, passport for Cyprian Sterry and John Smith, Jr., 24 September 1779, *PBFDE*.

deeply divided Revolutionary "America." His identity as a Bostonian, at least by lineage, and, implicitly, a citizen of Massachusetts, came only at the end, as part of his epithetical social location and personal history.

At the same time, Speakman, in the course of his letter, elided any distinction between the social identity of an American and the political identity of a U.S. citizen. In doing so he evoked the transitional nature of the U.S. citizenship—sprung from British imperial subjecthood—by describing himself as "an American Subject." Ultimately, even as he articulated this compound identity for himself, he evidently considered that his "Wife & Children," the latter unspecified in number and sex, need only be identified as such, in terms of their relation to him and their status as his dependents. Any relevant political or legal identities they bore were necessarily determined by their status as the wife and children of a man identified legally and politically in his own right.[100]

Examples of each of the two main forms of the U.S. passport abroad in turn identified the bearers to varying degrees and in a variety of terms, either adjusting the manuscript text or inserting chosen details in the blanks of the printed forms. Very little of the personal identities of the bearers was specified in the standardized forms. Even their nationality, subjecthood, or citizenship was typically left to be inserted, if at all, in manuscript. Individual passports might identify the named individual as a citizen or subject of the United States, or as a subject of another nation or empire. But there were many cases in which these specifics were omitted, whether or not the bearer was in fact considered by Franklin or another U.S. agent to be a U.S. citizen or an American. The passport issued to Burdy identified him by name alone, while the corrections that the French authorities had requested to the passport Franklin issued to Paradise and Jones suggest that the two men's places of birth, nationalities, and subjecthoods or citizenships had been omitted by Franklin in the original passport. The omission of the point from the standardized forms made them suitable to be issued,

---

[100] See Adams to Governor of Corunna, 18 December 1779, Wharton, III: 432, as a possible exception.

as they were, to both U.S. citizens and foreign nationals. This omission, and the widely varying terms and degree of specification when included, may also reflect the continuing fluidity of "American" or U.S. citizenship as a category, both at home and abroad.

Beyond the question of citizenship or subjecthood, the letter to the commanders would sometimes add further details concerning the bearer's background, connections, family, service to the cause, or any property they might be permitted to transport. As with instruments discussed in preceding chapters, they were likewise generally structured and issued on the assumption that servants, slaves, wives, and children would not legitimately travel alone or in their own right, with their own instruments of identification and mobility, but that "households," "families," or "suites" would travel and be identified as units. Thus Franklin's passport for John Adams covered Adams himself and "his son and a Servant."[101] The amended American passport for Paradise and Jones was to include the note that Jones would be travelling with "one valet de chambre."[102] Even in Lee's passport for the widow Ann Norton, she was described as travelling (as the head of the household) with her "Family," which was not further described.[103]

Beyond these details, the passports provided very little that described the grantee or otherwise tied the document and the identity it certified closely to the intended bearer. Neither form included the signature or physical description of the bearer, which would become standard devices in early-national U.S. passports issued abroad.[104] Physical descriptions at this time, in both

---

[101] Franklin, passport for John Adams et al., 7 March 1779, *PBFDE*.

[102] Paradise and Jones to Franklin, 1 June 1779, *PBFDE*.

[103] Arthur Lee, Passport for Ann Norton, 3 May 1779, Transcripts of Letters from Arthur Lee, William Lee, Ralph Izard, and the Joint Commissioners of the United States to France, 1776-80, *PCC*, NARA M247, r128, i102, v3, p23-24.

[104] See examples in Originals and Copies of Passports, 1794-1901, RG 59, Entry 518, Box 1, NARA. See also *The United States Passport: Past, Present, Future*, (Washington, DC: U.S. Government Printing Office, 1976), 32.

Europe and America, were used largely to identify subordinates and dependents.[105] For that reason,

they were likely considered degrading and out of keeping with the respect due to the "gentlemen"

for whom many of the passports were intended.

Both forms of passports were limited, on a less visceral level, by the federalism of the newly

forming confederation.[106] Because each of the new sovereign states claimed full authority over entry,

exit, and movement within its borders, the passports Congress and its agents abroad issued could

only claim authority abroad.[107] And in so far as they identified the individuals they named as citizens

or subjects of the United States, they dealt in an identity of tenuous substance, as was made still

clearer by, among other things, the debates among U.S. agents abroad over the nature of the oaths

of allegiance on which these passports were often founded.[108]

---

[105] See Samuel Bixby, Diary, 1775-1776, 3 July 1775, Mss. Octavo Volumes, AAS; 6th Massachusetts Regiment, Orderly Book, Verplanck's Point, 1782, U.S. Revolution Collection, Folio Vol. 3, AAS. For physical descriptions of deserters from the Continental Navy, see John Paul Jones to John de Neufville & Son, 21 December 1779, *MPCC*, NARA M332, r4, f131 (descriptive list of deserters at f133). On the use of physical descriptions to monitor and govern criminals, seamen, slaves, and the poor in the early national United States and some discussion of practice and norms in earlier periods, see Sankar, "State Power"; Simon P. Newman, *Embodied History: The Lives of the Poor in Early Philadelphia*, (Philadelphia: University of Pennsylvania Press, 2003); Sally Hadden, *Slave Patrols: Law and Violence in Virginia and the Carolinas*, (Cambridge, MA: Harvard UP, 2001); David Waldstreicher, "Reading the Runaways: Self-Fashioning, Print Culture, and Confidence in the Eighteenth-Century Mid-Atlantic," *William and Mary Quarterly*, Series 3, Vol. 56, No. 2 (Apr., 1999), 243-272; Gwenda Morgan and Peter Rushton, "Visible Bodies: Power, Subordination and Identity in the Eighteenth-Century Atlantic World," *Journal of Social History*, Vol. 39, No. 1 (Autumn, 2005), 39-64; Jonathan Prude, "To Look upon the 'Lower Sort': Runaway Ads and the Appearance of Unfree Laborers in America, 1750-1800," *Journal of American History*, Vol. 78, No. 1 (Jun., 1991), 124-159. For similar practice in France, see Vincent Denis, *Une Histoire de l'Identité: France, 1715-1815*, (Seyssel: Champ Vallon, 2008); Robert Darnton, "A Police Inspector Sorts His Files: The Anatomy of the Republic of Letters," *The Great Cat Massacre, and Other Episodes in French Cultural History*, (New York: Vintage, 1984), 145-189 (esp. 160-162). For an example of the use of physical descriptions by the Paris police, in an investigation in part on behalf of the American commissioners, see Van Doren, *Secret History*, 83. For a deeper background for the use of physical descriptions for identification, see Valentin Groebner, *Who Are You? Identification, Deception, and Surveillance in Early Modern Europe*, (New York: Zone Books, 2007), esp. chs. 4-5.

[106] On the recommendatory nature of letters to commanders, see Franklin to Jonathan Williams Jr., 19 November 1781, *PBFDE*.

[107] See Samuel Huntington to Jonathan Trumbull, 1 September 1780, *PCC*, NARA M247, r24, i15, p90-92; Leonard S. Goodman, "Passports in Perspective," *Texas Law Review*, Vol. 45 (1966-1967), 240-244.

[108] For an early example of this connection, see Franklin, Adams, and Lee to William Moore, *PCC*, NARA M247, r128, i102, v4, p20-21. For Franklin's later insistence that oaths of allegiance were required of all those claiming passports from him as American citizens, see Franklin to John Paul Jones, 1 November 1780, *PBFDE*.

Identification of U.S. citizens abroad during the Revolution was at least as much an exercise in creative thinking and studied ambiguities, worked on paper in ink and wax, as it was a process of discovery and verification. Even as the states were still shaping themselves, Americans and the agents of Congress abroad struggled to construct United States citizenship as a practical identity, to make functional in practice an identity as yet nearly undefined. Their efforts, and the instruments in which they embodied them helped to shape the definition of U.S. citizenship and American identity. Whether wary of the implications or eager to realize them, the parties to these identifications created new identities and new chains of identification as much as they certified or perpetuated old ones. An ocean away from home, starved for information, and operating in a near policy vacuum, they worked ad hoc in the medium of necessary fictions.

Conclusion

Passport number 4182 was signed and sealed at Paris on the 17th of November 1810. A single sheet, somewhat taller than a piece of letter paper, it consisted of a printed form, completed in manuscript, all in French, with an ornamental border of clover framing the whole. The passport described two men. On its face it described a man of fifty-three years, moderate height, chestnut hair, grey eyes, aquiline nose, oval face, and a complexion either florid or dark ("coloré"). His eyebrows matched his hair, his forehead was un-obscured, his chin was round, and his mouth unremarkable ("moyenne"). The reverse of the document described a man both younger—at thirty years old—and shorter of stature, with curled black hair, a high forehead, black eyes and eyebrows, flat nose, "inflated" lips, black beard, [....?] chin, oval face, and black complexion. The passport was issued to "Mr. Jean François Mérieult, Merchant," bearing diplomatic dispatches to the United States minister in London, "going to Dieppe to embark" for England, "and Attended by a Colored Domestic." Merieult subscribed his signature—the "Signature of the Bearer"—below the description of his person on the front of the passport. The man described on the reverse, referred to there less ambiguously as a "Negro Domestic," was accorded no name and left no mark of his own on the instrument.[1]

The passport was issued at the American Legation in Paris by Jonathan Russell, chargé d'affaires of the United States to the court of Emperor Napoleon Bonaparte, in the absence of a U.S. Minister Plenipotentiary, whose title in the heading of the printed form Russell crossed out and replaced with his own. Russell subscribed his signature and stamped the seal of the legation at the foot of the passport, which was countersigned and stamped with a departmental seal in turn by

---

[1] Jonathan Russell, passport for Jean François Merieult, 17 November 1810, Colonial and Early Territorial Louisiana Collection (MSS 579), Box 1, Folder 12, HNOC. All translations from the French are my own unless otherwise noted.

deputies of the French Minister of Foreign Affairs. The form of the passport identified Merieult as a "Citizen of the United States," requested that all concerned allow him to pass freely and afford him aid and protection in case of need, offering "reciprocity in parallel circumstances." Merieult's nameless "domestic" was stateless as far as he was described by the passport, identified by no nation or civil estate. Nor was any protection, aid, or freedom of movement solicited on his behalf, except implicitly as a dependent or extension of the person of his designated master. Likely one of the many slaves Merieult owned under U.S. Law (and the Law of Nations), the "domestic" found himself subordinated to Merieult's identity and identified in his own right by his body and "race," but ascribed no personal identity. The passport's description of him, indeed, rather than facilitating his mobility and protecting him in a tumultuous international realm, would have served equally well to authorize his passage through customs barriers as an item of Merieult's "property" or his (dependent) "family," or to aid the search for him as a fugitive, if he were to seek freedom in England.

This was at least the third passport that Merieult had received from the U.S. representatives in France. Four years earlier, in 1806, Merieult had embarked for Europe from New Orleans, where he was a plantation owner, a prominent merchant, and one of the city's leading importers of slaves.[2] Born in France, Merieult had originally settled in New Orleans in the 1780s, under Spanish imperial rule. After the United States purchased Louisiana from France in 1803, Merieult had embraced the opportunity to become a U.S. citizen under the terms of the treaty of cession. In January of 1804, in fact, his name headed the list of signatories on a memorial from the merchants of New Orleans to

---

[2] William C.C. Claiborne, Certificate of Citizenship and Residence for Merieult, January 1804, Colonial and Early Territorial Louisiana Collection (MSS 579), Box 4 (Oversize), Folder 3 (MSS 579.1.3), HNOC; Claiborne to James Madison, 16 March 1804, *PJMDE*, Secretary of State, VI: 590-594, n2; Merieult, Deposition, 25 July 1809, Colonial and Early Territorial Louisiana Collection (MSS 579), Box 4 (Oversize), Folder 87 (MSS 579.3.16), HNOC.

the U.S. Congress, pressing for the full rights and protections due them as U.S. citizens.[3] Merieult

set out from New Orleans for Europe in 1806 to seek a "reclamation" against the Spanish

government. He carried with him, among other documents, a certificate of his United States

citizenship from Territorial Governor William C.C. Claiborne and a certified declaration of his

extensive property holdings and interests in New Orleans. After multiple trips between Madrid and

Paris, Merieult found his efforts at reclamation still frustrated and decided to profit from the delay

by travelling more widely in France. Before leaving on this trip he made a deposition in July 1809

before the U.S. consul at Paris in which he described his activities in Europe; reaffirmed his

citizenship and standing as a merchant and property owner in New Orleans; and insisted that, as he

intended to return to New Orleans, where he was domiciled, his extended travels in Europe "ought

not in any manner to prejudice his rights as a citizen of the United States."[4]

Merieult, and many other free inhabitants of the newly American Louisiana, needed to

venture far from home at a time when their citizenship remained uncertain, and when war among

the European powers would have made the prospect of being mistaken for a French subject

unnerving. Pierre Porteaux, like Merieult "an Inhabitant of the newly acquired Territory of

Louisiana," had set off for London in early 1804 to "seek redress of some losses." Going by way of

Philadelphia, he had presented to Secretary of State James Madison a letter of recommendation from

Philadelphian Chandler Price, who explained that Porteaux felt "a pleasure in considering himself a

Citizen of the United States" and was "desirous to avail himself of the protection of the

---

[3] Memorial, 9 January 1804, "Papers Relating to the First Administration of Governor Claiborne, 1803-1804," *The Territorial Papers of the United States,* Clarence Edwin Carter ed., (Washington, DC: GPO, 1934-1975), IX: 157-158.

[4] Certificate of citizenship and residence, Colonial and Early Territorial Louisiana Collection (MSS 579), Box 4 (Oversize), Folder 3 (MSS 579.1.3); Power of attorney, ibid., Folder 108 (MSS 579.3.37); Deposition, ibid., Folder 87 (MSS 579.3.16); Passport, ibid., Box 1, Folder 12, HNOC. I have employed the unaccented spelling of Merieult's surname, a spelling that Merieult used himself in at least some instances, which was employed by acquaintances and officials writing in both English and French, and which has been adopted by the major repository of his few remaining papers, the Historic New Orleans Collection. Merieult was referred to as both "Jean François" and "John Francis" by others (the HNOC has adopted "Jean-François"). In surviving documents, Merieult signed himself generally either "John Francis," "John F.," or "J.F."

Government of the United States" on his impending journey. Price enclosed in his letter to

Madison "a Certificate of protection" given by Claiborne, in favor of Porteaux, and expressed his

hope that Madison would "be pleased to add such acceptance or approval, or a Certificate in any

other form, as may be deemed proper and sufficient to protect the person of Mr Porteaux on the

high Seas & elsewhere." Price closed his appeal by suggesting to Madison that it would be "very

flattering to the Louisianians to feel themselves under the protection of the Government of the

United States."[5] Merieult and Porteaux both clearly felt unsure how durable and efficacious their

new, tenuous citizenship and the protection of their new government would prove in practice

beyond the shores of the United States. Merieult, at least, feared that the U.S. citizenship he claimed

might not survive his journey.

Merieult and Porteaux were caught up in echoes of the Revolutionary crisis of identification

that resounded well after the Revolutionary War was over. The ongoing, iterative challenges of

identification embraced more than the predicament of these Louisianans and their fellows. The

difficulty, if not impossibility, of distinguishing "American" from "Briton," U.S. citizen from British

subject by any outward means—the problem at the core of the Revolutionary crisis of

identification—continued to pose problems and raise disputes well into the nineteenth century.

This was most salient in the impressment controversy with Britain that stretched through the War of

1812 and beyond, when British authorities claimed, with some plausibility, to be unable to

distinguish American seamen from British deserters. This same difficulty posed problems for

Americans abroad and at sea when Britain went to war with France and other powers who were

inclined to suspect that ships, seamen, travelers, and others claiming to be Americans were in fact

Britons in disguise. When tensions rose between the United States and Britain, moreover, it was

---

[5] Chandler Price to James Madison, 21 February 1804, Letters Requesting Passports, 1791-1910, RG 59, Entry 509, Box 1, NARA.

unclear how enemy aliens and potential spies were to be identified. Similar challenges and questions dogged American citizens of other descent or extraction. The U.S. at its inception was already a polyglot nation. It only grew more so as the years of the Early Republic passed, as new immigrants arrived and as new peoples were incorporated. As a republic that had replaced natural, indelible allegiance with volitional citizenship and a process of naturalization open to any (free white) person willing to fulfill its terms, the United States by dint of its most basic nature had to face the question of how to identify its citizens (and their dependents) for itself and to the world. French-Americans like Merieult, or Anglo-American seamen threatened with impressment, were only two of many groups of Americans of the Early Republic who faced multi-sided challenges and threats to their identities, at home and abroad. These included those of African ancestry, whose freedom, self-identification, and even personhood were continually under threat.

To meet the challenges of identification in the Early Republic, the United States and individual Americans turned again and again to written and printed instruments of identification—some familiar from the Revolution and before, some new—to make legible a variety of inward or abstract identities, both official and unofficial, civil and social. They carried documents of many types, from many authorities—certificates, protections, passports, statements of property, depositions, and letters of introduction and recommendation to potential friends and patrons abroad, among others—a complex of instruments, used in various combinations by Americans of many descriptions to identify themselves, and by which they were identified. To meet the impressment crisis, first mariners on their own initiative then the United States by law adopted certificates of citizenship known as seamen's protections. Though the authority of these documents was often dismissed by skeptical British press gangs, they continued to be the principal defense against the challenge to the identities of American seamen. To protect other citizens abroad, the Department of State, individual state governments, and diplomatic representatives abroad issued increasing numbers of passports. (Both seamen's protections and passports, at least when the latter were issued abroad, soon came to include physical descriptions of the bearers as a matter of standard practice.) For new citizens, certificates of naturalization became essential instruments of identification—essential protection against the claims of other sovereigns and the key to the rights and privileges of citizenship, including access to other instruments, such as passports. Letters of introduction and recommendation continued to serve as the principal instruments of social, commercial, and even official mobility, access, and preferment. Meanwhile, as the institution of slavery not only persisted but actually expanded and strengthened during the Early Republic, the allied regime of written records and instruments of identification, including slave passes and certificates of freedom, only increased in importance and salience.

Americans of the Early Republic of all descriptions needed to secure their identities in the eyes of their own governments and countrymen and upon the world stage—on occasion at the same time—across the recurring episodes of challenge, verification, and renegotiation that constituted identities in practice. The general challenges of identification were complicated and intensified by the multiple revolutions and nearly continuous wars that embroiled the powers of the Atlantic world in this period, and for Americans more particularly by the peculiar circumstances of the United States as a newly independent power. The nation had only recently emerged from civil war and revolution. It had broken away from one of the warring European empires, incorporated territory and people from two others over the course of the period, and comprised populations of many different national or cultural extractions. Little wonder that Americans had to work to establish their credibility as sovereigns in the international realm, and struggle to practice republican citizenship in a world of subjecthood and monarchy. They needed to distinguish themselves (and their dependents and property, human and otherwise) from their former British compatriots (not readily distinguishable by language, dress, body, or manners), and from the peoples of other nations from which Americans hailed or descended and with which they shared languages, names, appearances, or culture. These efforts formed part of individuals' enterprises of self-determination, but also part of the general effort to establish the independent sovereignty of the US and the independent institution of U.S. citizenship.

To distinguish Americans from the subjects of other Atlantic powers was likewise crucial in order to distinguish Americans and Americans property as neutral, to prevent entanglement with the European wars of the period, and to take advantage of the potential commercial and other benefits that could be reaped as neutrals. And it was essential as well to protecting both American citizens, as individuals due protection, and the national resources of the United States, by preventing other states, most notably Britain, from appropriating Americans to their national service. At the same time, the wars and revolutions of the period gave rise to a pervasive fear of spies, infiltrators, and subversives—whether French radicals, Haitian racial revolutionaries, royalist or pro-slavery reactionaries, or others—bringing further urgency to the identification of Americans (and others) as particular individuals, as members of particular social and political networks, and as citizens or subjects of particular states, nations, or empires.

For those who were subordinated to the identities of others, claimed as property, or ascribed a stigmatized racial identity, the same geopolitical context presented a very different calculus of opportunity and danger. For Africans and African Americans, whether free or enslaved, distance from U.S. authorities and from their wonted communities and social settings could mean new possibilities for self-liberation and re-fashioning, through opportunities for flight or access to the support and protection of foreign African diasporic communities, more sympathetic or accessible foreign legal systems, or foreign states. But it could also mean greater danger of enslavement or further loss of autonomy, as the social resources they might have drawn upon at home grew more distant, or as fragile documentary instruments of freedom or identification were lost, stolen, or ignored.

Disparities of power continued to define American identification (and, indeed, identification more broadly) through the course of the Early Republic and beyond. Different persons wielded very different degrees of power over how they themselves were identified, including whether they were recognized or claimed as U.S. citizens or as Americans (of many different categories) and treated accordingly. Those persons with more social connections or greater influence could better support the authority of any instrument of identification they bore if it were disputed and could better maintain their claims to the identity they chose even in the absence of any instrument. Those who were well connected or of prominent social status could better supply the testimonials of accepted credibility needed to support an application for naturalization or a passport. The wealthy merchant, with many connections abroad, could better meet a challenge to his identity as an American than could an impressed American seaman, separated by an ocean from his family and most of his friends and with little social influence of his own. Women were rarely issued or assumed to need instruments of identification that would allow them to substantiate identities of their own choice and in their own right. Institutionalized paupers, invalids, and criminals had little say over how their identities were registered by increasingly record-based and surveillance oriented bureaucracies and institutions.[6]

Those with the least power—African and African-American slaves—were denied legal personhood and often, in practice, very nearly any personal identity, but were treated instead as extensions of the persons or as chattel property of others. Free African Americans were required to

---

[6] See Pamela Sankar, "State Power and Record-keeping: The History of Individualized Surveillance in the United States, 1790-1935," PhD diss., (University of Pennsylvania, 1992); Simon P. Newman, *Embodied History: The Lives of the Poor in Early Philadelphia*, (Philadelphia: University of Pennsylvania Press, 2003); John K. Alexander, *Render them Submissive: Responses to Poverty in Philadelphia, 1760-1800*, (Amherst, MA: University of Massachusetts Press, 1980).

carry instruments certifying their freedom, laying on them a greater burden of proof than on any group of "white" Americans. An African American whose freedom was disputed could rarely hope to bring influence and credibility to bear in court equal to that of an ostensible master. Those persons deemed to be slaves had perhaps the least power over their practical identities, though even they could turn the regimes of identification to serve their own ends and secure their liberation, escaping bondage, for instance, by means of stolen or forged passes. The "domestic" that Merieult took with him to England and who was described but not named (or accorded a nationality) on the back of the latter's passport, exercised little if any power over how he was identified or over his own mobility, at least as far as the coercive power of his "master" and the state extended. His relationship to the instrument on which his body was described and to the power that issued it were very different than those of Merieult, the bearer.

Numerous "Americans" of all descriptions in the era of the Early Republic drew on the records, the officials, and the diplomatic and consular representatives of the United States, of individual states and other authorities, as well as on their private social connections, to secure instruments of identification—official and unofficial—to persuade still other authorities, and to sustain the identities they claimed as they travelled the globe. While they shared the same broad challenges, the more particular threats they faced to their identities varied widely among different categories of Americans and among particular individuals according to their differential social resources and standing, their class, their race, gender, age, and lineage, among other factors.

Merieult, a man of evident and acknowledged French extraction, had ventured abroad and was preparing to travel from France to Great Britain at a time when the two empires were at war. British authorities felt threatened by subversives coming incognito from France, as well as by homegrown sympathizers with the French Revolution and Napoleon. Merieult was also a merchant, abroad on business, and with both general and particular interest in establishing and maintaining his identity as the citizen of a neutral power, at least notionally free to trade and its ships exempt from capture, albeit with a variety of qualifications. Apart from his explicit anxiety to preserve his American citizenship through the course of his extended travels, Merieult likely hoped that the passport he secured from Russell would allow him to demonstrate to British authorities, as clearly as possible, that he was in fact a (trusted) U.S. citizen—indeed a diplomatic courier, for present purposes—rather than a Frenchman.

At the same time, Merieult was not only travelling abroad with a "domestic"—risky enough for a slaveholder whose human property might flee in a foreign land—but was bringing him along on a trip to a country where the legality of slavery had been in serious doubt for nearly four decades, after the Somerset decision of 1772 denied another travelling slaveholder the right to depart England with a slave had he brought with him. On both counts, Merieult may have hoped that the inclusion and description of his bondman in the passport would help substantiate his claims to ownership. At the same time, by employing the not uncommon euphemism "domestic" (or "servant"), Merieult may well have been effectively manipulating, even falsifying, this man's identity, attempting to avoid drawing attention to his enslavement in this contentious context. This same instrument, this same context, and these same ambiguities could well have served this "domestic," quite conversely, as an opportunity to seek and certify his freedom. Though this individual does not appear to have attempted it, such manipulation and deployment of documents was a common strategy for enslaved Africans and African-Americans around the Atlantic world.

These and other dramas of identification played out amidst awareness of forgery and fraud in the use of instruments of identification, including passports. Reports of rampant fraud, for instance, had reached U.S. Secretary of State James Madison in the summer of 1804. American S. B. Wigginton, abroad in Bordeaux, France, wrote to decry the "abuse that arises from passports issued from the Office of Secretary of State." These "having no description of the person, neither age, height, Complexion, general outlines of features or color of Hair," he explained, "[they] become

transferable with so much ease that they are daily abused." Unauthorized persons, having purchased

or stolen the passports, could "either simply erase the *name* or assume the original, and thereby enjoy

all the rights & protection of Citizens without the smallest claim to it." Worse, "many of those

impostors" conducted themselves "in such a manner as to bring odium on our Character, and

render it less respectable in the eyes of all Europe." Wigginton recommended that passports include

minute physical descriptions of the persons to whom they were issued. But as Madison and his

predecessors in office knew too well, identity papers that already bore such physical descriptions—

the certificates of citizenship issued to protect American seamen from impressment into the Royal

Navy as British subjects—had hardly proven notably credible or immune to fraud. The U.S. Agent

for Seamen in London had advised Madison, just the year before, that, "It is known that [seamen's

protections] have been obtained with the utmost facility" and "they will therefore always be

considered as questionable Evidence." Indeed, "they are frequently sold or transferred; as

frequently worn out or lost; a change in the description of the person as to marks complexion or

otherwise may happen, & render the certificate on that ground questionable."[7]

As Madison read these discouraging reports, Philadelphia newspapers reported snippets of

other American dramas of identification playing out in the courts, galleries, homes, and streets of the

Early Republic. Consider the cases of the contentious trial, rife with conflicting identification of the

accused, of a New York man wrongfully charged with bigamy after being mistaken for another man;

the denunciation and description of "a vile cheat and swindler…who frequently changed his name,

for the nefarious purpose of executing his wicked schemes," among them forgery, theft, robbery,

seduction, and adultery; as well as numerous advertisements describing suspected criminals, escaped

prisoners, and the fugitive men and women claimed as slaves who strove to construct new identities

---

[7] Wigginton to Madison, 30 May 1804, *PJMDE*; George Erving to Madison, 9 November 1803, *PJMDE*, VI: 26-30.

as free people.[8] Throughout the republic and in the Atlantic world beyond, identities were continually under construction because the means of identification were continually contested.

Fraud and the suspicion it generated made it more difficult for individuals to make persuasive claims to particular identities. Such disputes undermined the credibility of instruments of identification and fueled quarrels among states over their relative authority in the identification of individuals and of categories of persons. And despite efforts at greater security, opportunities nevertheless continued for some to seek new identities or put old ones to new uses. But while fraud encouraged challenges to the legitimacy of particular instruments of identification, it did not demonstrate a fundamental inutility of such documents or cause Americans in the era of the Early Republic to dismiss the potential or actual efficacy of such instruments in general. If anything, the uncertainty contributed to greater demand for such instruments and the deployment of multiple instruments in combination.

As "Americans on Paper" has shown, to understand how the Revolution was lived and enacted requires that we understand the crisis of identification that pervaded it and the practical means used to meet that crisis. A similar understanding of the challenges and means of identification in colonial America and the Early Republic is needed if we are to fully comprehend the formation and practice of American identities and, indeed, the ways early American lives were lived day-to-day, on a practical level. Our growing knowledge of the makings and workings of inward identities in early America must be matched by our awareness of the ways those identities were practiced and demonstrated, within constraints, and in contest and negotiation with others. Any such understanding must include an appreciation of the ways that power over identification was very unequally distributed among Americans of different classes, "races," genders, and walks of life.

---

[8] *United States Gazette*, 5 July 1804; *Aurora General Advertiser*, 13 November 1805. *AHN.*